10

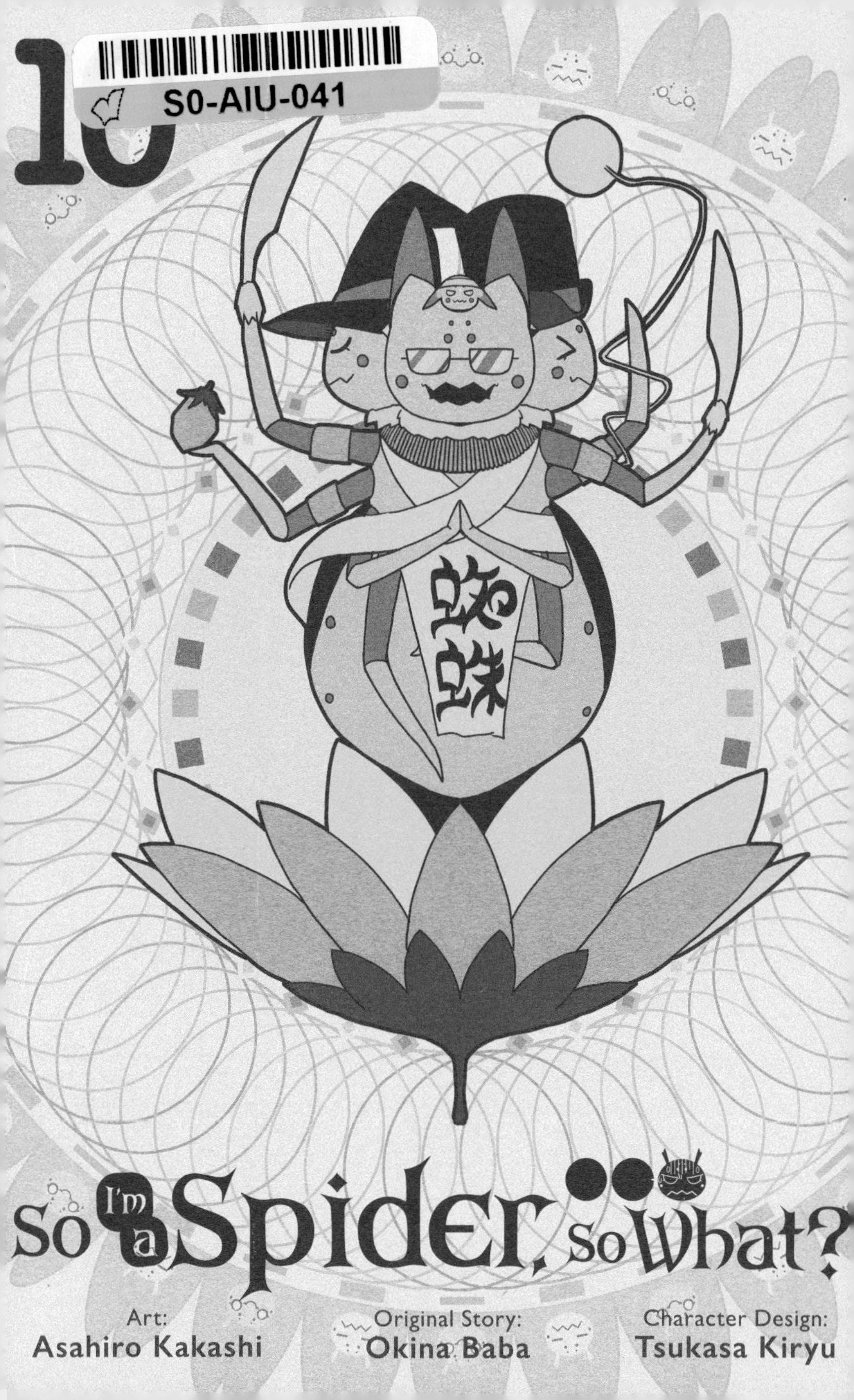
蜘蛛

So I'm a Spider, So What?

Art:
Asahiro Kakashi

Original Story:
Okina Baba

Character Design:
Tsukasa Kiryu

So I'm a Spider, So What?

CONTENTS

 So I'm a Spider, So What?

10

Art: **Asahiro Kakashi**

Original Story: **Okina Baba**

Character Design: **Tsukasa Kiryu**

Translation: Jenny McKeon Lettering: Bianca Pistillo

KUMO DESUGA, NANIKA? Volume 10
© Asahiro Kakashi 2021
© Okina Baba, Tsukasa Kiryu 2021
First published in Japan in 2021 by KADOKAWA CORPORATION, Tokyo.
English translation rights arranged with KADOKAWA CORPORATION, Tokyo, through TUTTLE-MORI AGENCY, INC.

English translation © 2021 by Yen Press, LLC

Yen Press
150 West 30th Street, 19th Floor
New York, NY 10001

Visit us at yenpress.com
facebook.com/yenpress
twitter.com/yenpress
yenpress.tumblr.com
instagram.com/yenpress

First Yen Press Print Edition: December 2021

Yen Press is an imprint of Yen Press, LLC.
The Yen Press name and logo are trademarks of Yen Press, LLC.

Library of Congress Control Number: 2017954138

ISBN: 978-1-9753-3983-8 (paperback)
978-1-9753-3984-5 (ebook)

10 9 8 7 6 5 4 3 2 1

WOR

Printed in the United States of America

so I'm a Spider, so What?

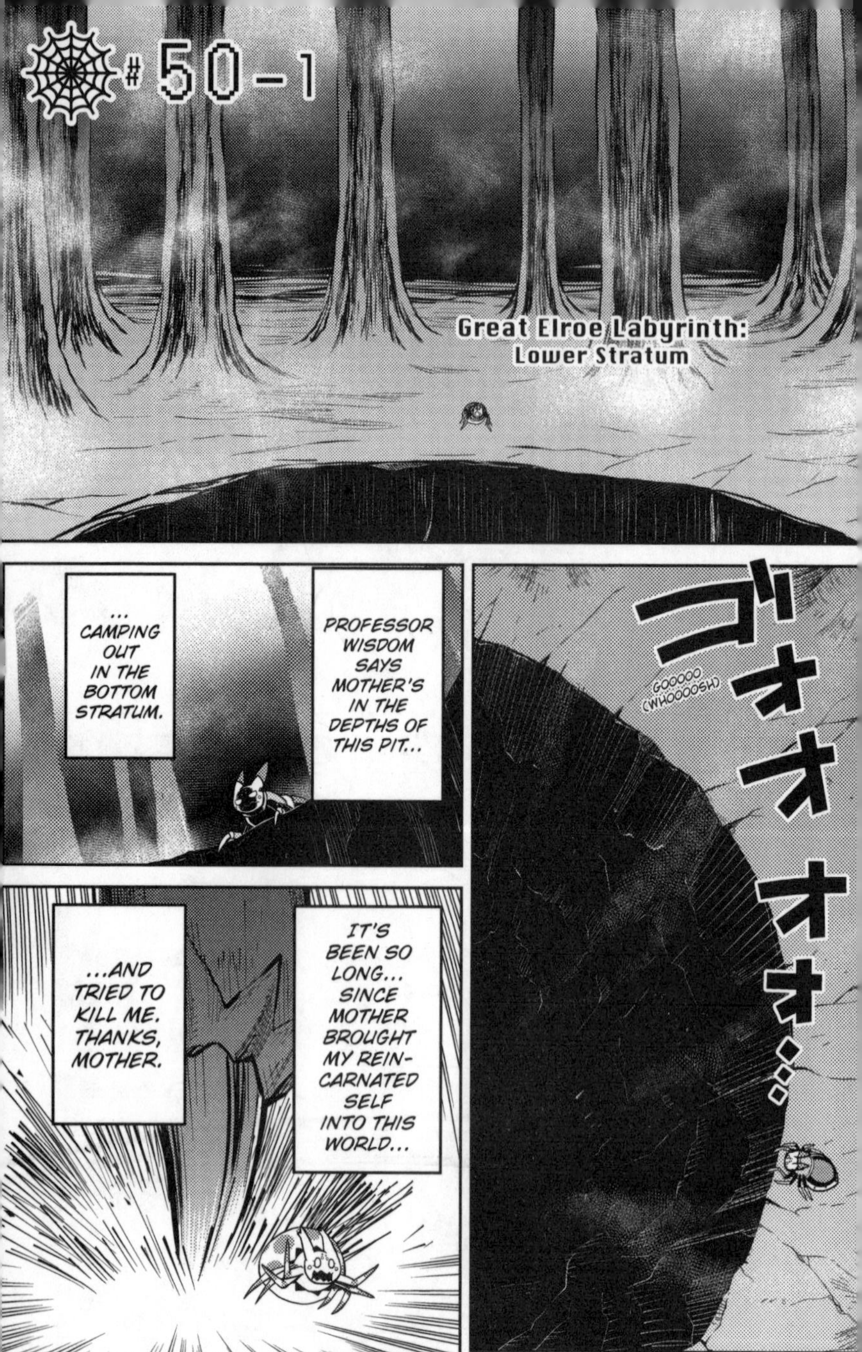
#50-1
Great Elroe Labyrinth: Lower Stratum
ゴオオオ…
GOOOOO (WHOOOOSH)
PROFESSOR WISDOM SAYS MOTHER'S IN THE DEPTHS OF THIS PIT...
...CAMPING OUT IN THE BOTTOM STRATUM.
IT'S BEEN SO LONG... SINCE MOTHER BROUGHT MY REIN-CARNATED SELF INTO THIS WORLD...
...AND TRIED TO KILL ME. THANKS, MOTHER.

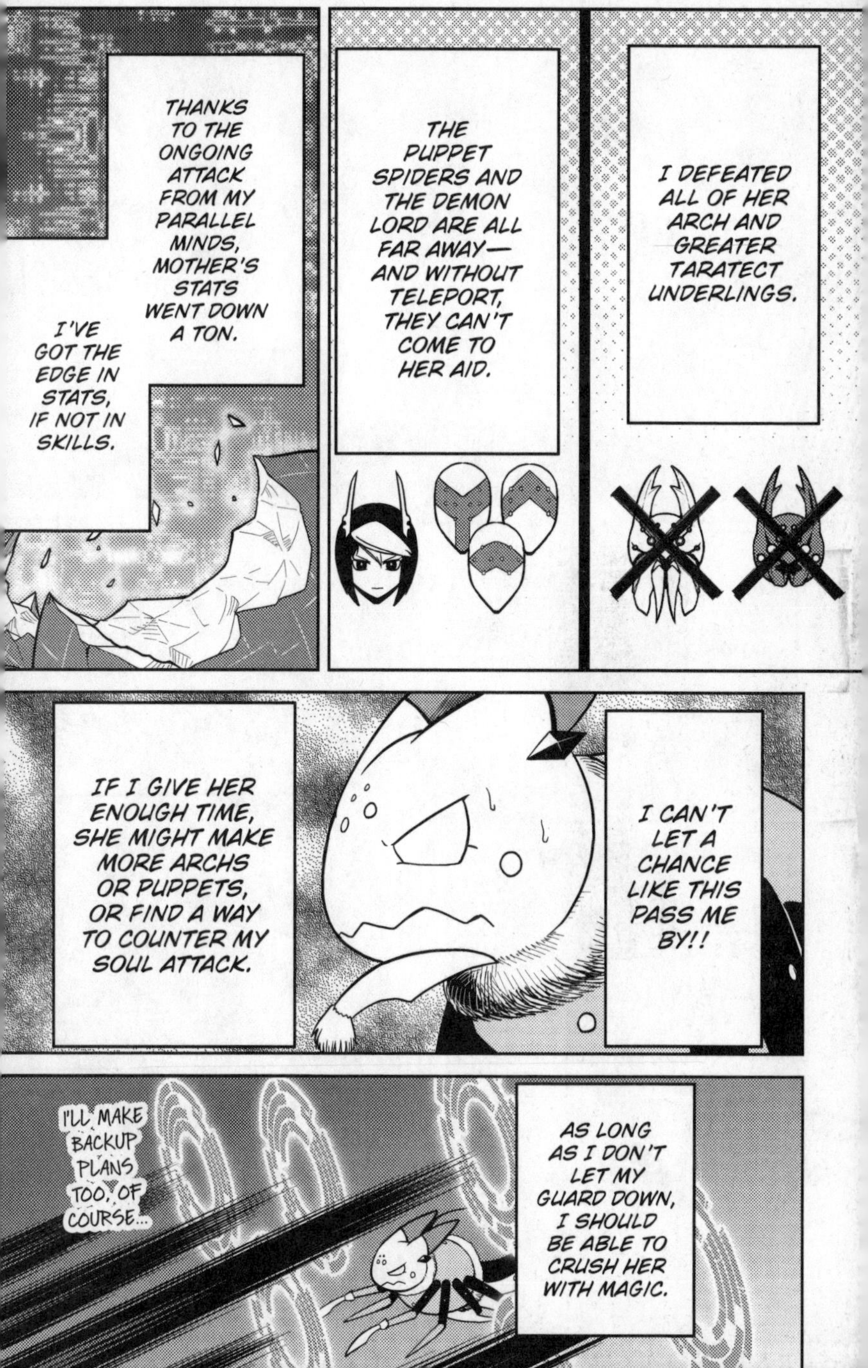
I DEFEATED ALL OF HER ARCH AND GREATER TARATECT UNDERLINGS.
THE PUPPET SPIDERS AND THE DEMON LORD ARE ALL FAR AWAY—AND WITHOUT TELEPORT, THEY CAN'T COME TO HER AID.
THANKS TO THE ONGOING ATTACK FROM MY PARALLEL MINDS, MOTHER'S STATS WENT DOWN A TON.
I'VE GOT THE EDGE IN STATS, IF NOT IN SKILLS.
I CAN'T LET A CHANCE LIKE THIS PASS ME BY!!
IF I GIVE HER ENOUGH TIME, SHE MIGHT MAKE MORE ARCHS OR PUPPETS, OR FIND A WAY TO COUNTER MY SOUL ATTACK.
AS LONG AS I DON'T LET MY GUARD DOWN, I SHOULD BE ABLE TO CRUSH HER WITH MAGIC.
I'LL MAKE BACKUP PLANS TOO, OF COURSE...

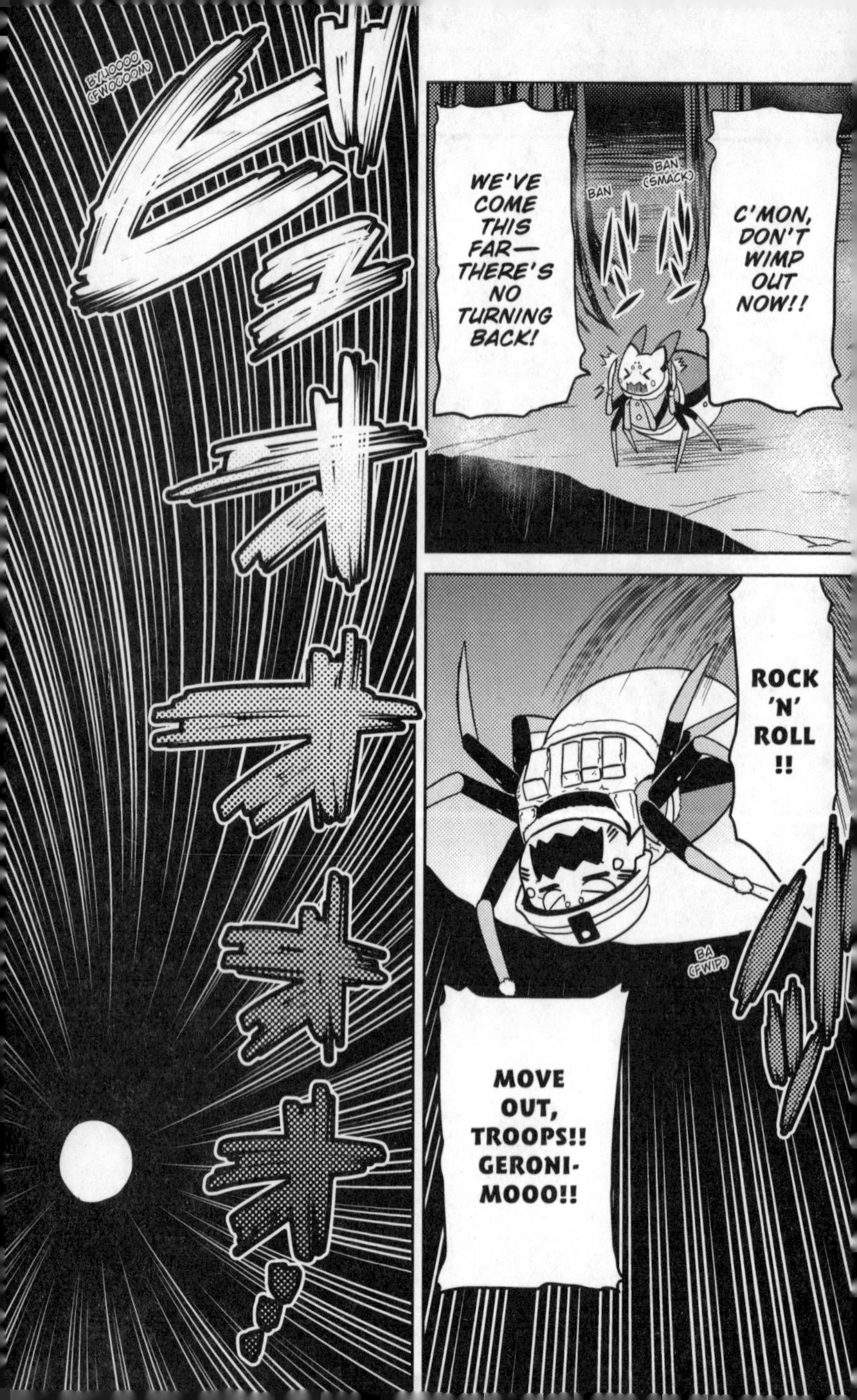
C'MON, DON'T WIMP OUT NOW!!
BAN (SMACK)
BAN
WE'VE COME THIS FAR— THERE'S NO TURNING BACK!
ROCK 'N' ROLL !!
BA (FWIP)
MOVE OUT, TROOPS!! GERONI-MOOO!!
BYUOOOO (FWOOOOM)

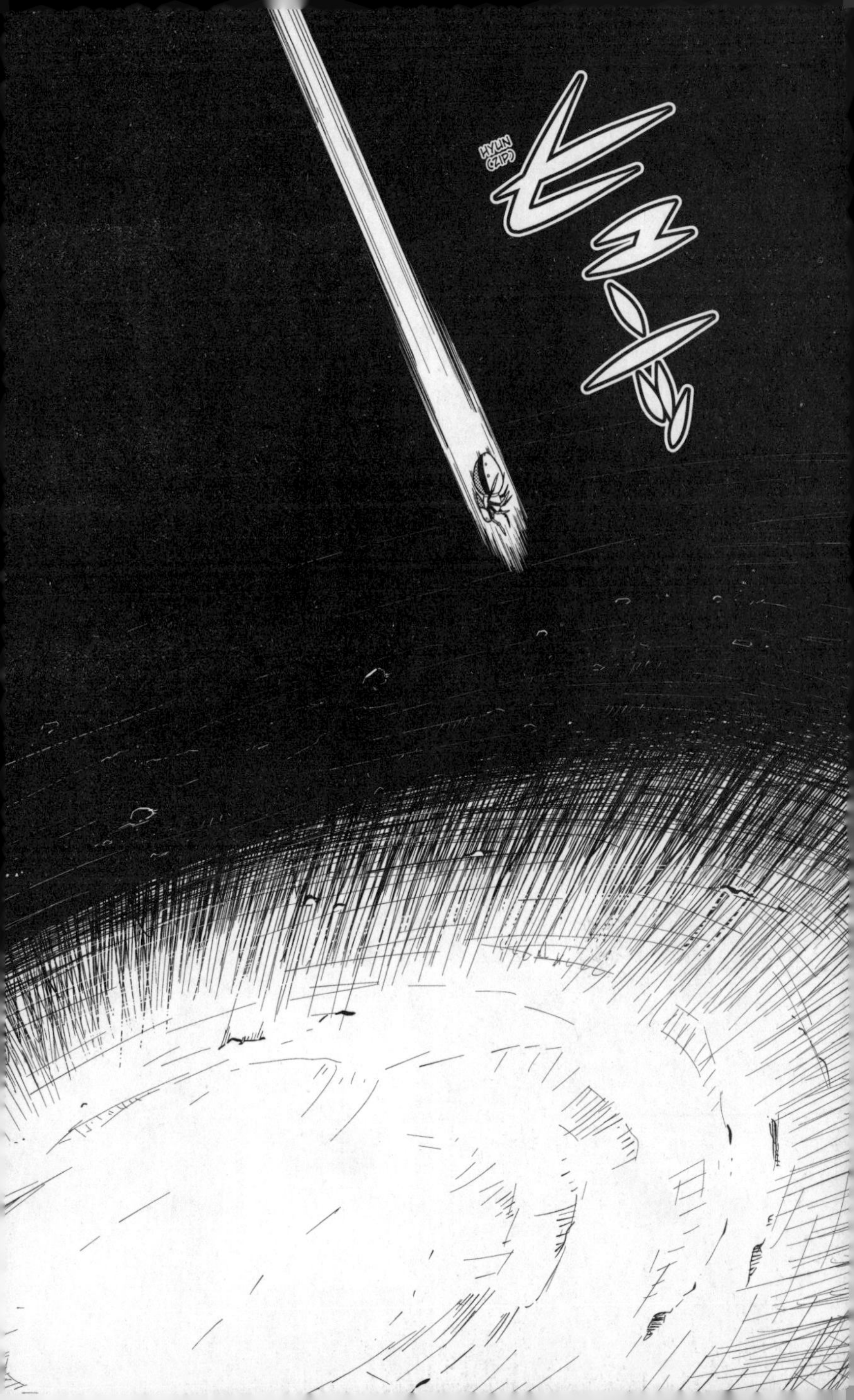
HYUN (ZIP)

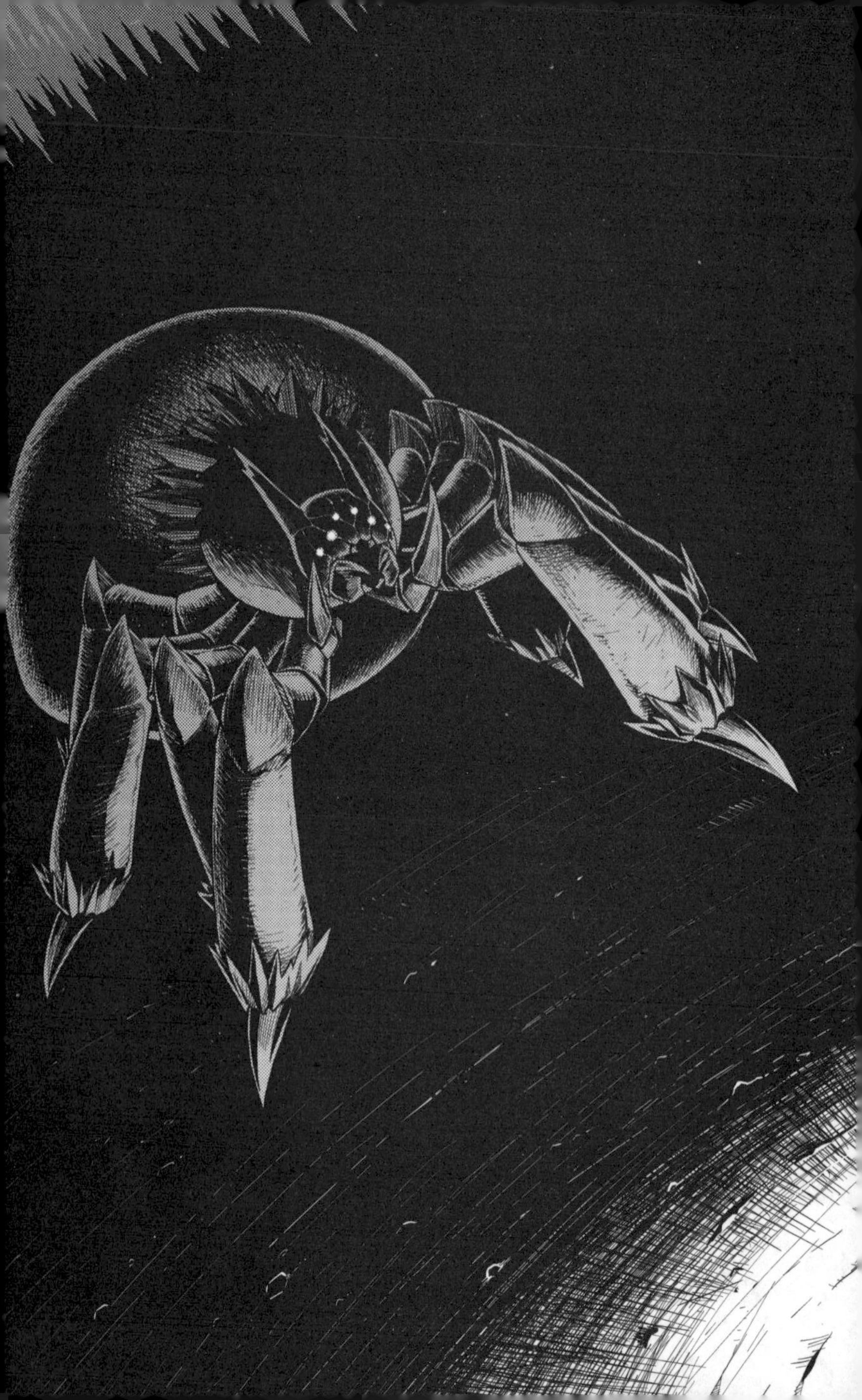

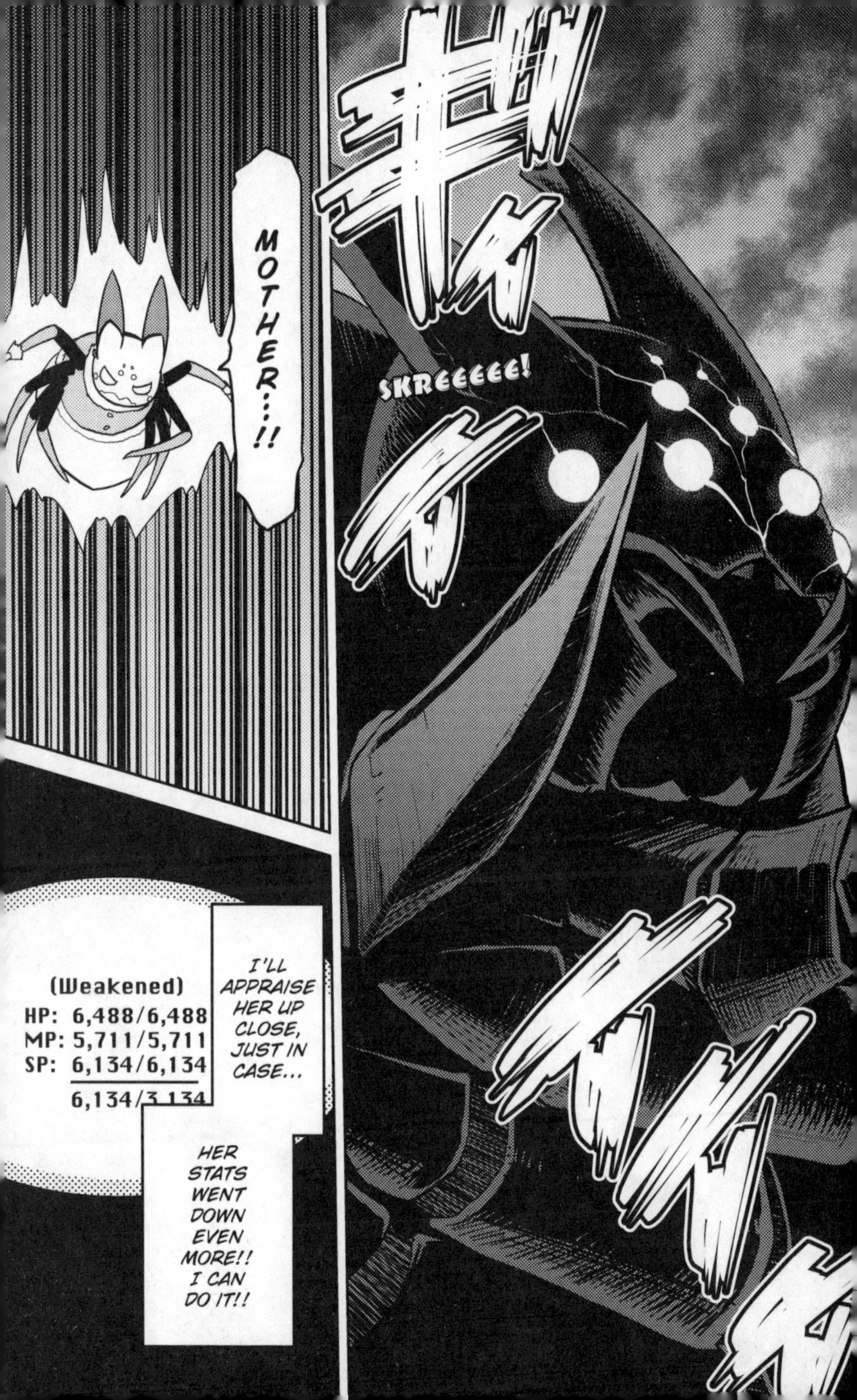
SKREEEEEE!
MOTHER...!!
I'LL APPRAISE HER UP CLOSE, JUST IN CASE...
(Weakened)
HP: 6,488/6,488
MP: 5,711/5,711
SP: 6,134/6,134
6,134/3,134
HER STATS WENT DOWN EVEN MORE!! I CAN DO IT!!

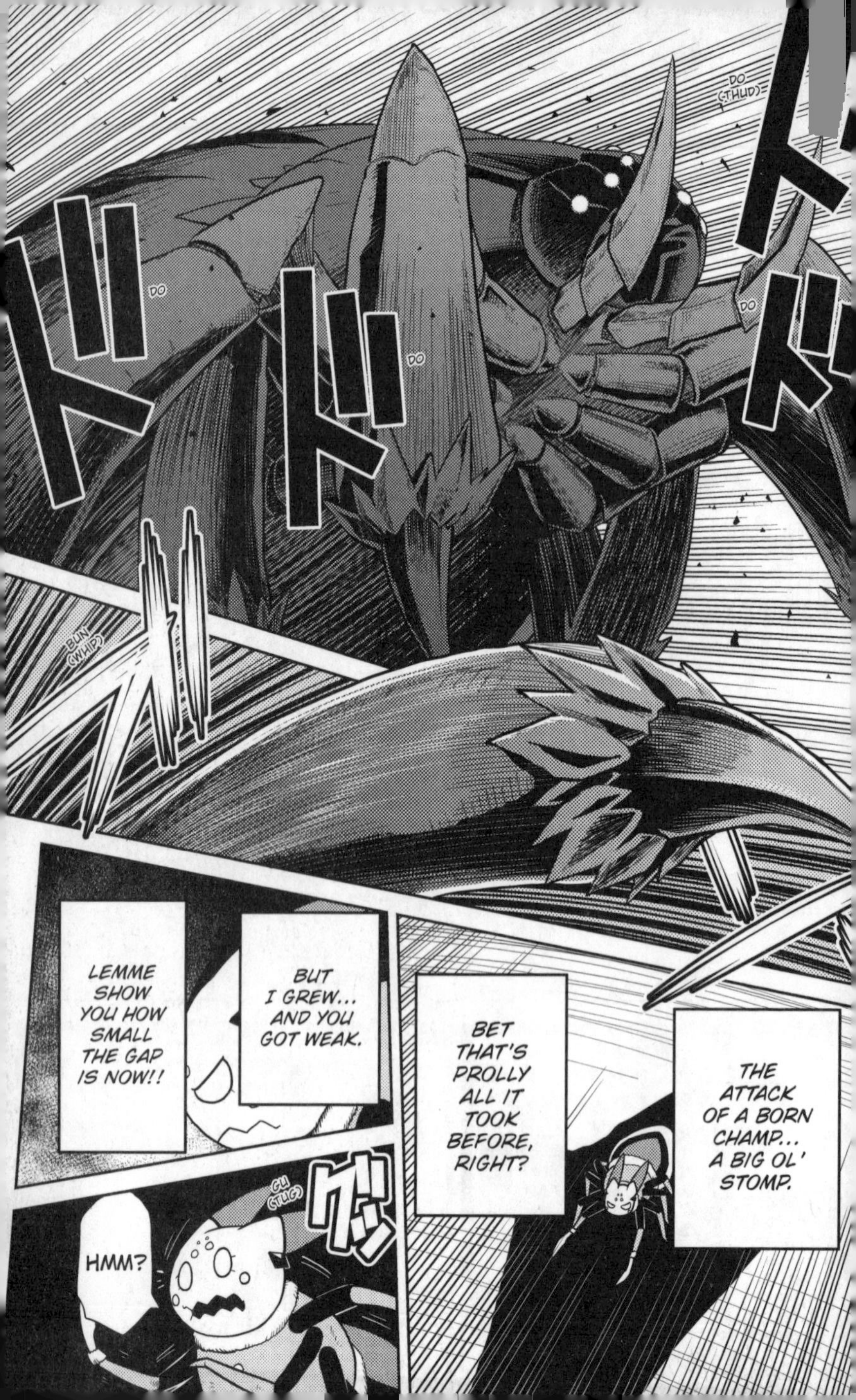
DO (THUD)
DO
DO
DO
BUN (WHIP)
THE ATTACK OF A BORN CHAMP... A BIG OL' STOMP.
BET THAT'S PROLLY ALL IT TOOK BEFORE, RIGHT?
BUT I GREW... AND YOU GOT WEAK.
LEMME SHOW YOU HOW SMALL THE GAP IS NOW!!
GU (TUG)
HMM?

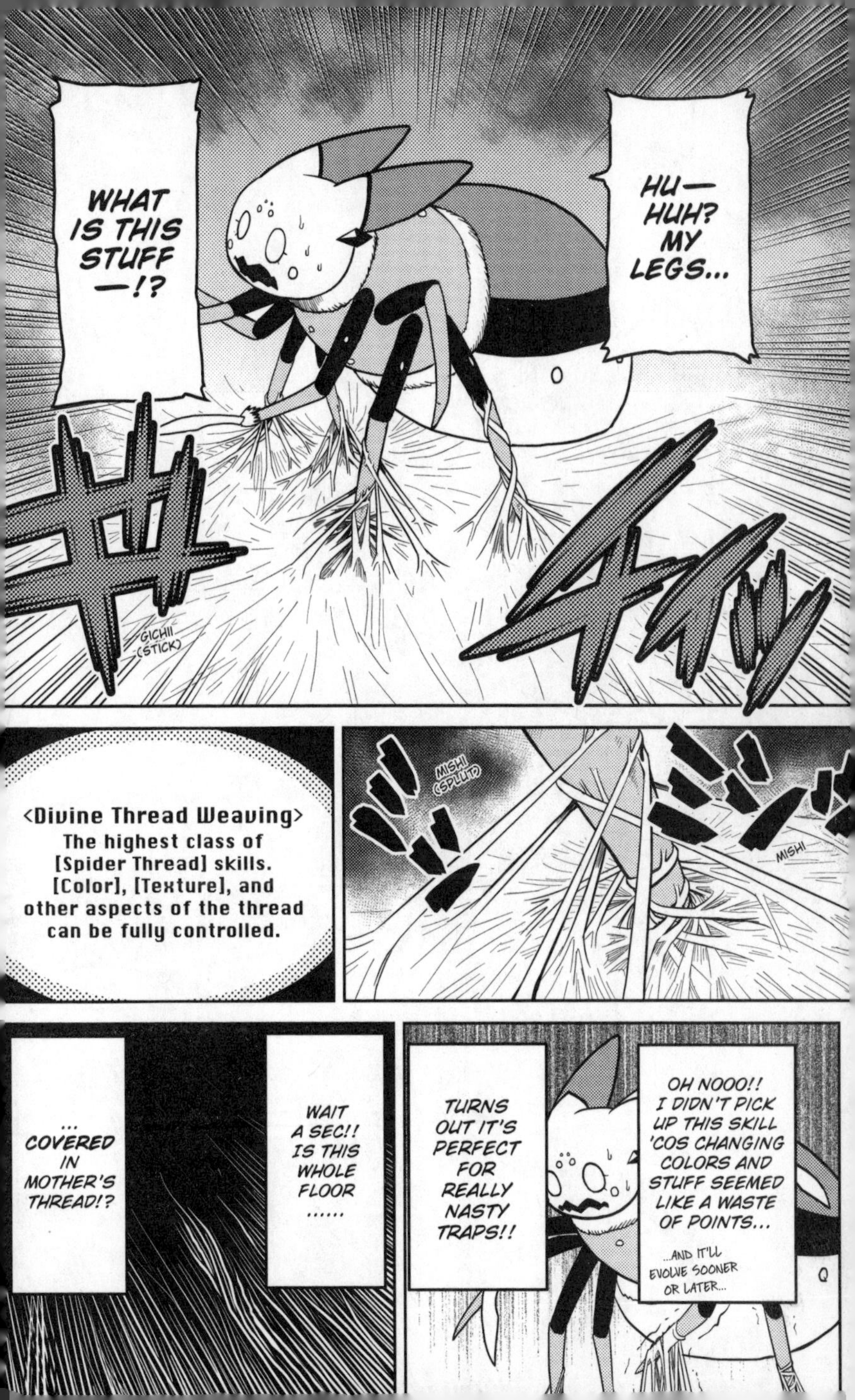
HU— HUH? MY LEGS...
WHAT IS THIS STUFF —!?
GICHII (STICK)
MISHI (SPLLLT)
MISHI
<Divine Thread Weaving> The highest class of [Spider Thread] skills. [Color], [Texture], and other aspects of the thread can be fully controlled.
OH NOOO!! I DIDN'T PICK UP THIS SKILL 'COS CHANGING COLORS AND STUFF SEEMED LIKE A WASTE OF POINTS...
...AND IT'LL EVOLVE SOONER OR LATER...
TURNS OUT IT'S PERFECT FOR REALLY NASTY TRAPS!!
WAIT A SEC!! IS THIS WHOLE FLOOR ......
... COVERED IN MOTHER'S THREAD!?

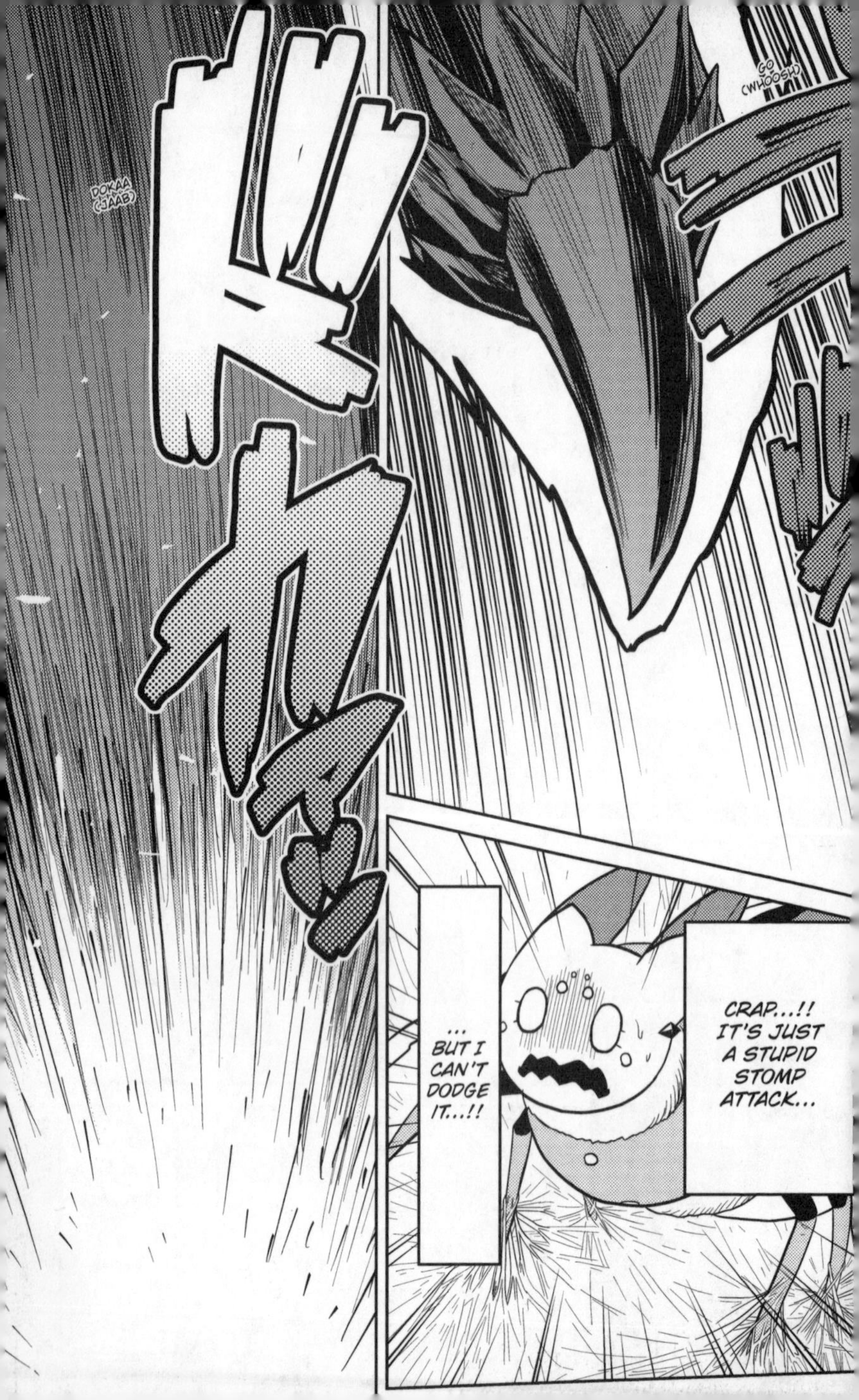
GO (WHOOSH)
CRAP...!! IT'S JUST A STUPID STOMP ATTACK...
... BUT I CAN'T DODGE IT...!!
DOKAA (JAAB)

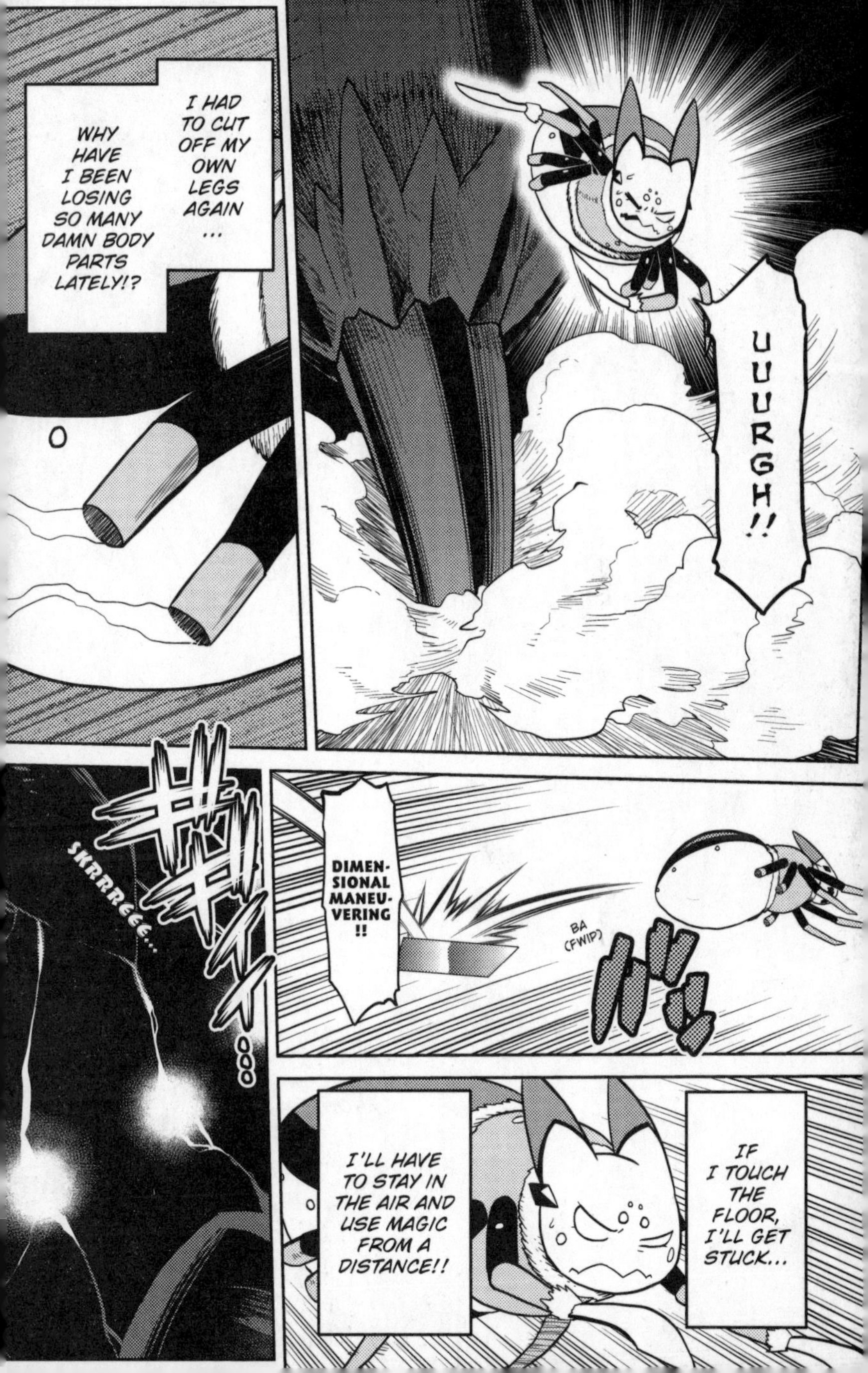
UUURGH!!
I HAD TO CUT OFF MY OWN LEGS AGAIN ...
WHY HAVE I BEEN LOSING SO MANY DAMN BODY PARTS LATELY!?
BA (FWIP)
DIMENSIONAL MANEUVERING!!
IF I TOUCH THE FLOOR, I'LL GET STUCK...
I'LL HAVE TO STAY IN THE AIR AND USE MAGIC FROM A DISTANCE!!
SKRRREEE...

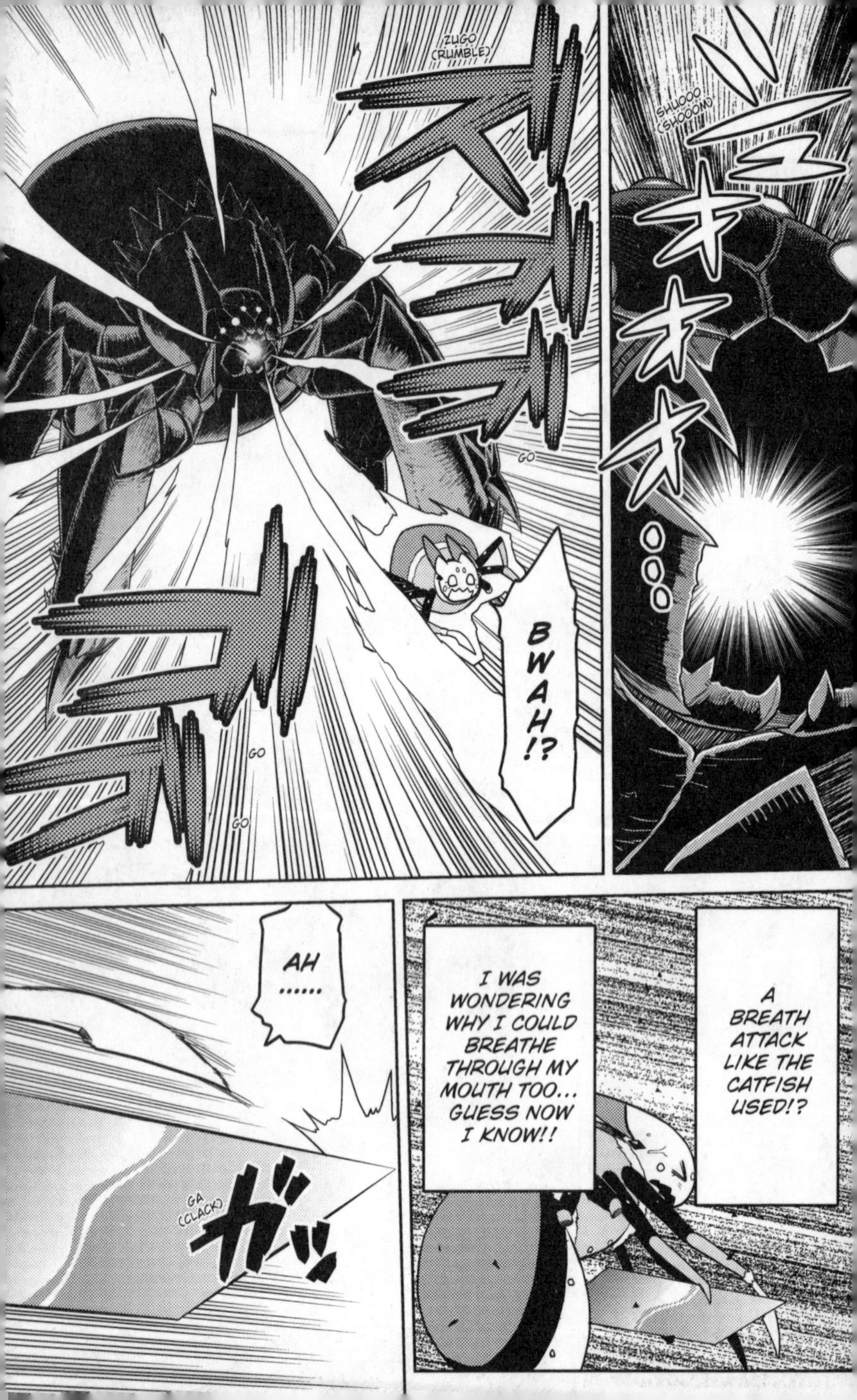
SHUOOO (SHOOOM)
ZUGO (RUMBLE)
GO
BWAH!?
GO
GO
A BREATH ATTACK LIKE THE CATFISH USED!?
I WAS WONDERING WHY I COULD BREATHE THROUGH MY MOUTH TOO... GUESS NOW I KNOW!!
AH ......
GA (CLACK)

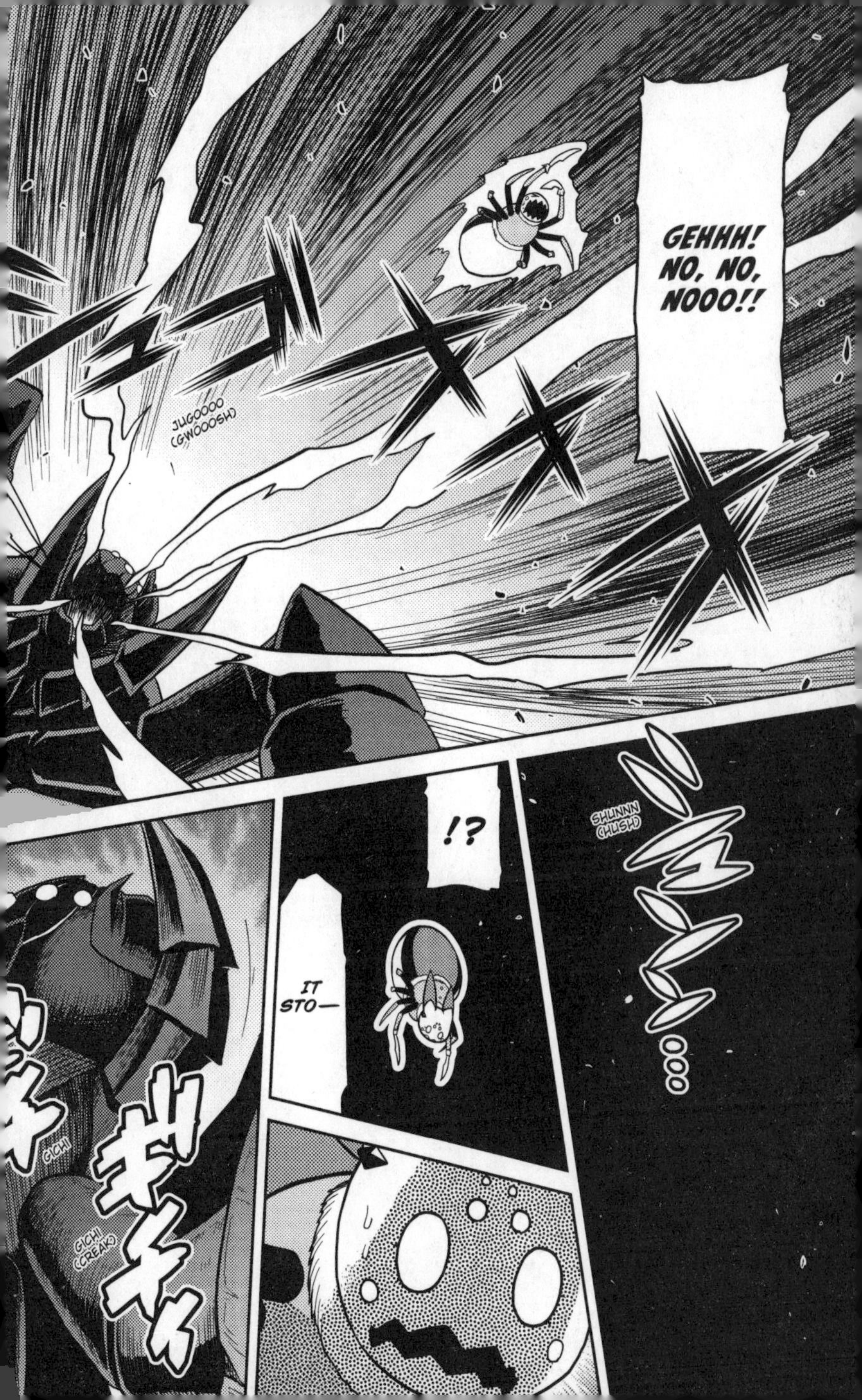
GEHHH! NO, NO, NOOO!!
JUGOOOO (GWOOOSH)
SHUNNN (HUSH)
!?
IT STO—
GICHI
GICHI (CREAK)

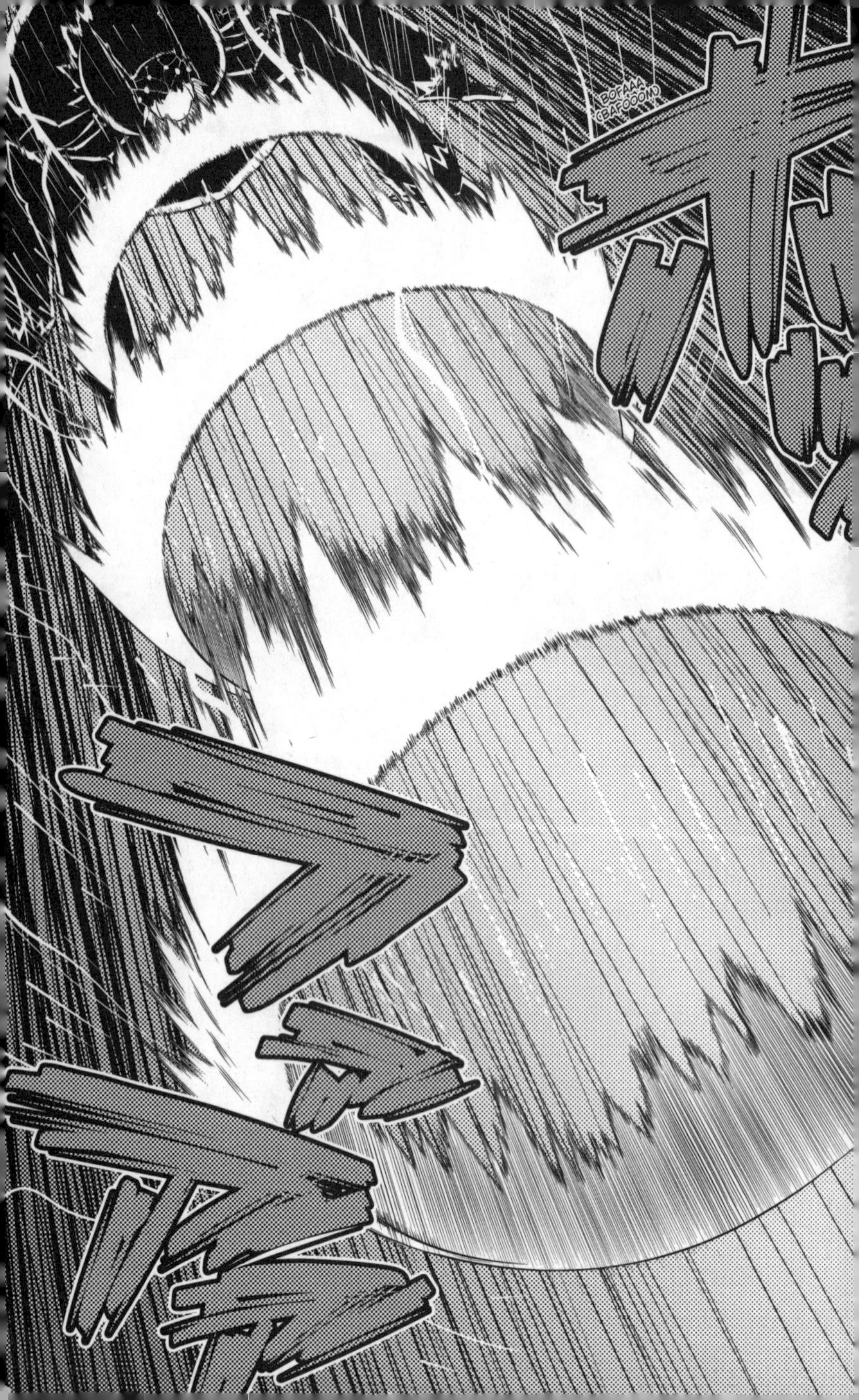
BOFAAA
(BAFOOOM)

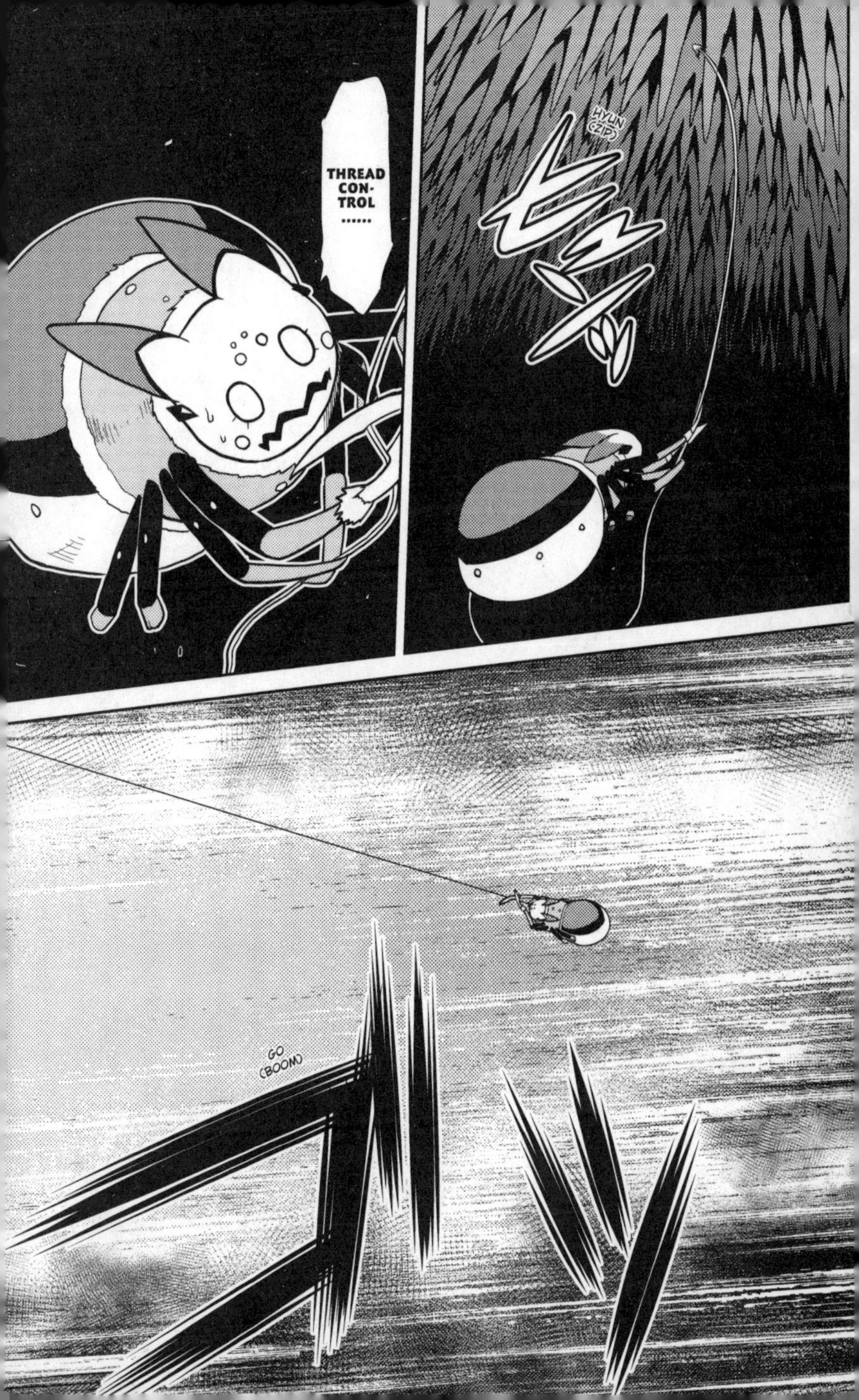
HYUN (ZIP)
THREAD CON-TROL ......
GO (BOOM)

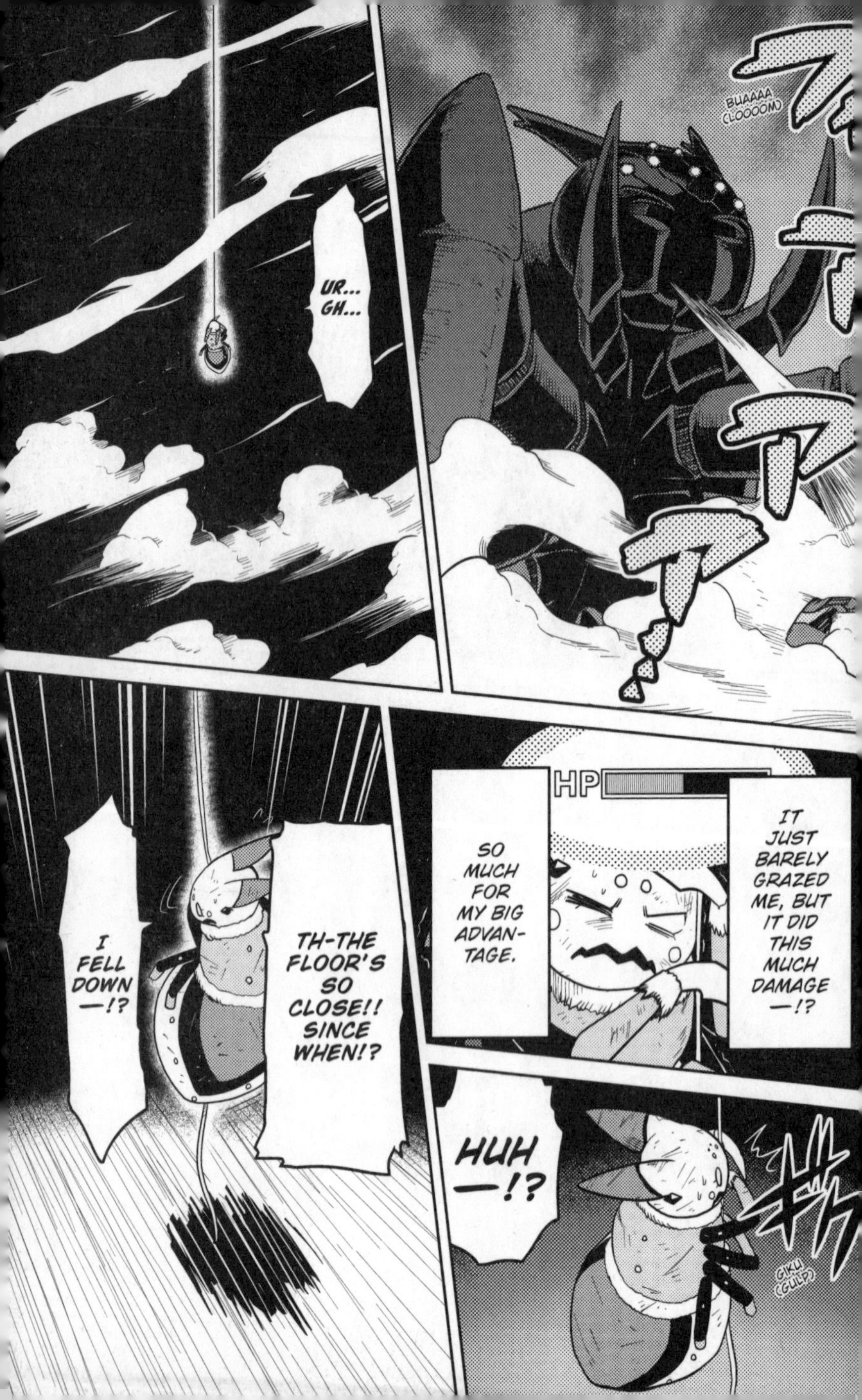
BUAAAA (LOOOOM)
UR... GH...
HP
IT JUST BARELY GRAZED ME, BUT IT DID THIS MUCH DAMAGE—!?
SO MUCH FOR MY BIG ADVAN-TAGE.
HUH—!?
GIKU (GULP)
TH-THE FLOOR'S SO CLOSE!! SINCE WHEN!?
I FELL DOWN—!?

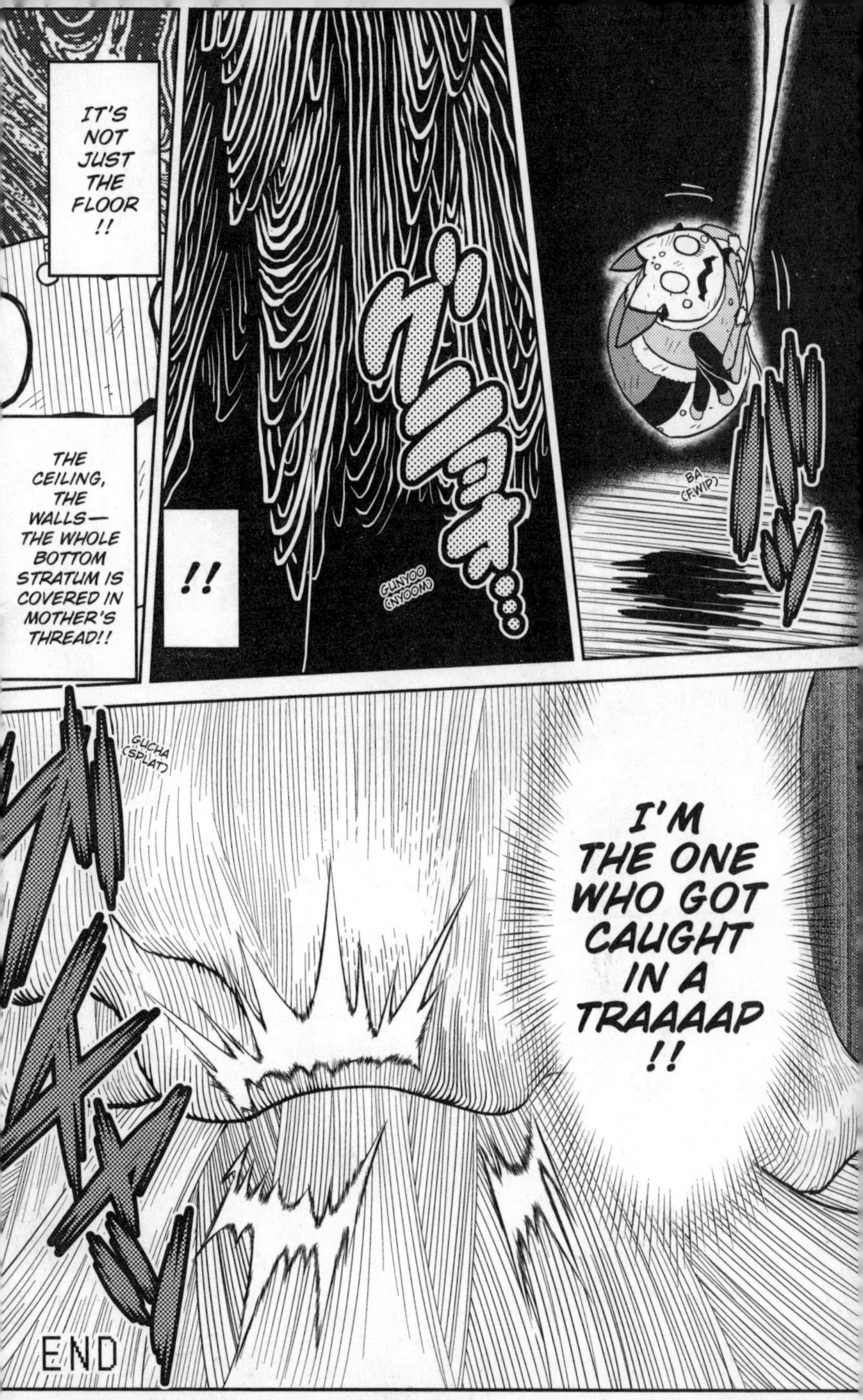
BA (F'WIP)
GUNYOO (NYOOM)
!!
IT'S NOT JUST THE FLOOR!!
THE CEILING, THE WALLS—THE WHOLE BOTTOM STRATUM IS COVERED IN MOTHER'S THREAD!!
I'M THE ONE WHO GOT CAUGHT IN A TRAAAAP!!
GUCHA (SPLAT)
END

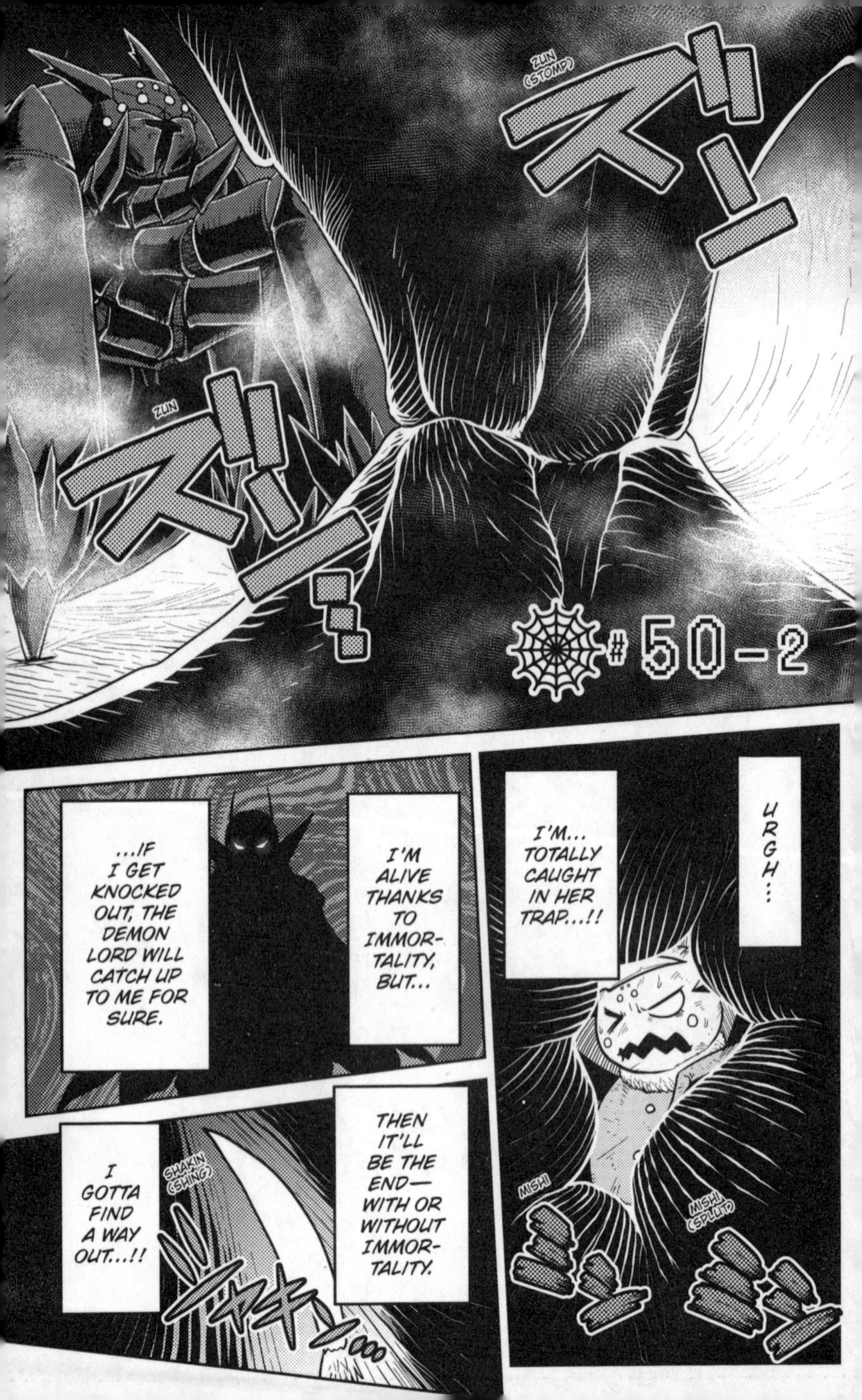
ZUN (STOMP)
ZUN
#50-2
URGH...
I'M... TOTALLY CAUGHT IN HER TRAP...!!
MISHI (SPLUT)
MISHI
I'M ALIVE THANKS TO IMMORTALITY, BUT...
...IF I GET KNOCKED OUT, THE DEMON LORD WILL CATCH UP TO ME FOR SURE.
THEN IT'LL BE THE END—WITH OR WITHOUT IMMORTALITY.
SHAKIN (SHING)
I GOTTA FIND A WAY OUT...!!

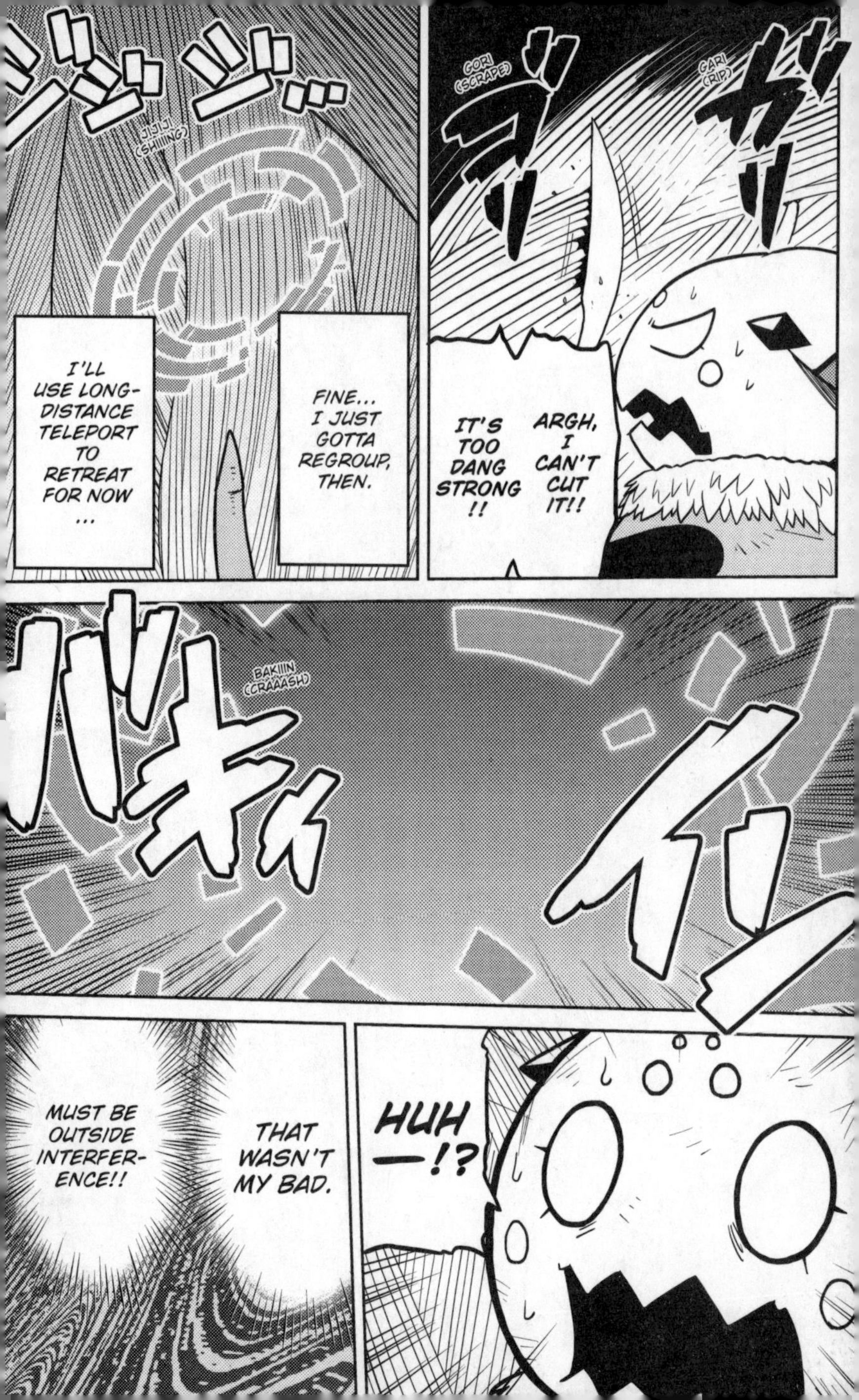
GARI (RIP)
GORI (SCRAPE)
ARGH, I CAN'T CUT IT!!
IT'S TOO DANG STRONG!!
JIJIJI (SHIIIING)
FINE... I JUST GOTTA REGROUP, THEN.
I'LL USE LONG-DISTANCE TELEPORT TO RETREAT FOR NOW...
BAKIIIN (CRAAASH)
HUH—!?
THAT WASN'T MY BAD.
MUST BE OUTSIDE INTERFERENCE!!

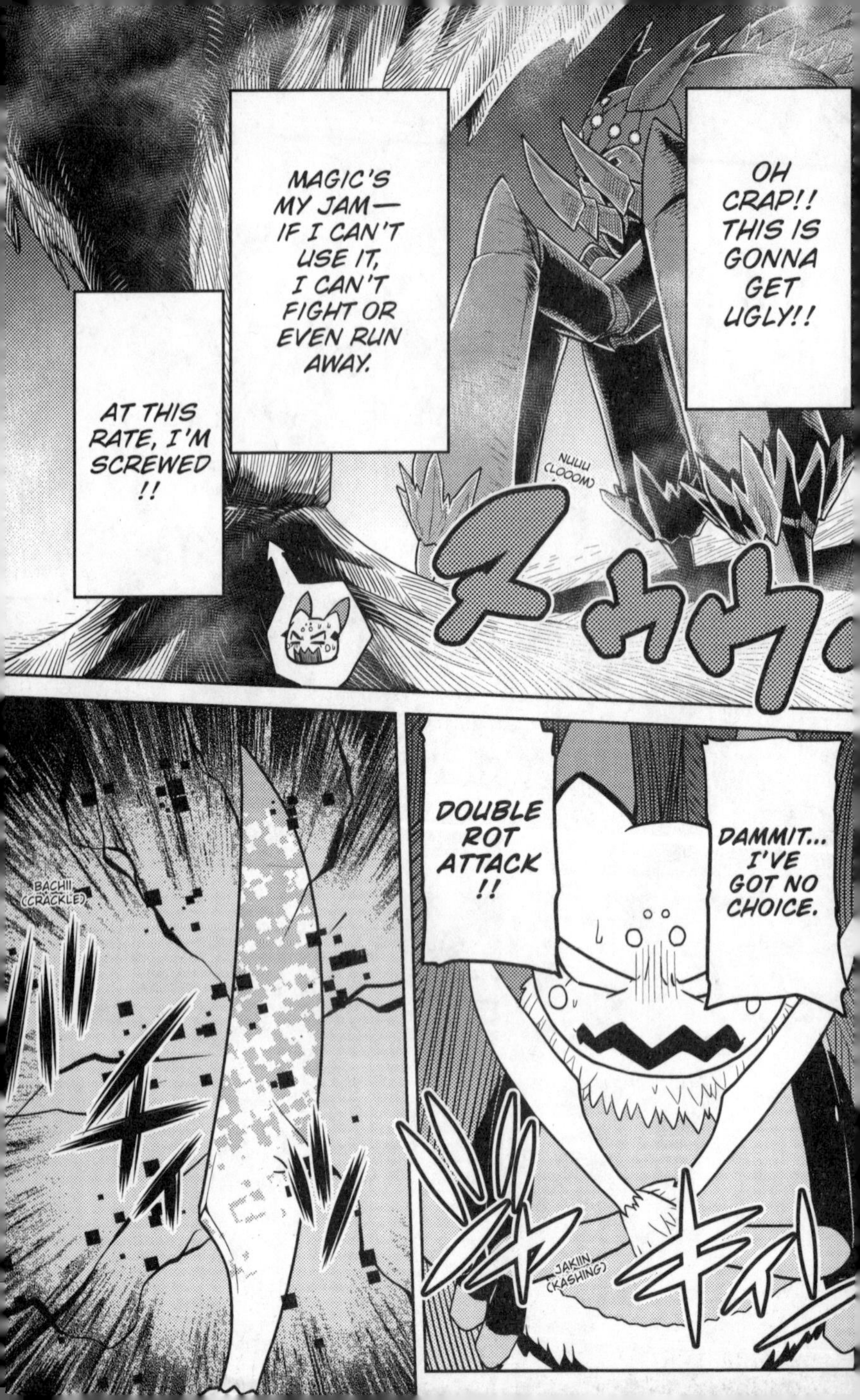
OH CRAP!! THIS IS GONNA GET UGLY!!
MAGIC'S MY JAM— IF I CAN'T USE IT, I CAN'T FIGHT OR EVEN RUN AWAY.
AT THIS RATE, I'M SCREWED!!
NUUU (LOOOM)
DAMMIT... I'VE GOT NO CHOICE.
DOUBLE ROT ATTACK!!
JAKIIN (KASHING)
BACHII (CRACKLE)

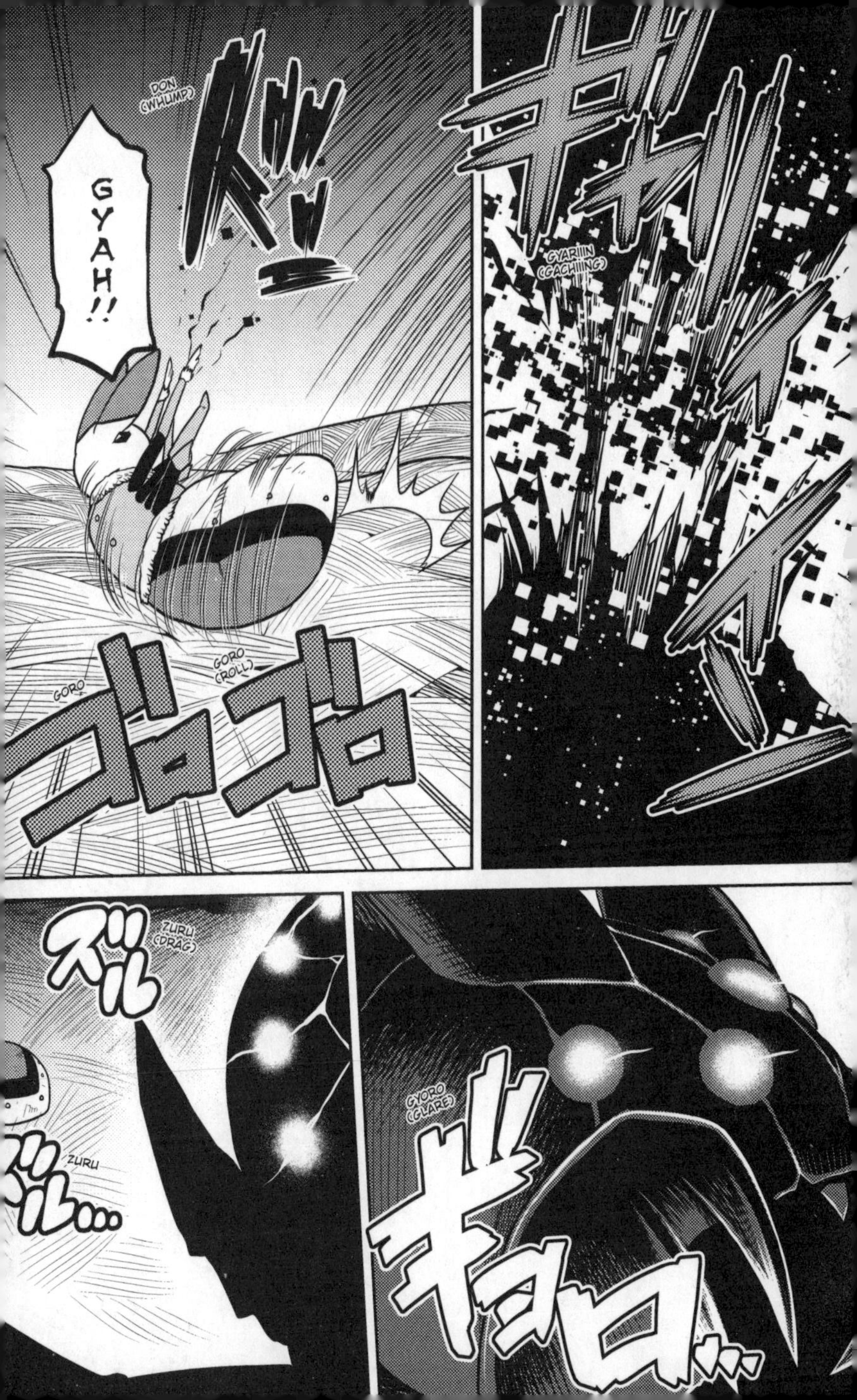
GYARIIN (GACHIING)
DON (WHUMP)
GYAH!!
GORO (ROLL)
GORO
ゴロゴロ
GYORO (GLARE)
ギョロ…
ZURU (DRAG)
ズル
ZURU
ズル…

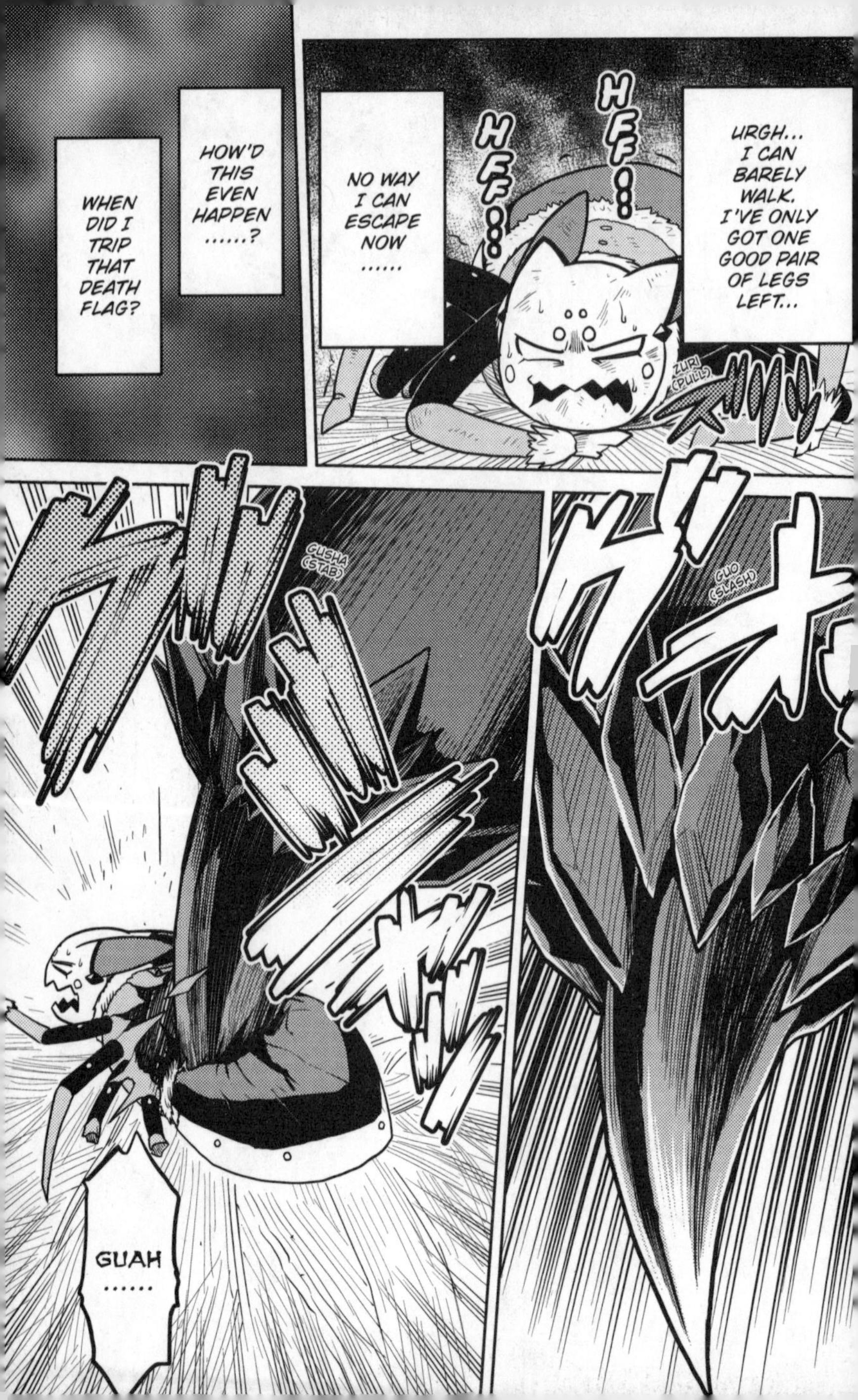
URGH... I CAN BARELY WALK. I'VE ONLY GOT ONE GOOD PAIR OF LEGS LEFT...
HFF...
HFF...
ZURI (PULL)
NO WAY I CAN ESCAPE NOW......
HOW'D THIS EVEN HAPPEN......?
WHEN DID I TRIP THAT DEATH FLAG?
GUO (SLASH)
GUSHA (STAB)
GUAH......

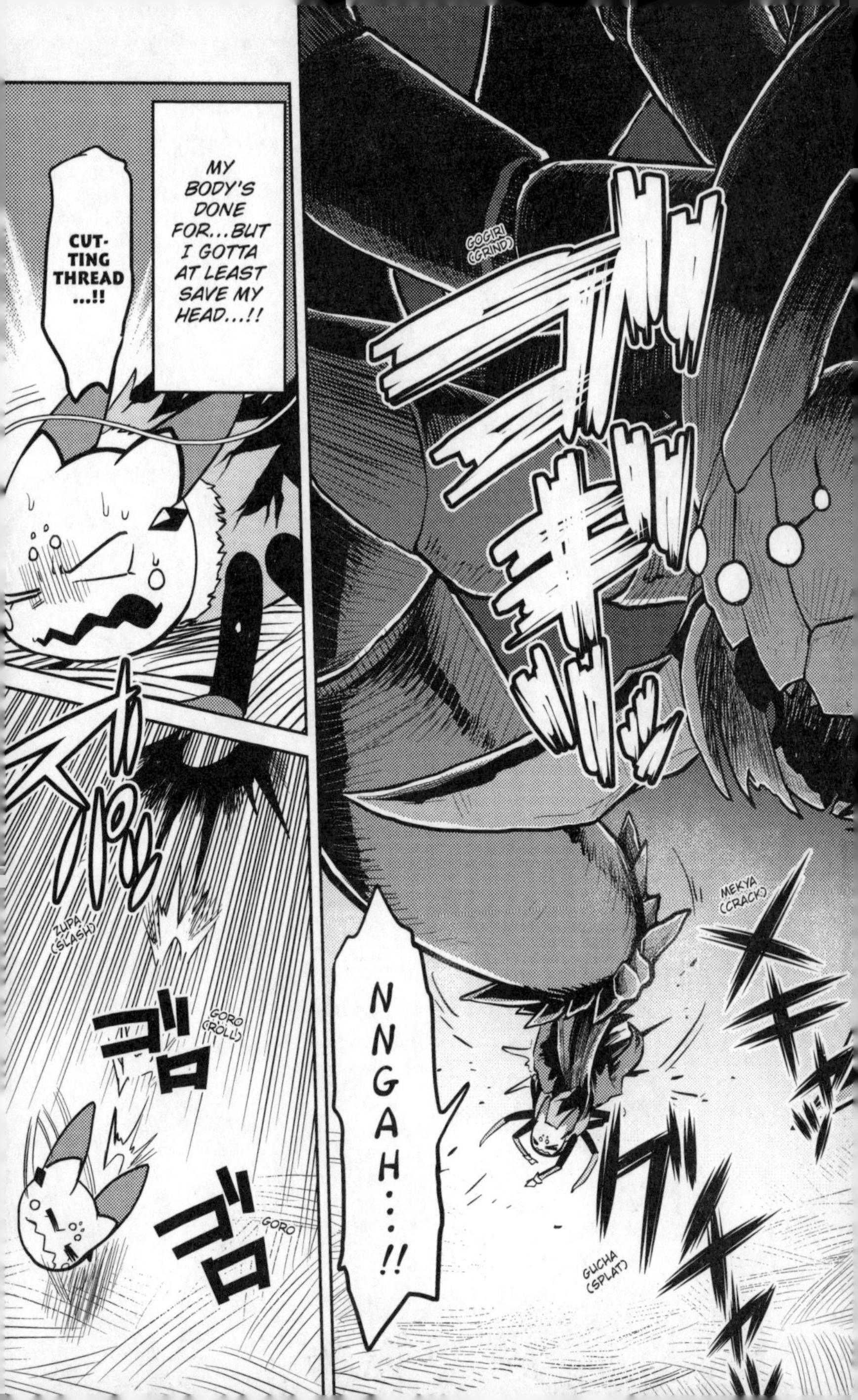
GOGIRI (GRIND)
MEKYA (CRACK)
NNGAH...!!
GUCHA (SPLAT)
MY BODY'S DONE FOR...BUT I GOTTA AT LEAST SAVE MY HEAD...!!
CUT-TING THREAD...!!
ZUPA (SLASH)
GORO (ROLL)
GORO

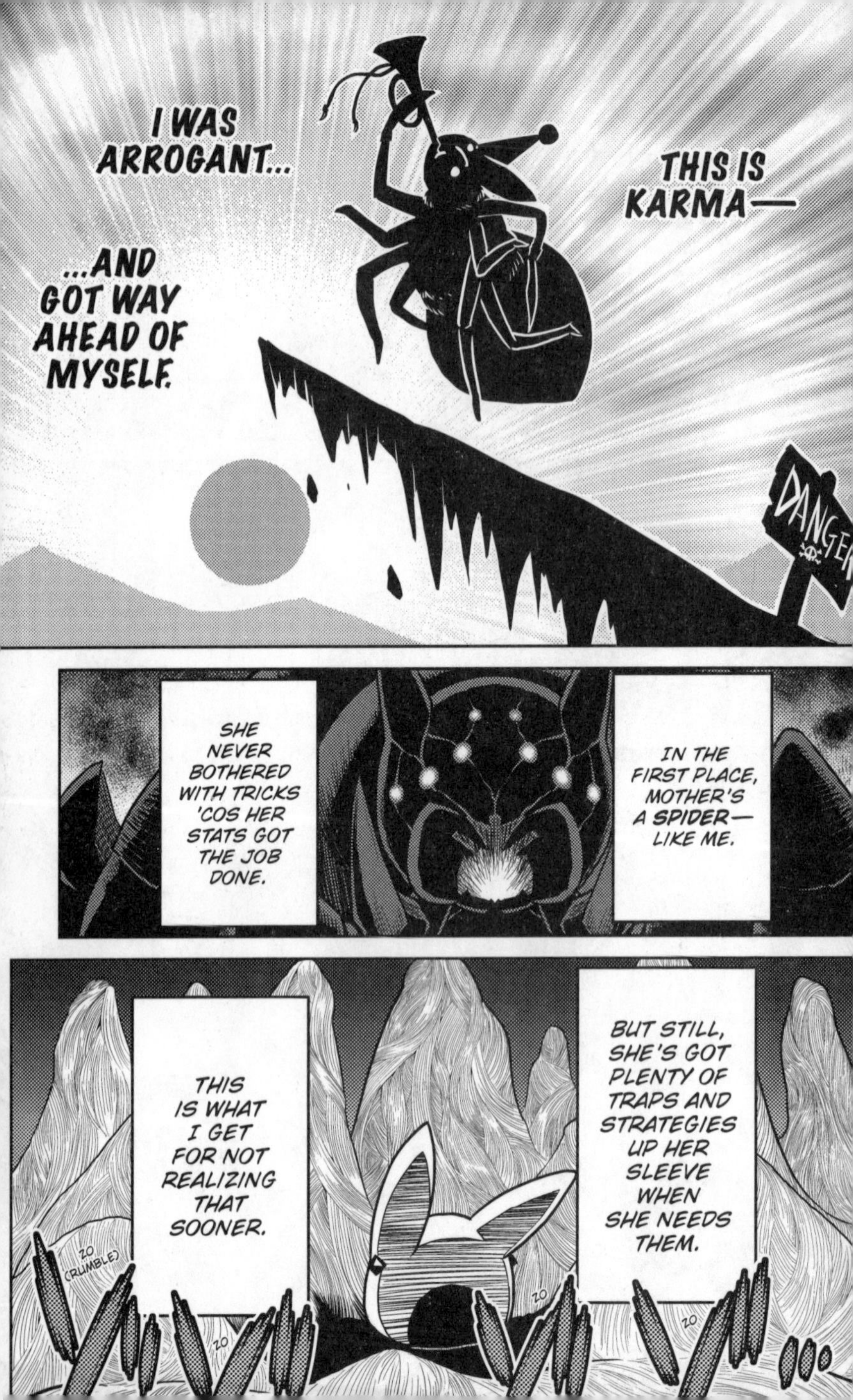
THIS IS KARMA—
I WAS ARROGANT...
...AND GOT WAY AHEAD OF MYSELF.
DANGER
IN THE FIRST PLACE, MOTHER'S A SPIDER—LIKE ME.
SHE NEVER BOTHERED WITH TRICKS 'COS HER STATS GOT THE JOB DONE.
BUT STILL, SHE'S GOT PLENTY OF TRAPS AND STRATEGIES UP HER SLEEVE WHEN SHE NEEDS THEM.
THIS IS WHAT I GET FOR NOT REALIZING THAT SOONER.
ZO (RUMBLE)
ZO
ZO
ZO

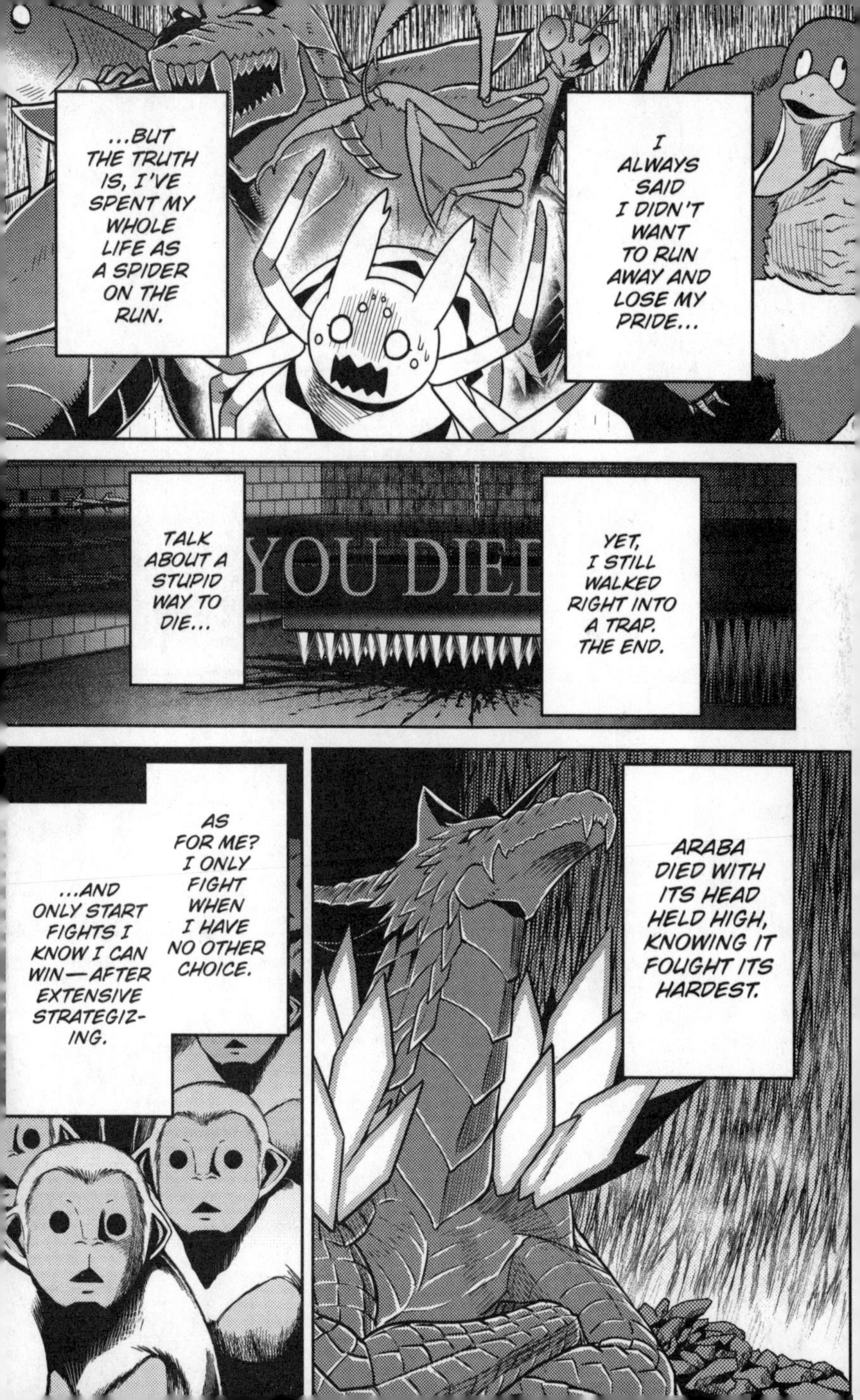
I ALWAYS SAID I DIDN'T WANT TO RUN AWAY AND LOSE MY PRIDE...
...BUT THE TRUTH IS, I'VE SPENT MY WHOLE LIFE AS A SPIDER ON THE RUN.
YET, I STILL WALKED RIGHT INTO A TRAP. THE END.
YOU DIE
TALK ABOUT A STUPID WAY TO DIE...
ARABA DIED WITH ITS HEAD HELD HIGH, KNOWING IT FOUGHT ITS HARDEST.
AS FOR ME? I ONLY FIGHT WHEN I HAVE NO OTHER CHOICE.
...AND ONLY START FIGHTS I KNOW I CAN WIN—AFTER EXTENSIVE STRATEGIZING.

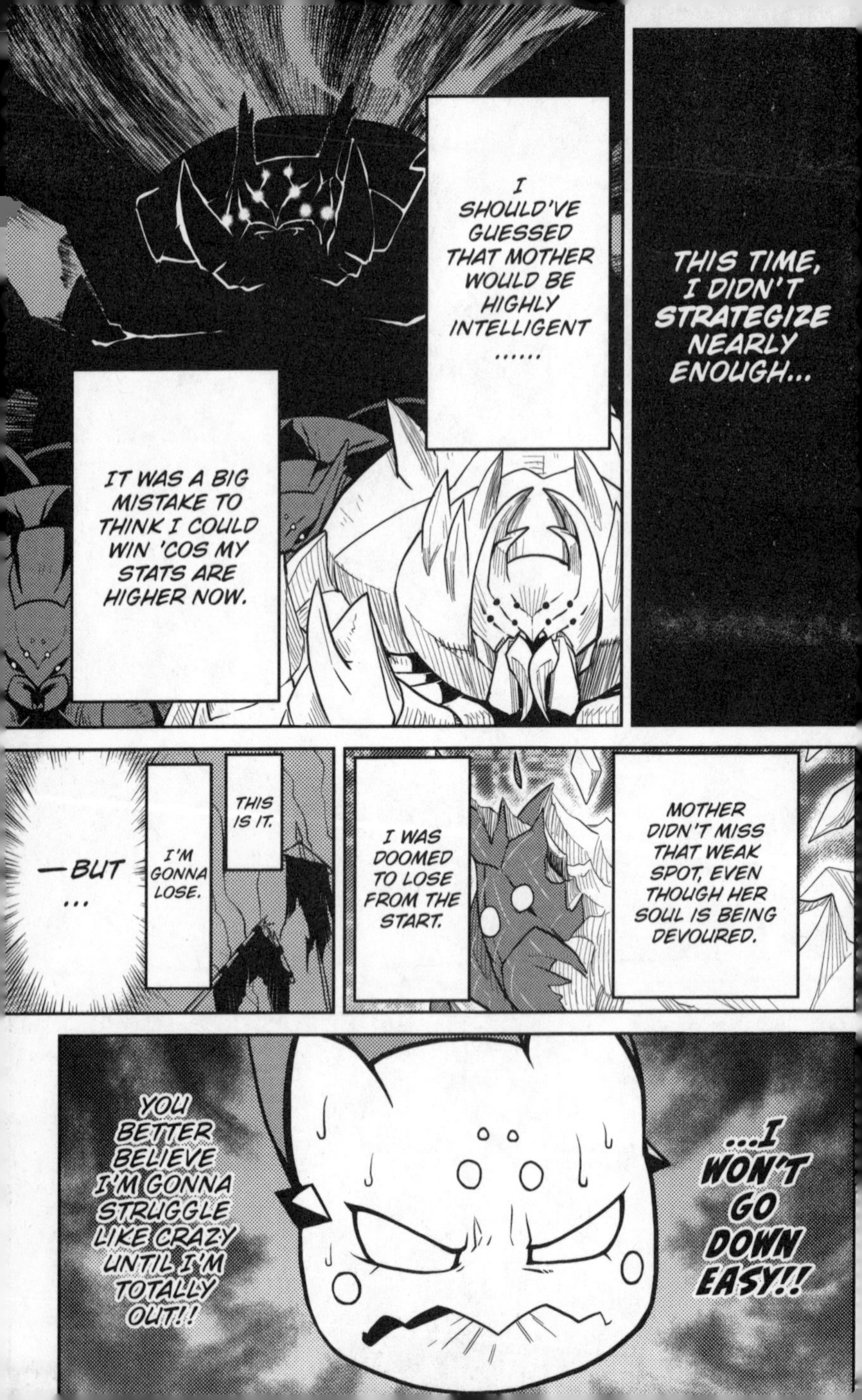
THIS TIME, I DIDN'T STRATEGIZE NEARLY ENOUGH...
I SHOULD'VE GUESSED THAT MOTHER WOULD BE HIGHLY INTELLIGENT ......
IT WAS A BIG MISTAKE TO THINK I COULD WIN 'COS MY STATS ARE HIGHER NOW.
MOTHER DIDN'T MISS THAT WEAK SPOT, EVEN THOUGH HER SOUL IS BEING DEVOURED.
I WAS DOOMED TO LOSE FROM THE START.
THIS IS IT.
I'M GONNA LOSE.
—BUT ...
...I WON'T GO DOWN EASY!!
YOU BETTER BELIEVE I'M GONNA STRUGGLE LIKE CRAZY UNTIL I'M TOTALLY OUT!!

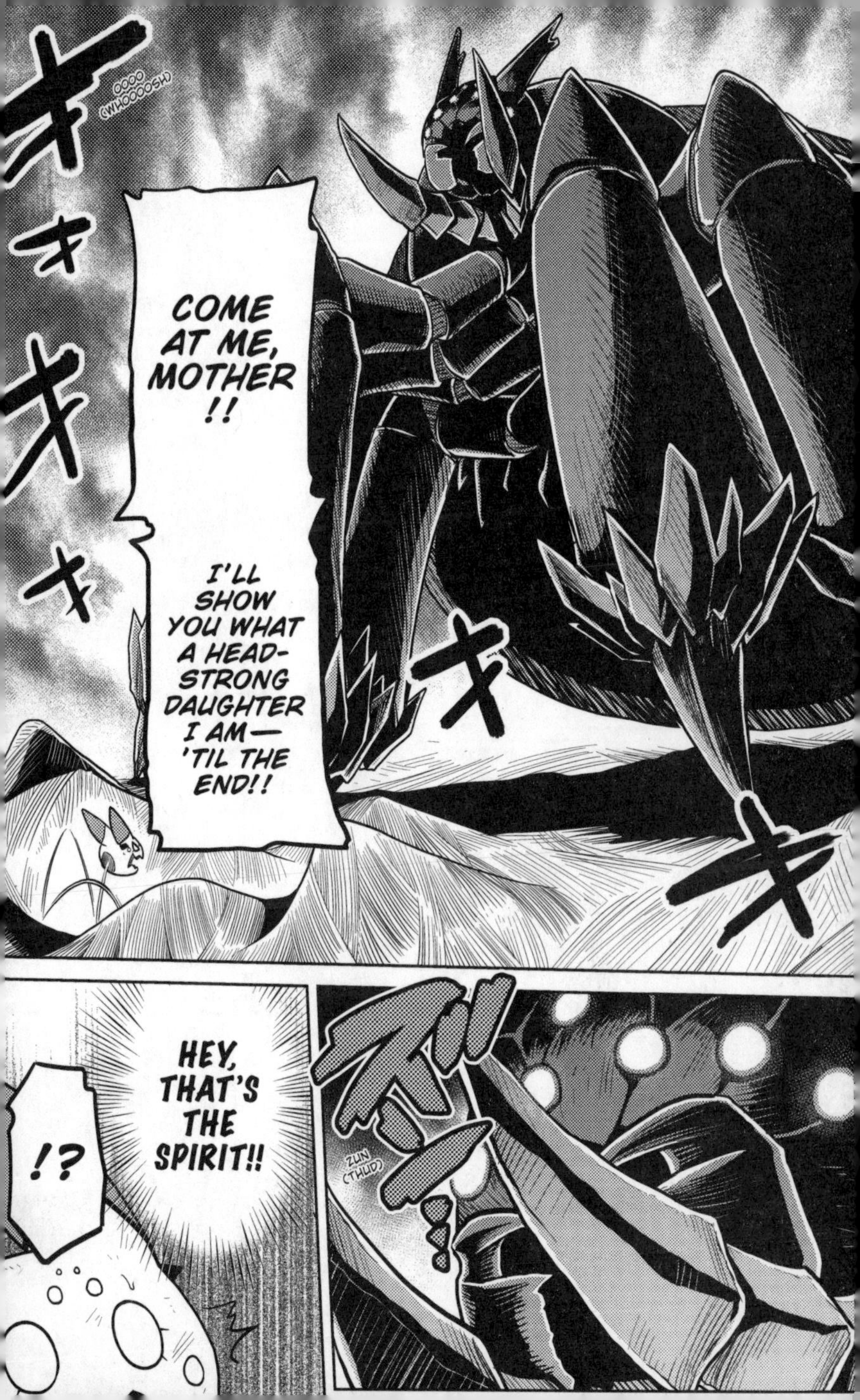
COME AT ME, MOTHER!!
I'LL SHOW YOU WHAT A HEAD-STRONG DAUGHTER I AM—'TIL THE END!!
(WHOOOOSH)
ZUN (THUD)
HEY, THAT'S THE SPIRIT!!
!?

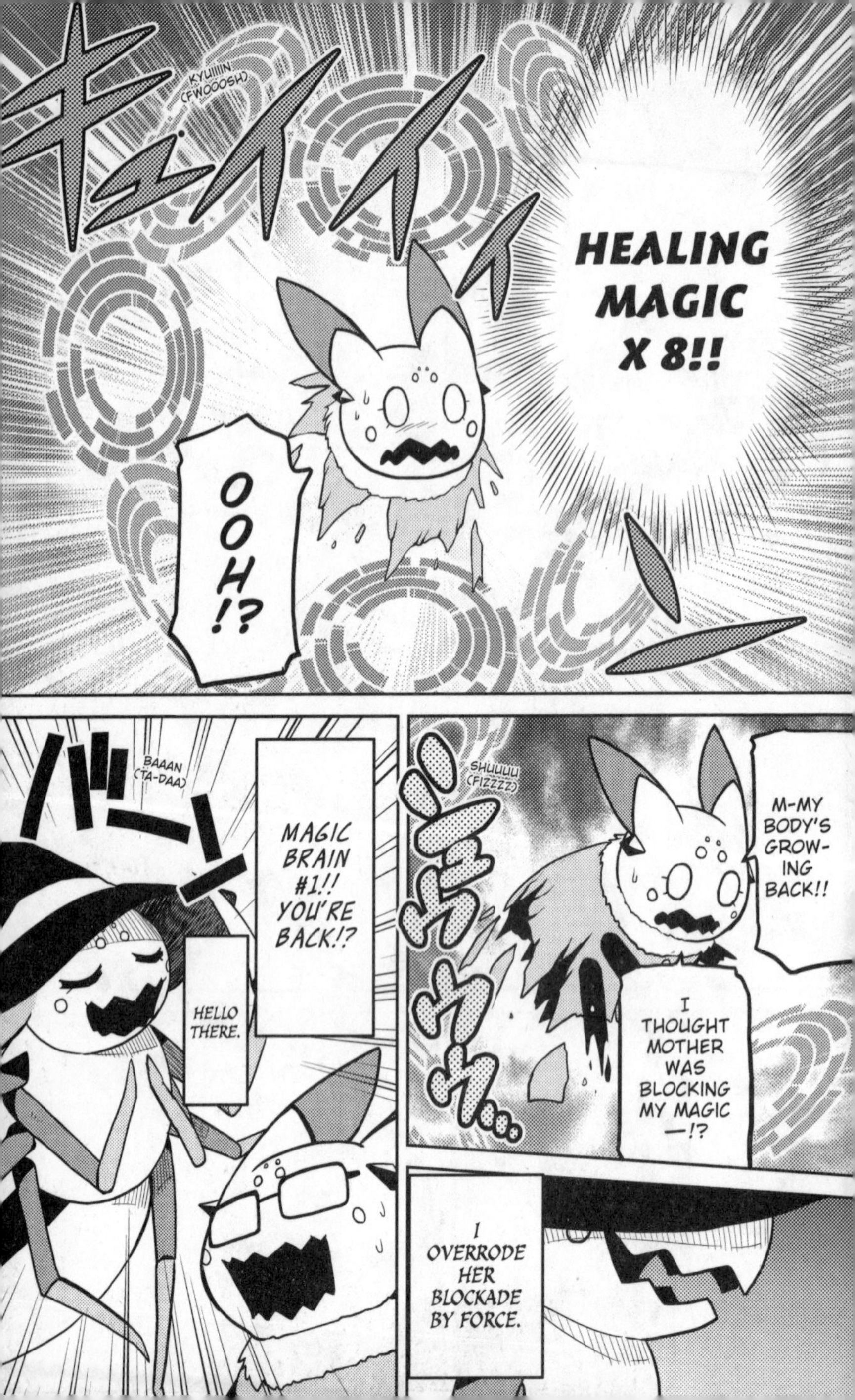
KYUIIIIN (FWOOOSH)
HEALING MAGIC X 8!!
OOH!?
SHUUUU (FIZZZZ)
M-MY BODY'S GROW-ING BACK!!
I THOUGHT MOTHER WAS BLOCKING MY MAGIC—!?
I OVERRODE HER BLOCKADE BY FORCE.
BAAAN (TA-DAA)
MAGIC BRAIN #1!! YOU'RE BACK!?
HELLO THERE.

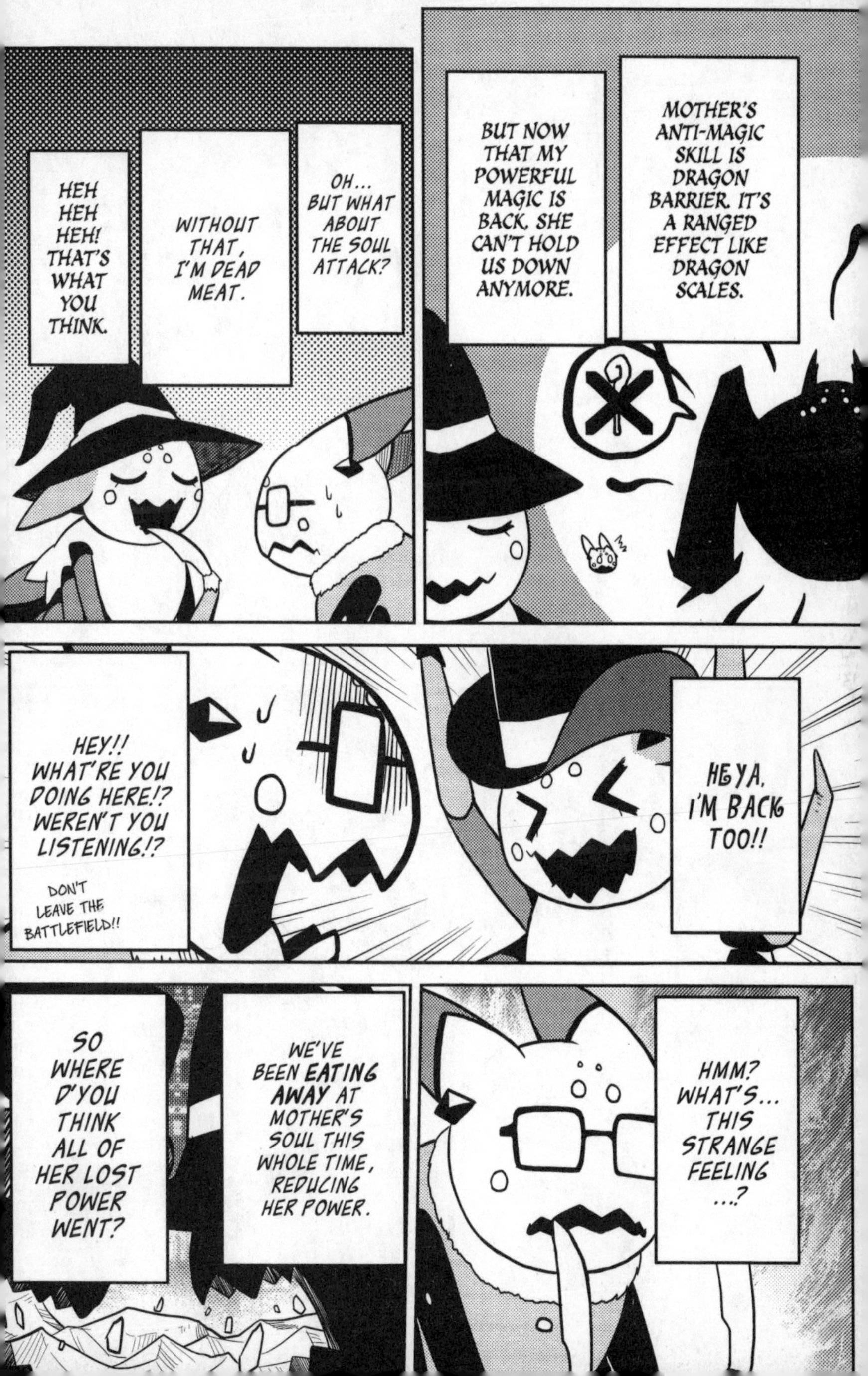
MOTHER'S ANTI-MAGIC SKILL IS DRAGON BARRIER. IT'S A RANGED EFFECT LIKE DRAGON SCALES.
BUT NOW THAT MY POWERFUL MAGIC IS BACK, SHE CAN'T HOLD US DOWN ANYMORE.
OH... BUT WHAT ABOUT THE SOUL ATTACK?
WITHOUT THAT, I'M DEAD MEAT.
HEH HEH HEH! THAT'S WHAT YOU THINK.
HEYA, I'M BACK TOO!!
HEY!! WHAT'RE YOU DOING HERE!? WEREN'T YOU LISTENING!?
DON'T LEAVE THE BATTLEFIELD!!
HMM? WHAT'S... THIS STRANGE FEELING...?
WE'VE BEEN EATING AWAY AT MOTHER'S SOUL THIS WHOLE TIME, REDUCING HER POWER.
SO WHERE D'YOU THINK ALL OF HER LOST POWER WENT?

«Zana Horowa LV 24 No Name»

Status
HP: 21,622/21,622 + 0 MP: 29,618/29,618 + 0
SP: 17,097/17,097: 4,111/17,097 + 0
ATK: 21,153 DEF: 21,104 MAG: 28,280
RES: 28,107 SPE:25,021

[HP Ultra-Fast Recovery LV 6]
[Height of Occultism] [Magic Divinity LV 7]
[Magic Power Conferment LV 10]
[Magic Power Super-Attack LV 2]
[SP Rapid Recovery LV 10]
[SP Minimized Consumption LV 10]
[Destruction Super-Enhancement LV 6]
[Impact Super-Enhancement LV 7]
[Cutting Super-Enhancement LV 4]
[Piercing Super-Enhancement LV 6]
[Shock Super-Enhancement LV 6]
[Status Condition Super-
Enhancement LV 10]
[Battle Divinity LV 10]
[Energy Conferment LV 10]
[Ability Conferment LV 7]
[Energy Super-Attack LV 4]
[Divine Dragon Power LV 7]
[Dragon Barrier LV 2]
[Deadly Poison
Attack LV 10]
[Enhanced Paralysis
Attack LV 10]
[Rot Attack LV 6]
[Heretic Attack LV 8]
[Poison
Synthesis LV 10]
[Medicine Synthesis LV 10]
[Thread Genius LV 10]
[Divine Thread Weaving]
[Thread Control LV 10]
[Psychokinesis LV 7]
[Throw LV 10] [Expel LV 10]
[Dimensional Maneuvering LV 10]
[Swim LV 2] [Kin Control LV 10]
[Egg-Laying LV 10] [Concentration LV 10]
[Thought Super-Acceleration LV 3]
[Future Sight LV 3] [Parallel Thinking LV 9]
[High-Speed Processing LV 10]
[Hit LV 10] [Evasion LV 10]
[Probability Super-Correction LV 10]
[Stealth LV 10] [Concealment LV 2]
[Silence LV 10] [Odorless LV 3] [Emperor]
[Conviction] [Hades] [Corruption] [Immortality]
[Heretic Magic LV 10] [Wind Magic LV 10]
[Gale Magic LV 1] [Earth Magic LV 10]
[Terrain Magic LV 3] [Shadow Magic LV 10]

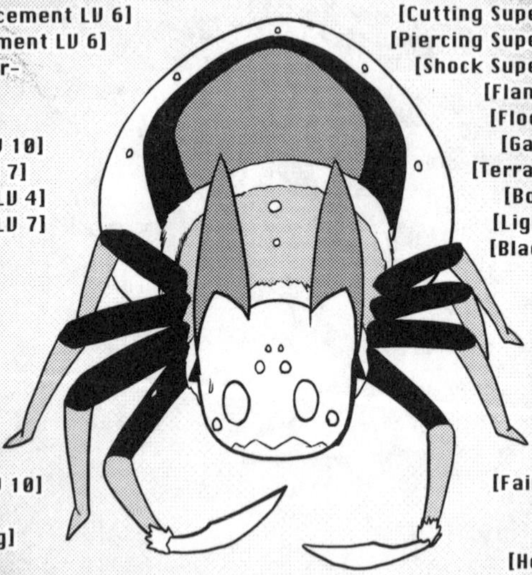

[Dark Magic LV 1
[Black Magic LV 7] [Poison Magic LV 1
[Healing Magic LV 10] [Spatial Magic LV 1
[Dimensional Magic LV 7] [Abyss Magic LV 1
[Demon Lord LV 8] [Perseveranc
[Pride] [Rage LV 2] [Usurp LV
[Satiation LV 10] [Sloth] [Wisdor
[Destruction Super-Resistance LV
[Impact Nullificatio
[Cutting Super-Resistance LV
[Piercing Super-Resistance LV
[Shock Super-Resistance LV
[Flame Resistance LV
[Flood Resistance LV
[Gale Resistance LV
[Terrain Resistance LV
[Bolt Resistance LV
[Light Resistance LV
[Black Resistance LV
[Heavy Supe
Resistance LV
[Status Conditic
Nullificatio
[Acid Supe
Resistance LV
[Rot Supe
Resistance LV
[Faint Resistance LV
[Fear Supe
Resistance LV
[Heresy Nullificatio
[Pain Nullificatio
[Suffering Nullificatio
[Night Vision LV 1
[Panoptic Vision LV
[Jinx Evil Eye LV
[Inert Evil Eye LV
[Repellent Evil Eye LV
[Annihilating Evil Eye LV
[Five Senses Super-Enhancement LV 1
[Perception Expansion LV
[Divinity Expansion LV
[Celestial Power] [Ultimate Life LV 1
[Ultimate Movement LV 1
[Fortune LV 10] [Fortitude LV 1
[Stronghold LV 10] [Skanda LV 1
[Taboo LV 10] [n%I = W

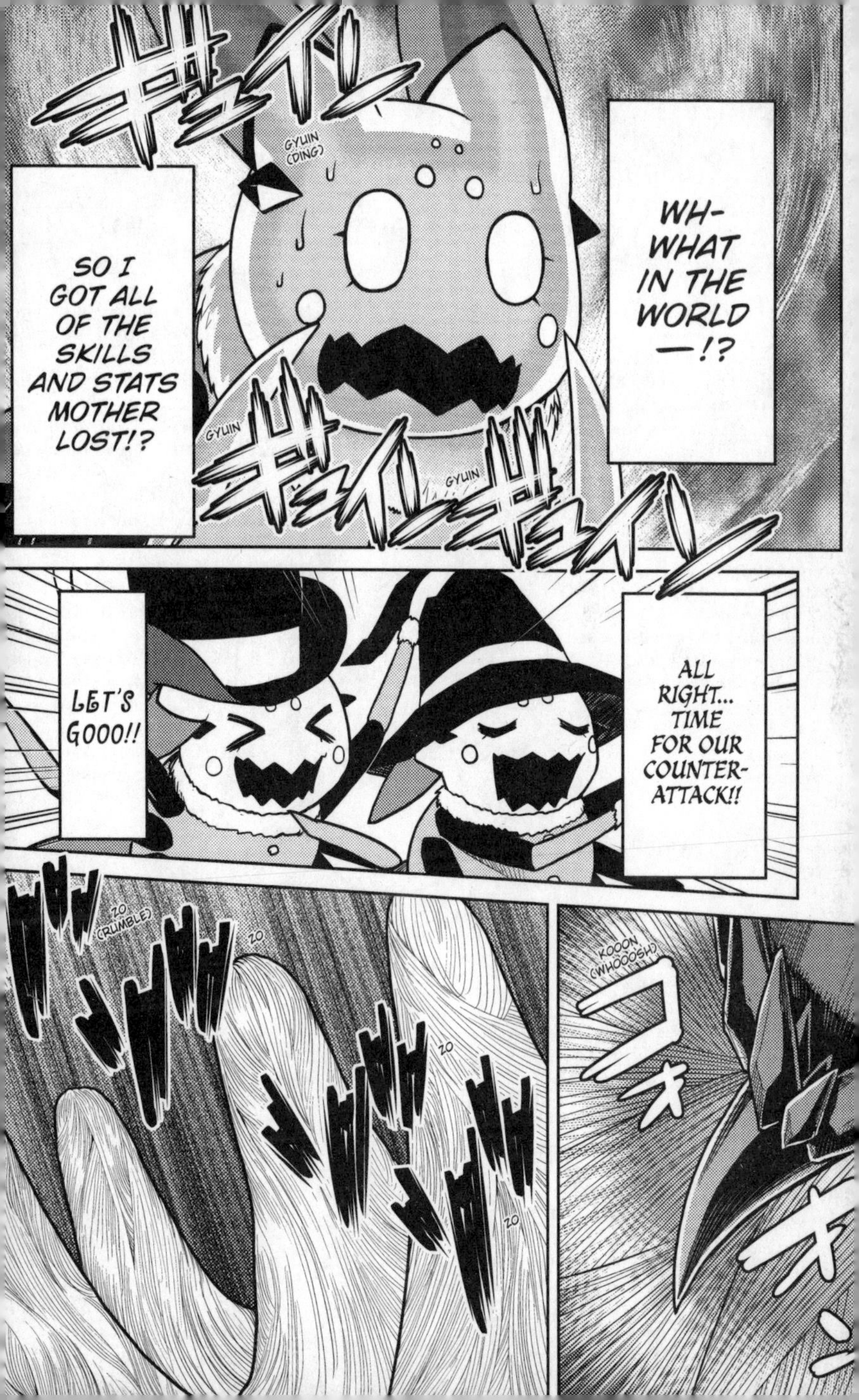
WH-WHAT IN THE WORLD—!?
GYUIN (DING)
SO I GOT ALL OF THE SKILLS AND STATS MOTHER LOST!?
GYUIN
GYUIN
ALL RIGHT... TIME FOR OUR COUNTER-ATTACK!!
LET'S GOOO!!
KOOON (WHOOOSH)
ZO (RUMBLE)
ZO
ZO
ZO

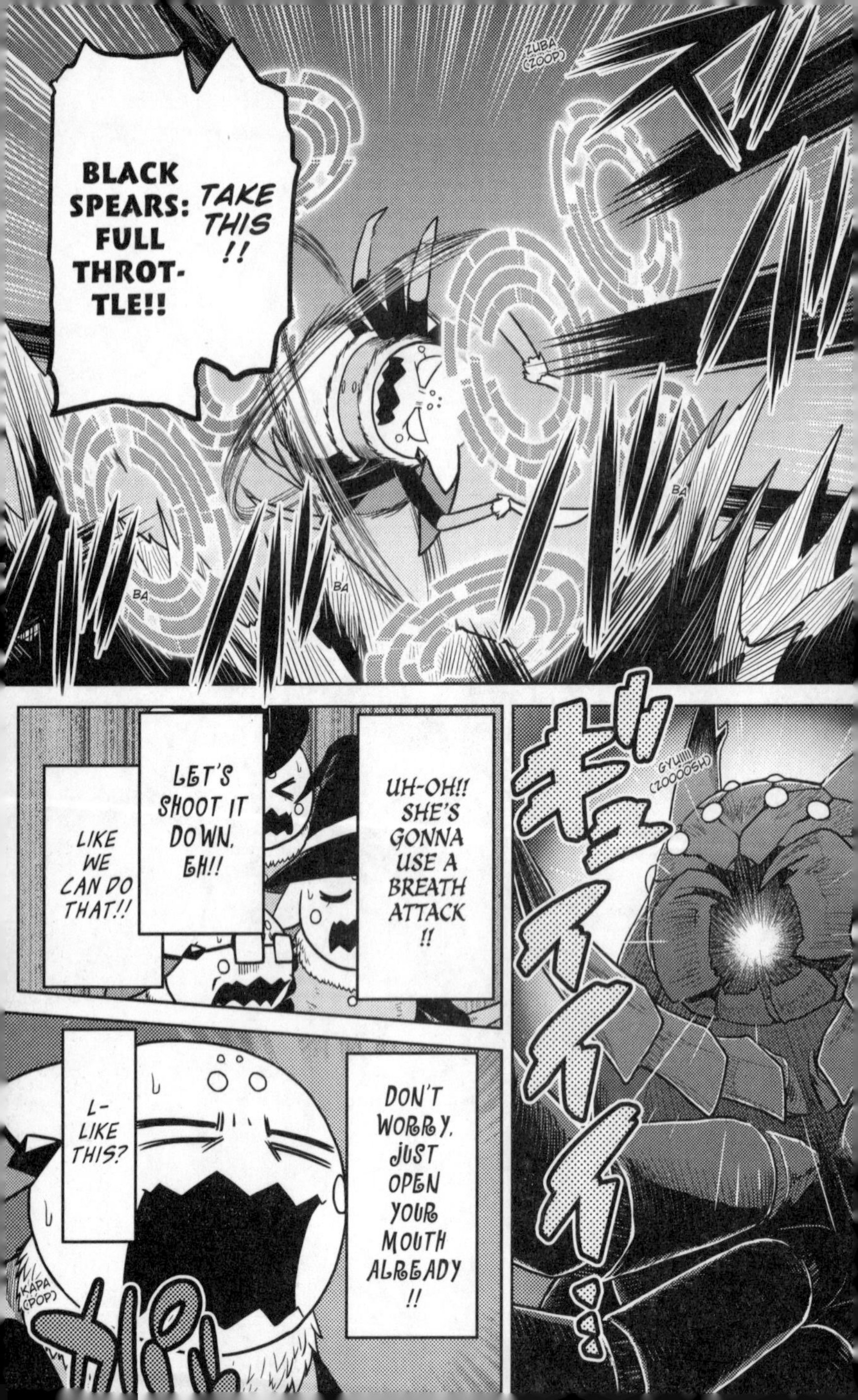
ZUBA (ZOOP)
TAKE THIS!!
BLACK SPEARS: FULL THROTTLE!!
BA
BA
BA
GYUIIII (ZOOOOSH)
UH-OH!! SHE'S GONNA USE A BREATH ATTACK!!
LET'S SHOOT IT DOWN, EH!!
LIKE WE CAN DO THAT!!
DON'T WORRY, JUST OPEN YOUR MOUTH ALREADY!!
L- LIKE THIS?
KAPA (POP)

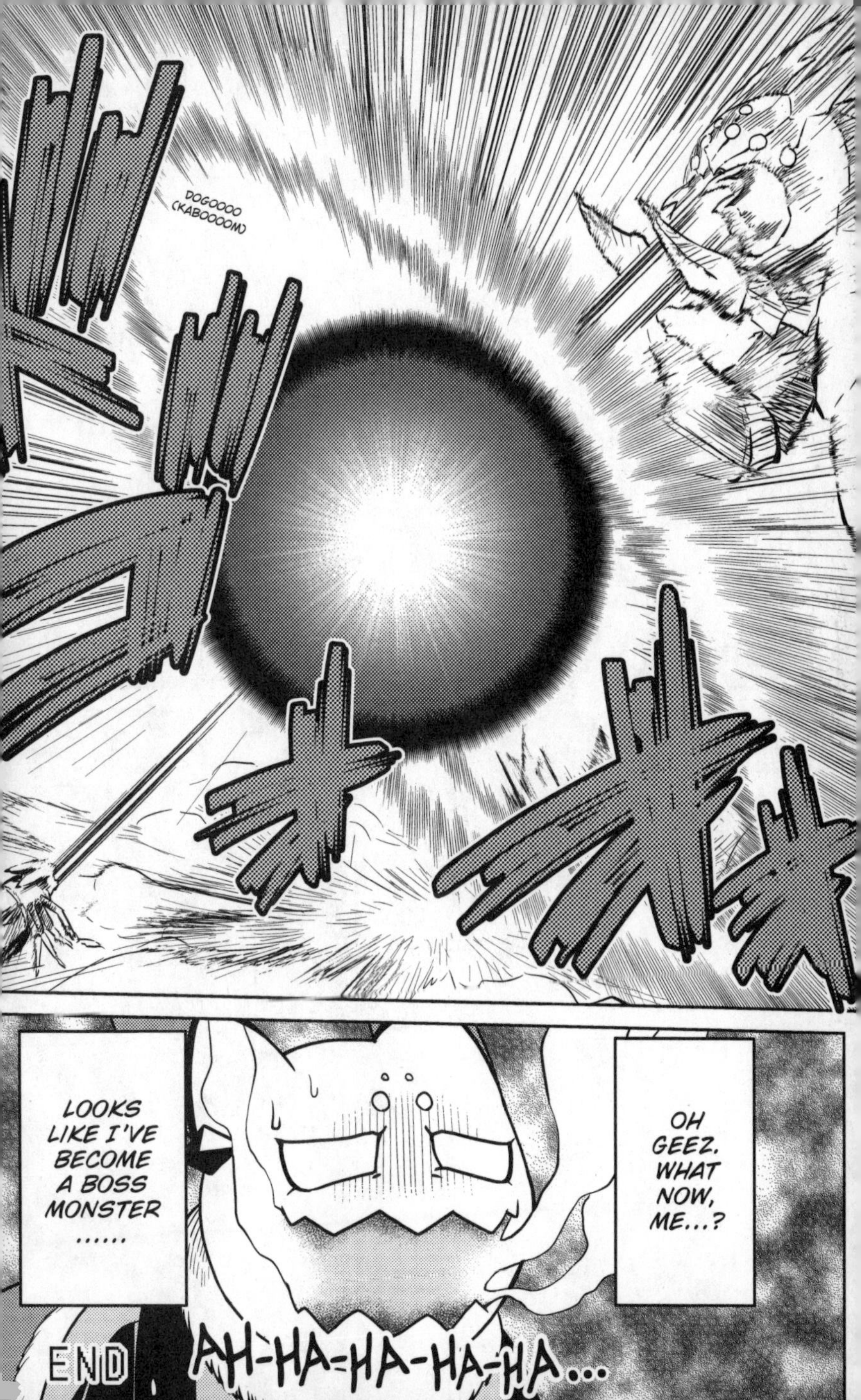
DOGOOOO (KABOOOOM)
OH GEEZ. WHAT NOW, ME...?
LOOKS LIKE I'VE BECOME A BOSS MONSTER ......
AH-HA-HA-HA-HA-HA...
END

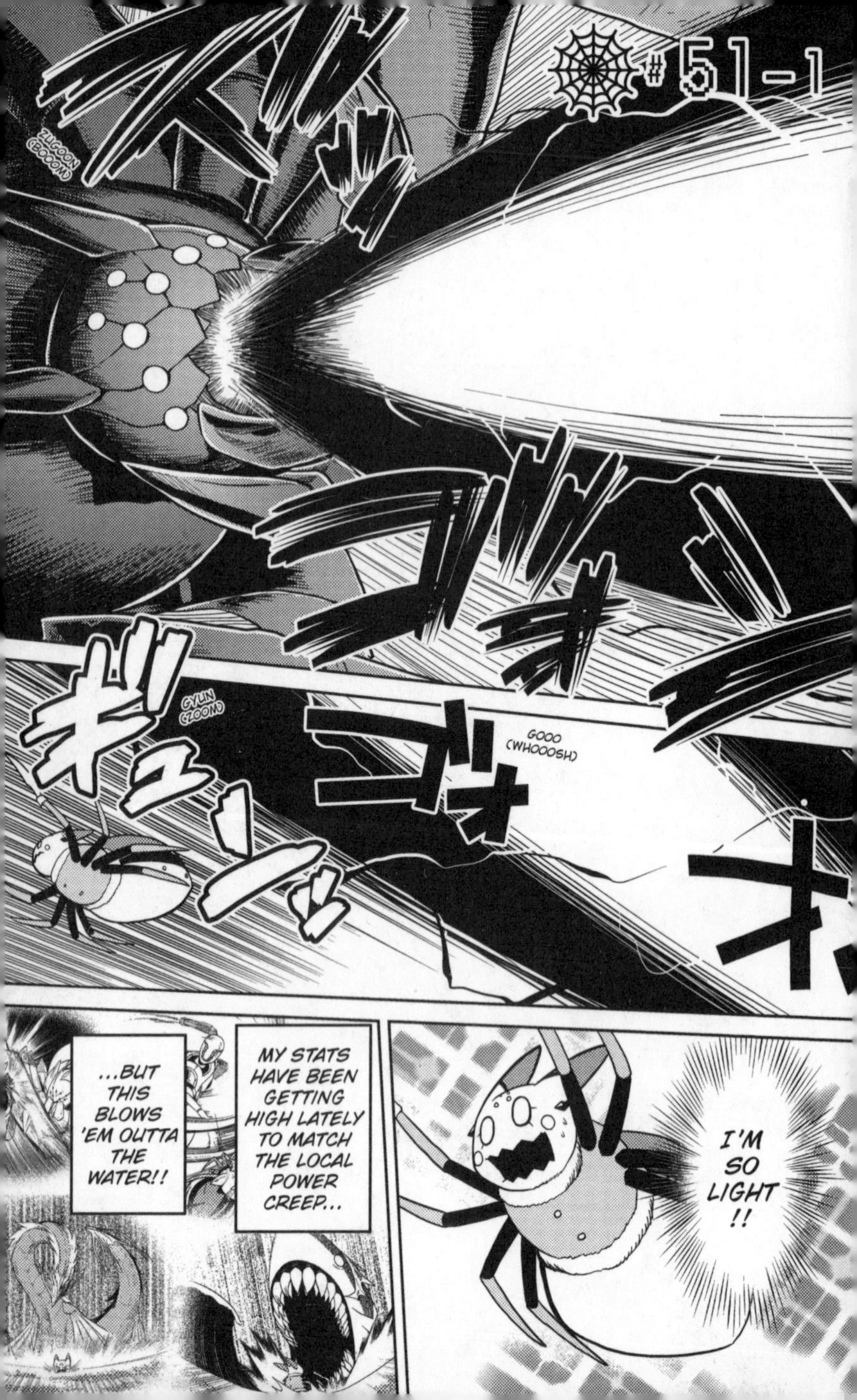
#51-1
ZUGOON (BOOOM)
GYUN (ZOOOM)
GOOO (WHOOOSH)
I'M SO LIGHT!!
MY STATS HAVE BEEN GETTING HIGH LATELY TO MATCH THE LOCAL POWER CREEP...
...BUT THIS BLOWS 'EM OUTTA THE WATER!!

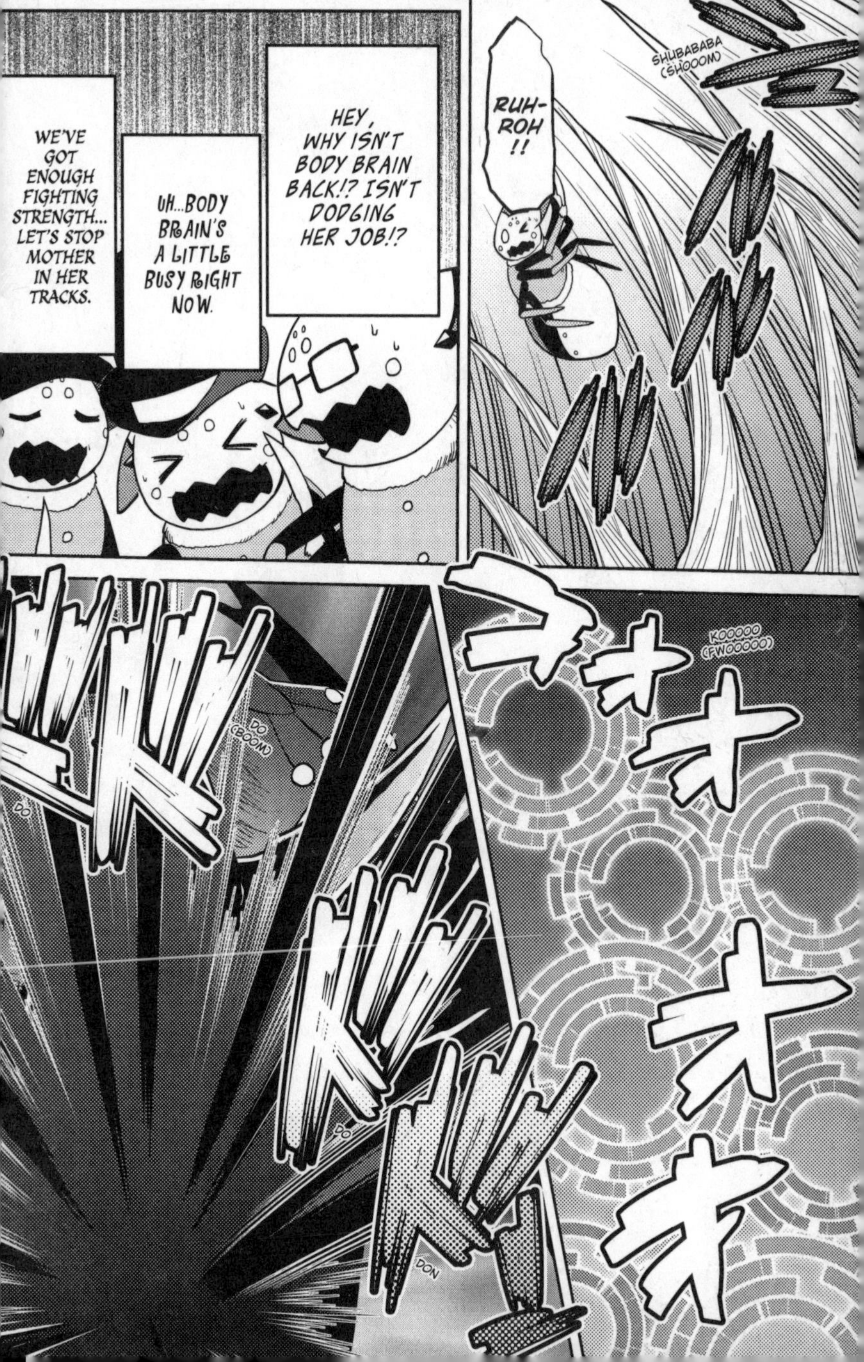
SHUBABABA (SHOOOM)
RUH-ROH !!
HEY, WHY ISN'T BODY BRAIN BACK!? ISN'T DODGING HER JOB!?
UH...BODY BRAIN'S A LITTLE BUSY RIGHT NOW.
WE'VE GOT ENOUGH FIGHTING STRENGTH... LET'S STOP MOTHER IN HER TRACKS.
KOOOOO (FWOOOOO)
DO (BOOM)
DO
DO
DON

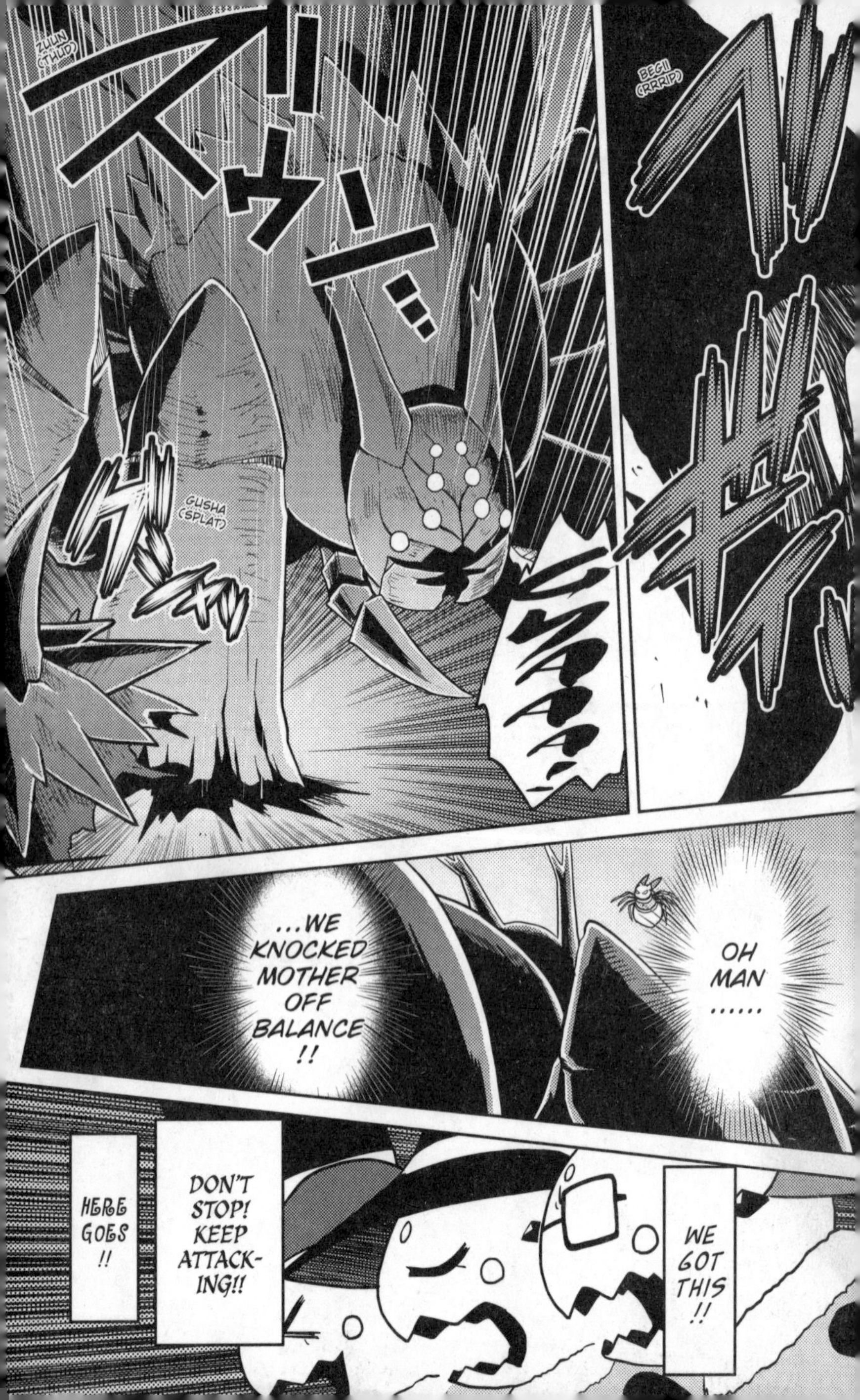
BEGII (RRRIP)
ZUUN (THUD)
GUSHA (SPLAT)
OH MAN……
…WE KNOCKED MOTHER OFF BALANCE!!
WE GOT THIS!!
DON'T STOP! KEEP ATTACK-ING!!
HERE GOES!!

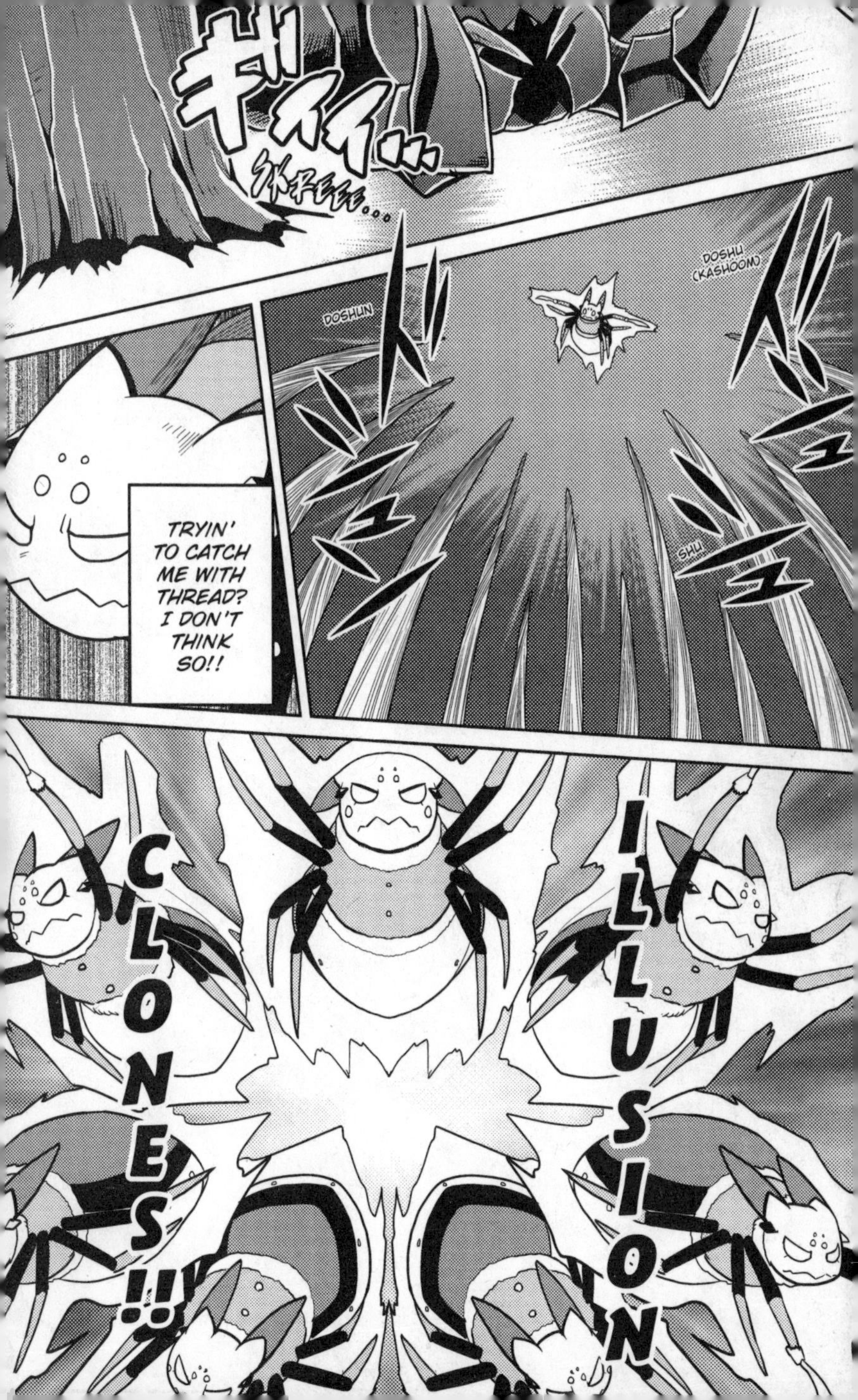

SKREEE...
DOSHU (KASHOOM)
DOSHUN
SHU
TRYIN' TO CATCH ME WITH THREAD? I DON'T THINK SO!!
ILLUSION
CLONES!!

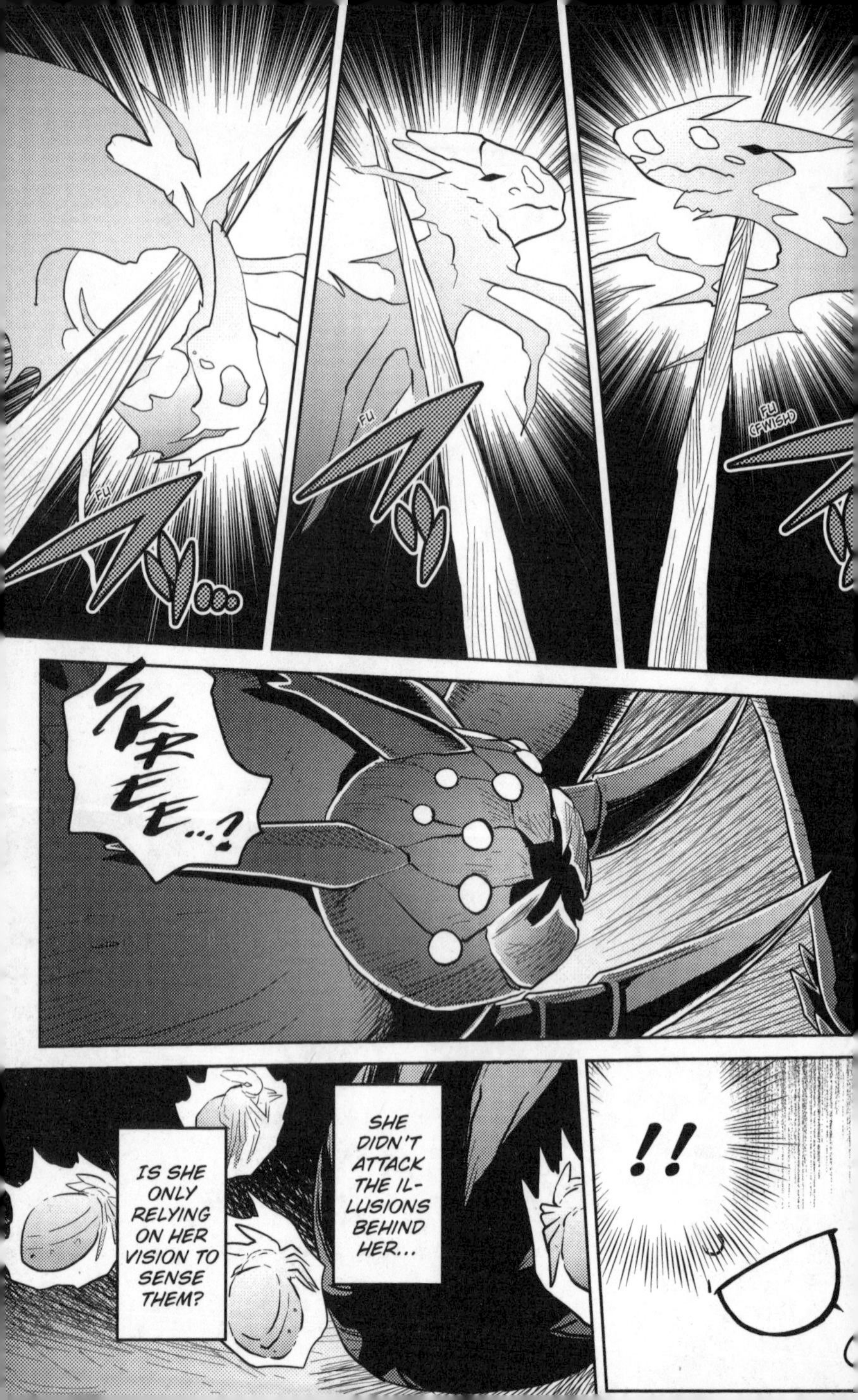
FU
(FWISH)
FU
FU
SKREEE...!?
!!
SHE DIDN'T ATTACK THE IL-LUSIONS BEHIND HER...
IS SHE ONLY RELYING ON HER VISION TO SENSE THEM?

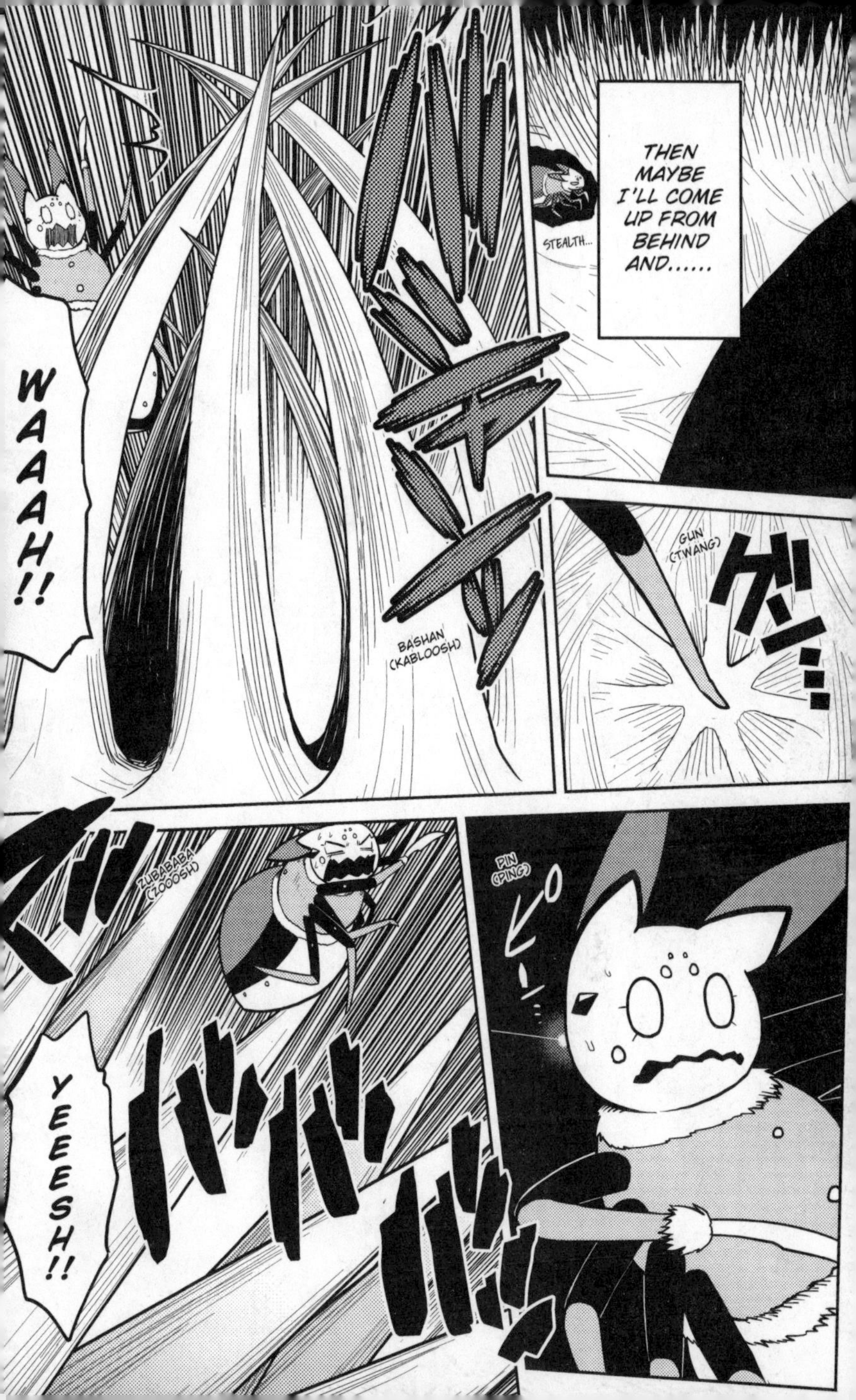
THEN MAYBE I'LL COME UP FROM BEHIND AND......
STEALTH...
GUN (TWANG)
WAAAAH!!
BASHAN (KABLOOSH)
PIN (PING)
ZUBABABA (ZOOOSH)
YEEEESH!!

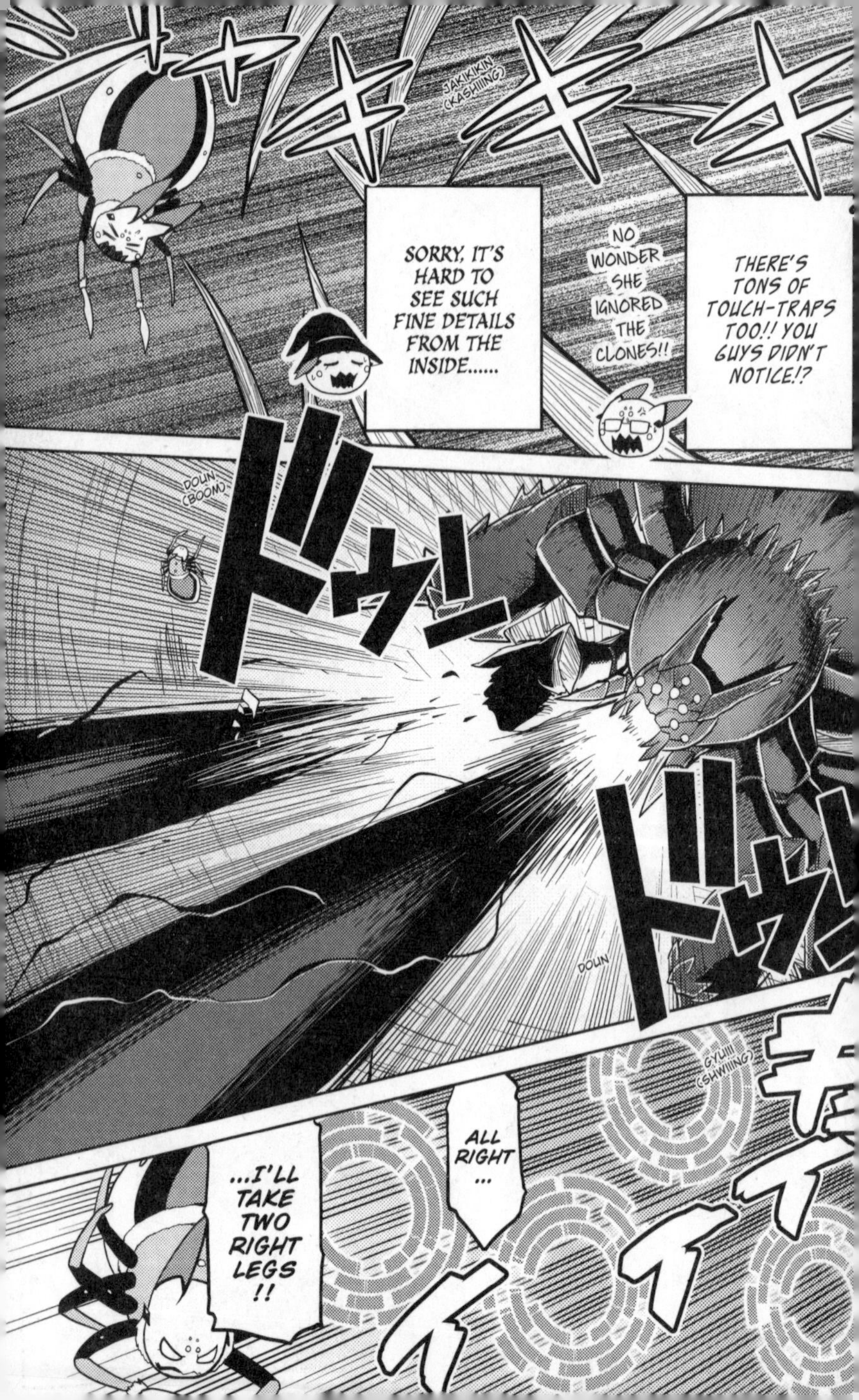
JAKIKIKIN (KASHIIING)
THERE'S TONS OF TOUCH-TRAPS TOO!! YOU GUYS DIDN'T NOTICE!?
NO WONDER SHE IGNORED THE CLONES!!
SORRY, IT'S HARD TO SEE SUCH FINE DETAILS FROM THE INSIDE......
DOUN (BOOM)
DOUN
GYUIIII (SHWIIING)
ALL RIGHT...
...I'LL TAKE TWO RIGHT LEGS!!

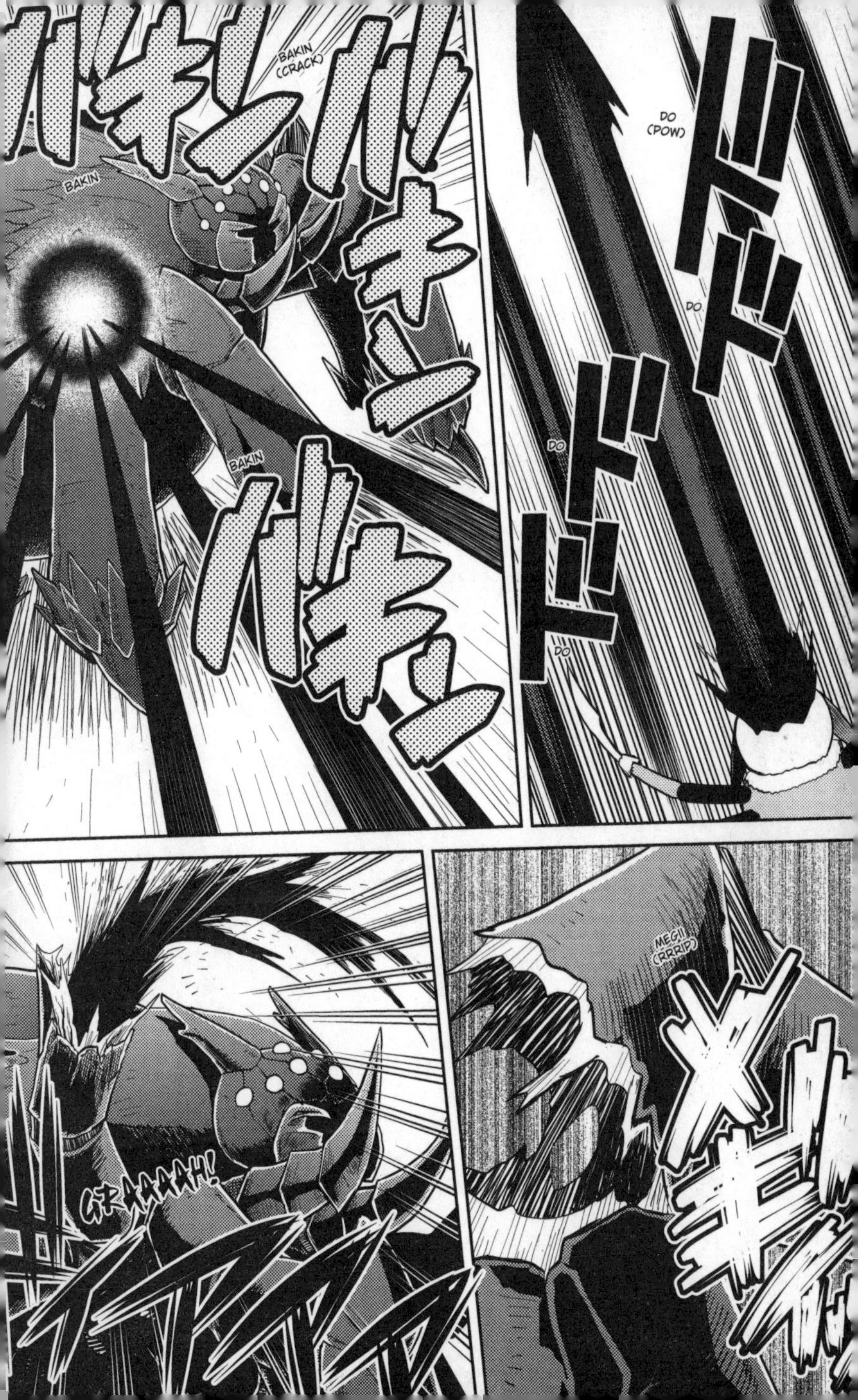
DO
(POW)
DO
DO
DO
BAKIN
(CRACK)
BAKIN
BAKIN
MEGII
(RRRIP)
GRAAAAH!

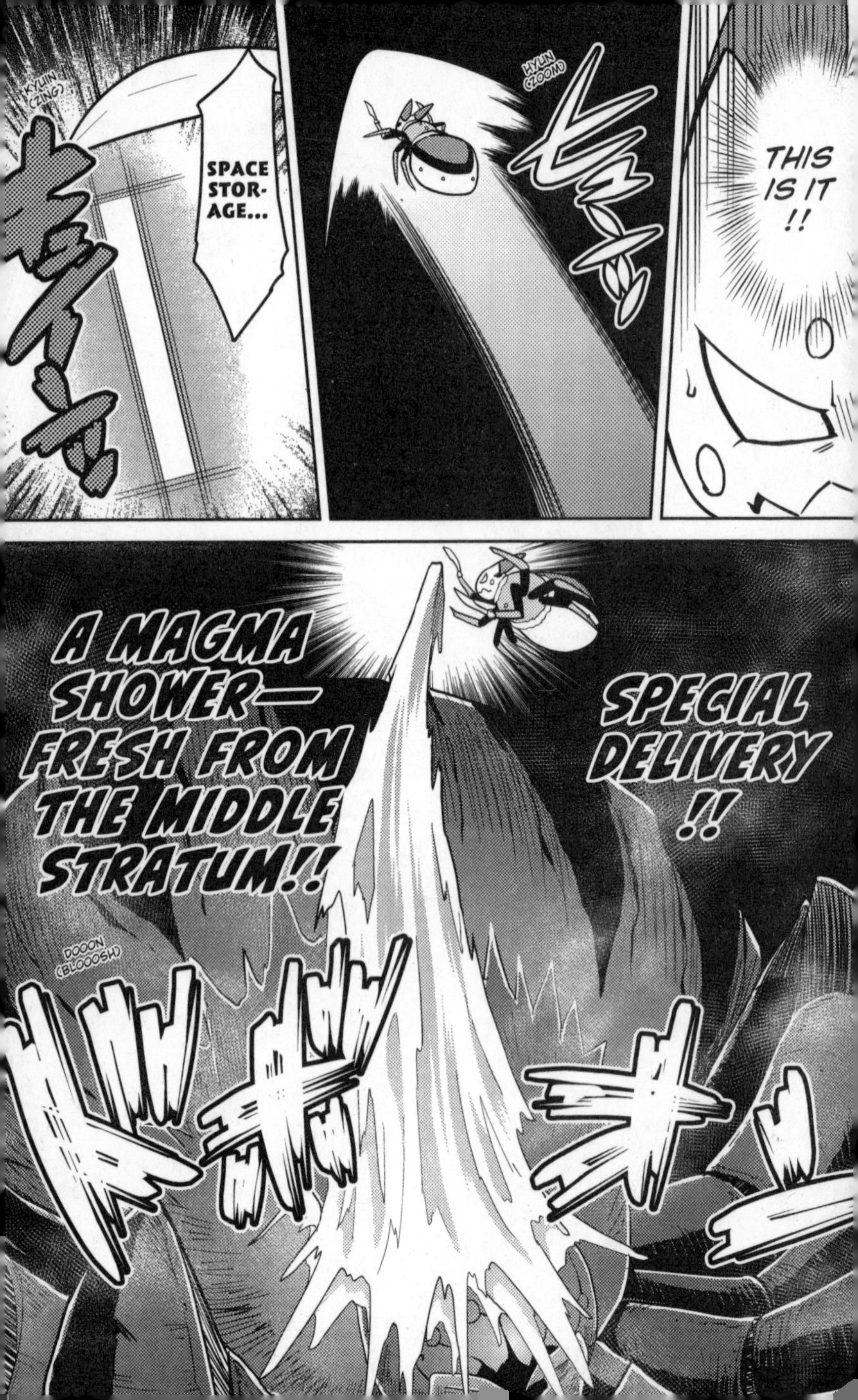
THIS IS IT !!
KYUN (ZOOM)
KYUIN (ZING)
SPACE STOR-AGE...
SPECIAL DELIVERY !!
A MAGMA SHOWER— FRESH FROM THE MIDDLE STRATUM!!
DOOON (BLOOOSH)

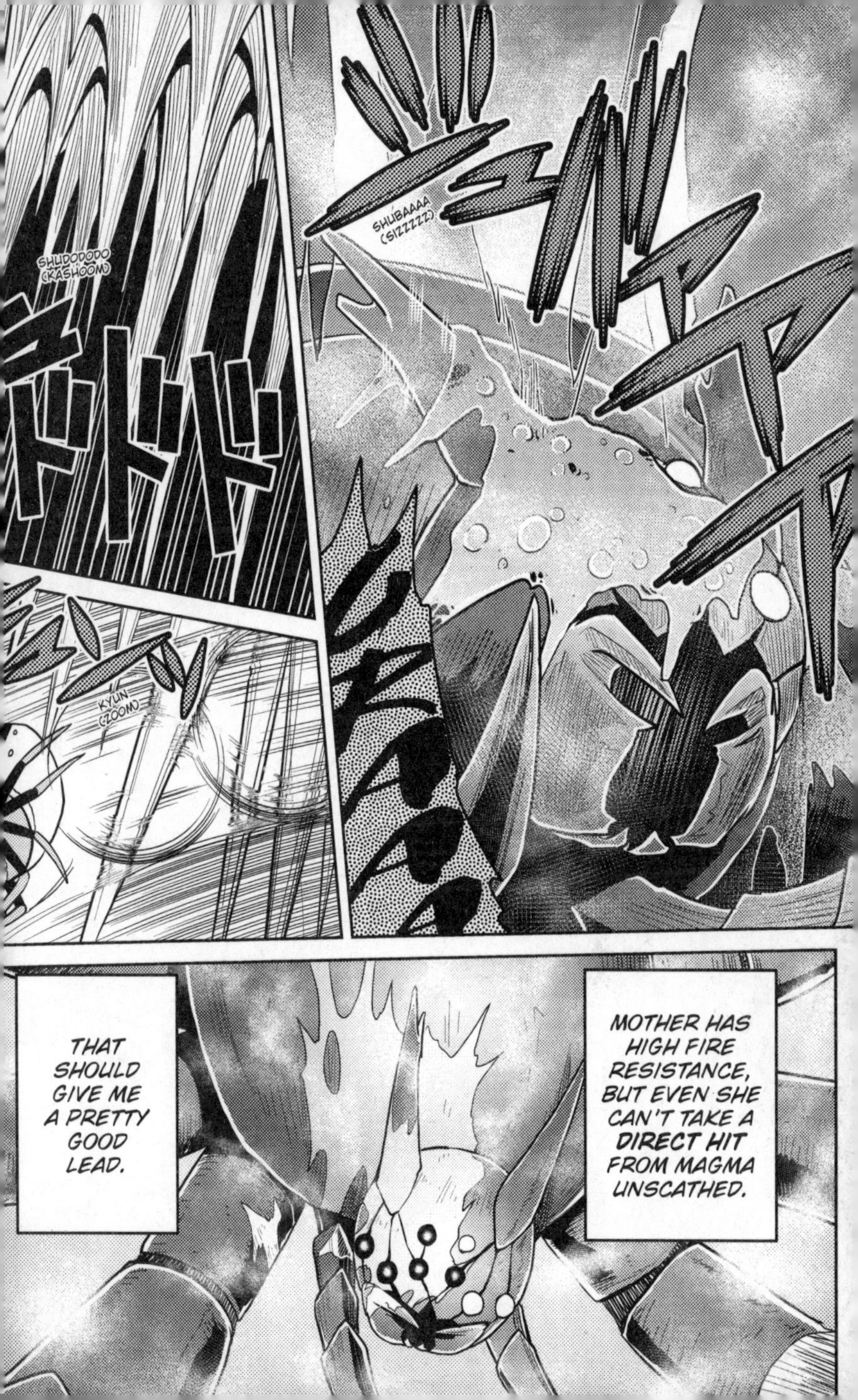
SHUBAAAA (SIZZZZZ)
SHUDODODO (KASHOOM)
KYUN (ZOOM)
MOTHER HAS HIGH FIRE RESISTANCE, BUT EVEN SHE CAN'T TAKE A **DIRECT HIT** FROM MAGMA UNSCATHED.
THAT SHOULD GIVE ME A PRETTY GOOD LEAD.

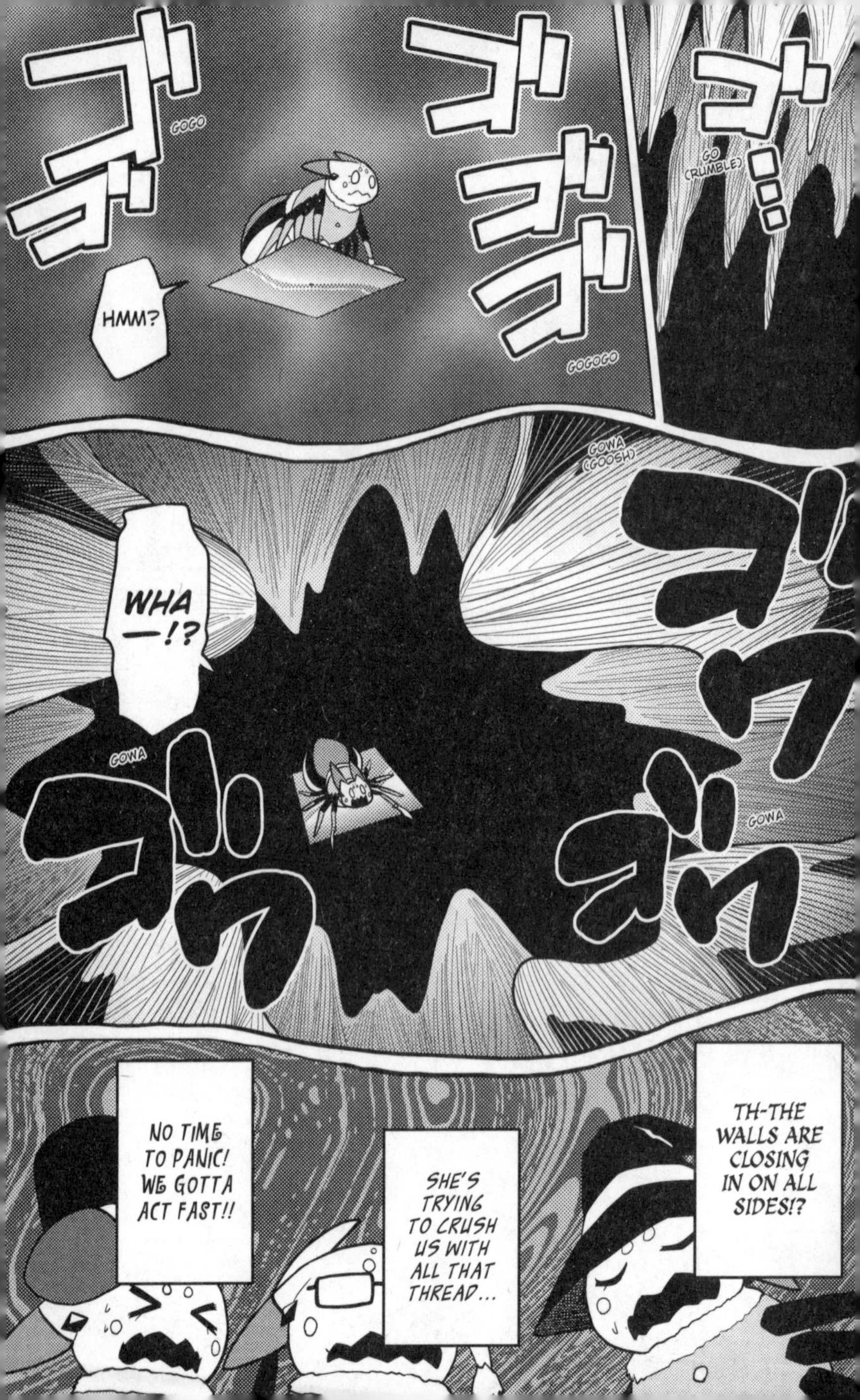
ゴ…
GO (RUMBLE)
ゴゴゴ
GOGOGO
ゴゴ
GOGO
HMM?
ゴワッ
GOWA (GOOSH)
GOWA
WHA—!?
ゴワッ
GOWA
ゴワッ
TH-THE WALLS ARE CLOSING IN ON ALL SIDES!?
SHE'S TRYING TO CRUSH US WITH ALL THAT THREAD...
NO TIME TO PANIC! WE GOTTA ACT FAST!!

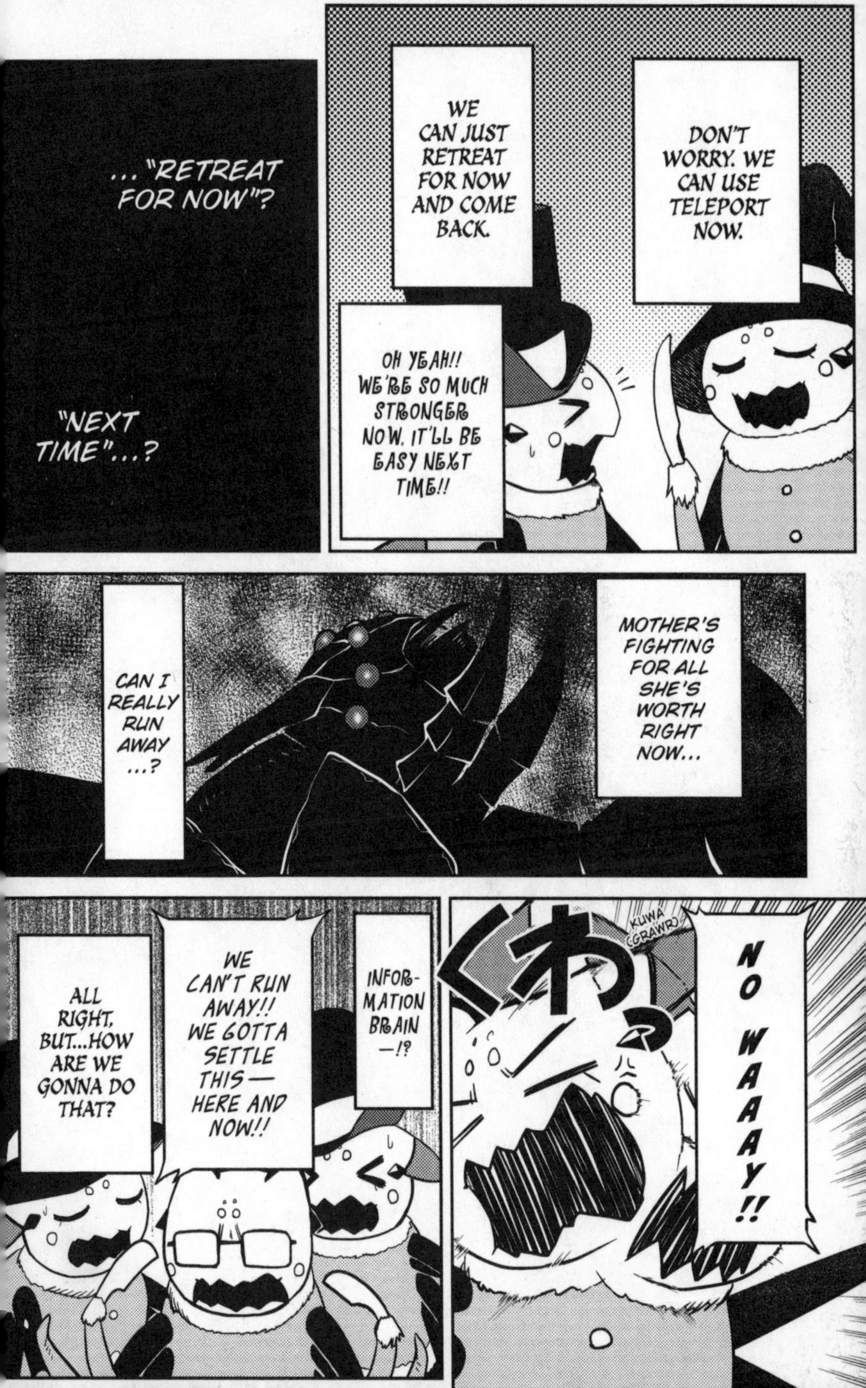
DON'T WORRY. WE CAN USE TELEPORT NOW.
WE CAN JUST RETREAT FOR NOW AND COME BACK.
OH YEAH!! WE'RE SO MUCH STRONGER NOW. IT'LL BE EASY NEXT TIME!!
..."RETREAT FOR NOW"?
"NEXT TIME"...?
MOTHER'S FIGHTING FOR ALL SHE'S WORTH RIGHT NOW...
CAN I REALLY RUN AWAY ...?
NO WAAAAAY!!
KUWA (GRAWR)
くわっ
INFOR-MATION BRAIN —!?
WE CAN'T RUN AWAY!! WE GOTTA SETTLE THIS— HERE AND NOW!!
ALL RIGHT, BUT...HOW ARE WE GONNA DO THAT?

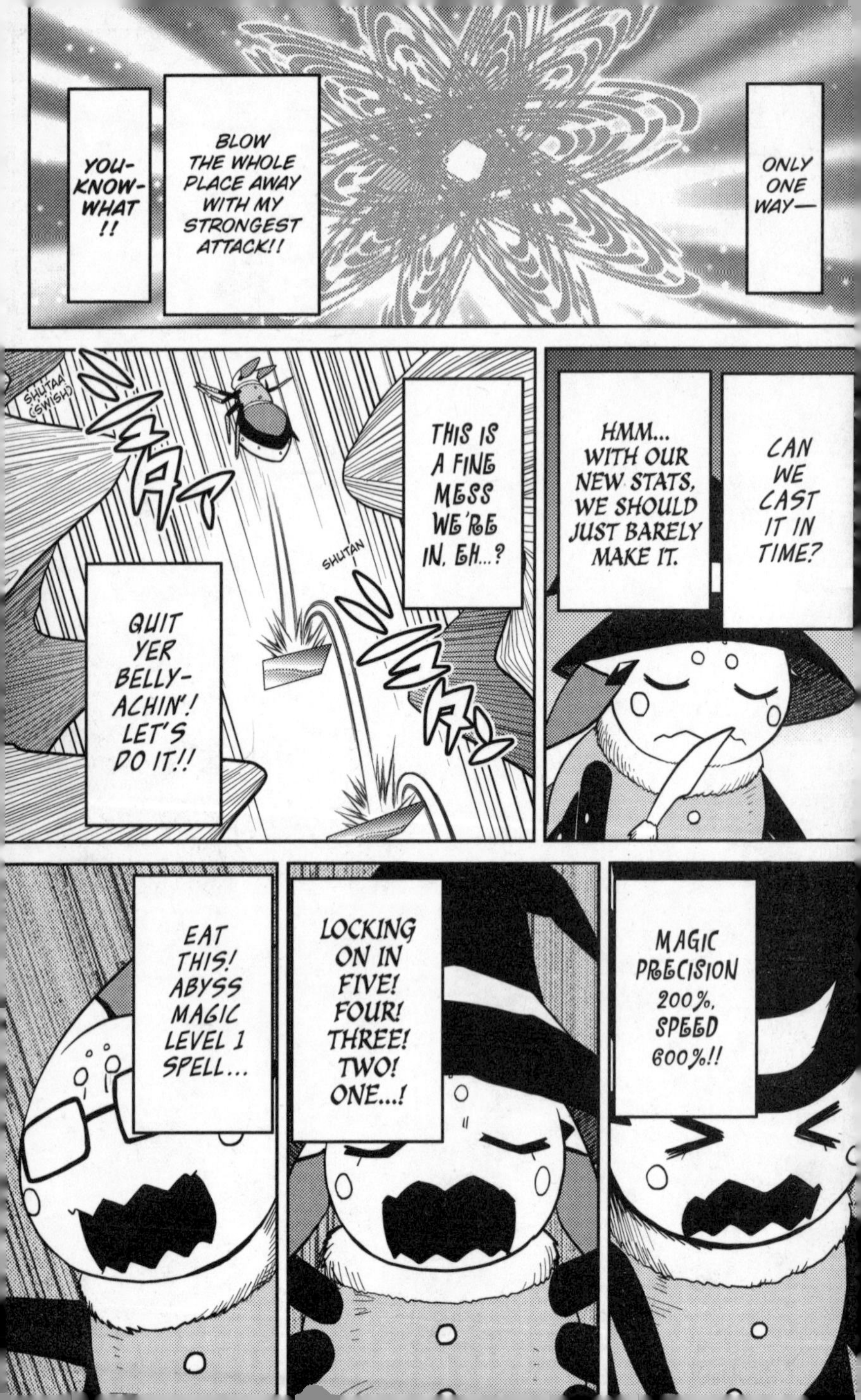
ONLY ONE WAY—
BLOW THE WHOLE PLACE AWAY WITH MY STRONGEST ATTACK!!
YOU-KNOW-WHAT!!
CAN WE CAST IT IN TIME?
HMM... WITH OUR NEW STATS, WE SHOULD JUST BARELY MAKE IT.
THIS IS A FINE MESS WE'RE IN, EH...?
SHUTAA (SWISH)
SHUTAN
QUIT YER BELLY-ACHIN'! LET'S DO IT!!
MAGIC PRECISION 200%, SPEED 600%!!
LOCKING ON IN FIVE! FOUR! THREE! TWO! ONE...!
EAT THIS! ABYSS MAGIC LEVEL 1 SPELL...

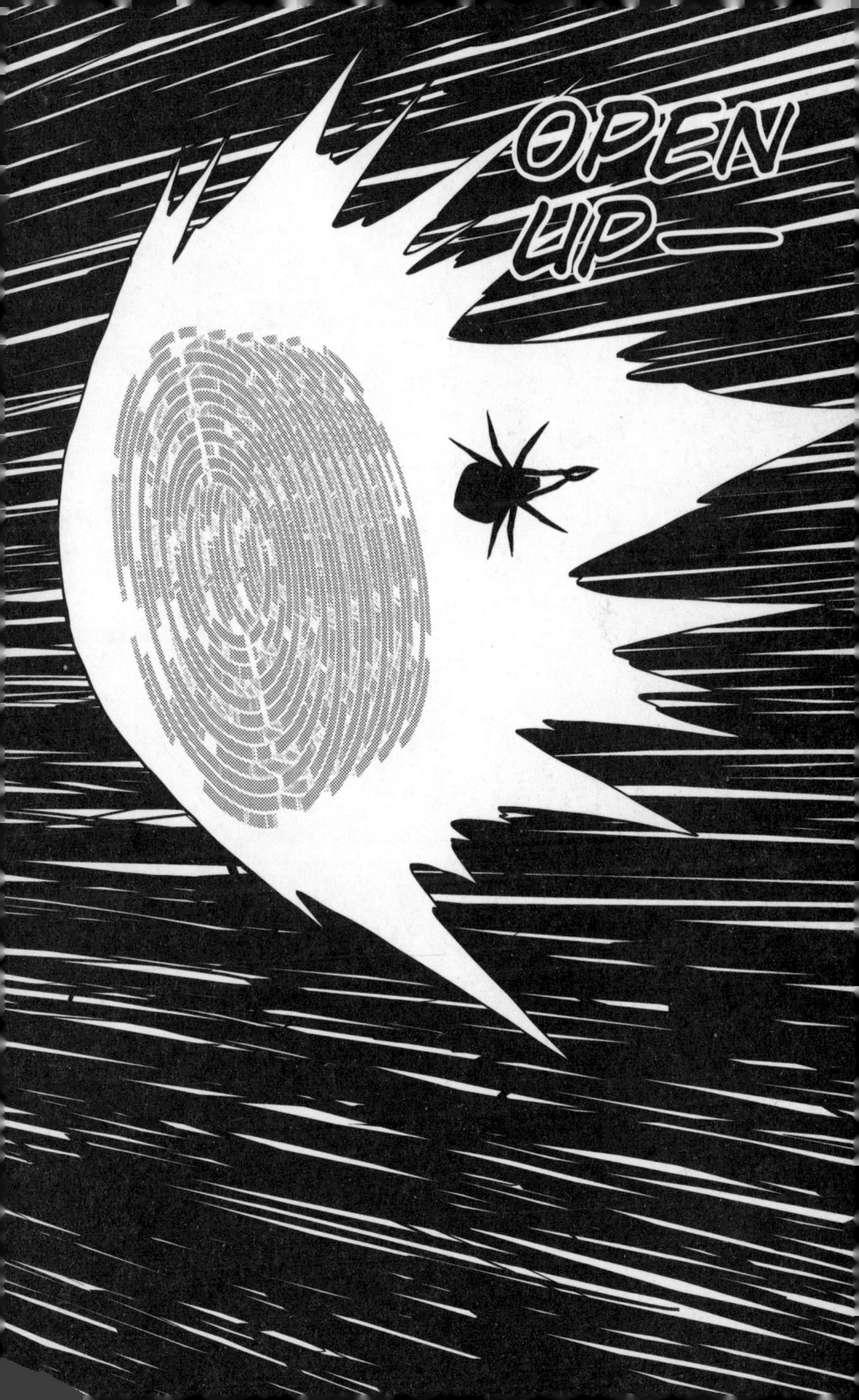
OPEN UP—

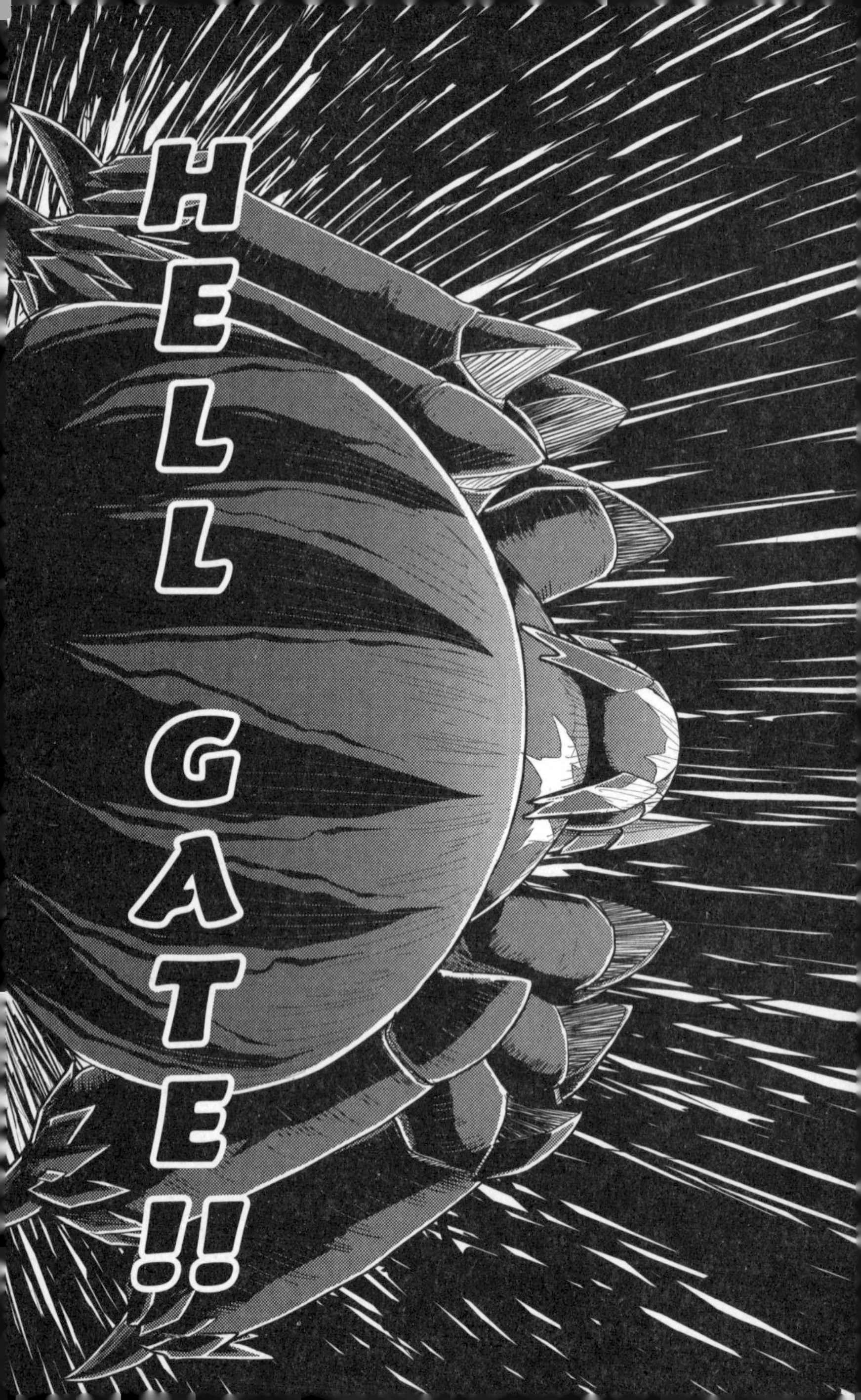
HELL GATE!!

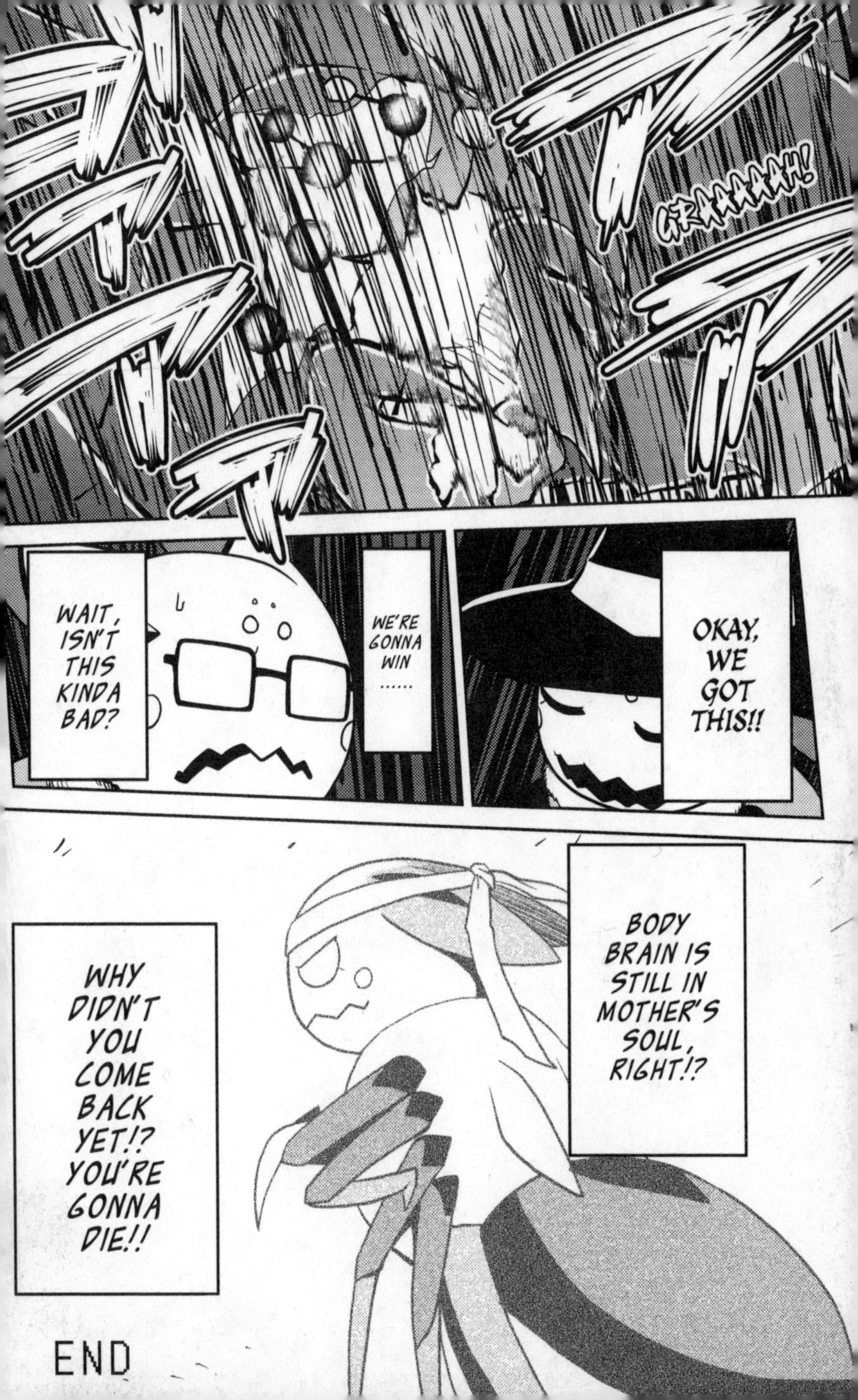
GRAAAAAH!
OKAY, WE GOT THIS!!
WE'RE GONNA WIN ......
WAIT, ISN'T THIS KINDA BAD?
BODY BRAIN IS STILL IN MOTHER'S SOUL, RIGHT!?
WHY DIDN'T YOU COME BACK YET!? YOU'RE GONNA DIE!!
END

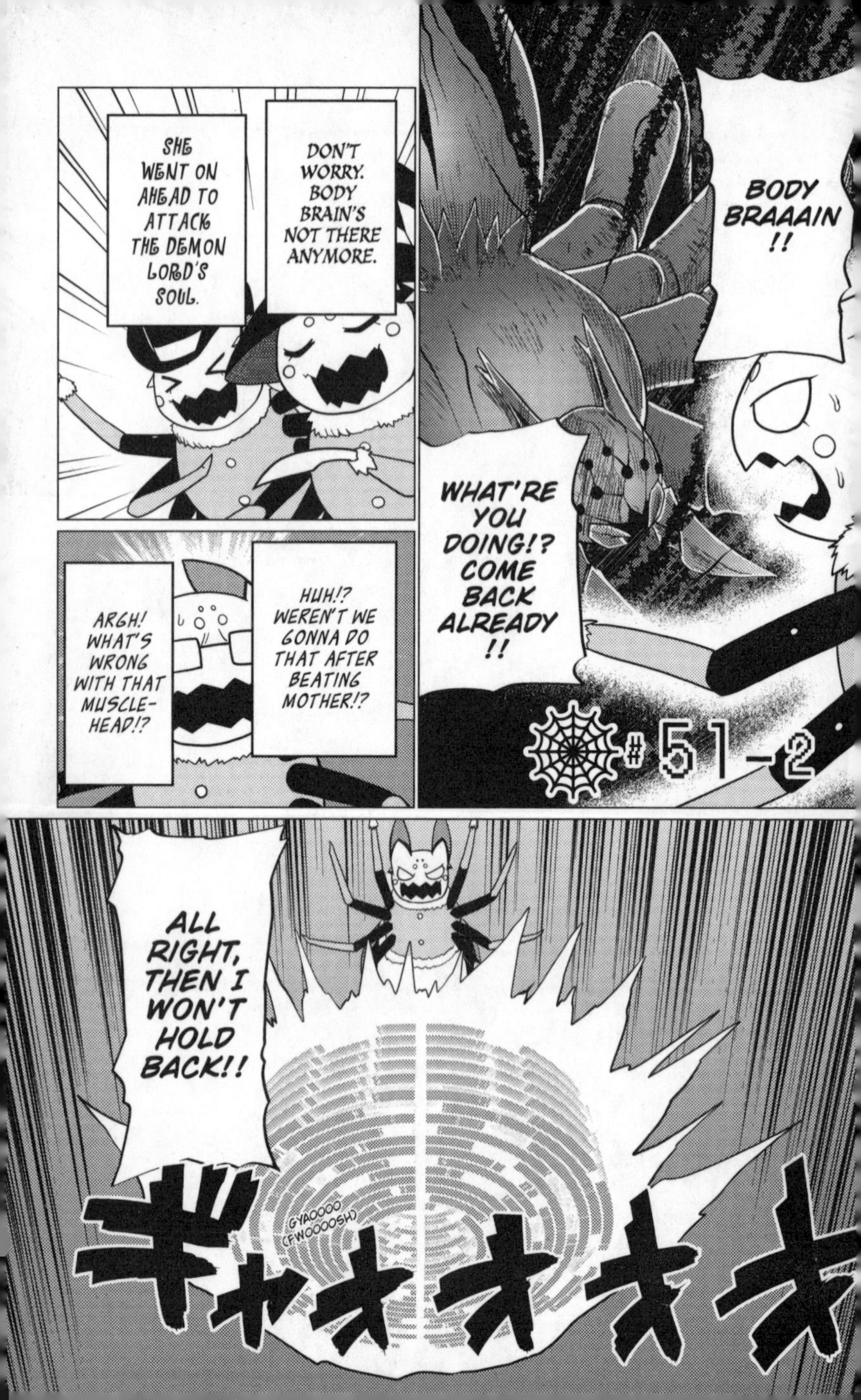
BODY BRAAAIN!!
WHAT'RE YOU DOING!? COME BACK ALREADY!!
#51-2
DON'T WORRY. BODY BRAIN'S NOT THERE ANYMORE.
SHE WENT ON AHEAD TO ATTACK THE DEMON LORD'S SOUL.
HUH!? WEREN'T WE GONNA DO THAT AFTER BEATING MOTHER!?
ARGH! WHAT'S WRONG WITH THAT MUSCLE-HEAD!?
ALL RIGHT, THEN I WON'T HOLD BACK!!
ギャオオオオ
GYAOOOO (FWOOOOSH)

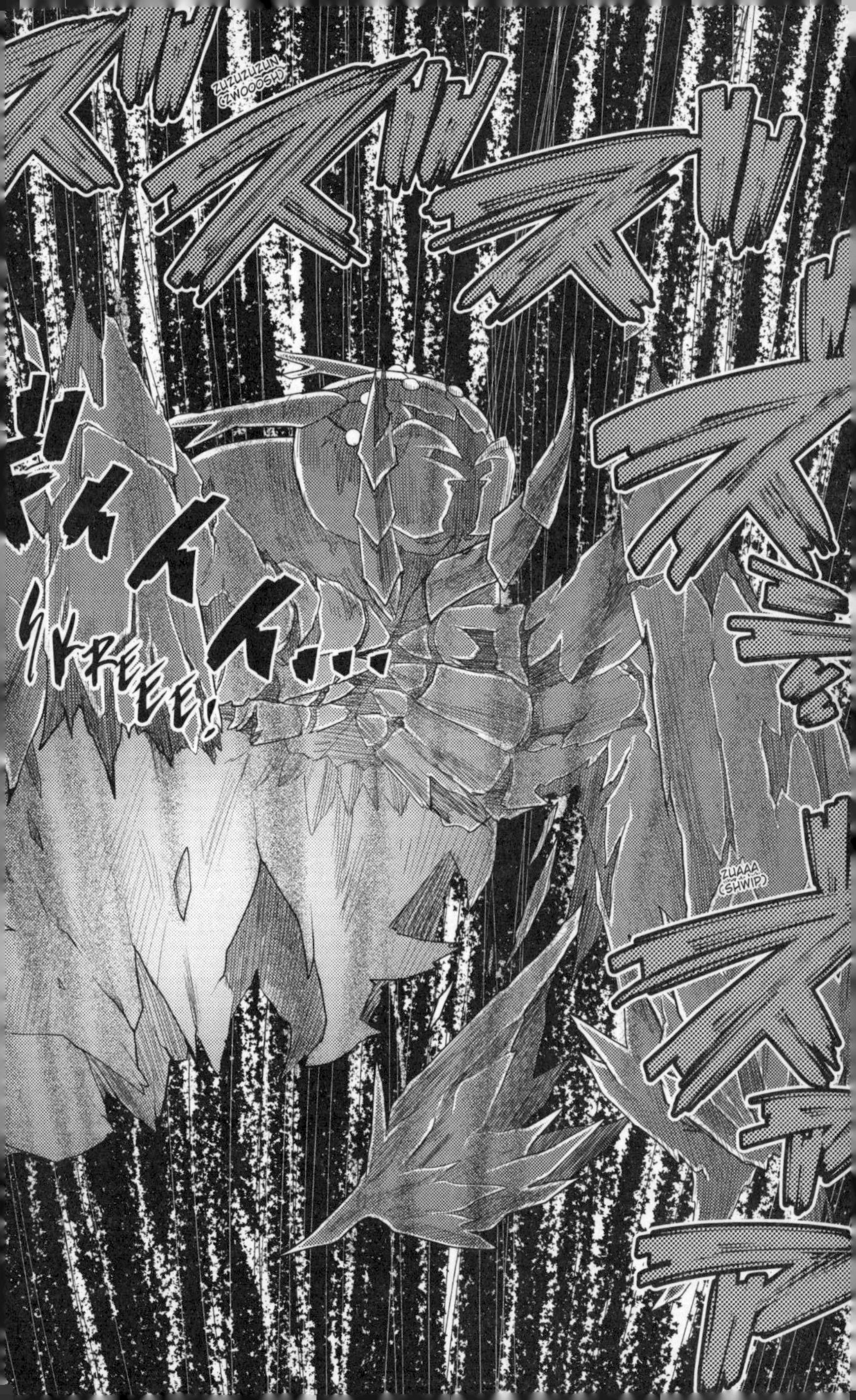
ZUZUZUZUN (ZWOOOSH)
SKREEEE!
ZUAAA (SHWIP)

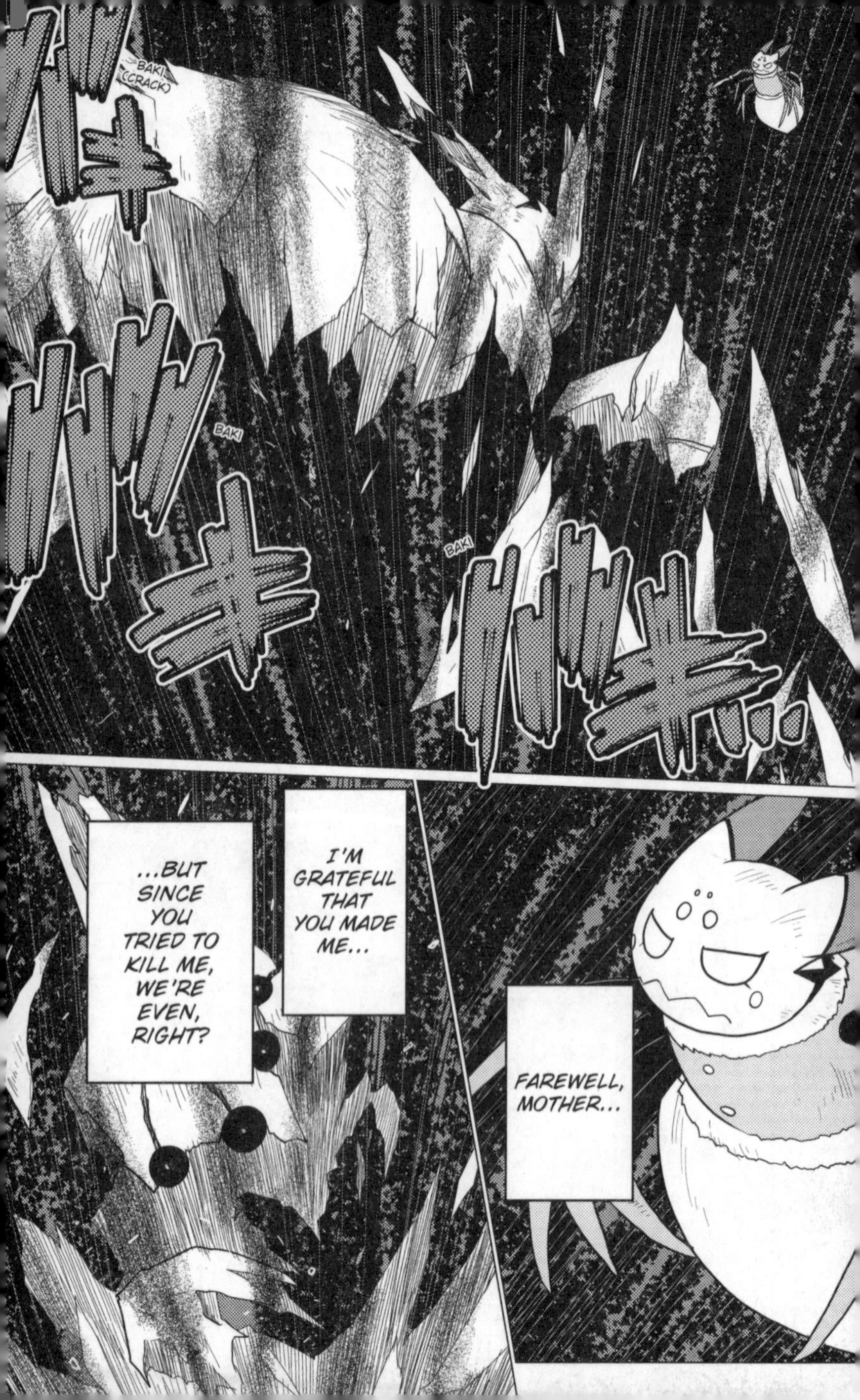
BAKI (CRACK)
BAKI
BAKI
FAREWELL, MOTHER...
I'M GRATEFUL THAT YOU MADE ME...
...BUT SINCE YOU TRIED TO KILL ME, WE'RE EVEN, RIGHT?

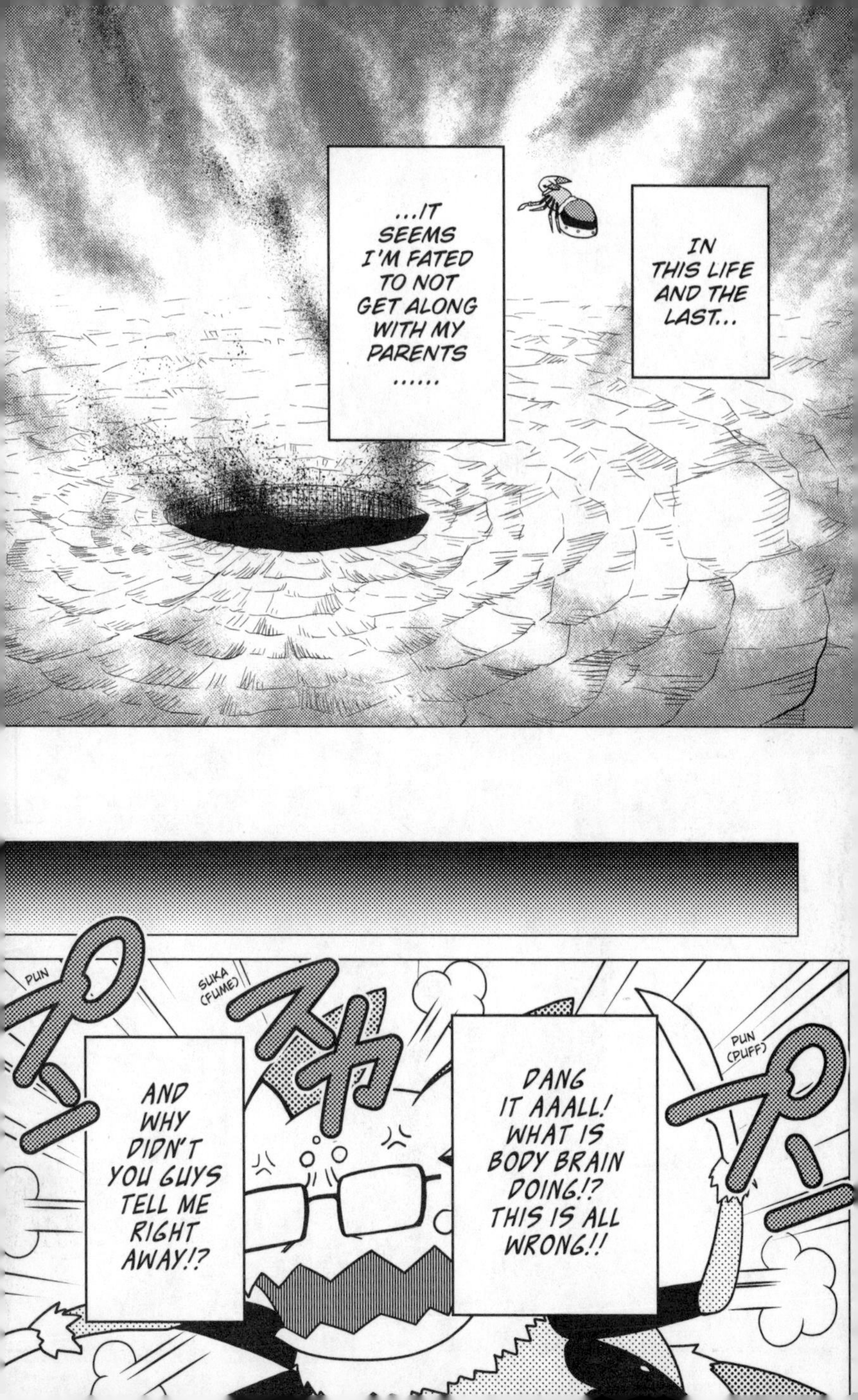
IN THIS LIFE AND THE LAST...
...IT SEEMS I'M FATED TO NOT GET ALONG WITH MY PARENTS ......
PUN (PUFF)
DANG IT AAALL! WHAT IS BODY BRAIN DOING!? THIS IS ALL WRONG!!
SUKA (FUME)
AND WHY DIDN'T YOU GUYS TELL ME RIGHT AWAY!?
PUN

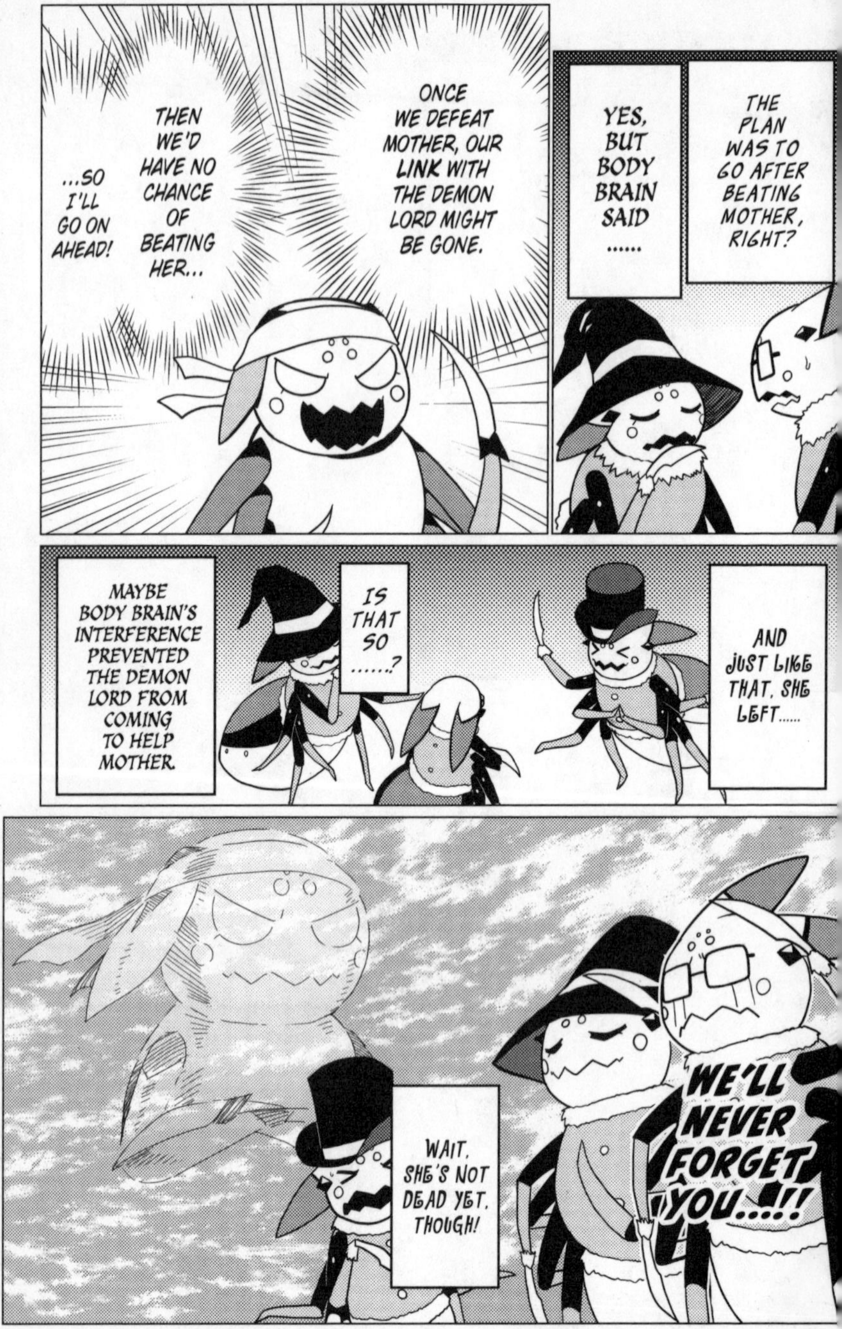
THE PLAN WAS TO GO AFTER BEATING MOTHER, RIGHT?
YES, BUT BODY BRAIN SAID ......
ONCE WE DEFEAT MOTHER, OUR LINK WITH THE DEMON LORD MIGHT BE GONE.
THEN WE'D HAVE NO CHANCE OF BEATING HER...
...SO I'LL GO ON AHEAD!
AND JUST LIKE THAT, SHE LEFT......
IS THAT SO ......?
MAYBE BODY BRAIN'S INTERFERENCE PREVENTED THE DEMON LORD FROM COMING TO HELP MOTHER.
WE'LL NEVER FORGET YOU...!!
WAIT, SHE'S NOT DEAD YET, THOUGH!

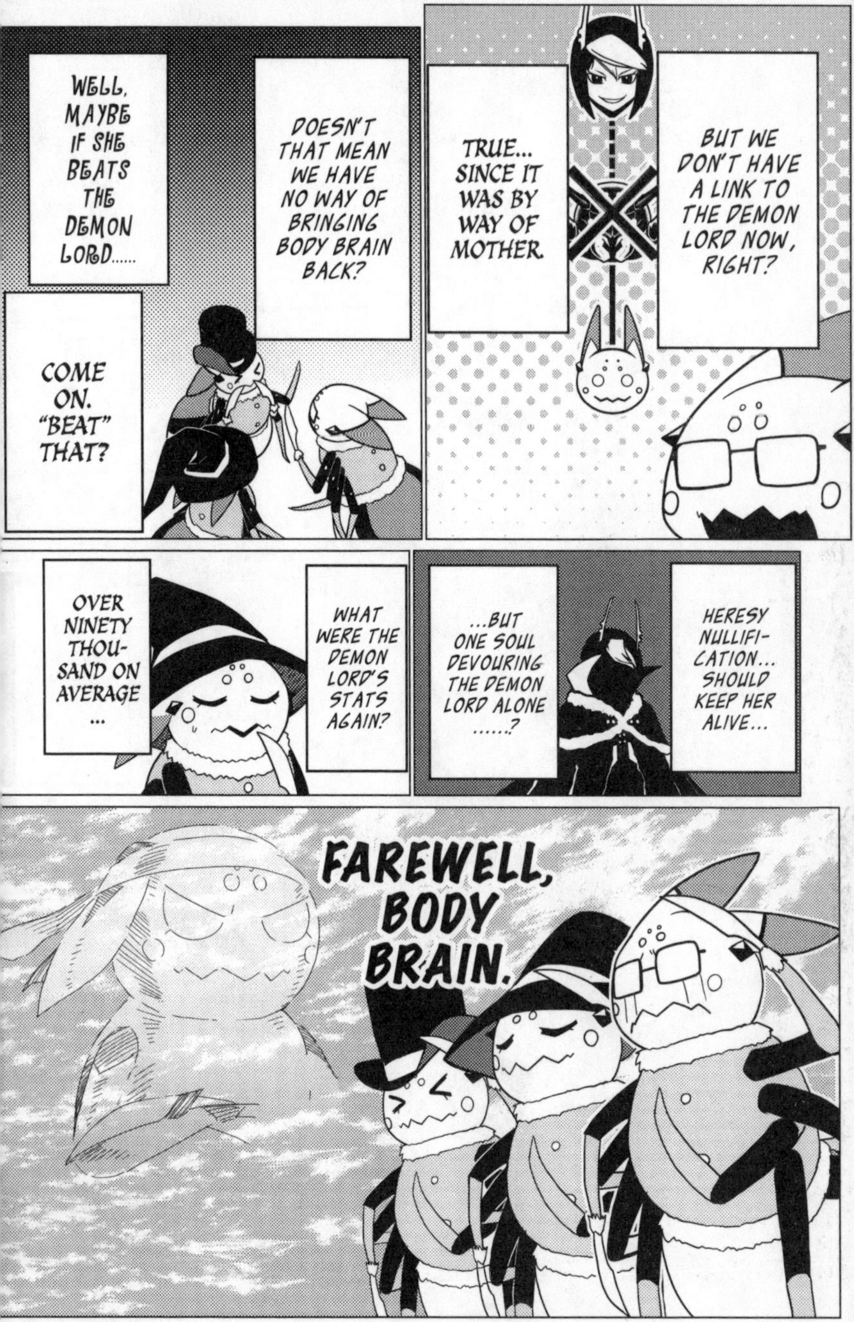
BUT WE DON'T HAVE A LINK TO THE DEMON LORD NOW, RIGHT?
TRUE... SINCE IT WAS BY WAY OF MOTHER.
DOESN'T THAT MEAN WE HAVE NO WAY OF BRINGING BODY BRAIN BACK?
WELL, MAYBE IF SHE BEATS THE DEMON LORD......
COME ON. "BEAT" THAT?
HERESY NULLIFICATION... SHOULD KEEP HER ALIVE...
...BUT ONE SOUL DEVOURING THE DEMON LORD ALONE ......?
WHAT WERE THE DEMON LORD'S STATS AGAIN?
OVER NINETY THOUSAND ON AVERAGE ...
FAREWELL, BODY BRAIN.

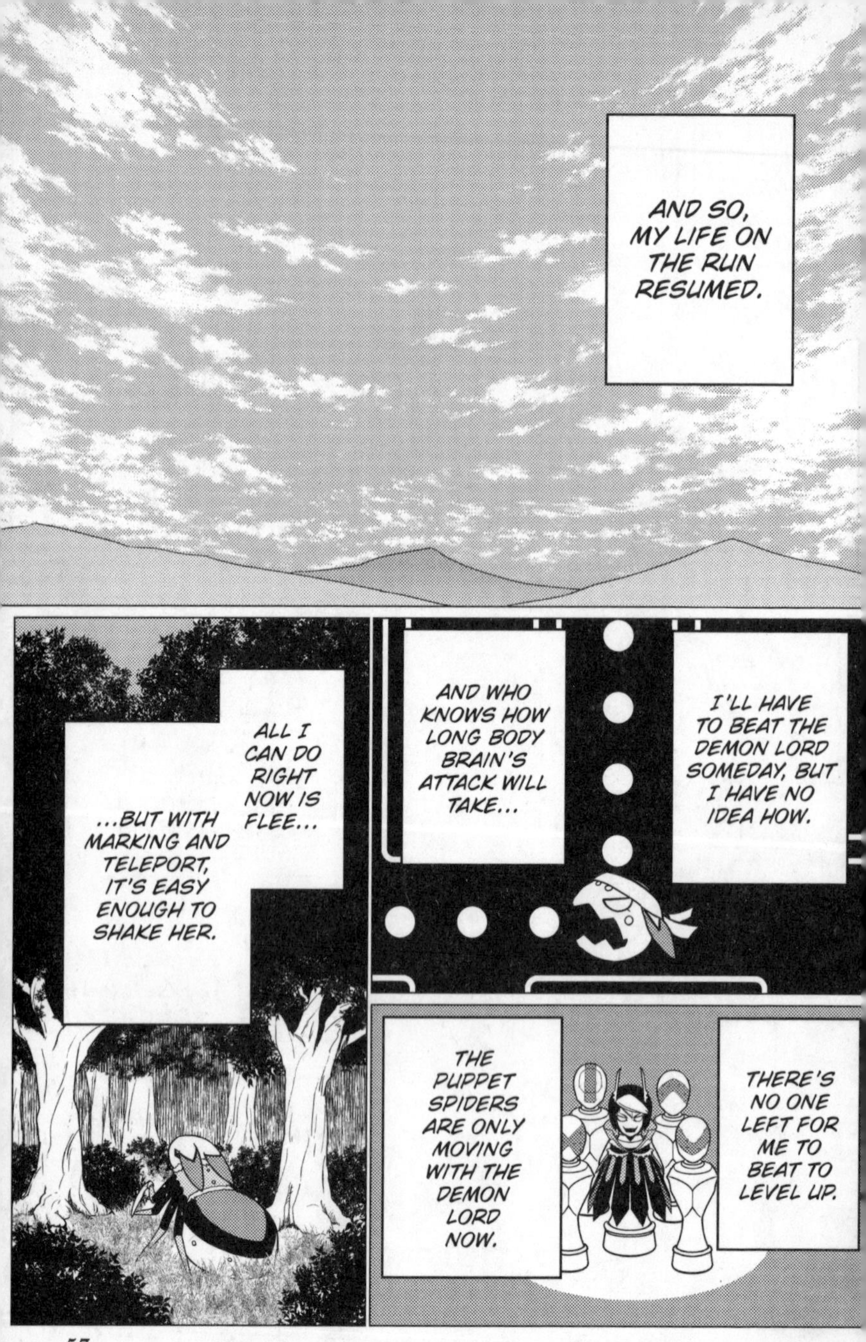
AND SO, MY LIFE ON THE RUN RESUMED.
I'LL HAVE TO BEAT THE DEMON LORD SOMEDAY, BUT I HAVE NO IDEA HOW.
AND WHO KNOWS HOW LONG BODY BRAIN'S ATTACK WILL TAKE...
THERE'S NO ONE LEFT FOR ME TO BEAT TO LEVEL UP.
THE PUPPET SPIDERS ARE ONLY MOVING WITH THE DEMON LORD NOW.
ALL I CAN DO RIGHT NOW IS FLEE...
...BUT WITH MARKING AND TELEPORT, IT'S EASY ENOUGH TO SHAKE HER.

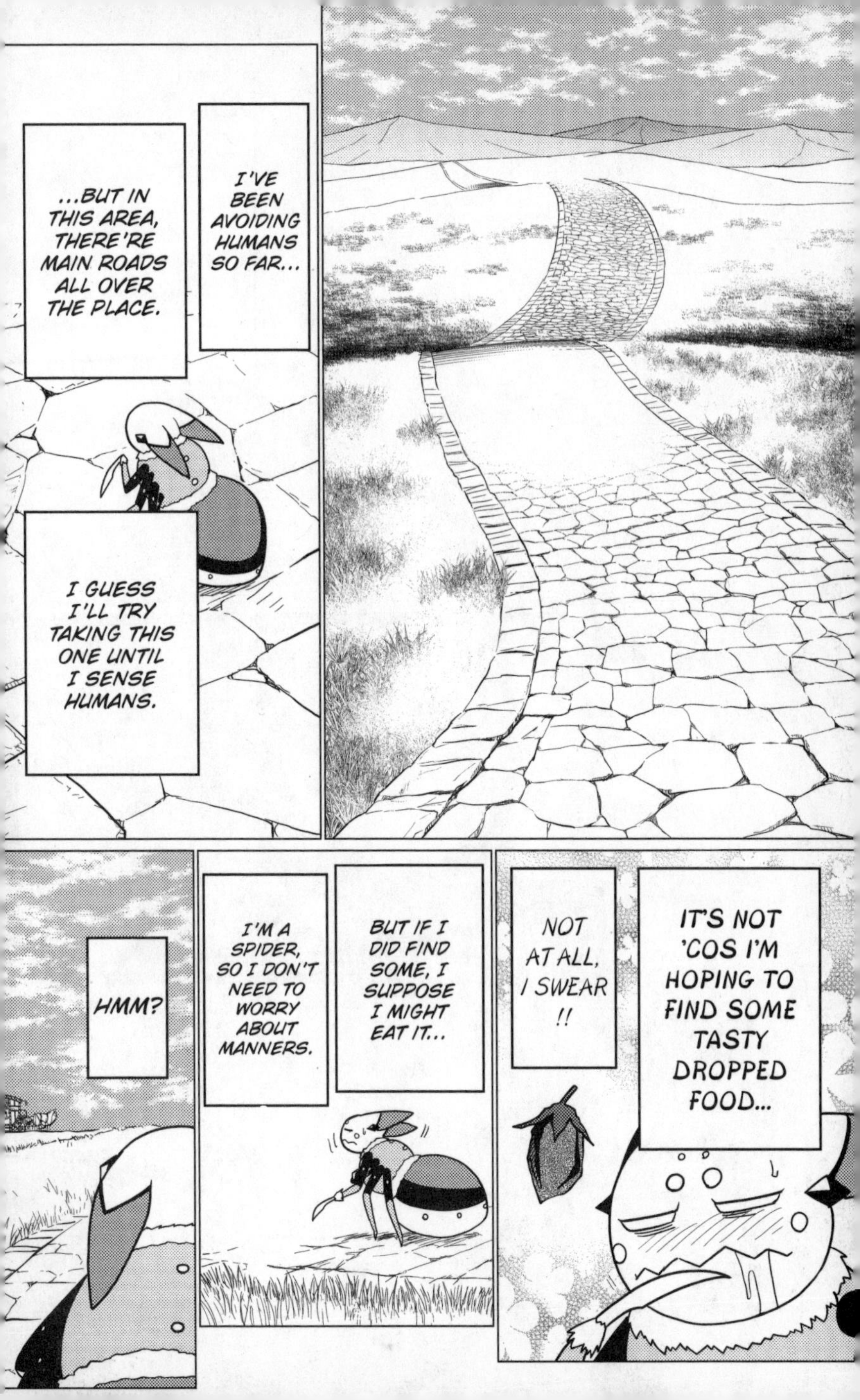
I'VE BEEN AVOIDING HUMANS SO FAR...
...BUT IN THIS AREA, THERE'RE MAIN ROADS ALL OVER THE PLACE.
I GUESS I'LL TRY TAKING THIS ONE UNTIL I SENSE HUMANS.
IT'S NOT 'COS I'M HOPING TO FIND SOME TASTY DROPPED FOOD...
NOT AT ALL, I SWEAR!!
BUT IF I DID FIND SOME, I SUPPOSE I MIGHT EAT IT...
I'M A SPIDER, SO I DON'T NEED TO WORRY ABOUT MANNERS.
HMM?

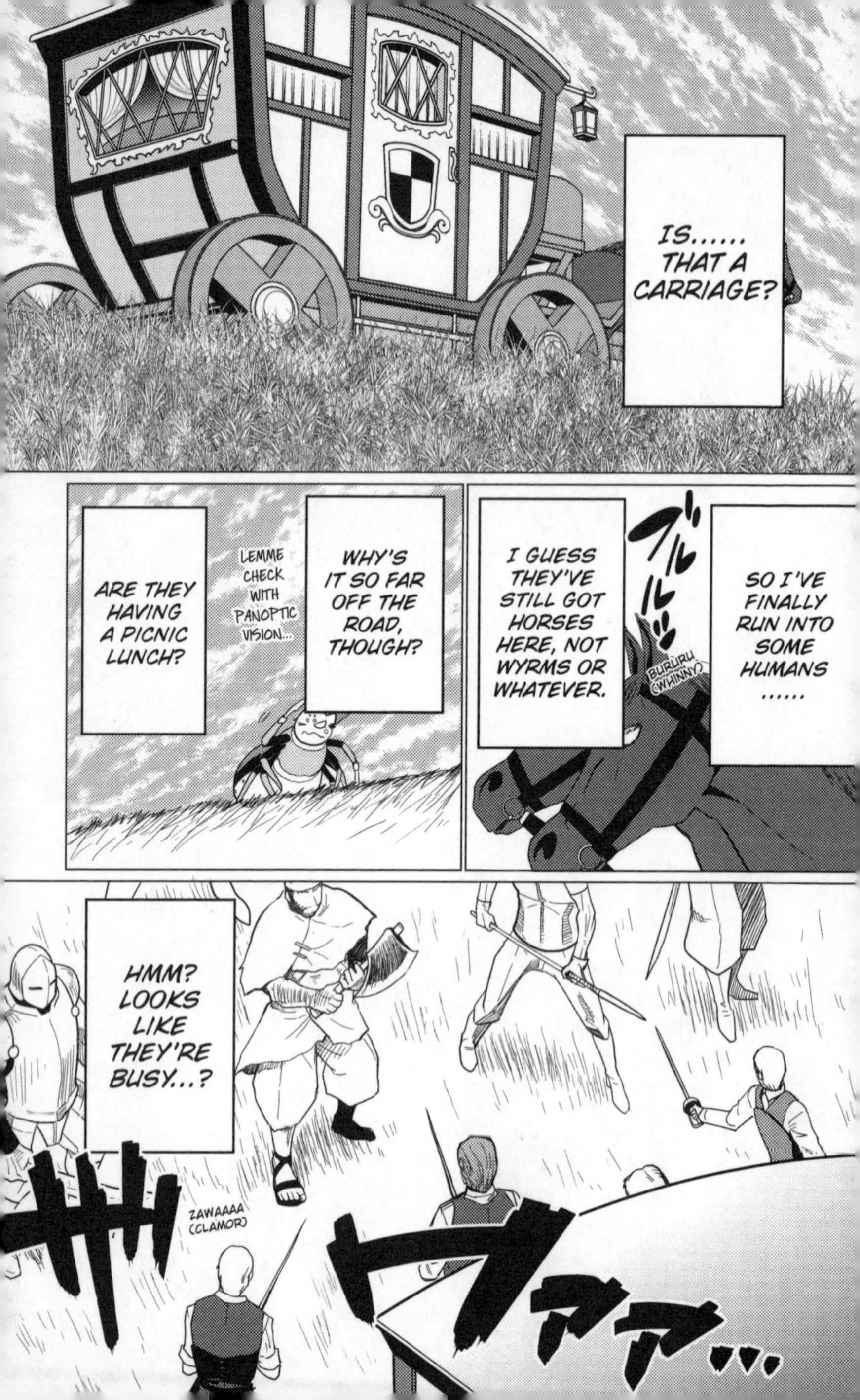
IS...... THAT A CARRIAGE?
SO I'VE FINALLY RUN INTO SOME HUMANS ......
BURURU (WHINNY)
I GUESS THEY'VE STILL GOT HORSES HERE, NOT WYRMS OR WHATEVER.
WHY'S IT SO FAR OFF THE ROAD, THOUGH?
LEMME CHECK WITH PANOPTIC VISION...
ARE THEY HAVING A PICNIC LUNCH?
HMM? LOOKS LIKE THEY'RE BUSY...?
ZAWAAAA (CLAMOR)

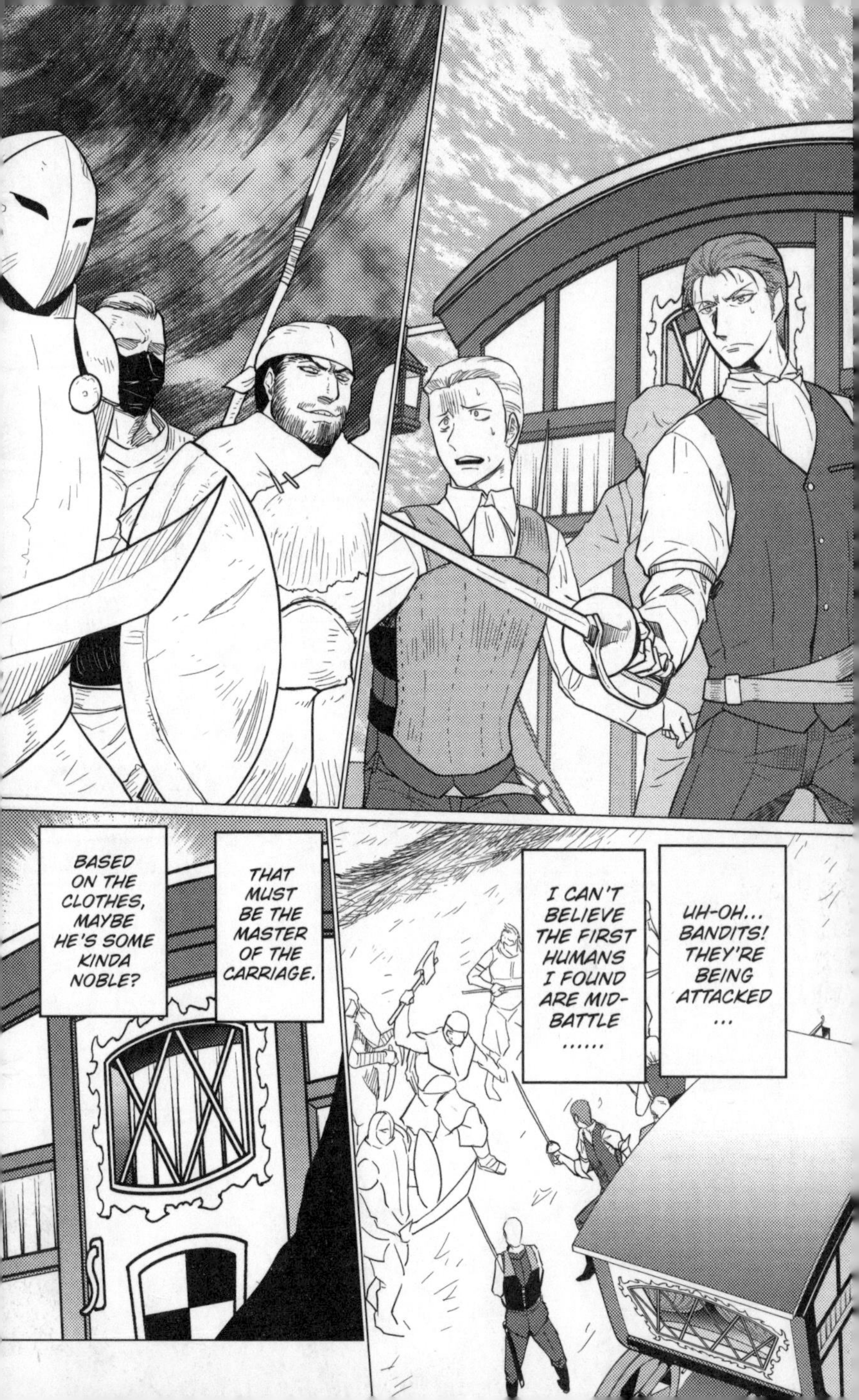
UH-OH... BANDITS! THEY'RE BEING ATTACKED ...
I CAN'T BELIEVE THE FIRST HUMANS I FOUND ARE MID-BATTLE ......
THAT MUST BE THE MASTER OF THE CARRIAGE.
BASED ON THE CLOTHES, MAYBE HE'S SOME KINDA NOBLE?

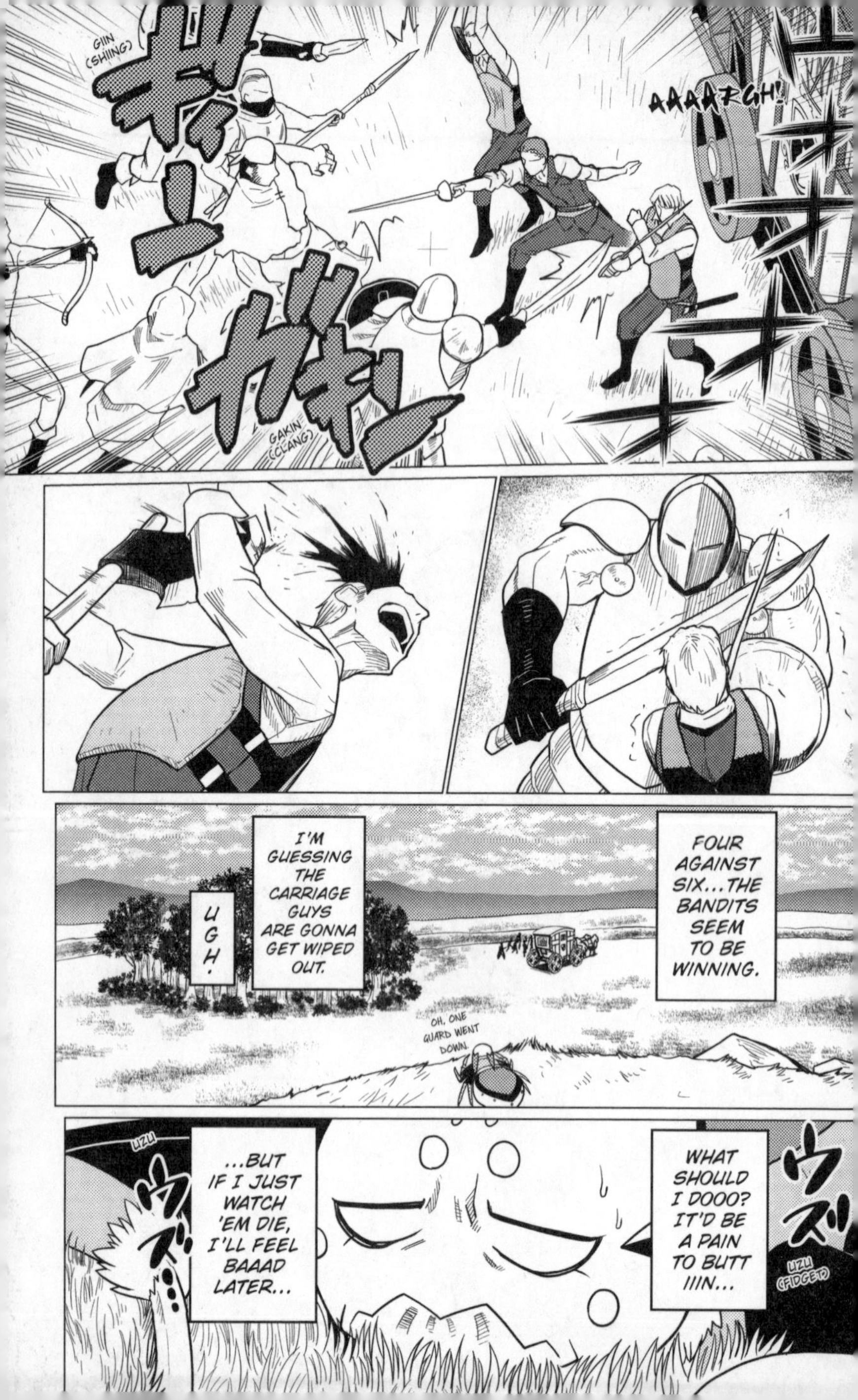
AAAARGH!
GIIN (SHIING)
GAKIN (CLANG)
FOUR AGAINST SIX...THE BANDITS SEEM TO BE WINNING.
I'M GUESSING THE CARRIAGE GUYS ARE GONNA GET WIPED OUT.
UGH!
OH, ONE GUARD WENT DOWN.
WHAT SHOULD I DOOO? IT'D BE A PAIN TO BUTT IIIN...
UZU (FIDGET)
...BUT IF I JUST WATCH 'EM DIE, I'LL FEEL BAAAD LATER...
UZU

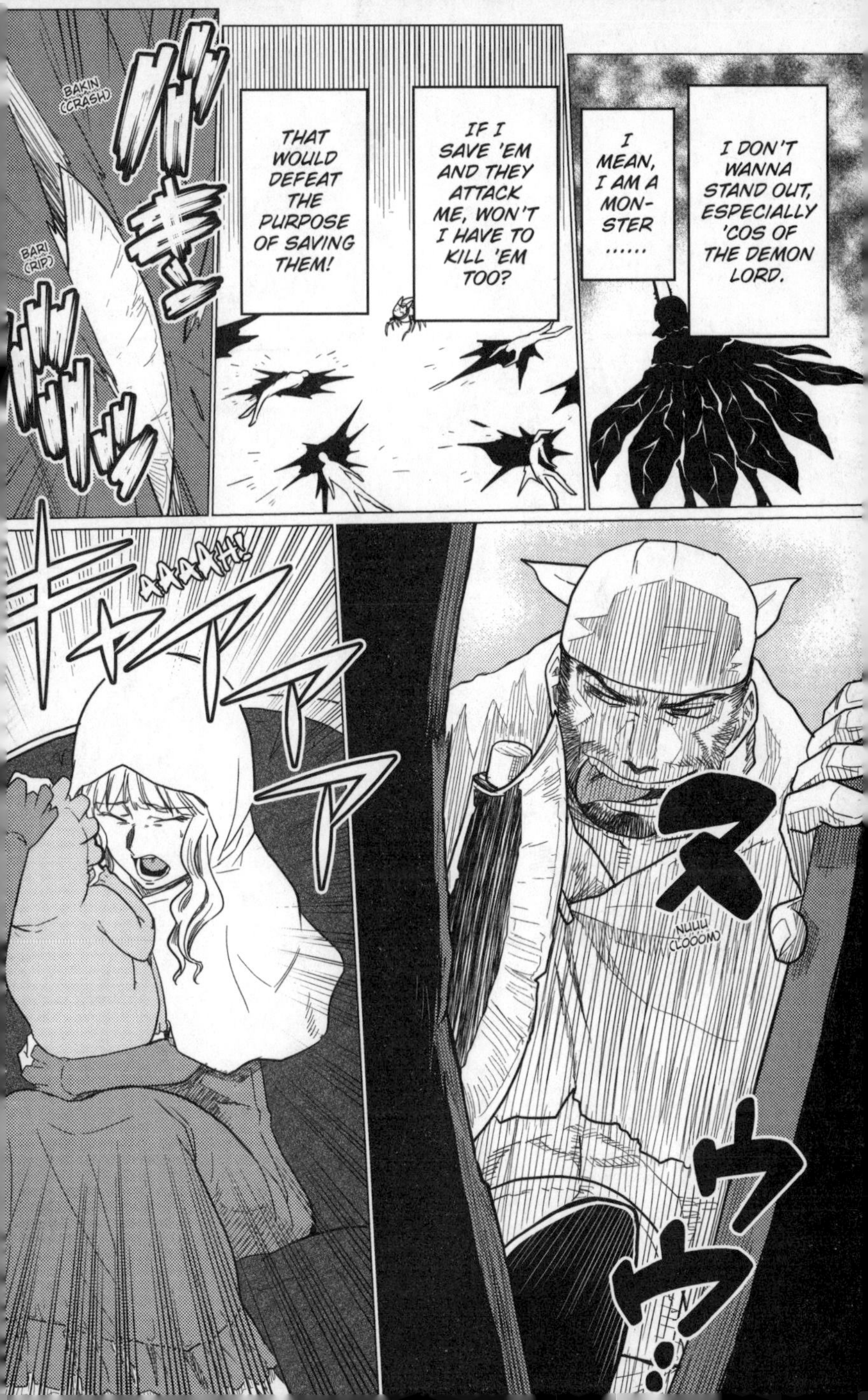
I DON'T WANNA STAND OUT, ESPECIALLY 'COS OF THE DEMON LORD.
I MEAN, I AM A MON-STER......
IF I SAVE 'EM AND THEY ATTACK ME, WON'T I HAVE TO KILL 'EM TOO?
THAT WOULD DEFEAT THE PURPOSE OF SAVING THEM!
BAKIN (CRASH)
BARI (RIP)
NUUU (CLOOOM)
AAAAAH!

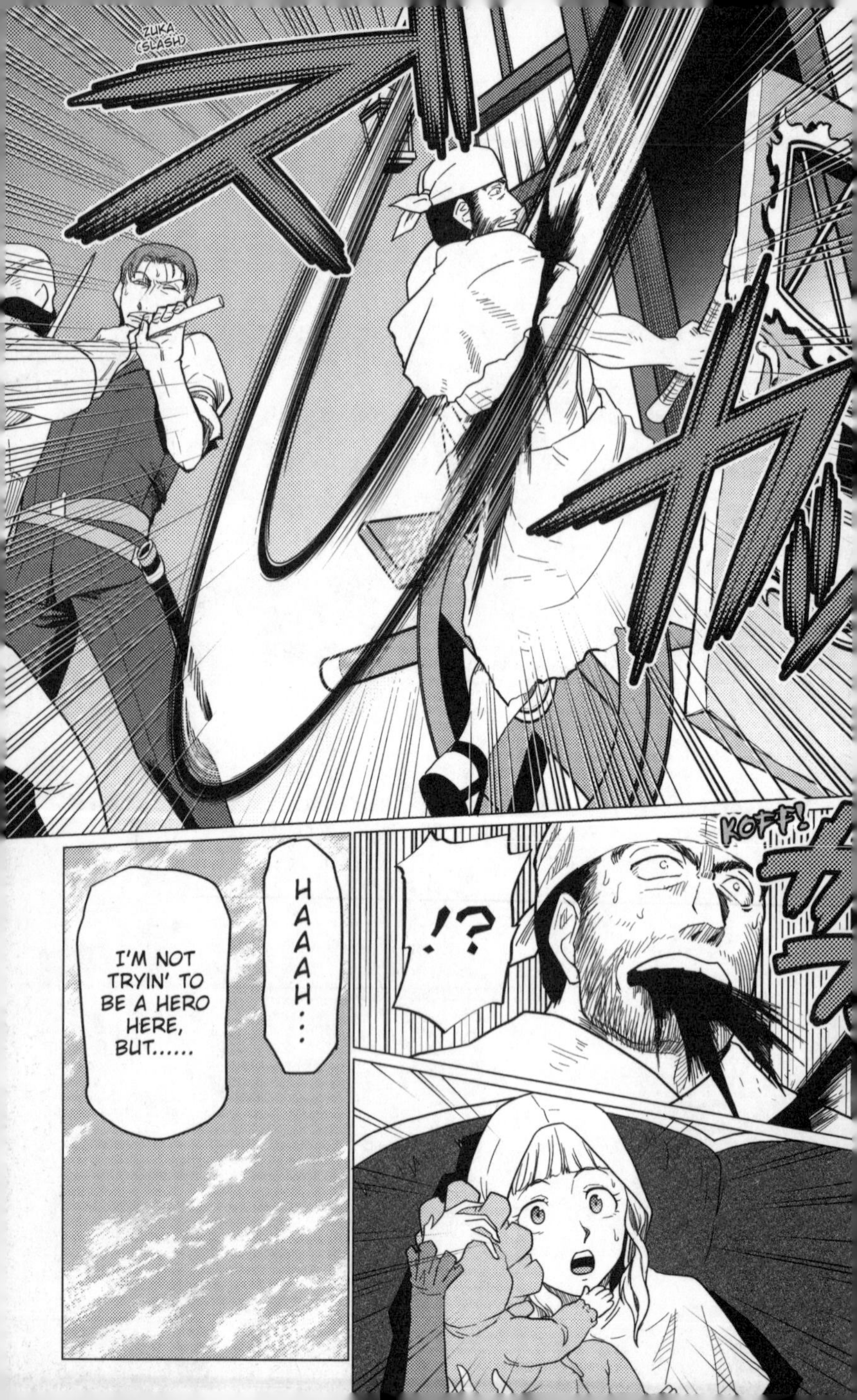
ZUKA
(SLASH)
KOFF!
!?
HAAAAH...
I'M NOT TRYIN' TO BE A HERO HERE, BUT......

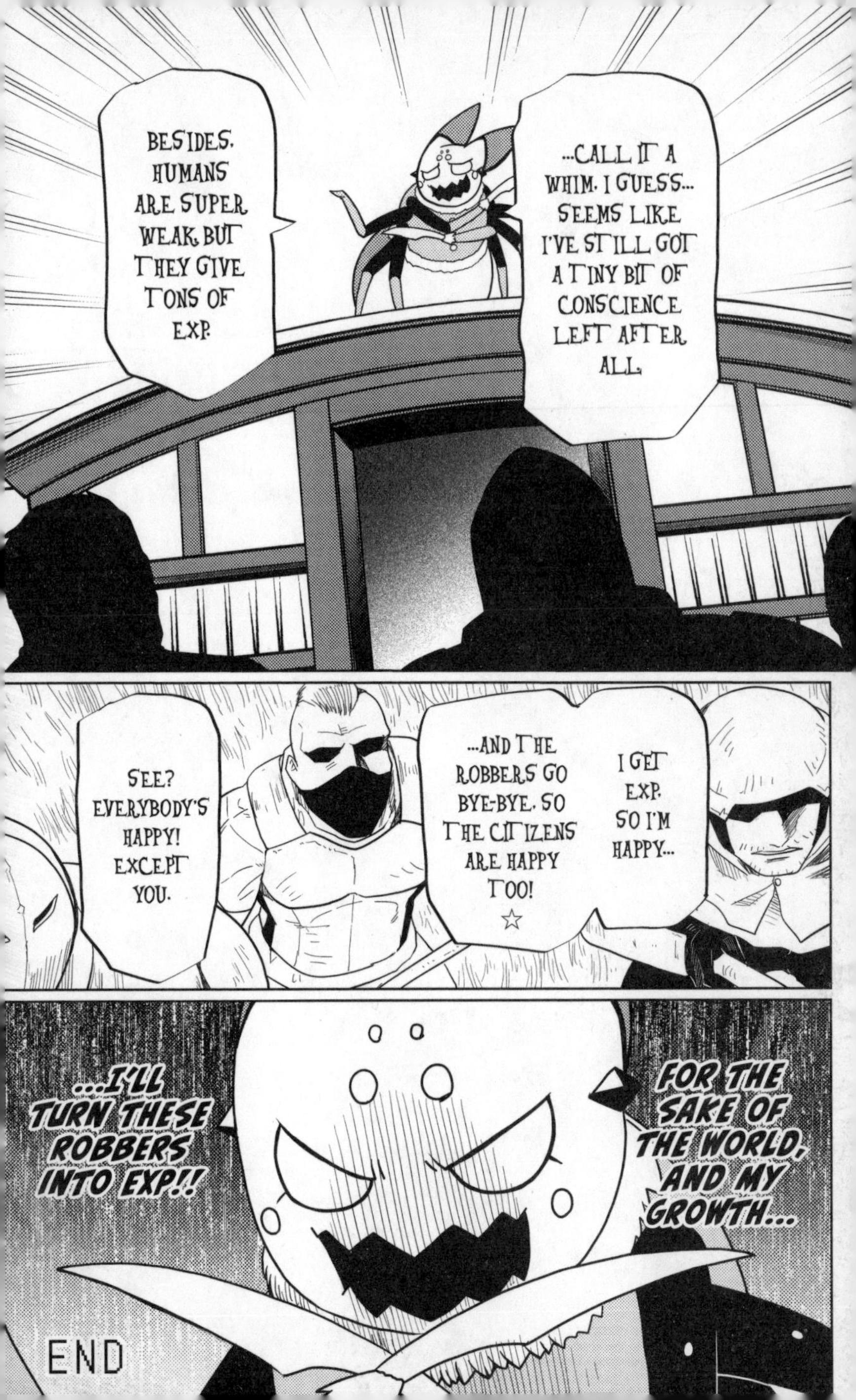
...CALL IT A WHIM, I GUESS... SEEMS LIKE I'VE STILL GOT A TINY BIT OF CONSCIENCE LEFT AFTER ALL.
BESIDES, HUMANS ARE SUPER WEAK, BUT THEY GIVE TONS OF EXP.
I GET EXP, SO I'M HAPPY...
...AND THE ROBBERS GO BYE-BYE, SO THE CITIZENS ARE HAPPY TOO! ☆
SEE? EVERYBODY'S HAPPY! EXCEPT YOU.
FOR THE SAKE OF THE WORLD, AND MY GROWTH...
...I'LL TURN THESE ROBBERS INTO EXP!!
END

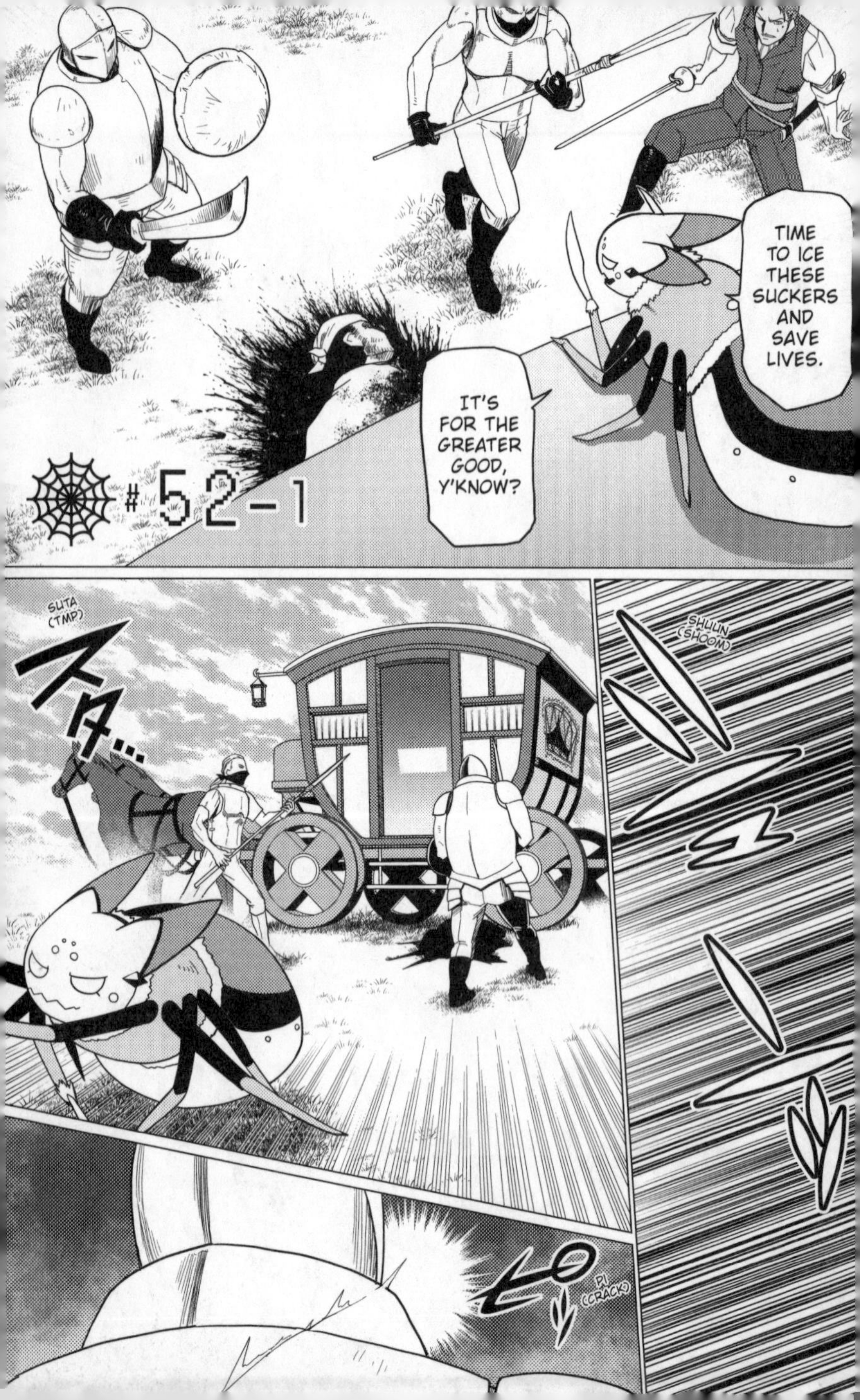
TIME TO ICE THESE SUCKERS AND SAVE LIVES.
IT'S FOR THE GREATER GOOD, Y'KNOW?
#52-1
SHUUN (SHOOM)
SUTA (TMP)
PI (CRACK)

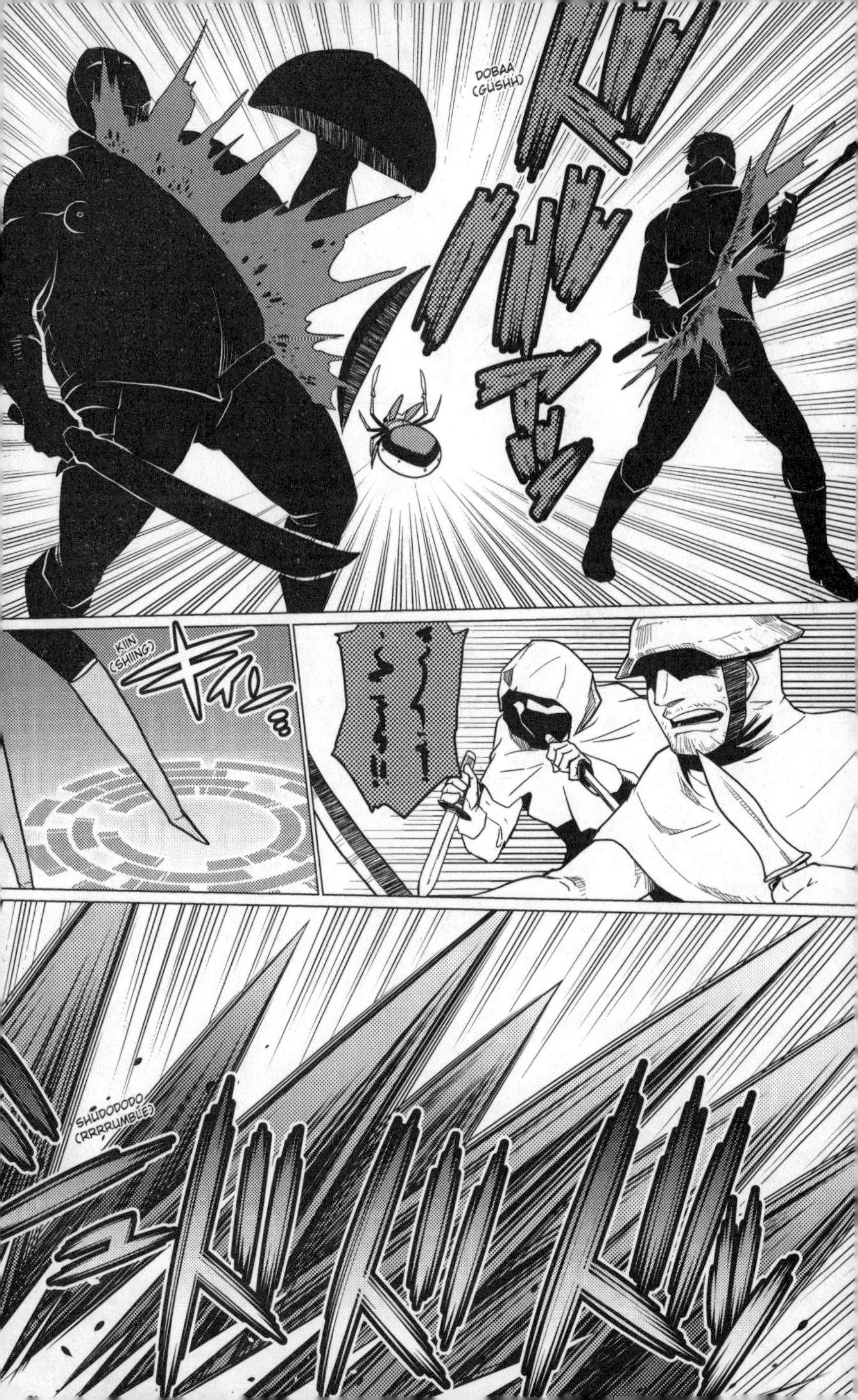
DOBAA (GUSHH)
KIN (SHIING)
SHUDODODO (RRRRUMBLE)

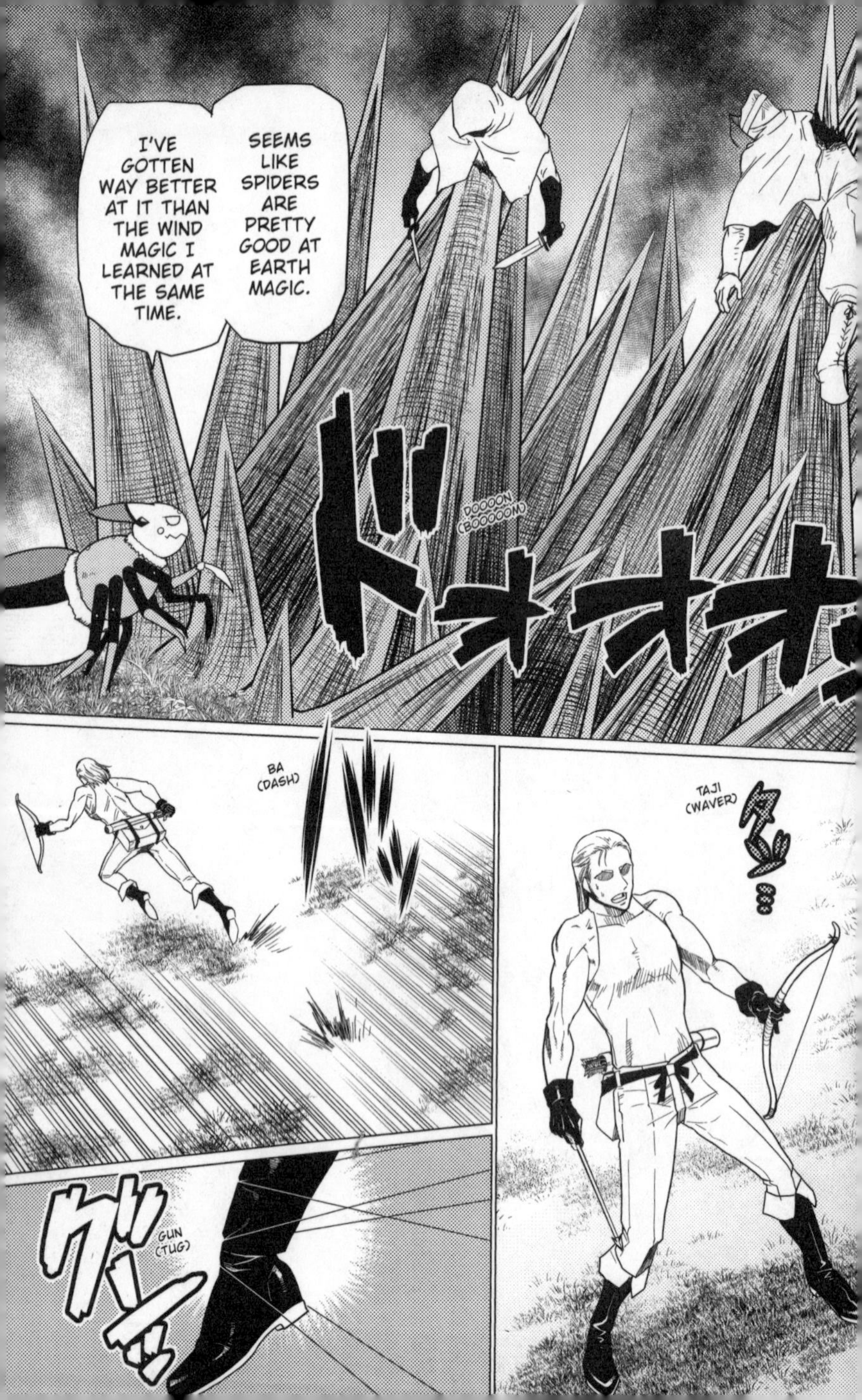
SEEMS LIKE SPIDERS ARE PRETTY GOOD AT EARTH MAGIC.
I'VE GOTTEN WAY BETTER AT IT THAN THE WIND MAGIC I LEARNED AT THE SAME TIME.
DOOOON (BOOOOOM)
TAJI (WAVER)
BA (DASH)
GUN (TUG)

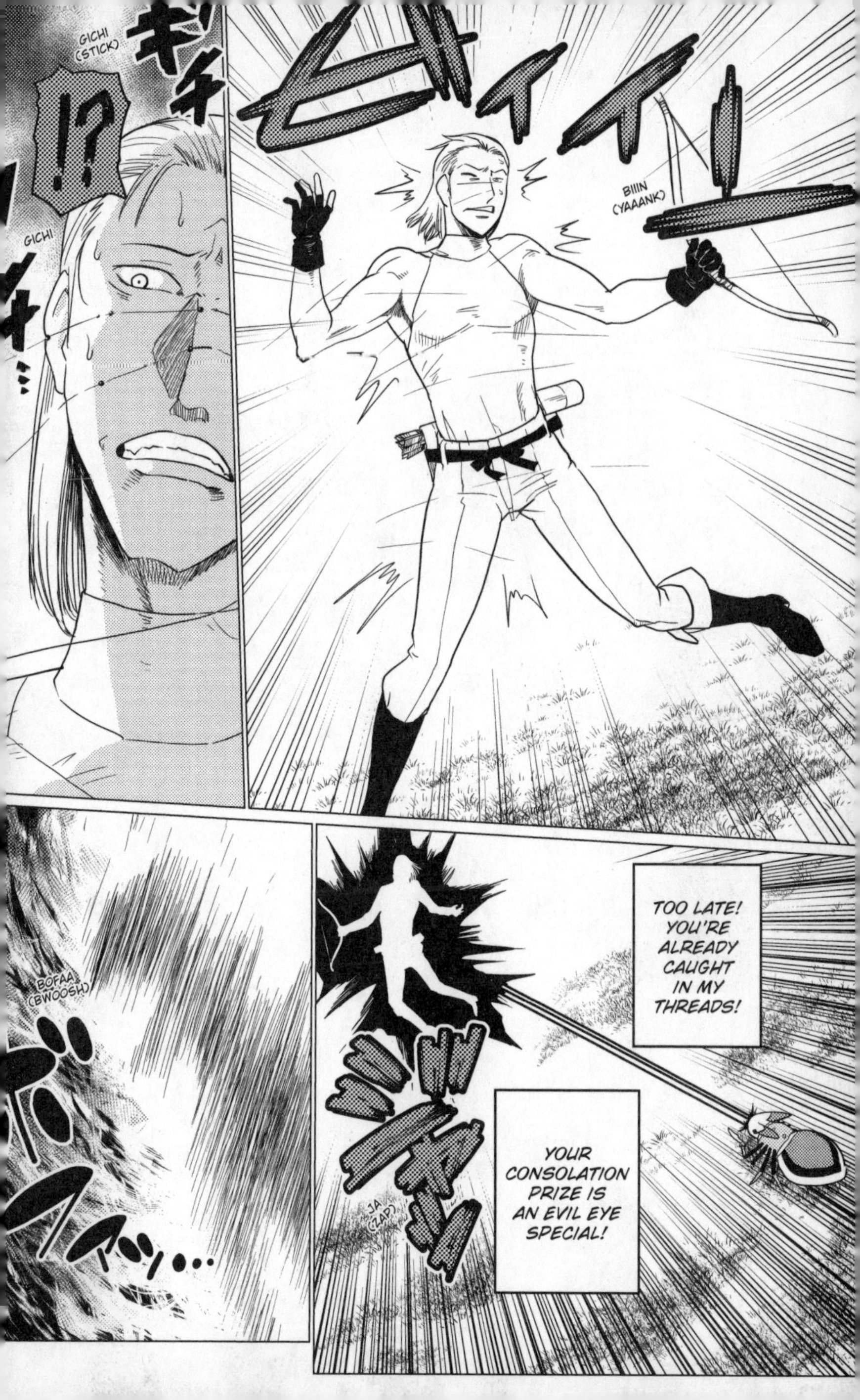
BIIIN (YAAANK)
GICHI (STICK)
!?
GICHI
TOO LATE! YOU'RE ALREADY CAUGHT IN MY THREADS!
YOUR CONSOLATION PRIZE IS AN EVIL EYE SPECIAL!
JA (ZAP)
BOFAA (BWOOSH)

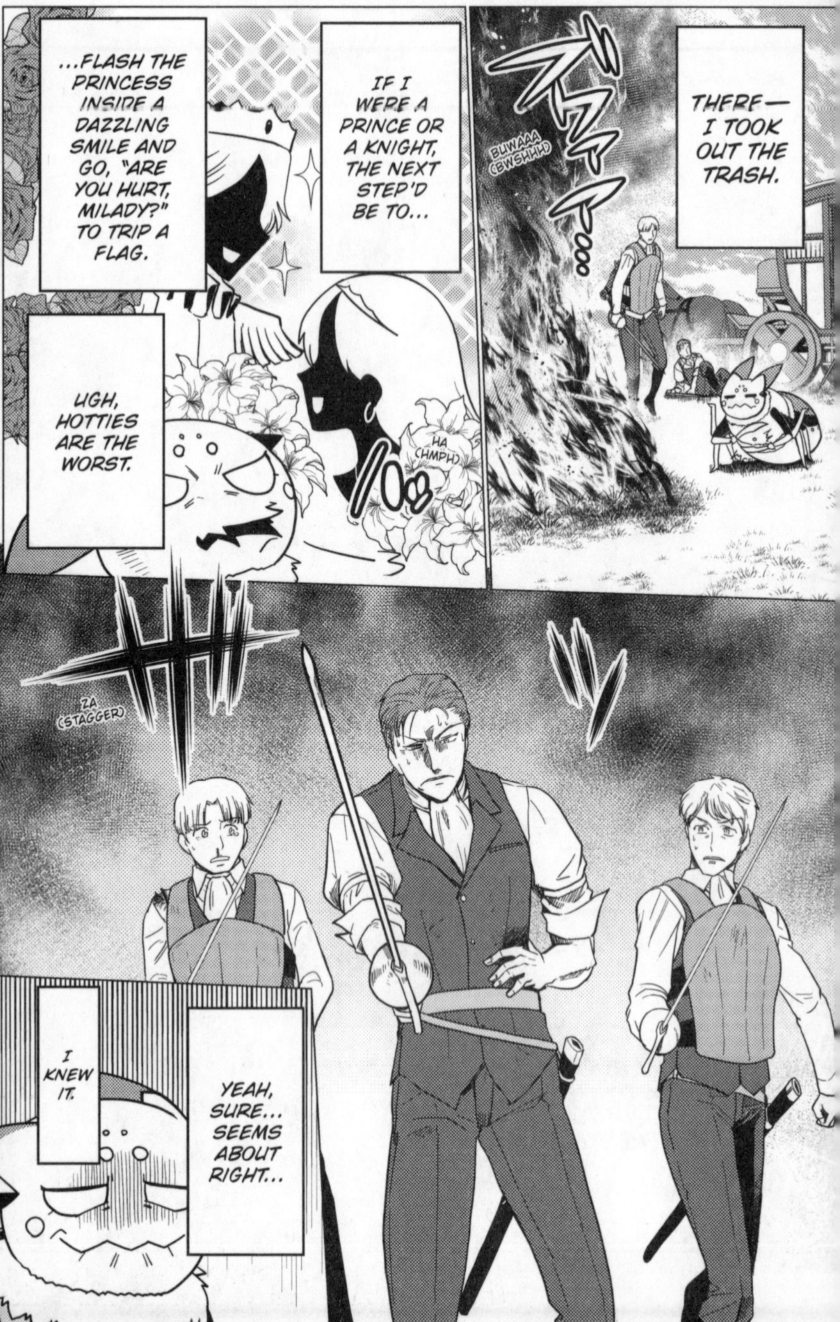
THERE—
I TOOK OUT THE TRASH.
BUWAAA (BWSHHH)
IF I WERE A PRINCE OR A KNIGHT, THE NEXT STEP'D BE TO...
...FLASH THE PRINCESS INSIDE A DAZZLING SMILE AND GO, "ARE YOU HURT, MILADY?" TO TRIP A FLAG.
HA (HMPH)
UGH, HOTTIES ARE THE WORST.
ZA (STAGGER)
YEAH, SURE... SEEMS ABOUT RIGHT...
I KNEW IT.

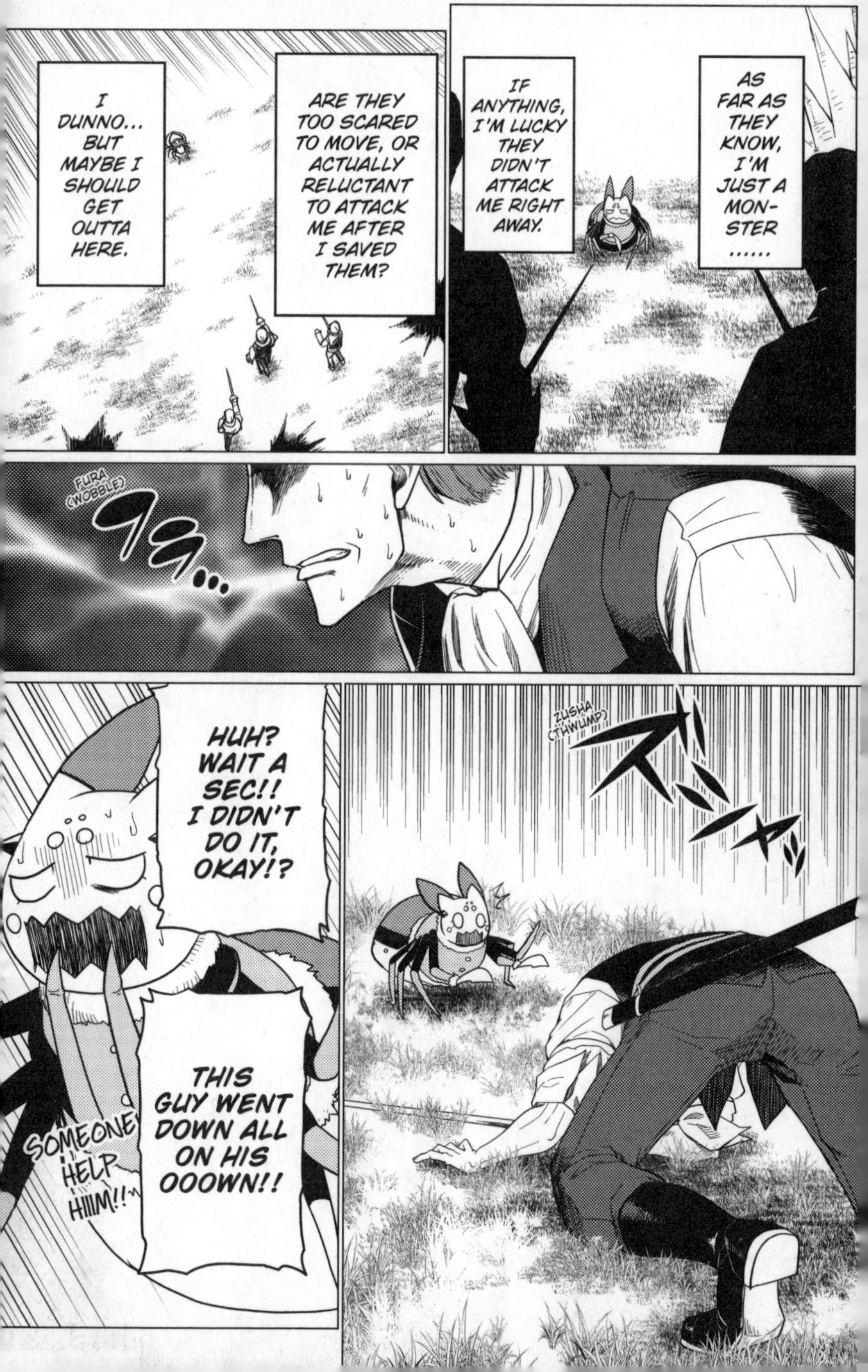
AS FAR AS THEY KNOW, I'M JUST A MON-STER......
IF ANYTHING, I'M LUCKY THEY DIDN'T ATTACK ME RIGHT AWAY.
ARE THEY TOO SCARED TO MOVE, OR ACTUALLY RELUCTANT TO ATTACK ME AFTER I SAVED THEM?
I DUNNO... BUT MAYBE I SHOULD GET OUTTA HERE.
FURA (WOBBLE)
ZUSHA (THWUMP)
HUH? WAIT A SEC!! I DIDN'T DO IT, OKAY!?
THIS GUY WENT DOWN ALL ON HIS OOOWN!!
SOMEONE HELP HIIIM!!

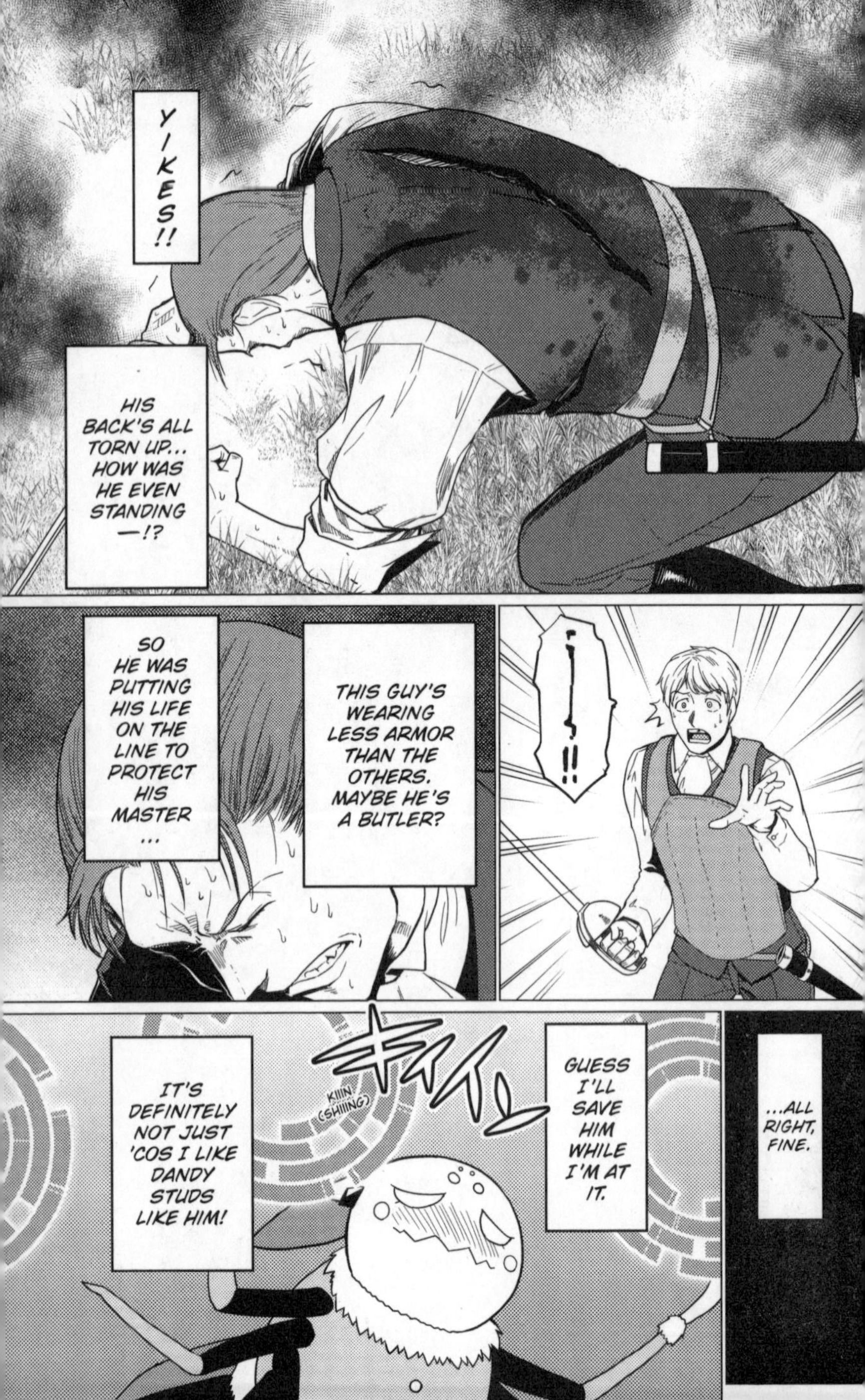
YIKES!!
HIS BACK'S ALL TORN UP... HOW WAS HE EVEN STANDING—!?
—!!
THIS GUY'S WEARING LESS ARMOR THAN THE OTHERS. MAYBE HE'S A BUTLER?
SO HE WAS PUTTING HIS LIFE ON THE LINE TO PROTECT HIS MASTER...
...ALL RIGHT, FINE.
GUESS I'LL SAVE HIM WHILE I'M AT IT.
KIIIN (SHIIING)
IT'S DEFINITELY NOT JUST 'COS I LIKE DANDY STUDS LIKE HIM!

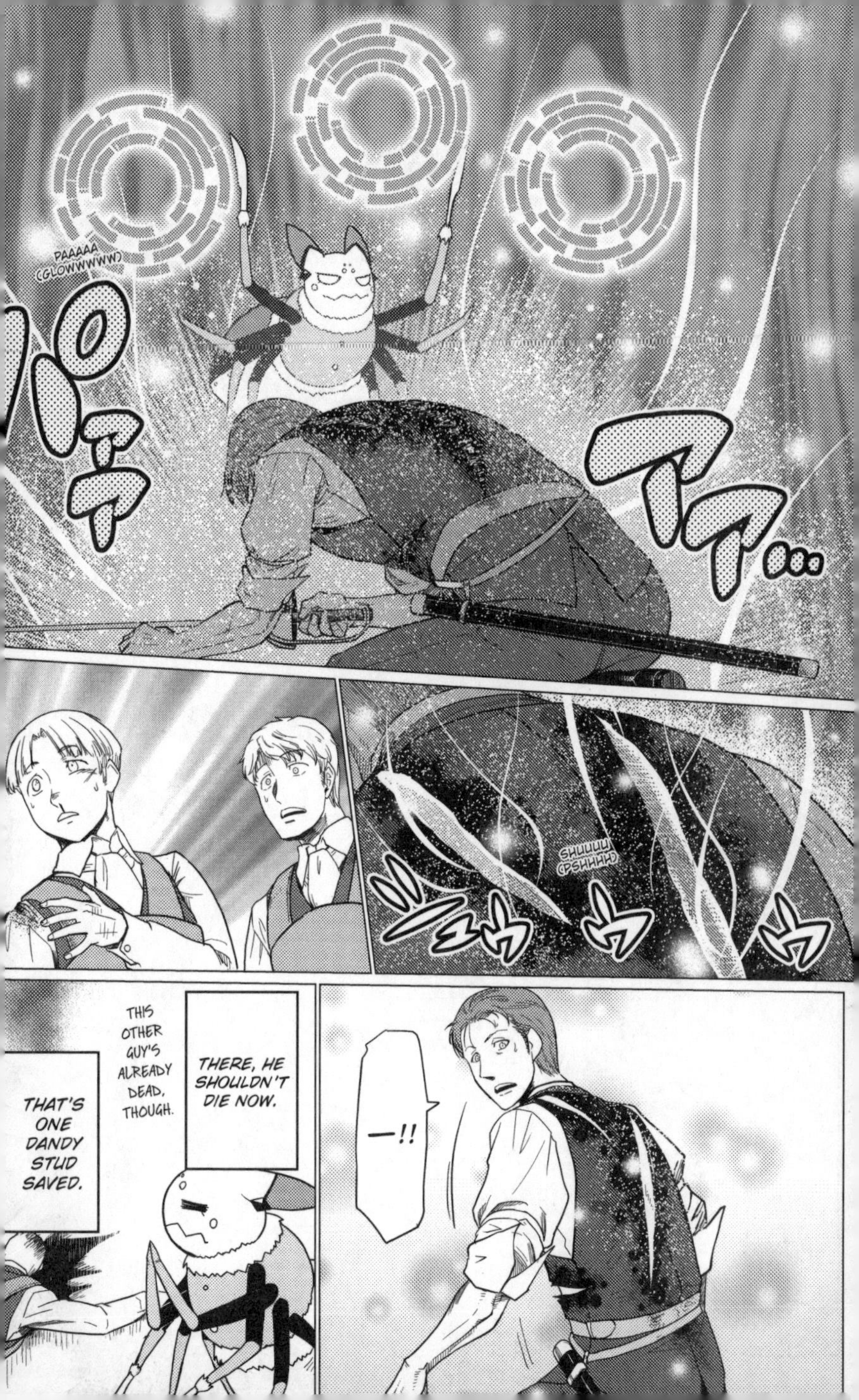
PAAAAA (GLOWWWWW)
SHUUUUU (PSHHHHH)
—!!
THERE, HE SHOULDN'T DIE NOW.
THIS OTHER GUY'S ALREADY DEAD, THOUGH.
THAT'S ONE DANDY STUD SAVED.

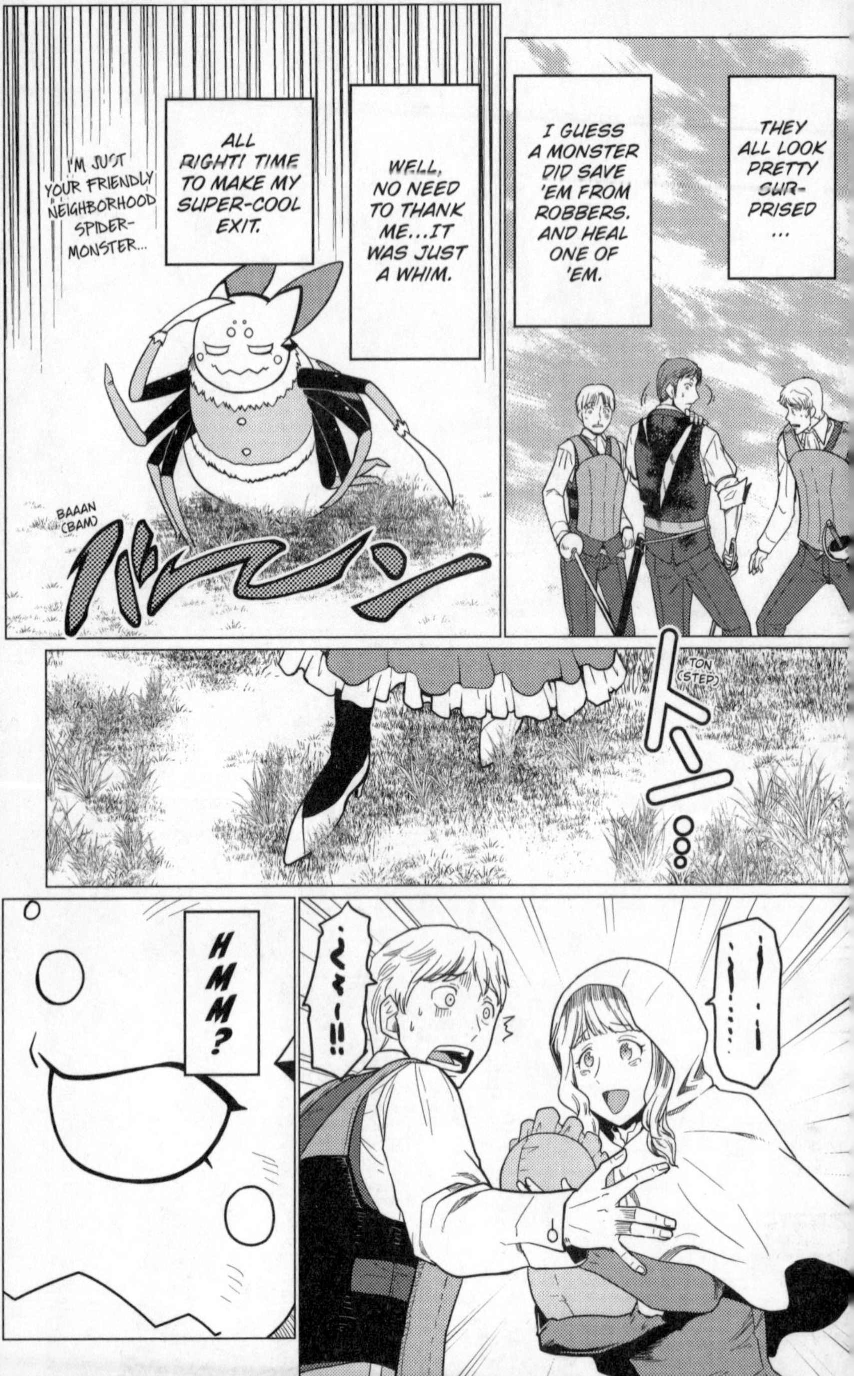
THEY ALL LOOK PRETTY SUR-PRISED...
I GUESS A MONSTER DID SAVE 'EM FROM ROBBERS. AND HEAL ONE OF 'EM.
WELL, NO NEED TO THANK ME...IT WAS JUST A WHIM.
ALL RIGHT! TIME TO MAKE MY SUPER-COOL EXIT.
I'M JUST YOUR FRIENDLY NEIGHBORHOOD SPIDER-MONSTER...
BAAAN (BAM)
TON (STEP)
HMM?

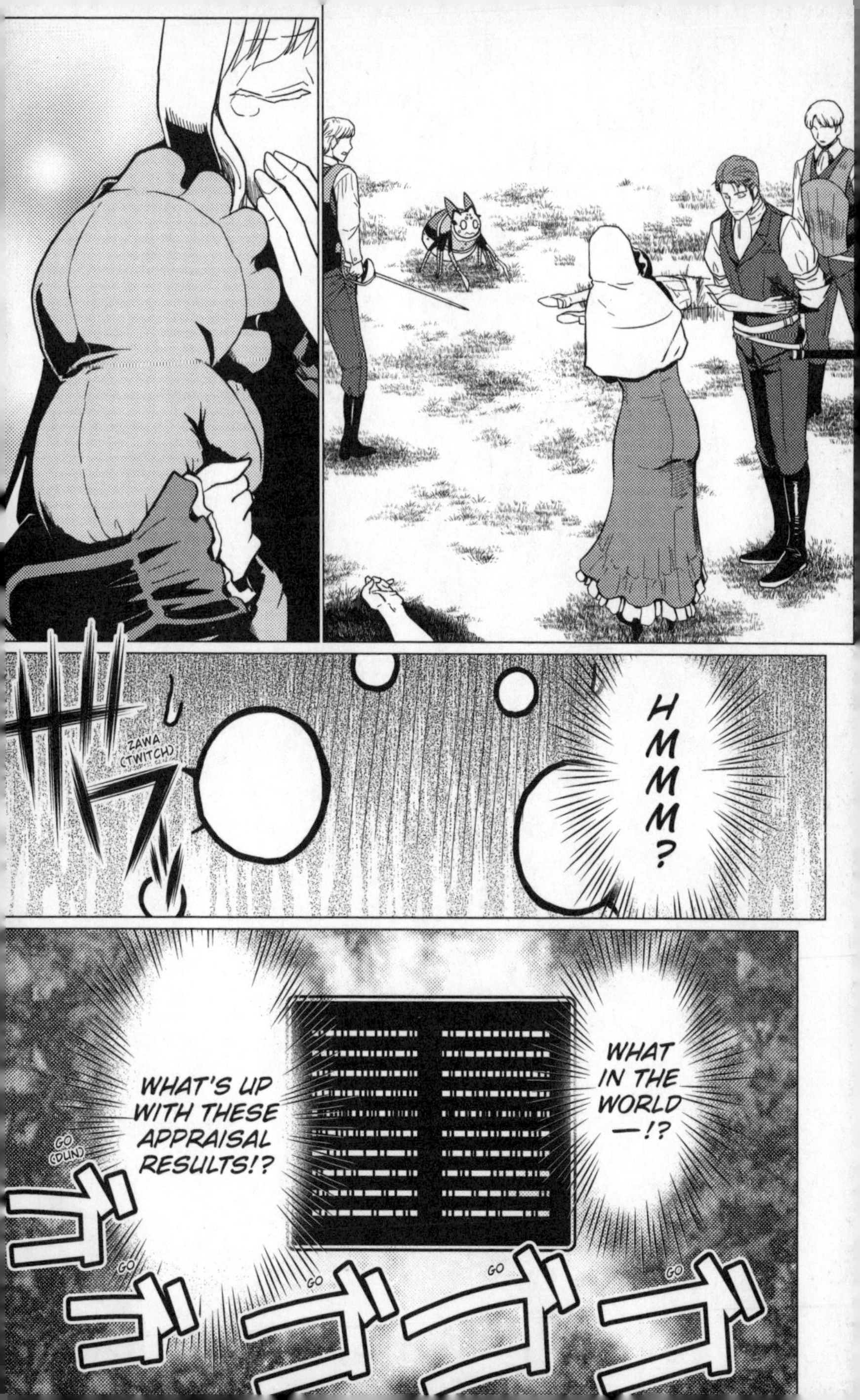
HMMMM?
ZAWA (TWITCH)
WHAT IN THE WORLD—!?
WHAT'S UP WITH THESE APPRAISAL RESULTS!?
GO (DUN)
GO
GO
GO
GO

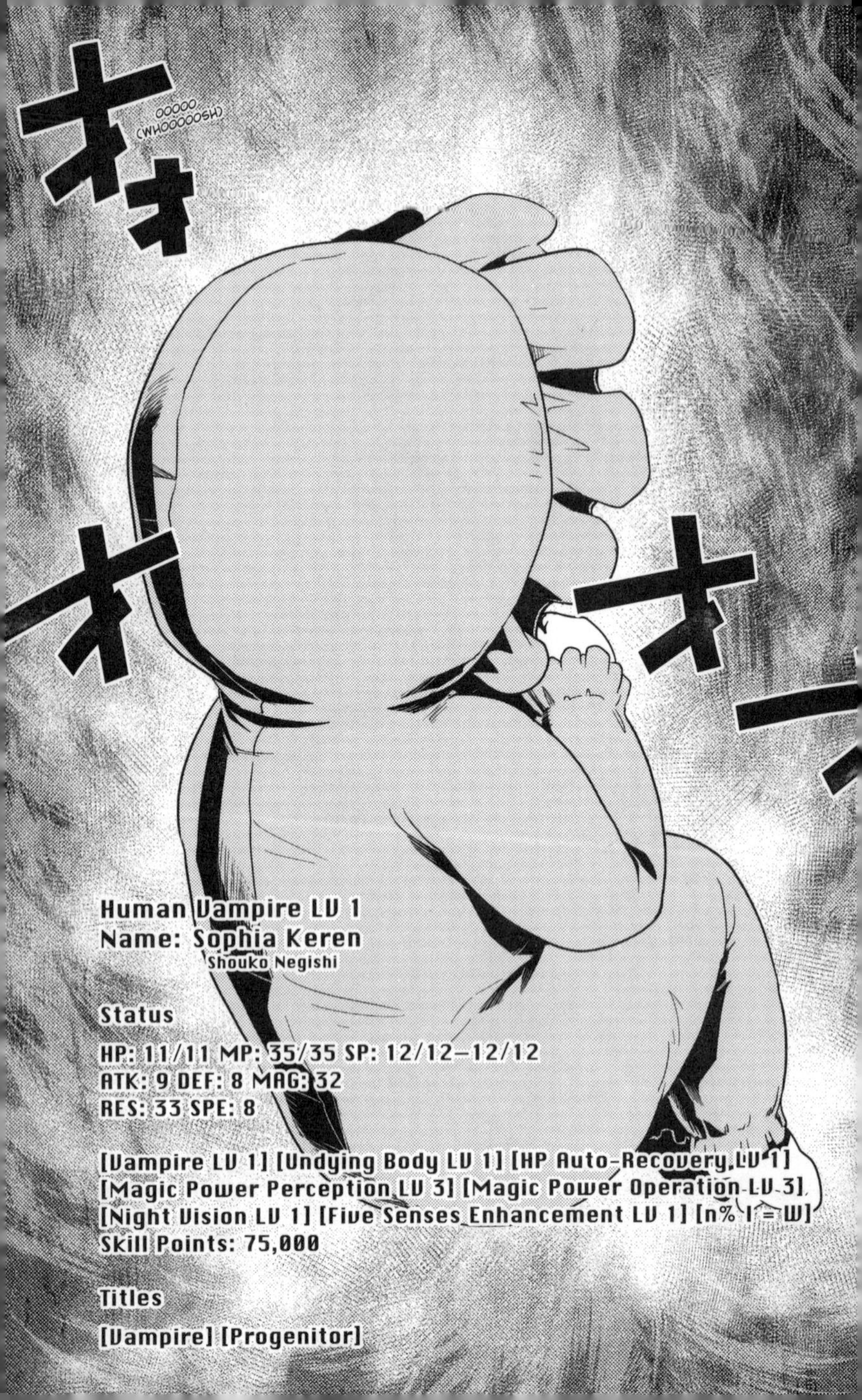
OOOOO (WHOOOOOSH)
Human Vampire LV 1
Name: Sophia Keren
Shouko Negishi
Status
HP: 11/11 MP: 35/35 SP: 12/12–12/12
ATK: 9 DEF: 8 MAG: 32
RES: 33 SPE: 8
[Vampire LV 1] [Undying Body LV 1] [HP Auto-Recovery LV 1]
[Magic Power Perception LV 3] [Magic Power Operation LV 3]
[Night Vision LV 1] [Five Senses Enhancement LV 1] [n% I = W]
Skill Points: 75,000
Titles
[Vampire] [Progenitor]

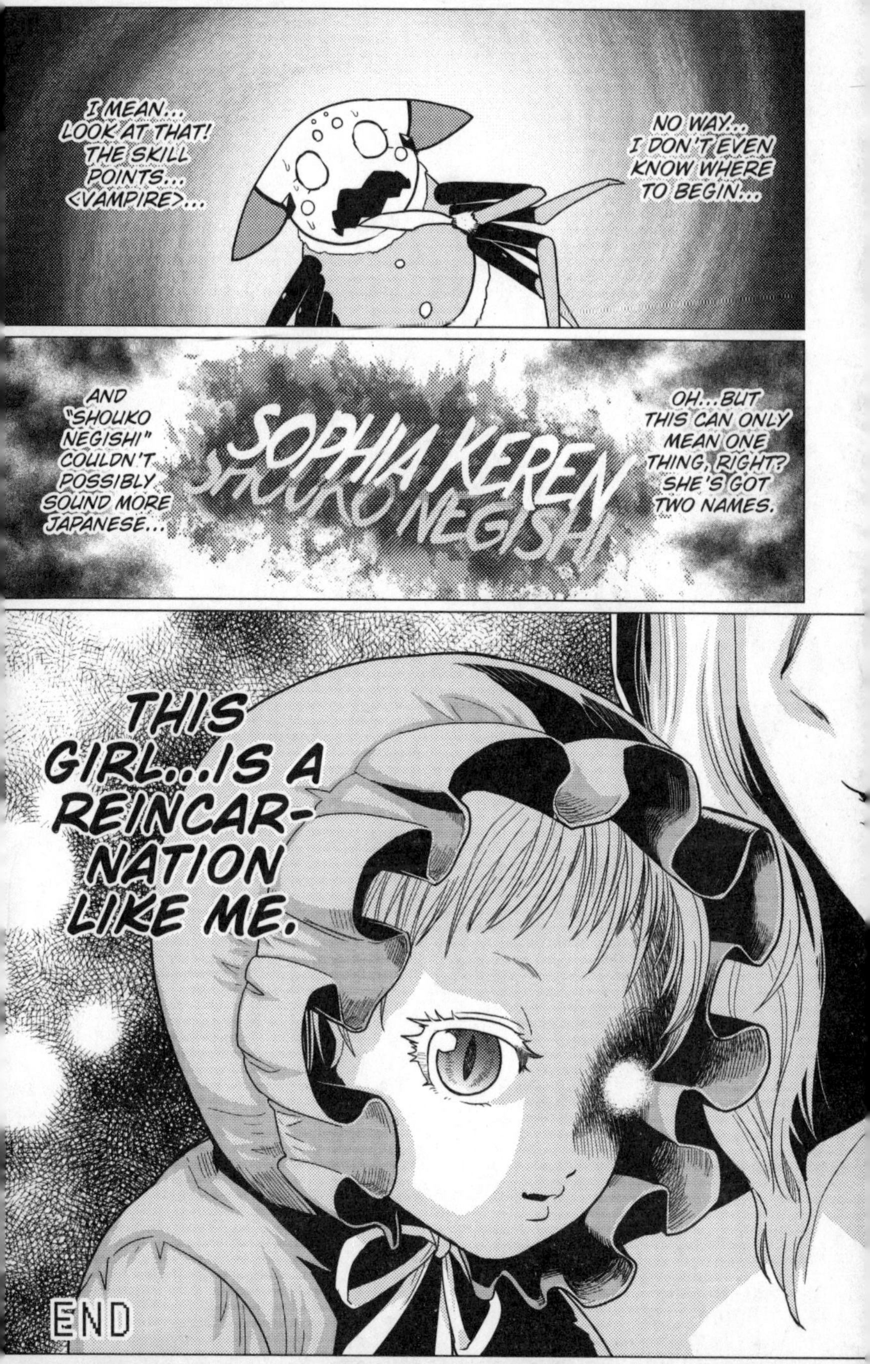
NO WAY... I DON'T EVEN KNOW WHERE TO BEGIN...
I MEAN... LOOK AT THAT! THE SKILL POINTS... <VAMPIRE>...
OH...BUT THIS CAN ONLY MEAN ONE THING, RIGHT? SHE'S GOT TWO NAMES.
SOPHIA KEREN
SHOUKO NEGISHI
AND "SHOUKO NEGISHI" COULDN'T POSSIBLY SOUND MORE JAPANESE...
THIS GIRL...IS A REINCAR-NATION LIKE ME.
END

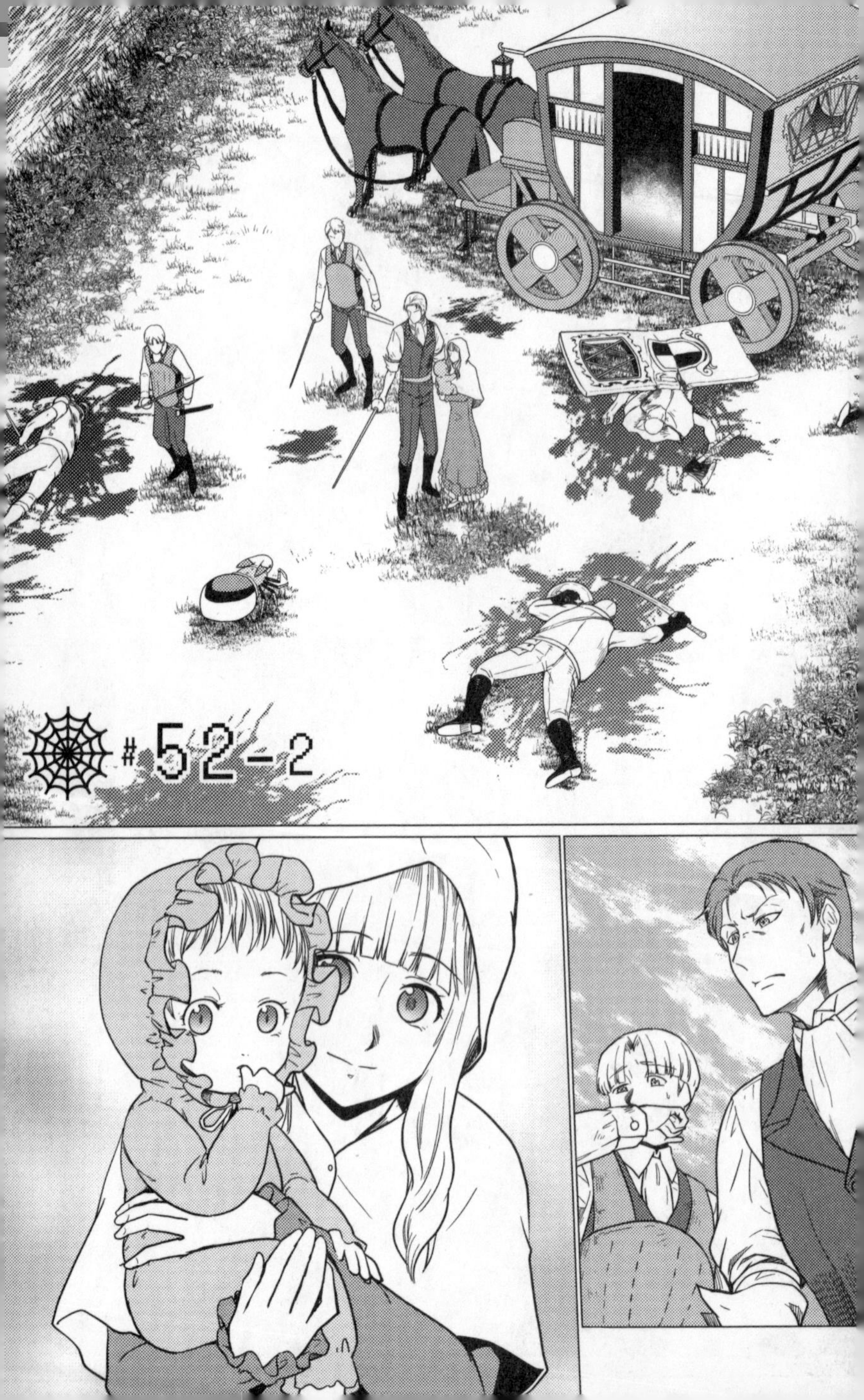
#52-2

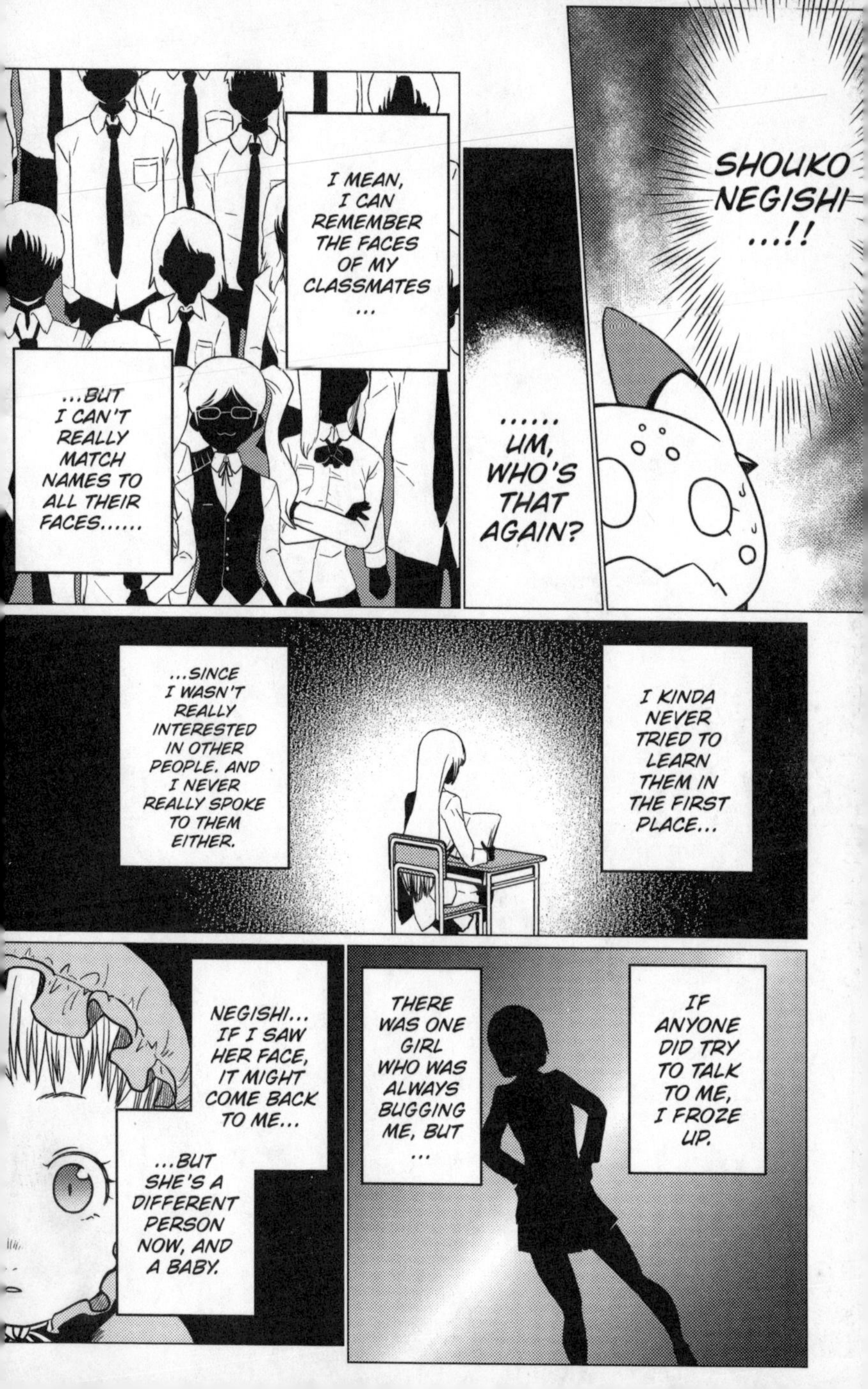
SHOUKO NEGISHI ...!!
...... UM, WHO'S THAT AGAIN?
I MEAN, I CAN REMEMBER THE FACES OF MY CLASSMATES ...
...BUT I CAN'T REALLY MATCH NAMES TO ALL THEIR FACES......
I KINDA NEVER TRIED TO LEARN THEM IN THE FIRST PLACE...
...SINCE I WASN'T REALLY INTERESTED IN OTHER PEOPLE. AND I NEVER REALLY SPOKE TO THEM EITHER.
IF ANYONE DID TRY TO TALK TO ME, I FROZE UP.
THERE WAS ONE GIRL WHO WAS ALWAYS BUGGING ME, BUT ...
NEGISHI... IF I SAW HER FACE, IT MIGHT COME BACK TO ME...
...BUT SHE'S A DIFFERENT PERSON NOW, AND A BABY.

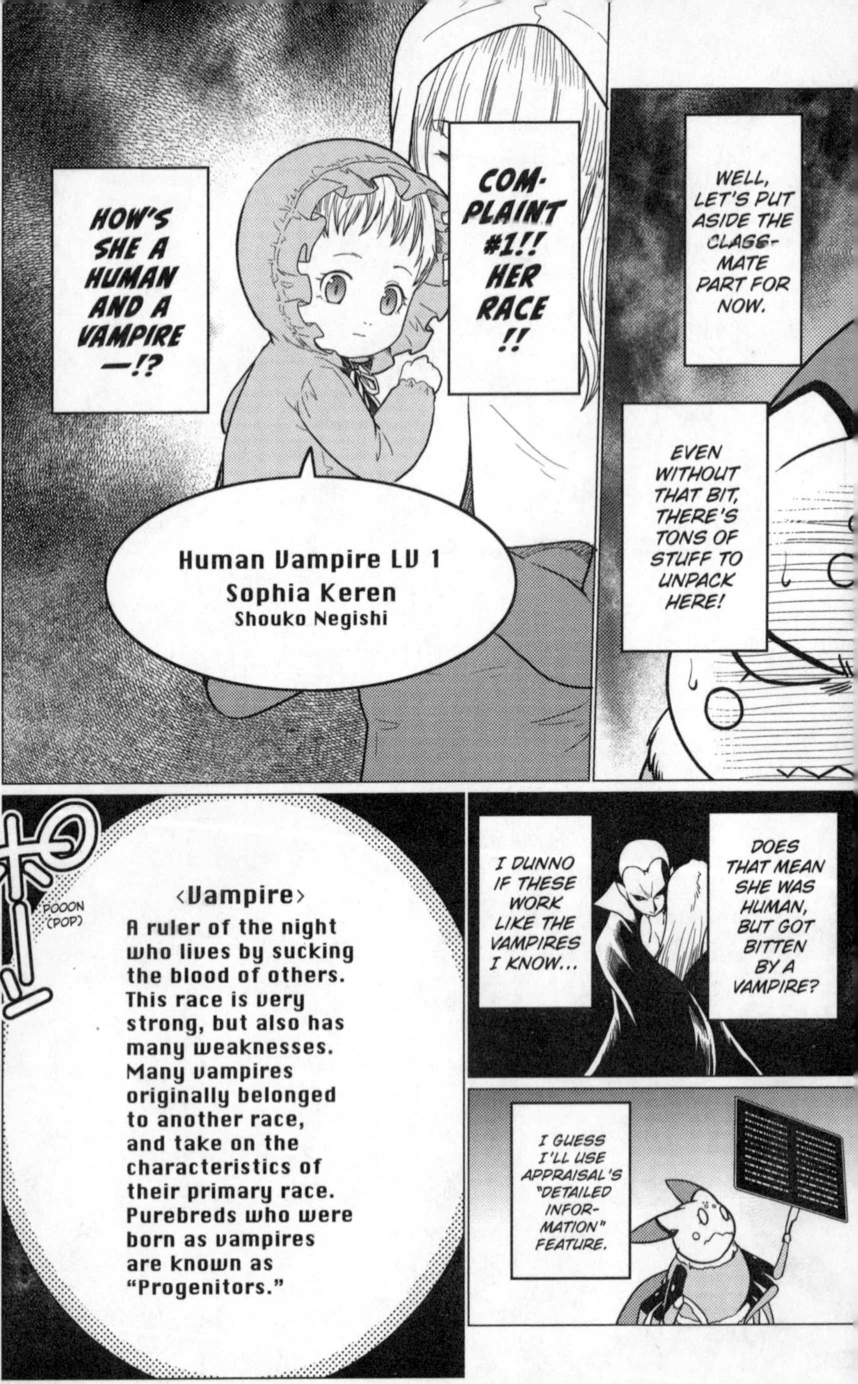
WELL, LET'S PUT ASIDE THE CLASSMATE PART FOR NOW.
EVEN WITHOUT THAT BIT, THERE'S TONS OF STUFF TO UNPACK HERE!
COM-PLAINT #1!! HER RACE!!
HOW'S SHE A HUMAN AND A VAMPIRE—!?
Human Vampire LV 1 Sophia Keren Shouko Negishi
DOES THAT MEAN SHE WAS HUMAN, BUT GOT BITTEN BY A VAMPIRE?
I DUNNO IF THESE WORK LIKE THE VAMPIRES I KNOW...
I GUESS I'LL USE APPRAISAL'S "DETAILED INFORMATION" FEATURE.
POOON (POP)
‹Vampire›
A ruler of the night who lives by sucking the blood of others. This race is very strong, but also has many weaknesses. Many vampires originally belonged to another race, and take on the characteristics of their primary race. Purebreds who were born as vampires are known as "Progenitors."

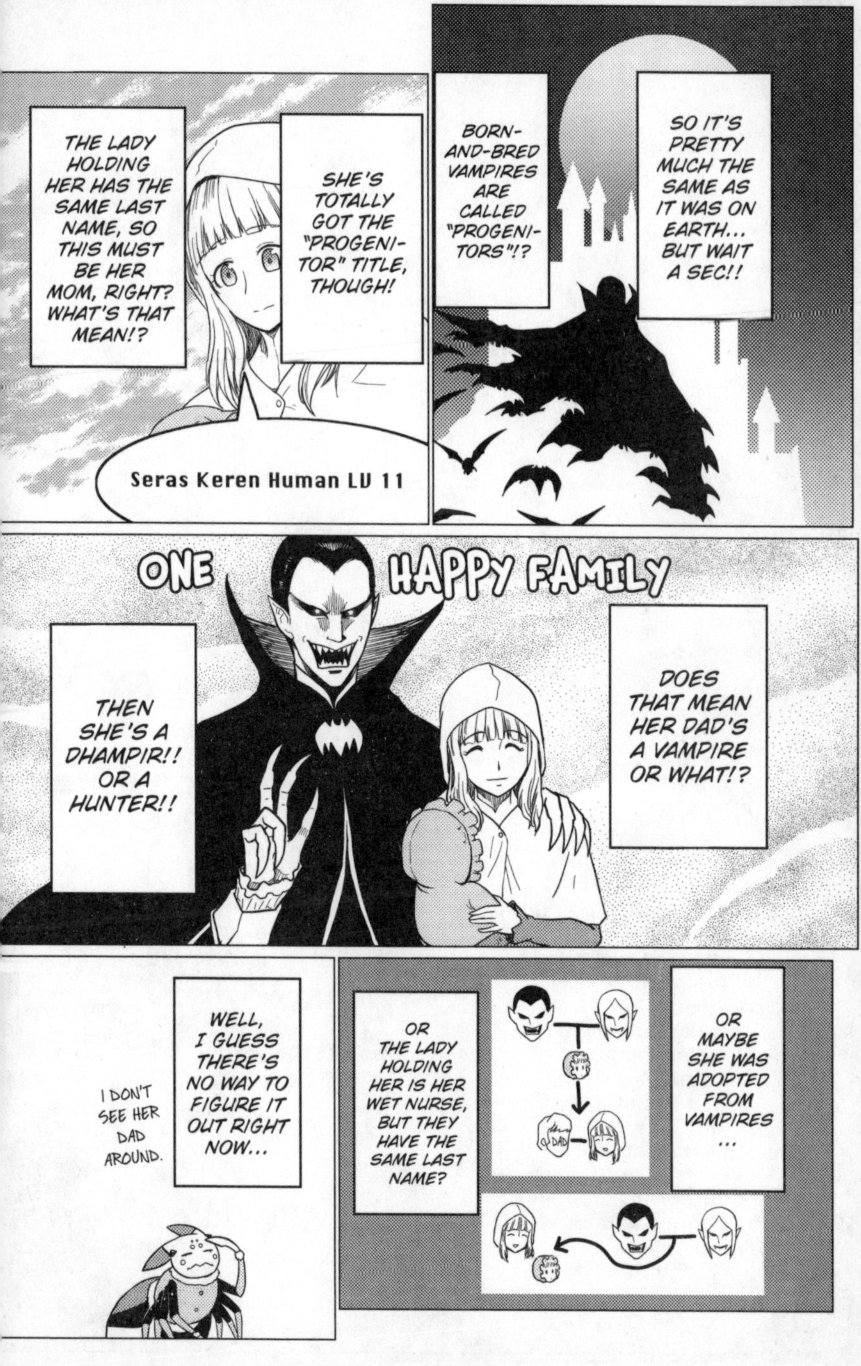
SO IT'S PRETTY MUCH THE SAME AS IT WAS ON EARTH... BUT WAIT A SEC!!
BORN-AND-BRED VAMPIRES ARE CALLED "PROGENITORS"!?
SHE'S TOTALLY GOT THE "PROGENITOR" TITLE, THOUGH!
THE LADY HOLDING HER HAS THE SAME LAST NAME, SO THIS MUST BE HER MOM, RIGHT? WHAT'S THAT MEAN!?
Seras Keren Human LV 11
ONE HAPPY FAMILY
DOES THAT MEAN HER DAD'S A VAMPIRE OR WHAT!?
THEN SHE'S A DHAMPIR!! OR A HUNTER!!
OR MAYBE SHE WAS ADOPTED FROM VAMPIRES...
DAD
OR THE LADY HOLDING HER IS HER WET NURSE, BUT THEY HAVE THE SAME LAST NAME?
WELL, I GUESS THERE'S NO WAY TO FIGURE IT OUT RIGHT NOW...
I DON'T SEE HER DAD AROUND.

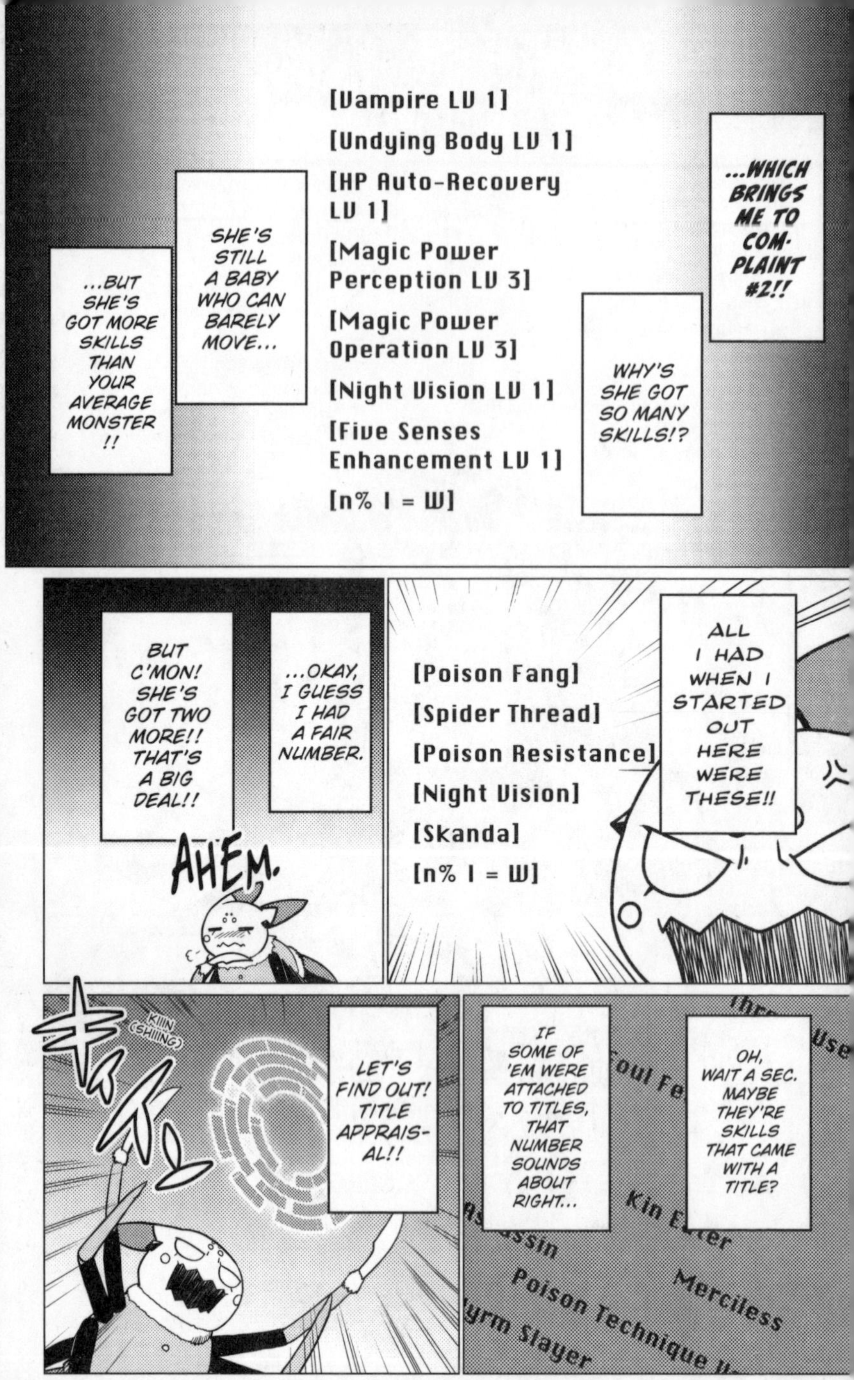
...WHICH BRINGS ME TO COMPLAINT #2!!
[Vampire LV 1]
[Undying Body LV 1]
[HP Auto-Recovery LV 1]
[Magic Power Perception LV 3]
[Magic Power Operation LV 3]
[Night Vision LV 1]
[Five Senses Enhancement LV 1]
[n% I = W]
WHY'S SHE GOT SO MANY SKILLS!?
SHE'S STILL A BABY WHO CAN BARELY MOVE...
...BUT SHE'S GOT MORE SKILLS THAN YOUR AVERAGE MONSTER!!
ALL I HAD WHEN I STARTED OUT HERE WERE THESE!!
[Poison Fang]
[Spider Thread]
[Poison Resistance]
[Night Vision]
[Skanda]
[n% I = W]
...OKAY, I GUESS I HAD A FAIR NUMBER.
BUT C'MON! SHE'S GOT TWO MORE!! THAT'S A BIG DEAL!!
AHEM.
OH, WAIT A SEC. MAYBE THEY'RE SKILLS THAT CAME WITH A TITLE?
IF SOME OF 'EM WERE ATTACHED TO TITLES, THAT NUMBER SOUNDS ABOUT RIGHT...
Merciless
Poison Technique
Slayer
LET'S FIND OUT! TITLE APPRAISAL!!
KIIN (SHIIING)

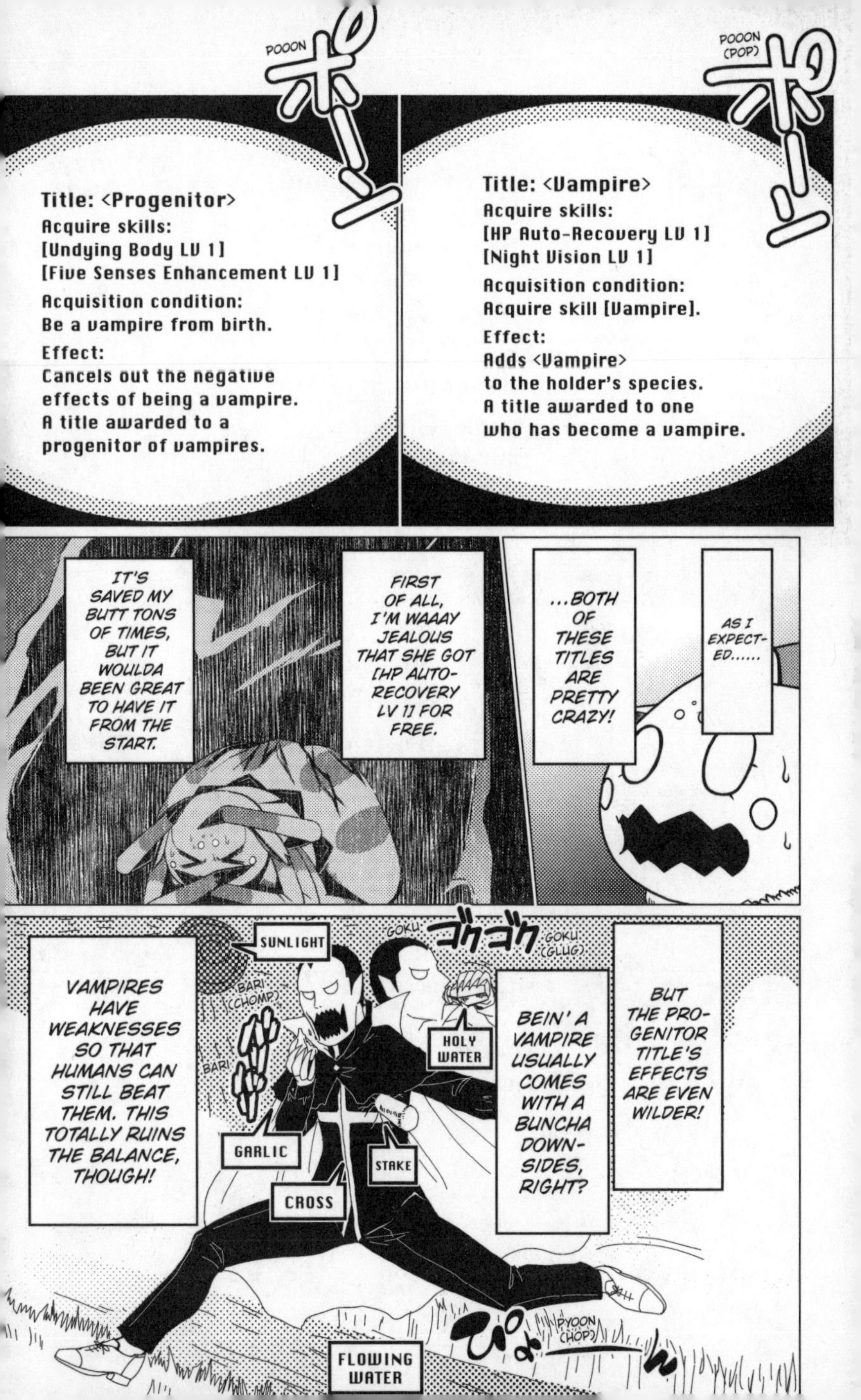
POOON (POP)
Title: <Vampire>
Acquire skills:
[HP Auto-Recovery LV 1]
[Night Vision LV 1]
Acquisition condition:
Acquire skill [Vampire].
Effect:
Adds <Vampire>
to the holder's species.
A title awarded to one
who has become a vampire.
POOON
Title: <Progenitor>
Acquire skills:
[Undying Body LV 1]
[Five Senses Enhancement LV 1]
Acquisition condition:
Be a vampire from birth.
Effect:
Cancels out the negative
effects of being a vampire.
A title awarded to a
progenitor of vampires.
AS I EXPECTED......
...BOTH OF THESE TITLES ARE PRETTY CRAZY!
FIRST OF ALL, I'M WAAAY JEALOUS THAT SHE GOT [HP AUTO-RECOVERY LV 1] FOR FREE.
IT'S SAVED MY BUTT TONS OF TIMES, BUT IT WOULDA BEEN GREAT TO HAVE IT FROM THE START.
BUT THE PROGENITOR TITLE'S EFFECTS ARE EVEN WILDER!
BEIN' A VAMPIRE USUALLY COMES WITH A BUNCHA DOWNSIDES, RIGHT?
GOKU GOKU (GLUG)
SUNLIGHT
HOLY WATER
BARI (CHOMP)
BARI
VAMPIRES HAVE WEAKNESSES SO THAT HUMANS CAN STILL BEAT THEM. THIS TOTALLY RUINS THE BALANCE, THOUGH!
STAKE
GARLIC
CROSS
PYOON (HOP)
FLOWING WATER

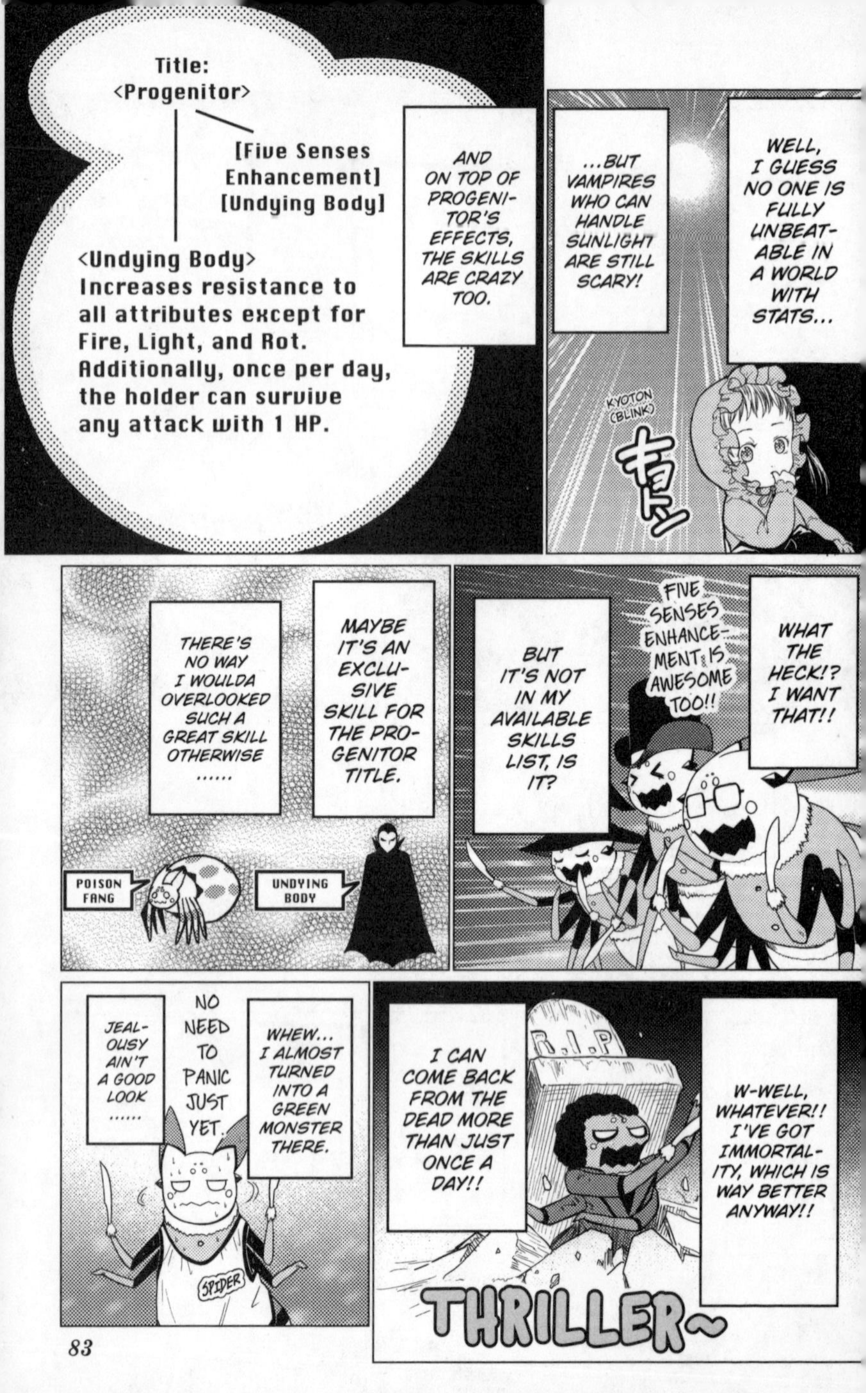
WELL, I GUESS NO ONE IS FULLY UNBEATABLE IN A WORLD WITH STATS...
...BUT VAMPIRES WHO CAN HANDLE SUNLIGHT ARE STILL SCARY!
KYOTON (BLINK)
AND ON TOP OF PROGENITOR'S EFFECTS, THE SKILLS ARE CRAZY TOO.
Title: <Progenitor>
[Five Senses Enhancement]
[Undying Body]
<Undying Body> Increases resistance to all attributes except for Fire, Light, and Rot. Additionally, once per day, the holder can survive any attack with 1 HP.
WHAT THE HECK!? I WANT THAT!!
FIVE SENSES ENHANCEMENT IS AWESOME TOO!!
BUT IT'S NOT IN MY AVAILABLE SKILLS LIST, IS IT?
MAYBE IT'S AN EXCLUSIVE SKILL FOR THE PROGENITOR TITLE.
THERE'S NO WAY I WOULDA OVERLOOKED SUCH A GREAT SKILL OTHERWISE ......
UNDYING BODY
POISON FANG
W-WELL, WHATEVER!! I'VE GOT IMMORTALITY, WHICH IS WAY BETTER ANYWAY!!
I CAN COME BACK FROM THE DEAD MORE THAN JUST ONCE A DAY!!
R.I.P
THRILLER~
WHEW... I ALMOST TURNED INTO A GREEN MONSTER THERE.
NO NEED TO PANIC JUST YET.
JEALOUSY AIN'T A GOOD LOOK ......
SPIDER

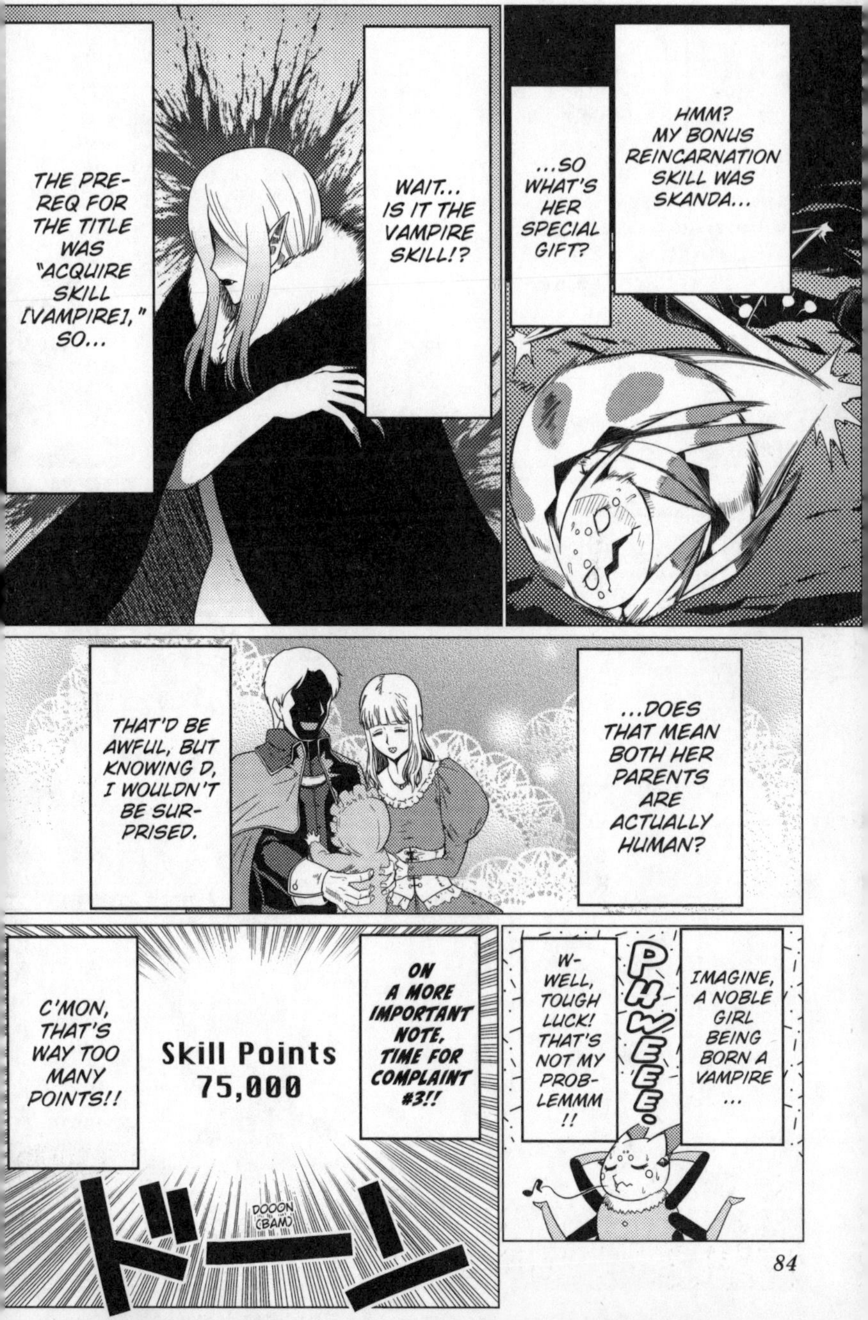
HMM? MY BONUS REINCARNATION SKILL WAS SKANDA...
...SO WHAT'S HER SPECIAL GIFT?
WAIT... IS IT THE VAMPIRE SKILL!?
THE PRE-REQ FOR THE TITLE WAS "ACQUIRE SKILL [VAMPIRE]," SO...
...DOES THAT MEAN BOTH HER PARENTS ARE ACTUALLY HUMAN?
THAT'D BE AWFUL, BUT KNOWING D, I WOULDN'T BE SURPRISED.
IMAGINE, A NOBLE GIRL BEING BORN A VAMPIRE...
PHWEEE
W-WELL, TOUGH LUCK! THAT'S NOT MY PROBLEMMM!!
ON A MORE IMPORTANT NOTE, TIME FOR COMPLAINT #3!!
Skill Points 75,000
C'MON, THAT'S WAY TOO MANY POINTS!!
DOOON (BAM)

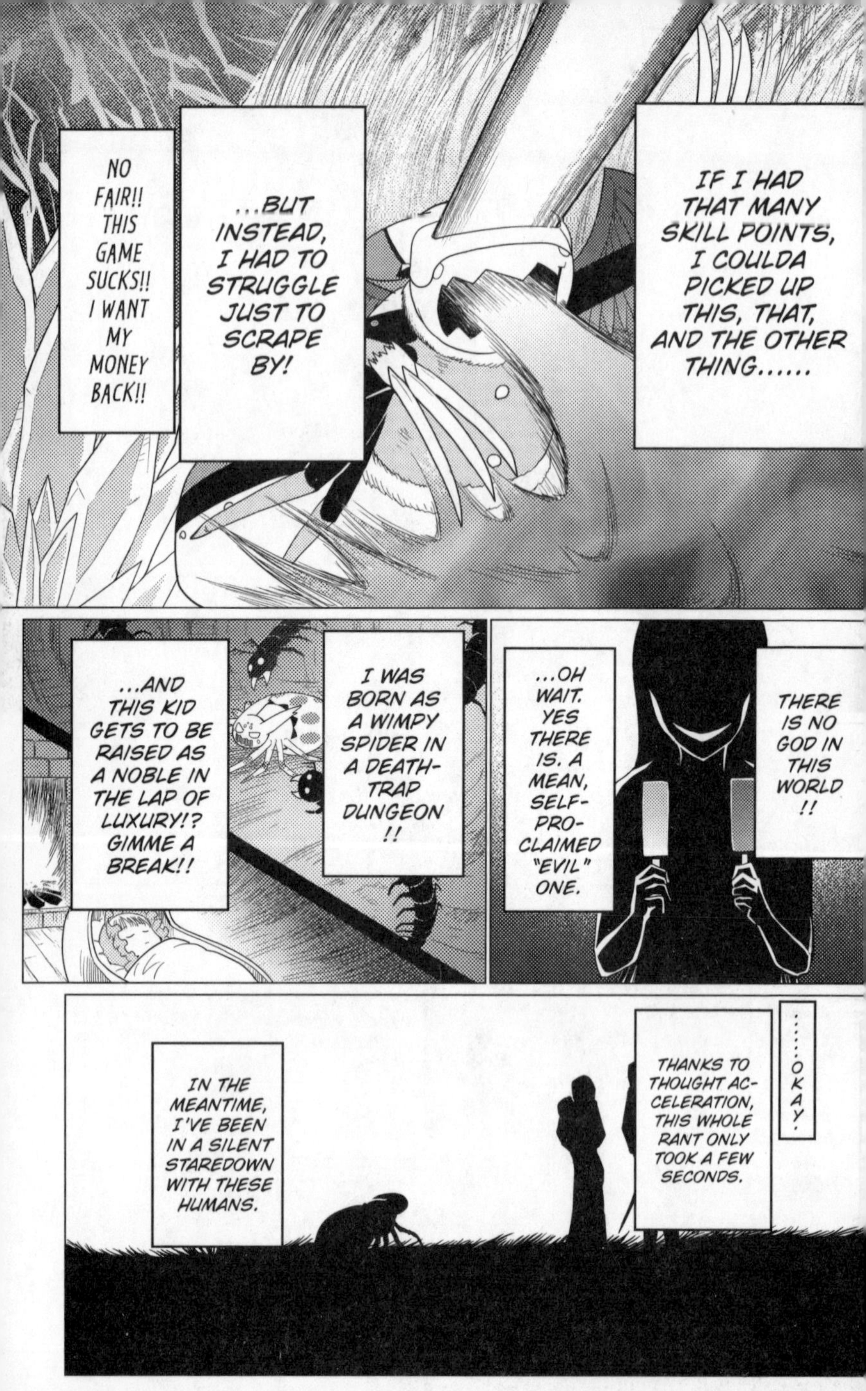
IF I HAD THAT MANY SKILL POINTS, I COULDA PICKED UP THIS, THAT, AND THE OTHER THING......
...BUT INSTEAD, I HAD TO STRUGGLE JUST TO SCRAPE BY!
NO FAIR!! THIS GAME SUCKS!! I WANT MY MONEY BACK!!
THERE IS NO GOD IN THIS WORLD !!
...OH WAIT. YES THERE IS. A MEAN, SELF-PROCLAIMED "EVIL" ONE.
I WAS BORN AS A WIMPY SPIDER IN A DEATH-TRAP DUNGEON !!
...AND THIS KID GETS TO BE RAISED AS A NOBLE IN THE LAP OF LUXURY!? GIMME A BREAK!!
......OKAY.
THANKS TO THOUGHT ACCELERATION, THIS WHOLE RANT ONLY TOOK A FEW SECONDS.
IN THE MEANTIME, I'VE BEEN IN A SILENT STAREDOWN WITH THESE HUMANS.

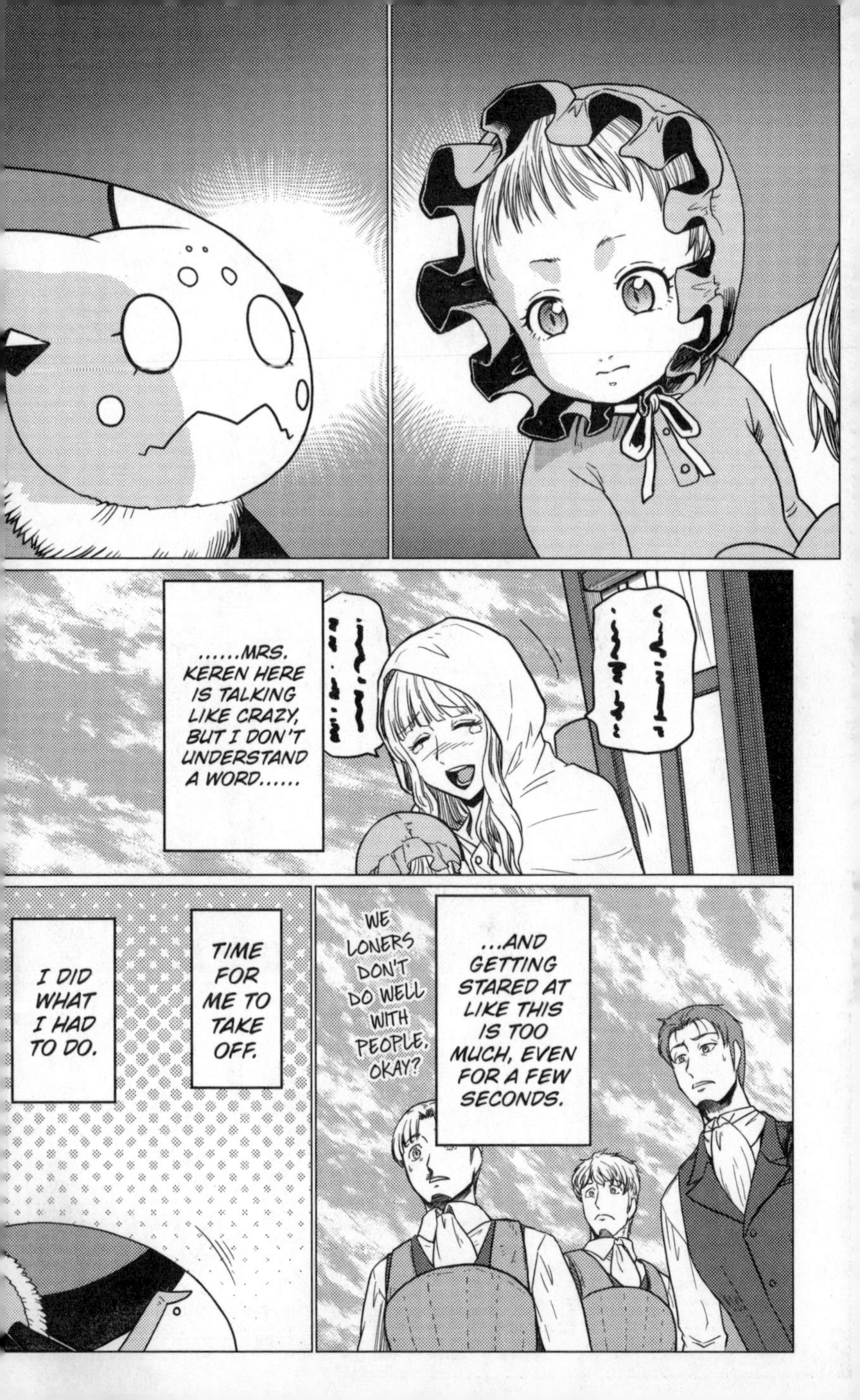
......MRS. KEREN HERE IS TALKING LIKE CRAZY, BUT I DON'T UNDERSTAND A WORD......
...AND GETTING STARED AT LIKE THIS IS TOO MUCH, EVEN FOR A FEW SECONDS.
WE LONERS DON'T DO WELL WITH PEOPLE, OKAY?
TIME FOR ME TO TAKE OFF.
I DID WHAT I HAD TO DO.

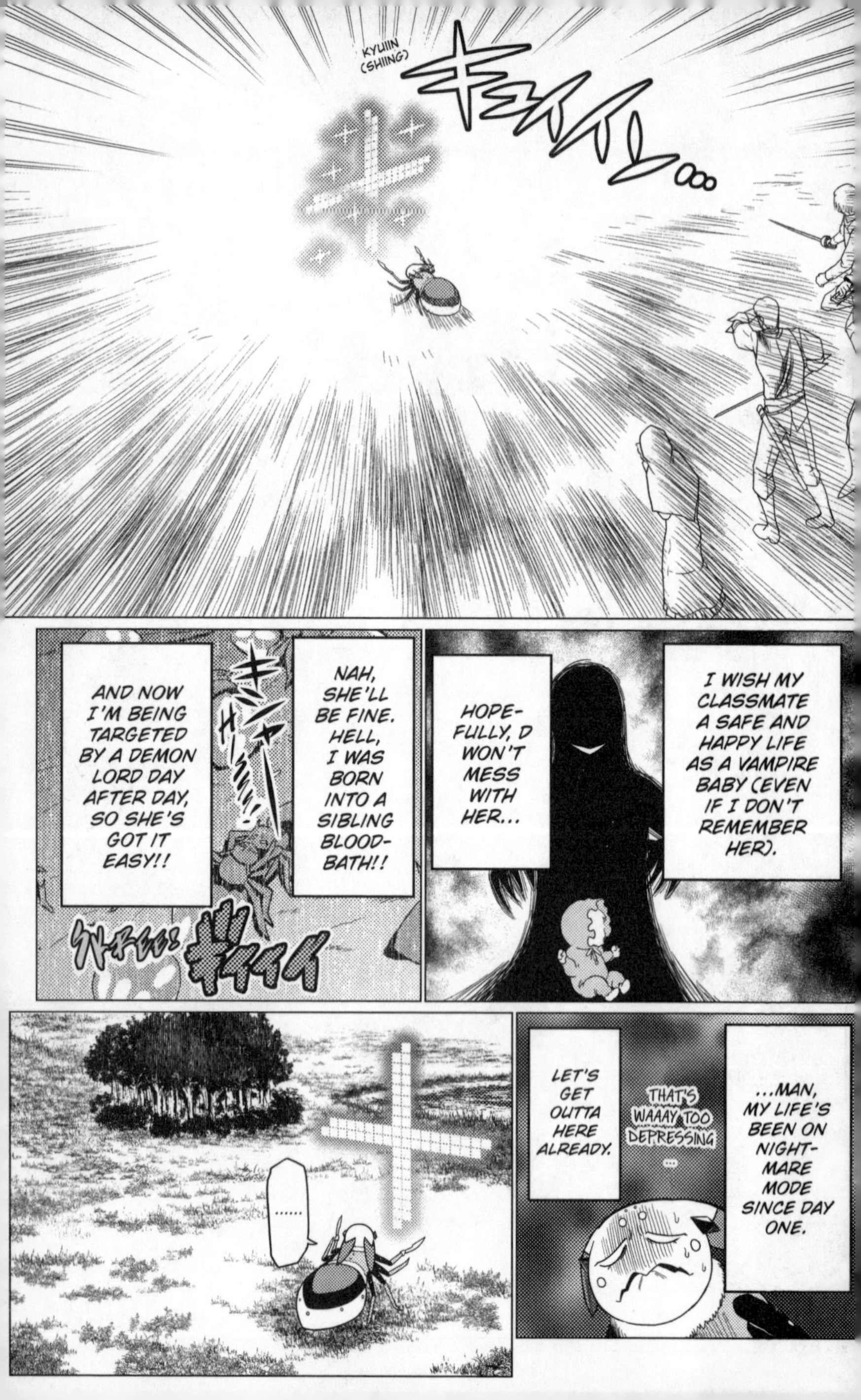
KYUIIN (SHIING)
I WISH MY CLASSMATE A SAFE AND HAPPY LIFE AS A VAMPIRE BABY (EVEN IF I DON'T REMEMBER HER).
HOPE-FULLY, D WON'T MESS WITH HER...
NAH, SHE'LL BE FINE. HELL, I WAS BORN INTO A SIBLING BLOOD-BATH!!
AND NOW I'M BEING TARGETED BY A DEMON LORD DAY AFTER DAY, SO SHE'S GOT IT EASY!!
...MAN, MY LIFE'S BEEN ON NIGHT-MARE MODE SINCE DAY ONE.
THAT'S WAAAY TOO DEPRESSING...
LET'S GET OUTTA HERE ALREADY.
......

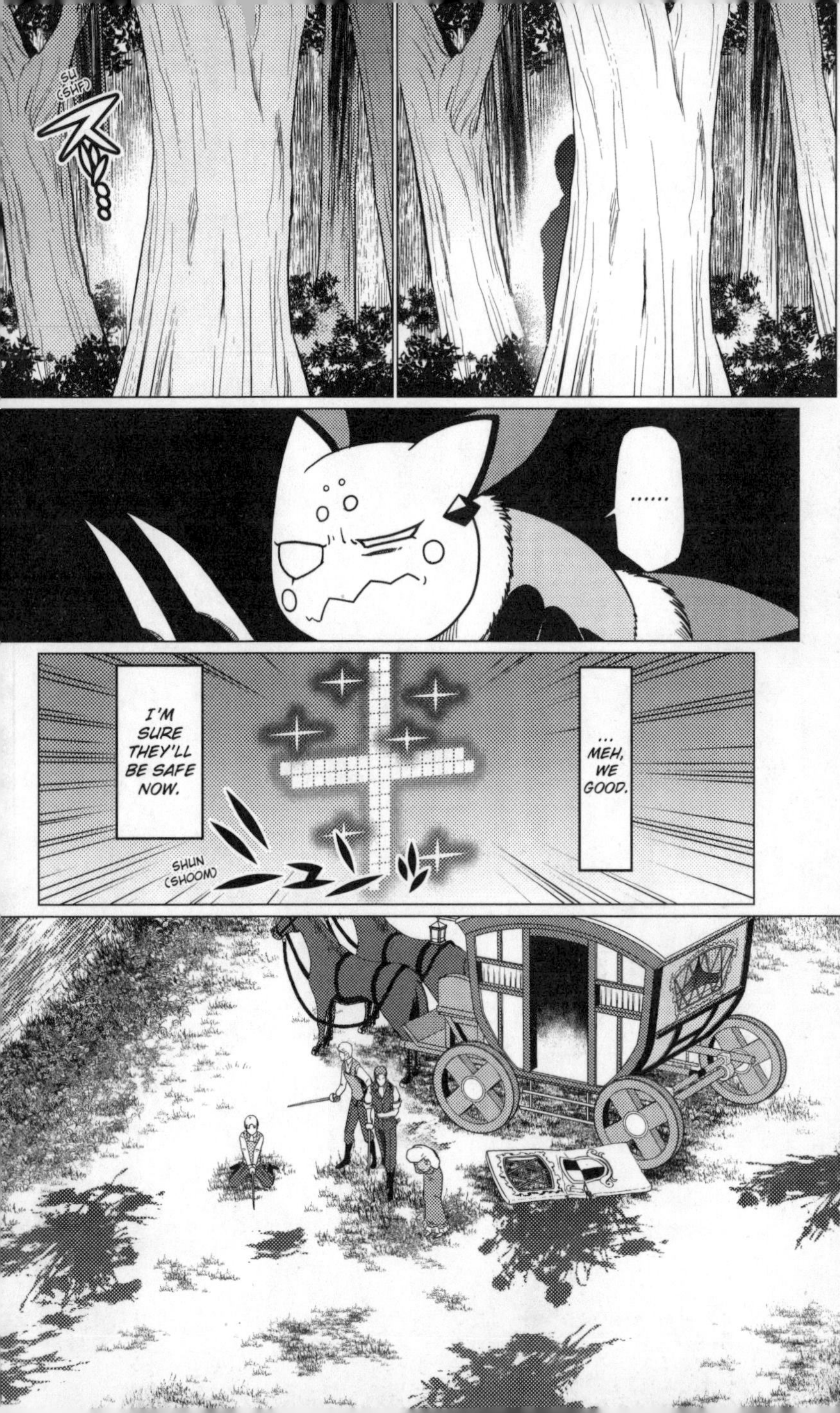
SU (SHF)
......
... MEH, WE GOOD.
I'M SURE THEY'LL BE SAFE NOW.
SHUN (SHOOM)

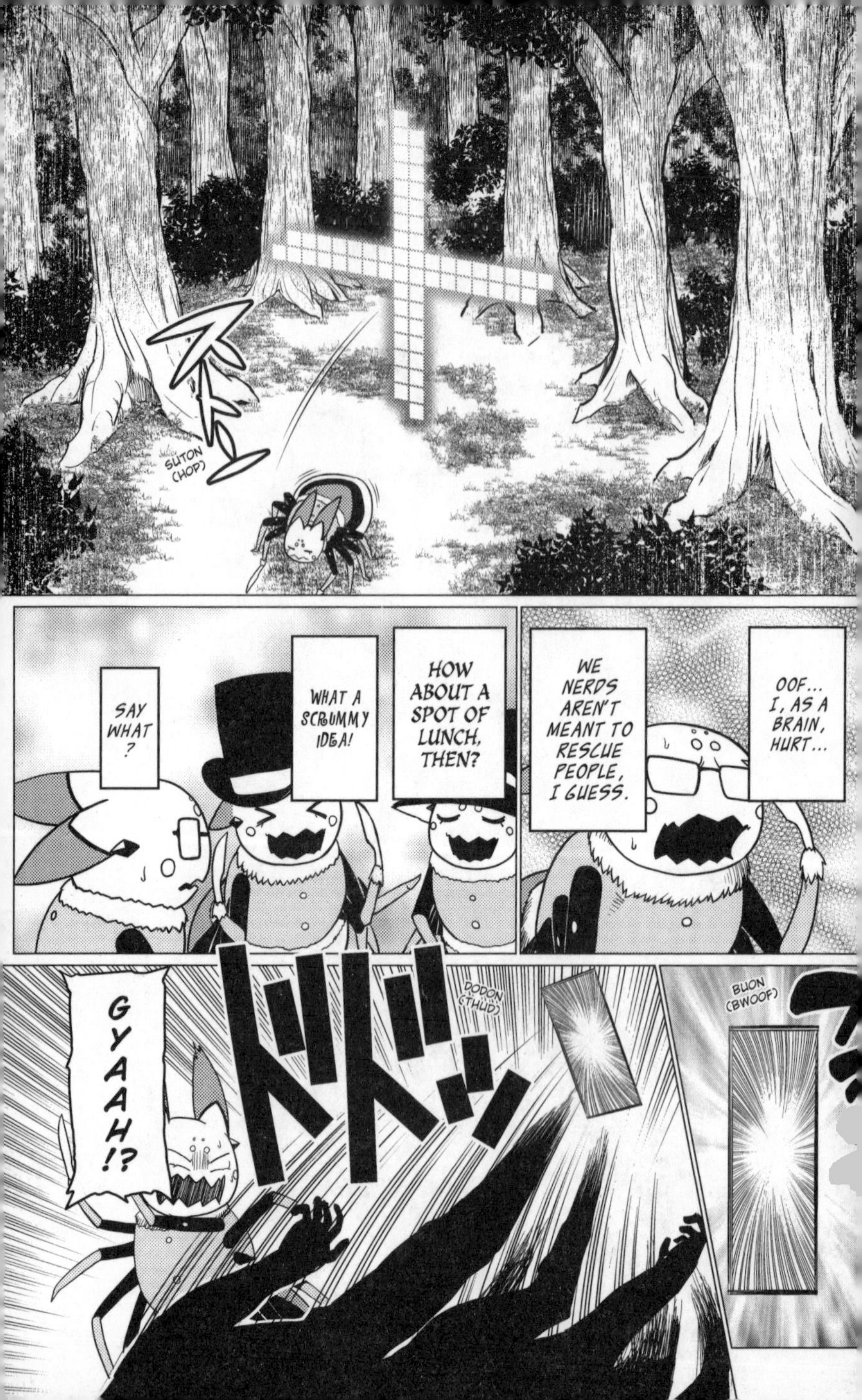
SUTON (HOP)
OOF... I, AS A BRAIN, HURT...
WE NERDS AREN'T MEANT TO RESCUE PEOPLE, I GUESS.
HOW ABOUT A SPOT OF LUNCH, THEN?
WHAT A SCRUMMY IDEA!
SAY WHAT?
BUON (BWOOF)
DODON (THUD)
GYAAH!?

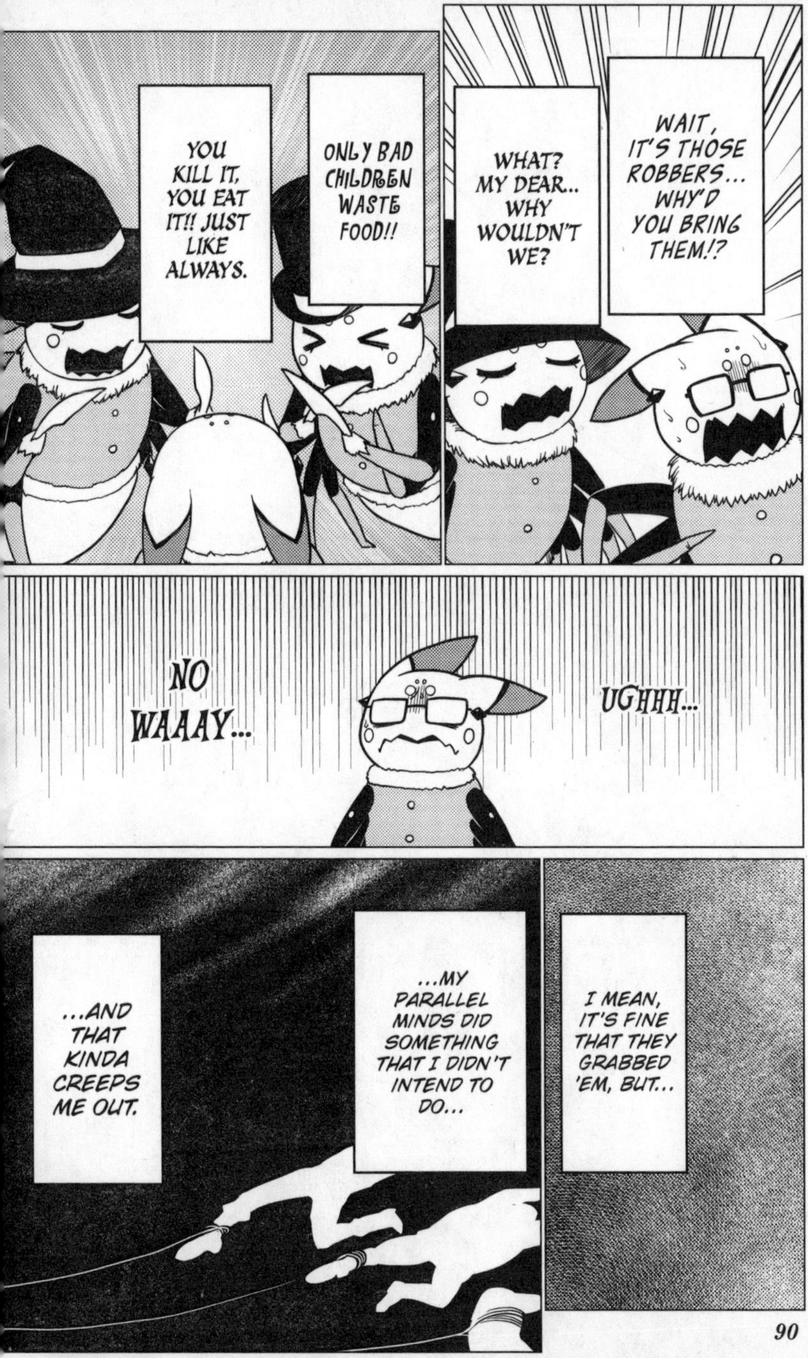
WAIT, IT'S THOSE ROBBERS... WHY'D YOU BRING THEM!?
WHAT? MY DEAR... WHY WOULDN'T WE?
ONLY BAD CHILDREN WASTE FOOD!!
YOU KILL IT, YOU EAT IT!! JUST LIKE ALWAYS.
UGHHH...
NO WAAAY...
I MEAN, IT'S FINE THAT THEY GRABBED 'EM, BUT...
...MY PARALLEL MINDS DID SOMETHING THAT I DIDN'T INTEND TO DO...
...AND THAT KINDA CREEPS ME OUT.

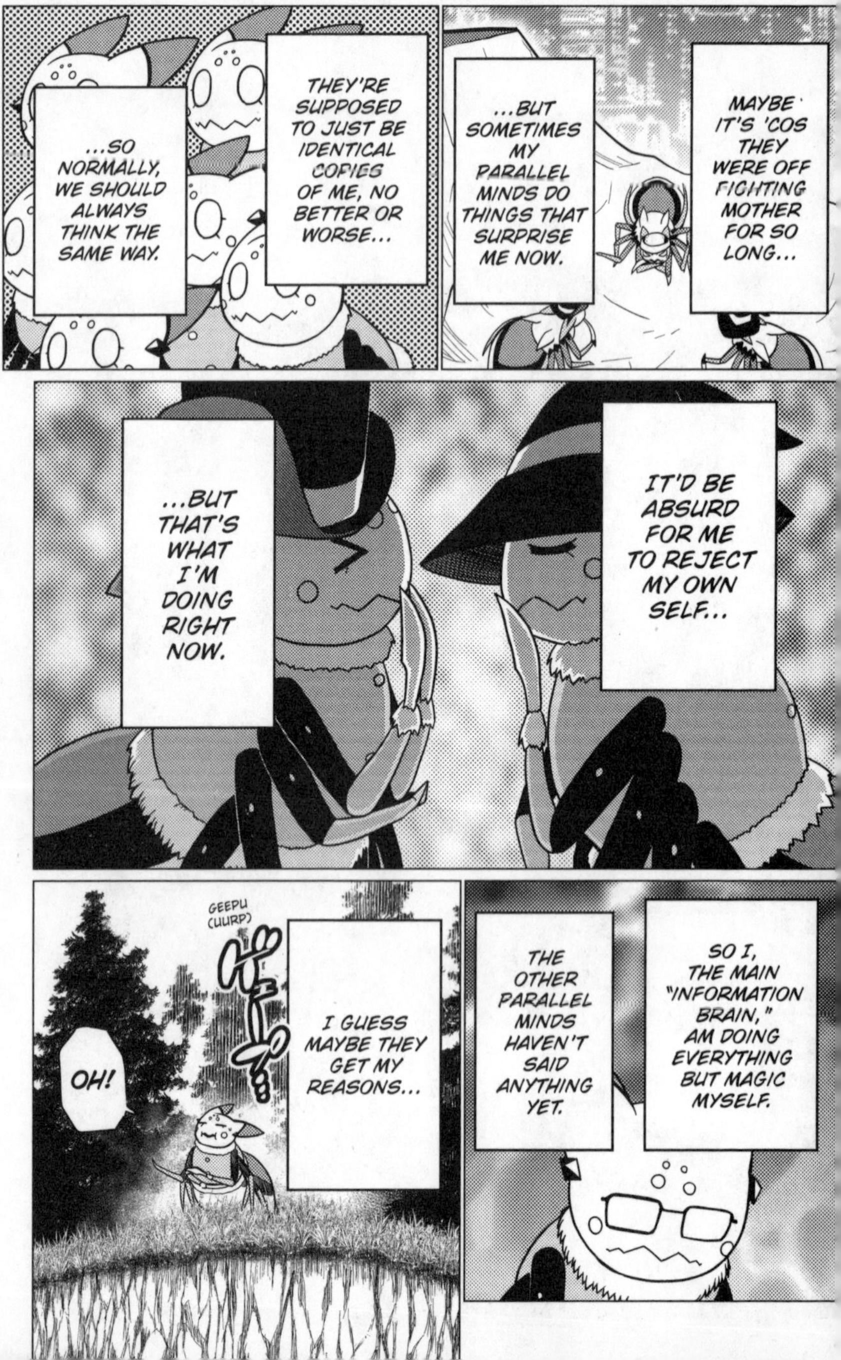
MAYBE IT'S 'COS THEY WERE OFF FIGHTING MOTHER FOR SO LONG...
...BUT SOMETIMES MY PARALLEL MINDS DO THINGS THAT SURPRISE ME NOW.
THEY'RE SUPPOSED TO JUST BE IDENTICAL COPIES OF ME, NO BETTER OR WORSE...
...SO NORMALLY, WE SHOULD ALWAYS THINK THE SAME WAY.
IT'D BE ABSURD FOR ME TO REJECT MY OWN SELF...
...BUT THAT'S WHAT I'M DOING RIGHT NOW.
SO I, THE MAIN "INFORMATION BRAIN," AM DOING EVERYTHING BUT MAGIC MYSELF.
THE OTHER PARALLEL MINDS HAVEN'T SAID ANYTHING YET.
I GUESS MAYBE THEY GET MY REASONS...
GEEPU (UURP)
OH!

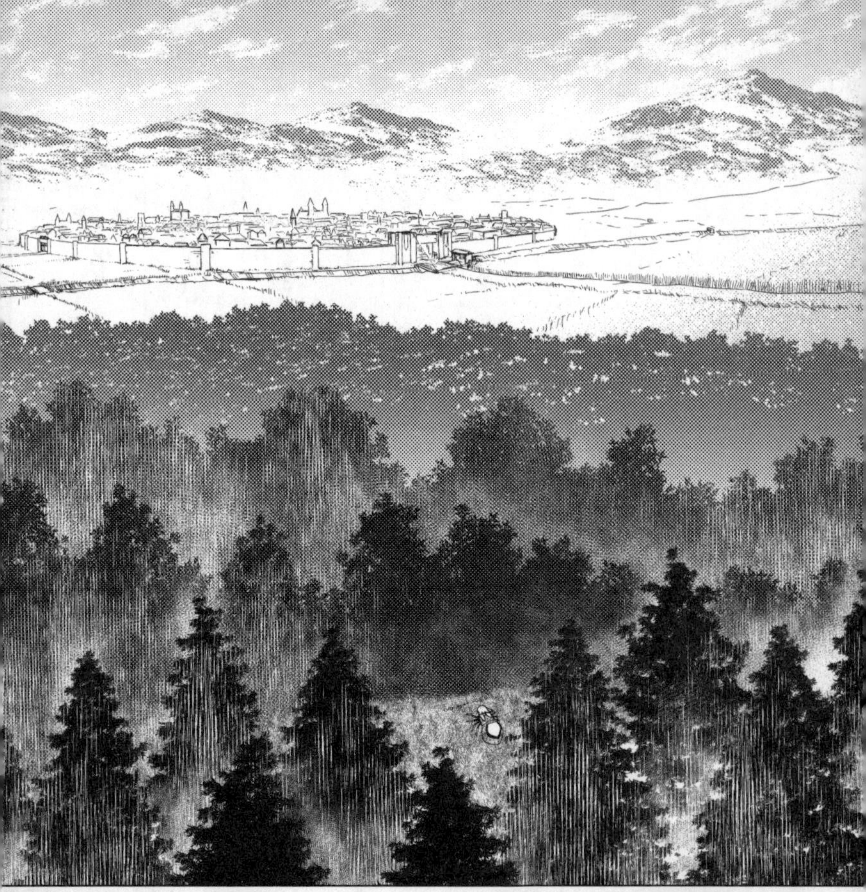

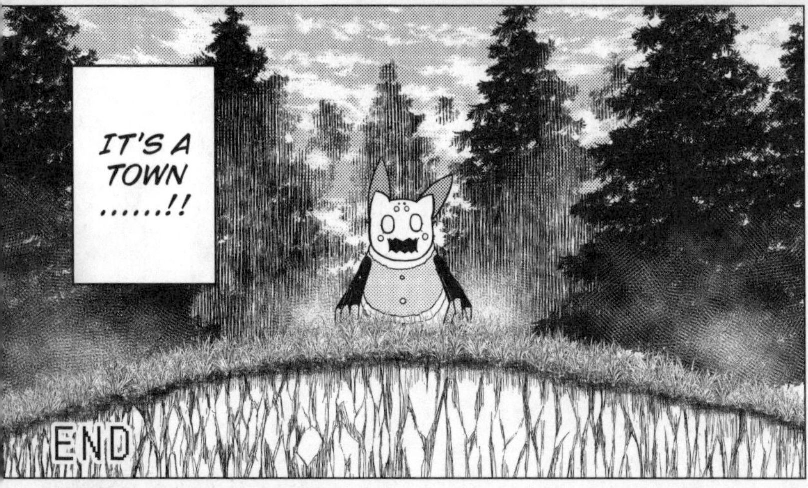
IT'S A TOWN ......!!
END

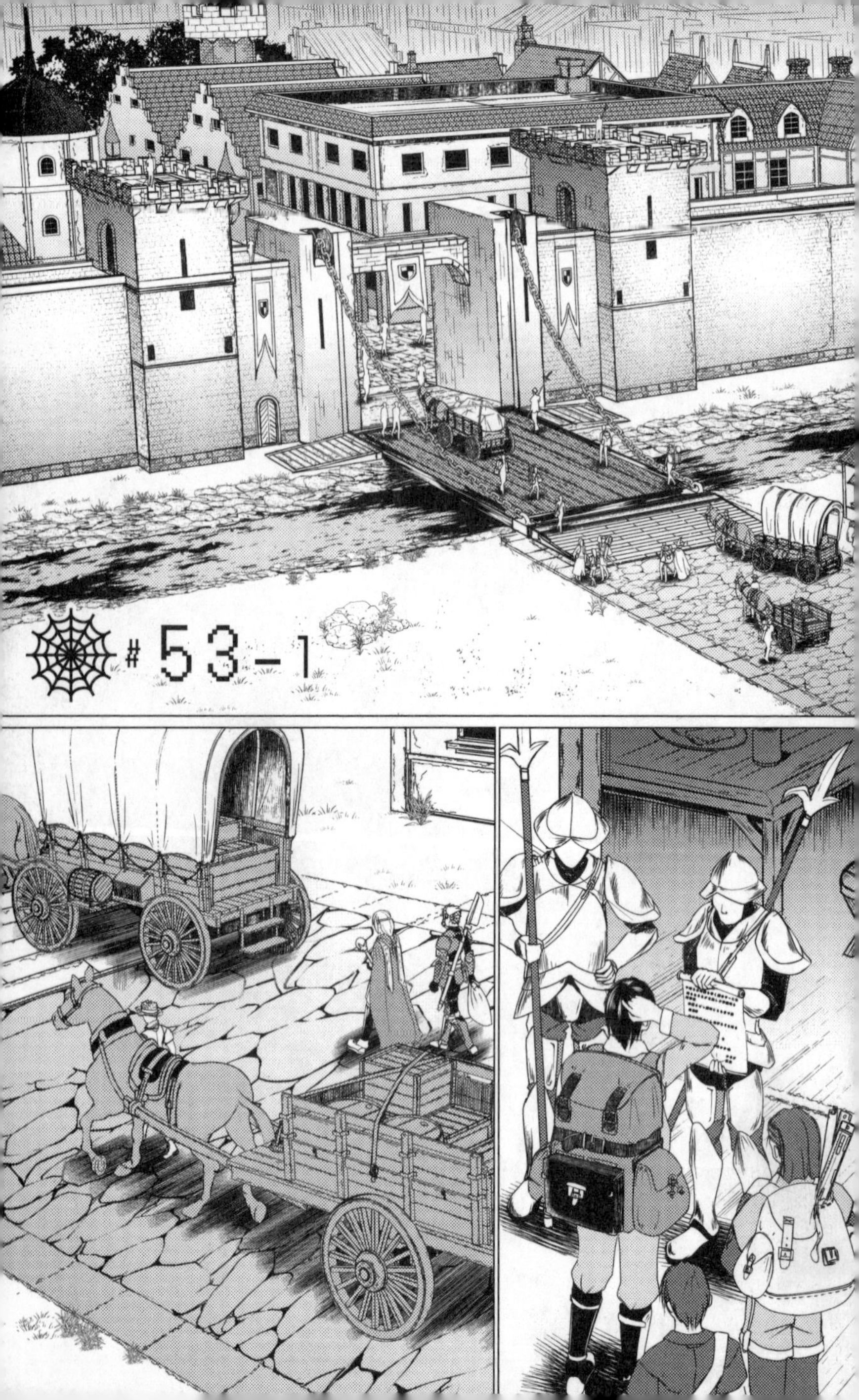
#53-1

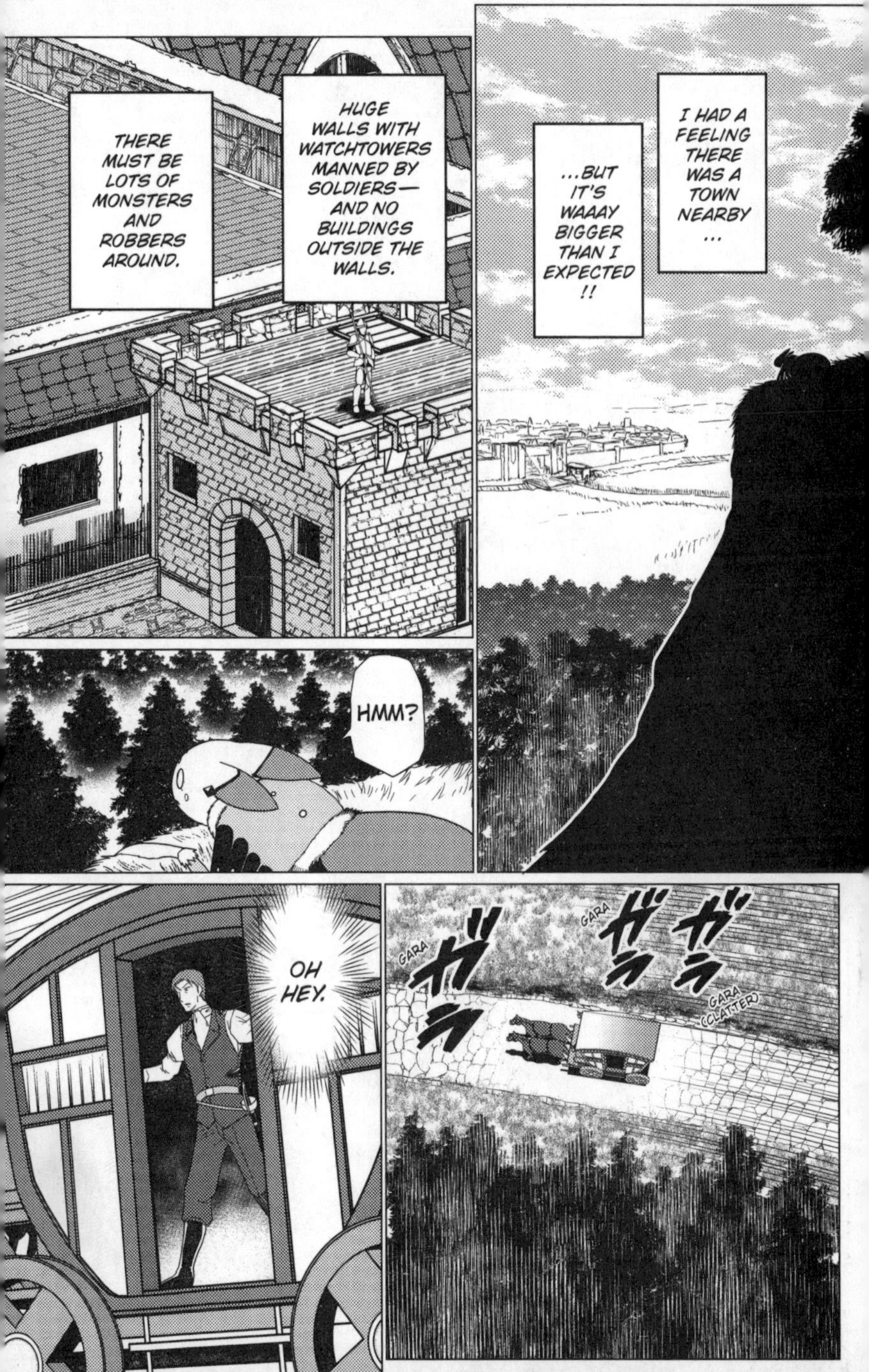
I HAD A FEELING THERE WAS A TOWN NEARBY ...
...BUT IT'S WAAAY BIGGER THAN I EXPECTED !!
HUGE WALLS WITH WATCHTOWERS MANNED BY SOLDIERS— AND NO BUILDINGS OUTSIDE THE WALLS.
THERE MUST BE LOTS OF MONSTERS AND ROBBERS AROUND.
HMM?
GARA (CLATTER)
GARA
GARA
OH HEY.

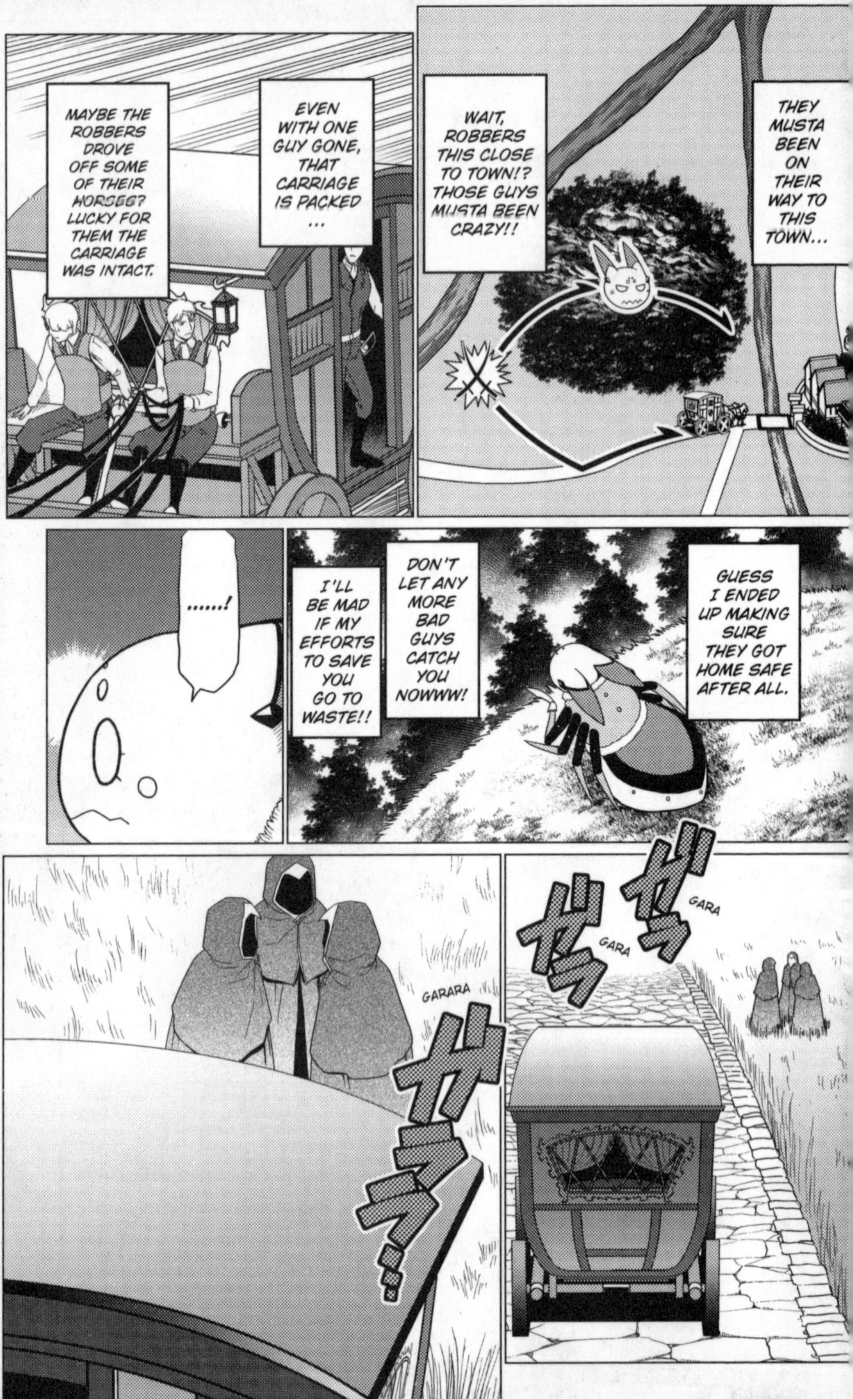
THEY MUSTA BEEN ON THEIR WAY TO THIS TOWN...
WAIT, ROBBERS THIS CLOSE TO TOWN!? THOSE GUYS MUSTA BEEN CRAZY!!
EVEN WITH ONE GUY GONE, THAT CARRIAGE IS PACKED...
MAYBE THE ROBBERS DROVE OFF SOME OF THEIR HORSES? LUCKY FOR THEM THE CARRIAGE WAS INTACT.
GUESS I ENDED UP MAKING SURE THEY GOT HOME SAFE AFTER ALL.
DON'T LET ANY MORE BAD GUYS CATCH YOU NOWWW!
I'LL BE MAD IF MY EFFORTS TO SAVE YOU GO TO WASTE!!
......!
GARA
GARA
GARARA

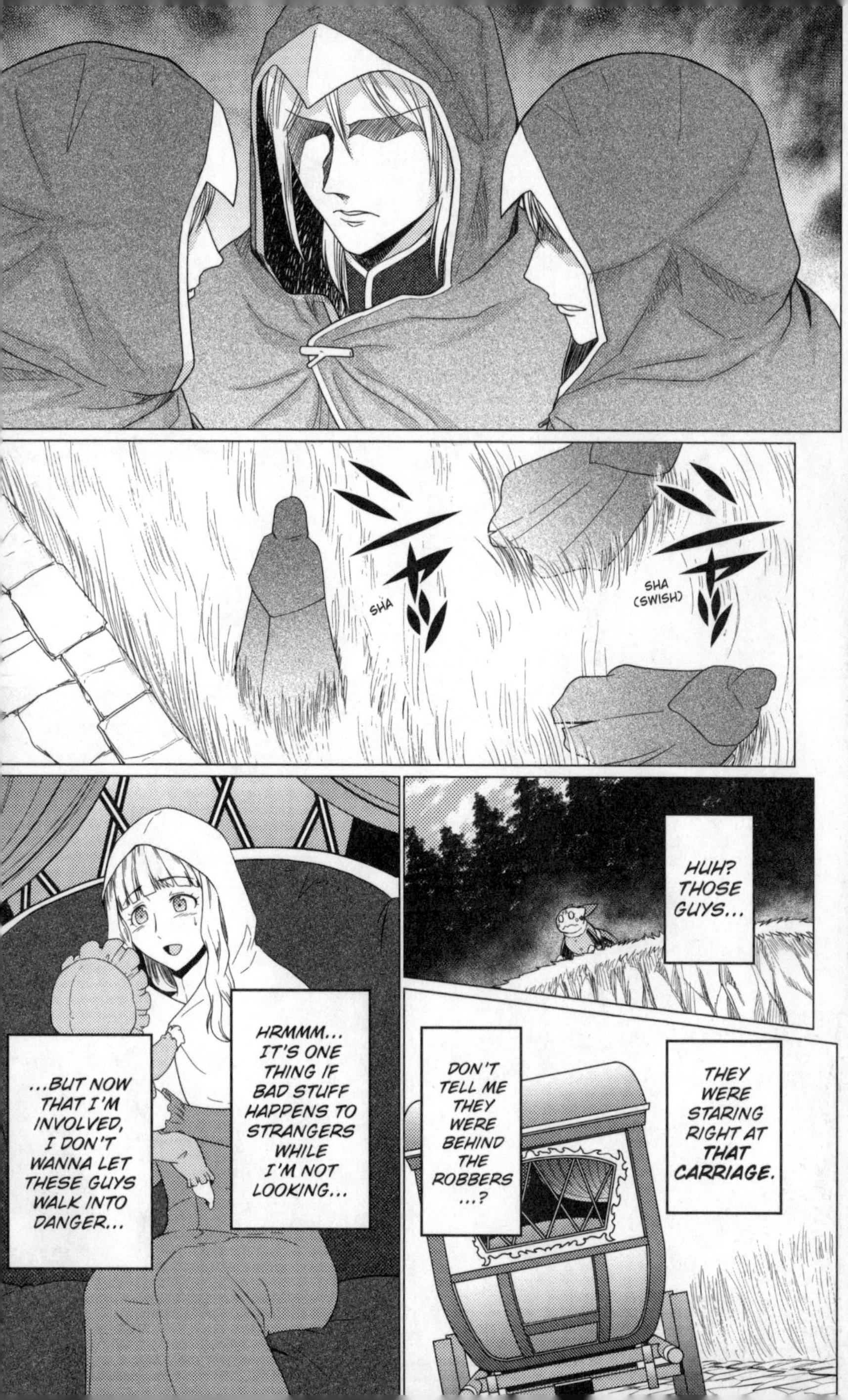
SHA (SWISH)
SHA
HUH? THOSE GUYS...
THEY WERE STARING RIGHT AT THAT CARRIAGE.
DON'T TELL ME THEY WERE BEHIND THE ROBBERS ...?
HRMMM... IT'S ONE THING IF BAD STUFF HAPPENS TO STRANGERS WHILE I'M NOT LOOKING...
...BUT NOW THAT I'M INVOLVED, I DON'T WANNA LET THESE GUYS WALK INTO DANGER...

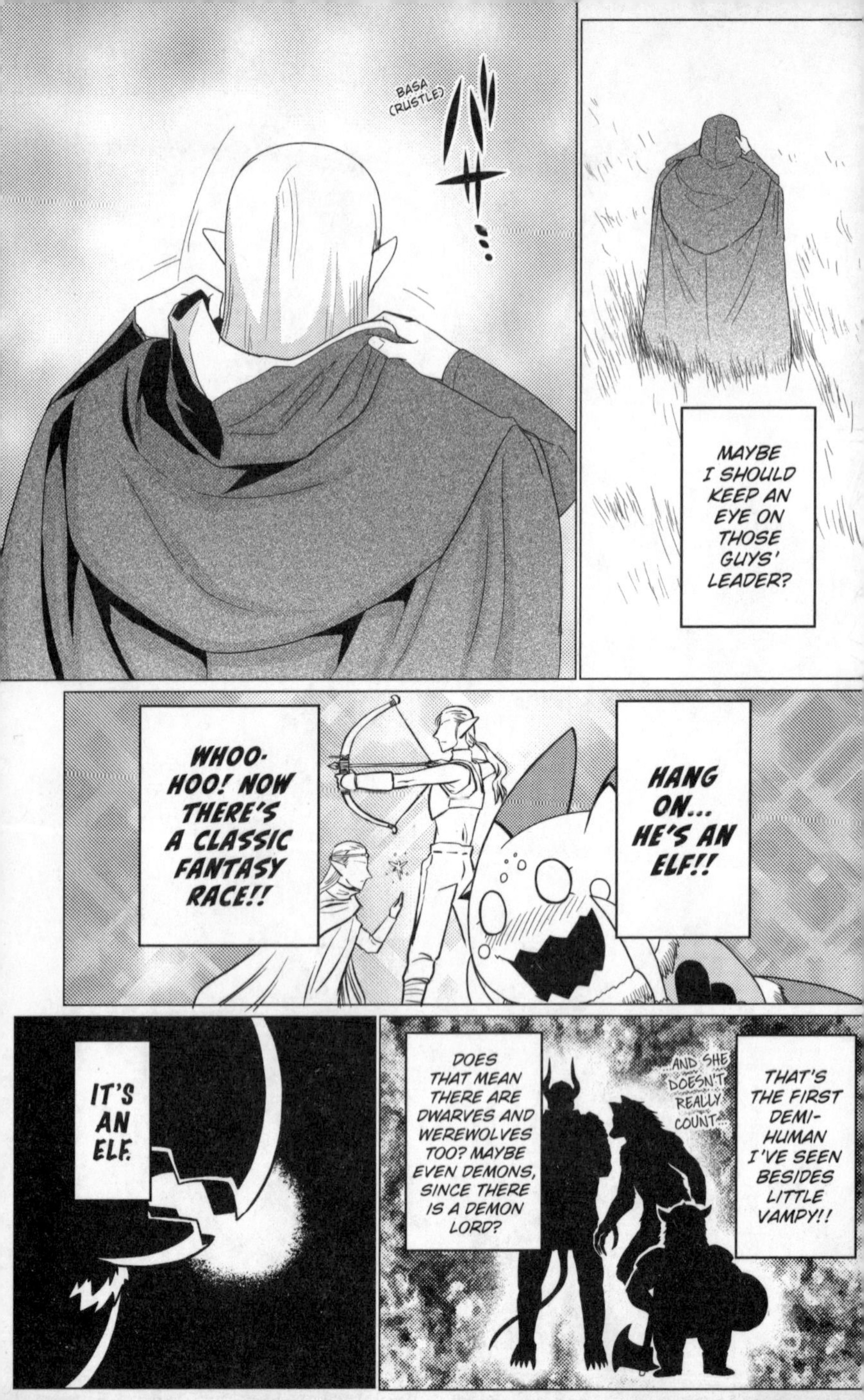
MAYBE I SHOULD KEEP AN EYE ON THOSE GUYS' LEADER?
BASA (RUSTLE)
HANG ON... HE'S AN ELF!!
WHOO-HOO! NOW THERE'S A CLASSIC FANTASY RACE!!
THAT'S THE FIRST DEMI-HUMAN I'VE SEEN BESIDES LITTLE VAMPY!!
AND SHE DOESN'T REALLY COUNT...
DOES THAT MEAN THERE ARE DWARVES AND WEREWOLVES TOO? MAYBE EVEN DEMONS, SINCE THERE IS A DEMON LORD?
IT'S AN ELF.

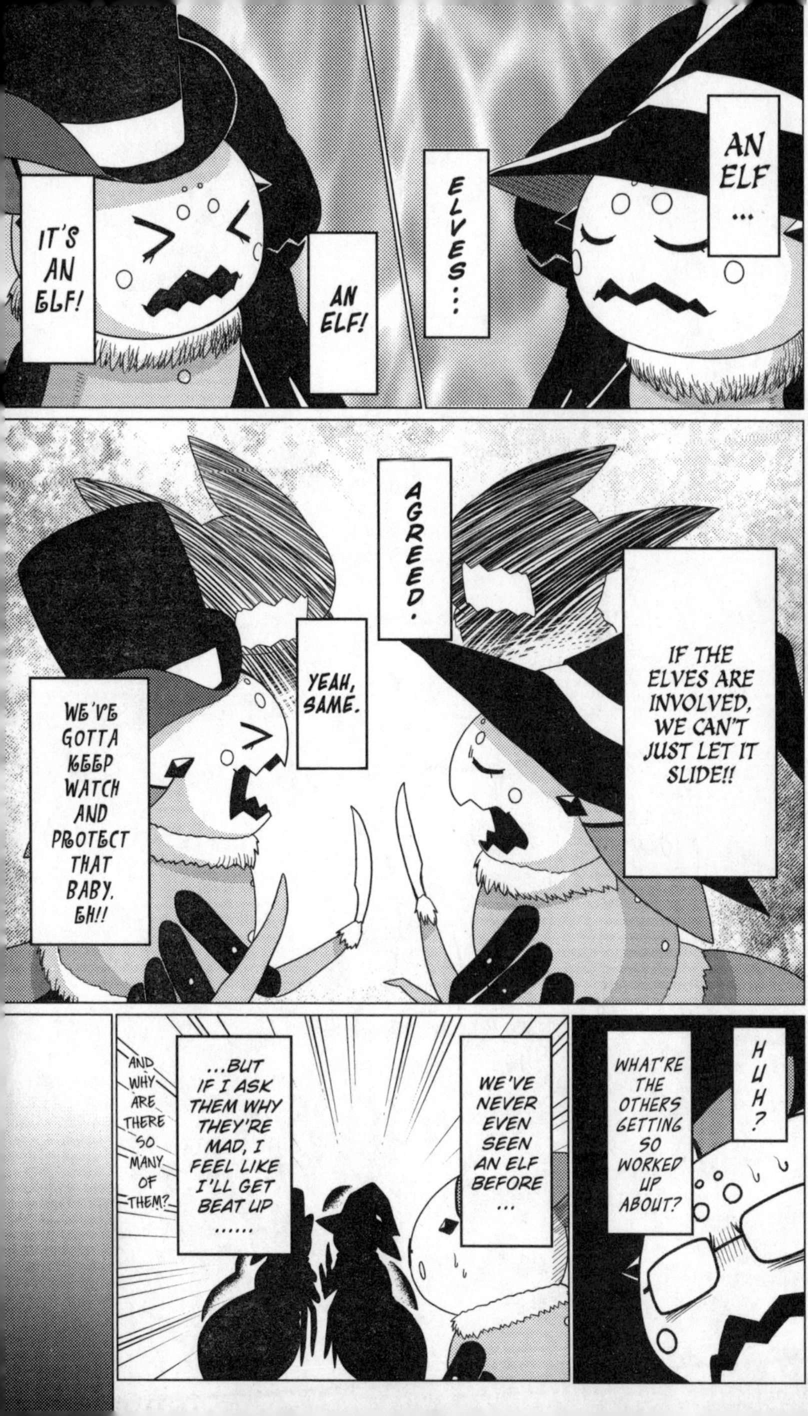

AN ELF …
ELVES…
AN ELF!
IT'S AN ELF!
IF THE ELVES ARE INVOLVED, WE CAN'T JUST LET IT SLIDE!!
AGREED.
YEAH, SAME.
WE'VE GOTTA KEEP WATCH AND PROTECT THAT BABY, EH!!
HUH?
WHAT'RE THE OTHERS GETTING SO WORKED UP ABOUT?
WE'VE NEVER EVEN SEEN AN ELF BEFORE …
…BUT IF I ASK THEM WHY THEY'RE MAD, I FEEL LIKE I'LL GET BEAT UP ……
AND WHY ARE THERE SO MANY OF THEM?

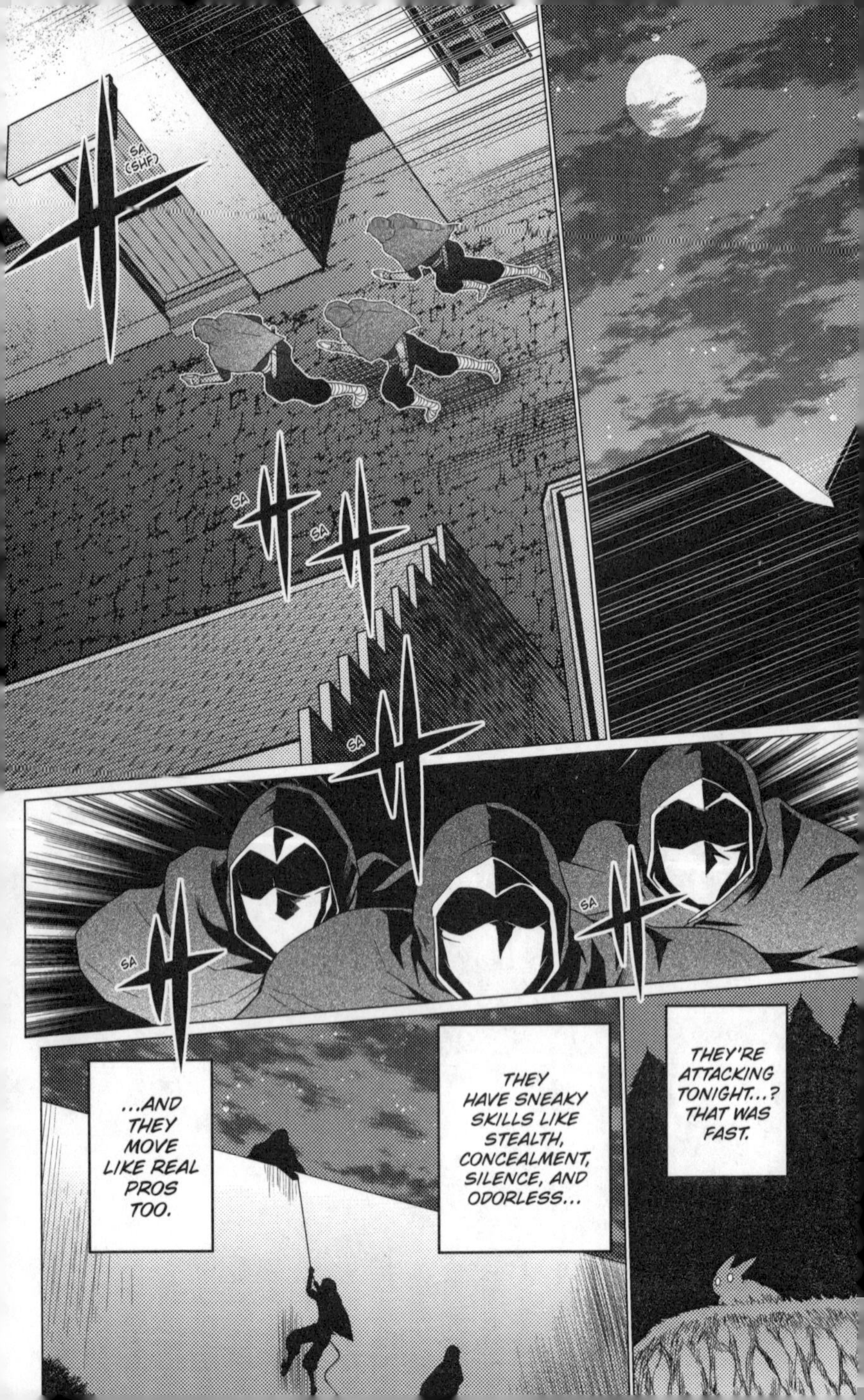
SA (SHF)
SA
SA
SA
SA
SA
THEY'RE ATTACKING TONIGHT...? THAT WAS FAST.
THEY HAVE SNEAKY SKILLS LIKE STEALTH, CONCEALMENT, SILENCE, AND ODORLESS...
...AND THEY MOVE LIKE REAL PROS TOO.

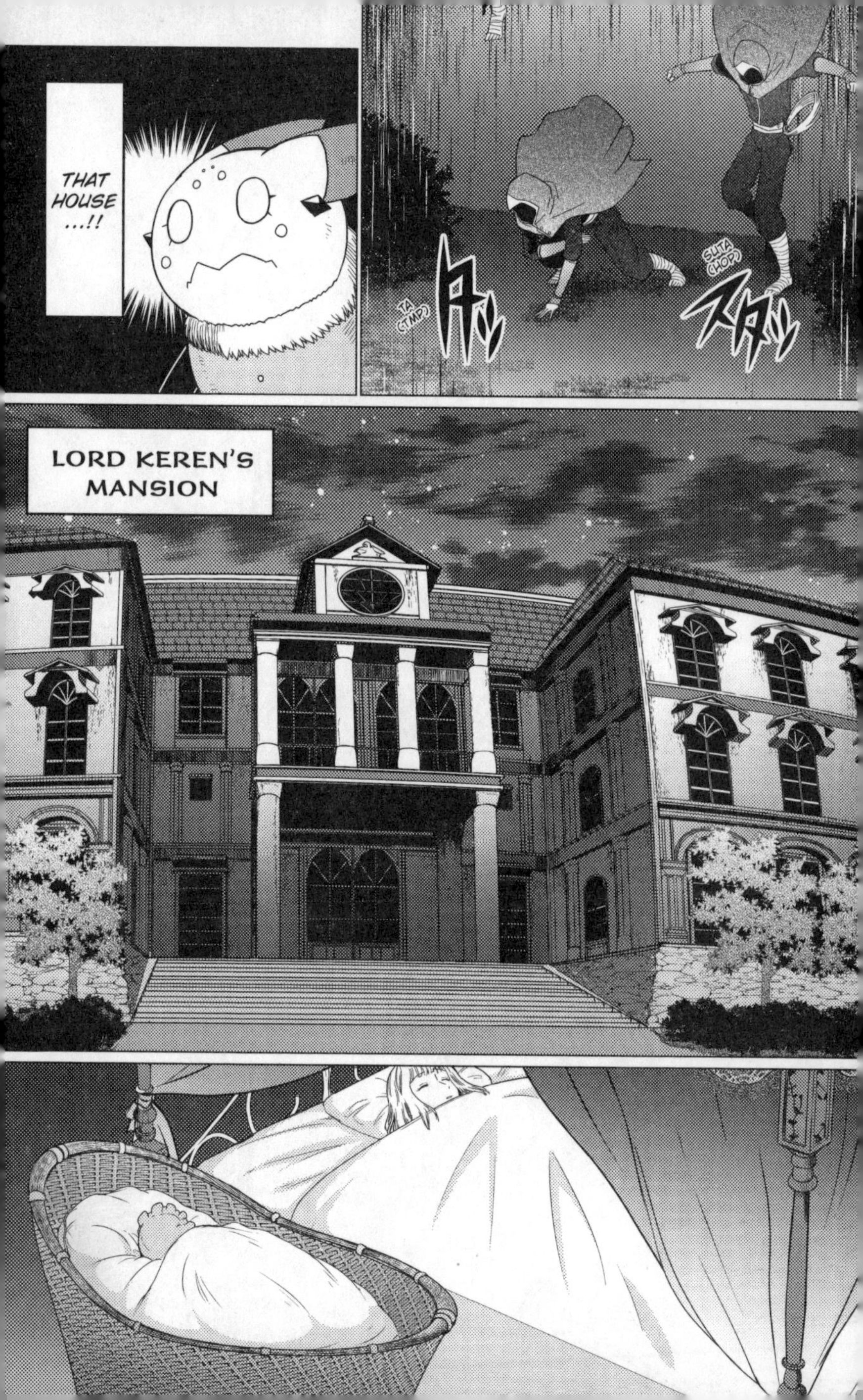
SUTA (HOP)
TA (STMP)
THAT HOUSE ...!!
LORD KEREN'S MANSION

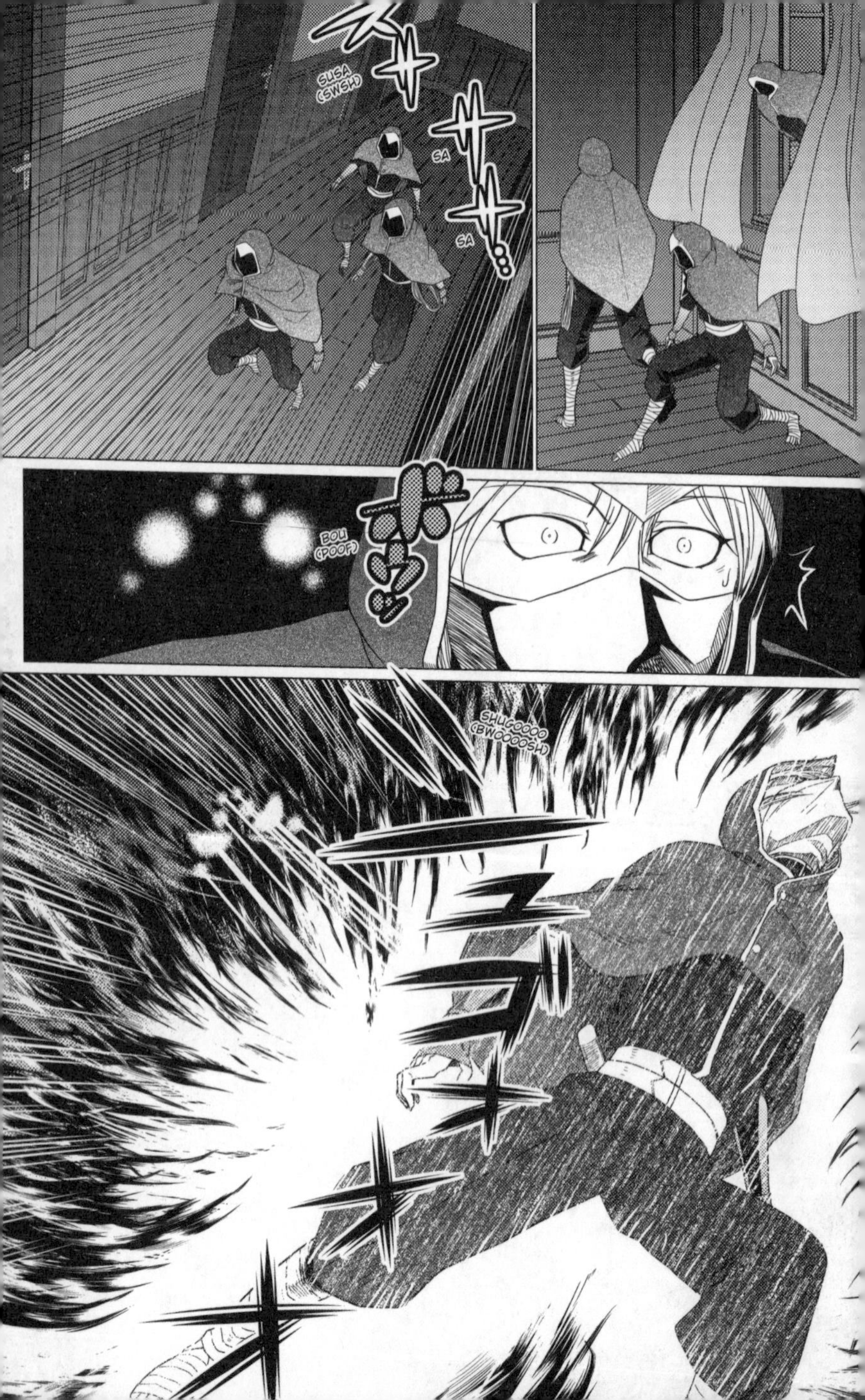
SUSA (SWSH)
SA
SA
BOU (POOF)
SHUGOOOO (BWOOOOSH)

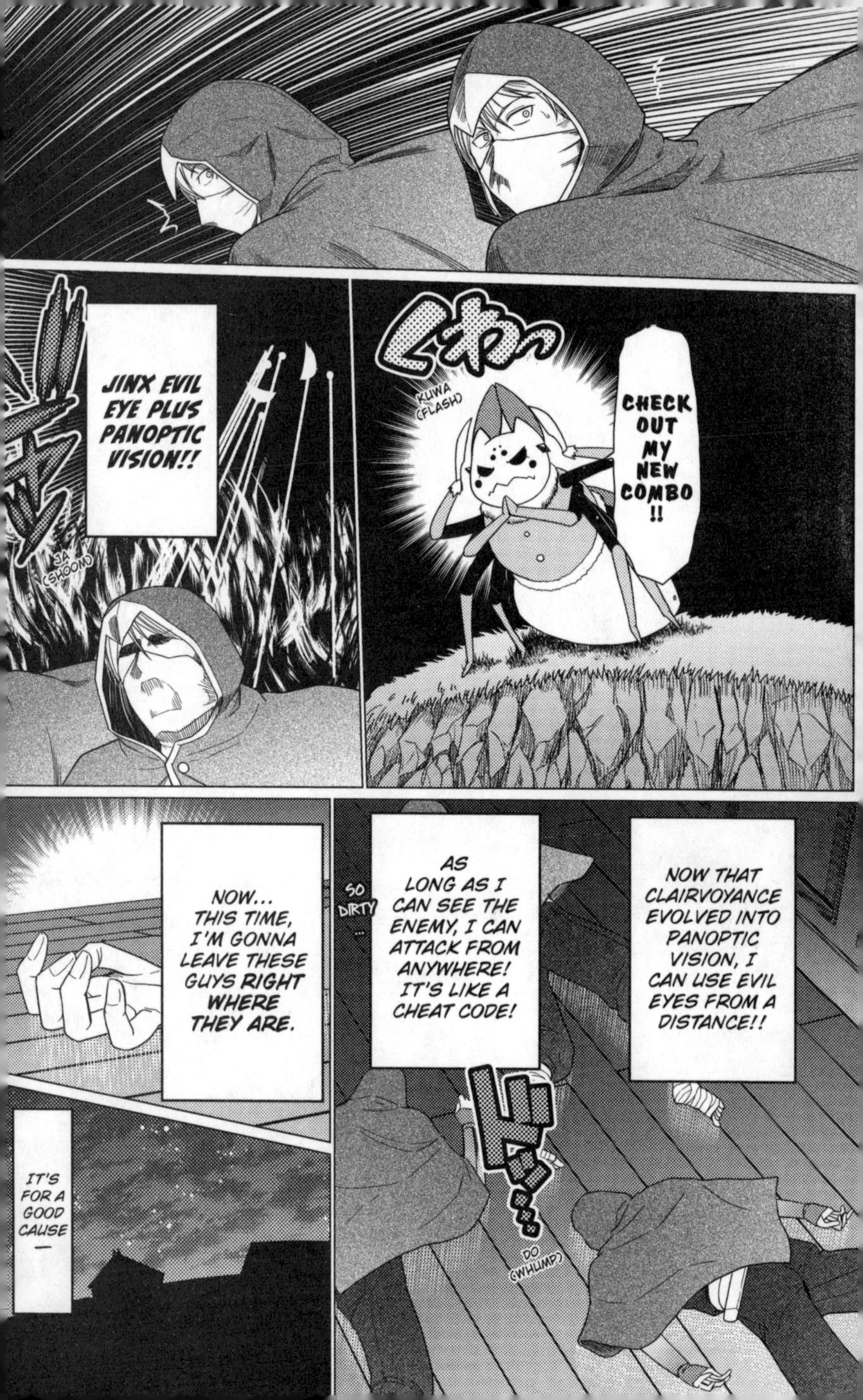
KUWA (FLASH)
CHECK OUT MY NEW COMBO!!
JINX EVIL EYE PLUS PANOPTIC VISION!!
JA (SHOOM)
NOW THAT CLAIRVOYANCE EVOLVED INTO PANOPTIC VISION, I CAN USE EVIL EYES FROM A DISTANCE!!
AS LONG AS I CAN SEE THE ENEMY, I CAN ATTACK FROM ANYWHERE! IT'S LIKE A CHEAT CODE!
SO DIRTY...
DO (WHUMP)
NOW... THIS TIME, I'M GONNA LEAVE THESE GUYS RIGHT WHERE THEY ARE.
IT'S FOR A GOOD CAUSE—

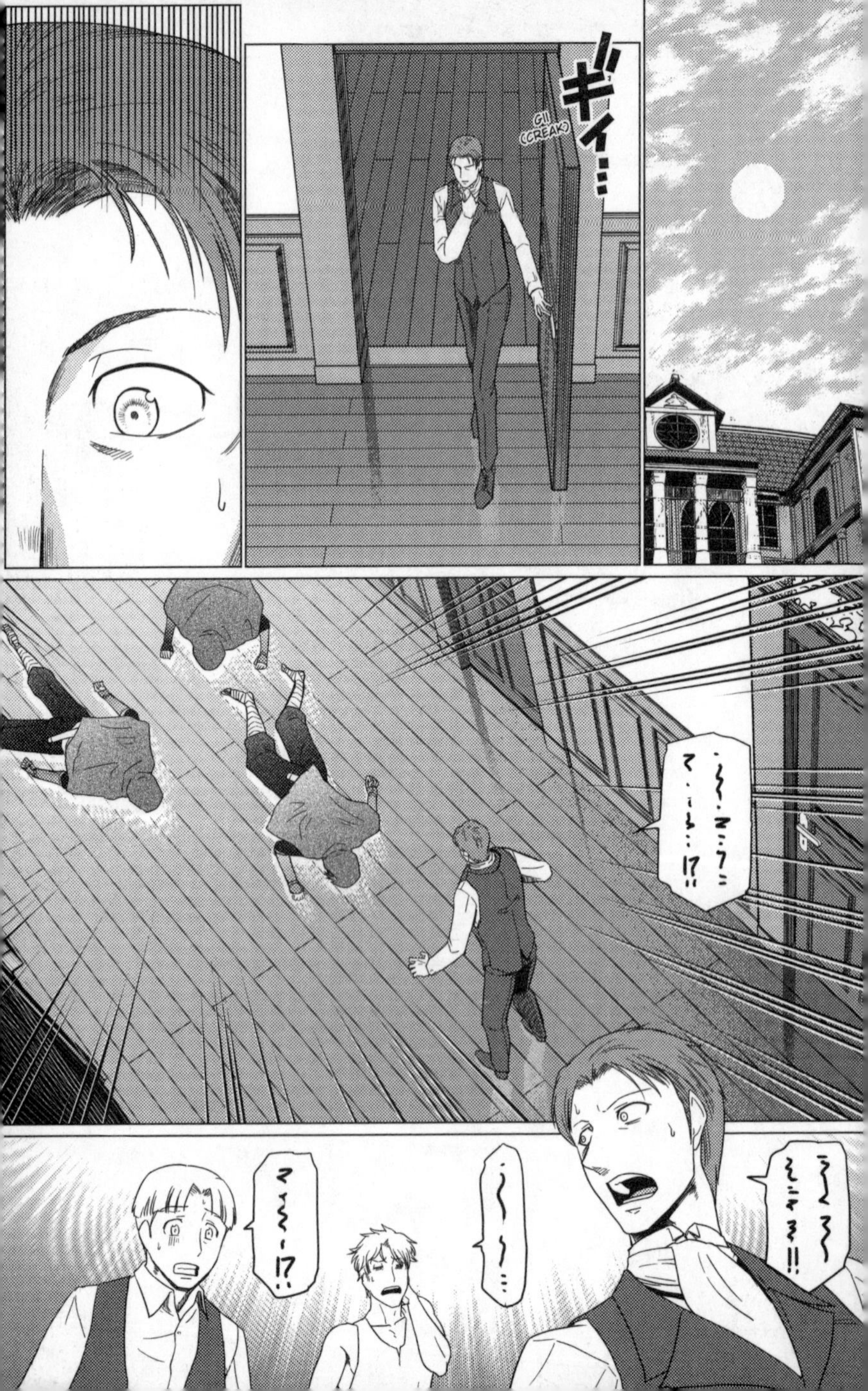

ギイ…
GII (CREAK)

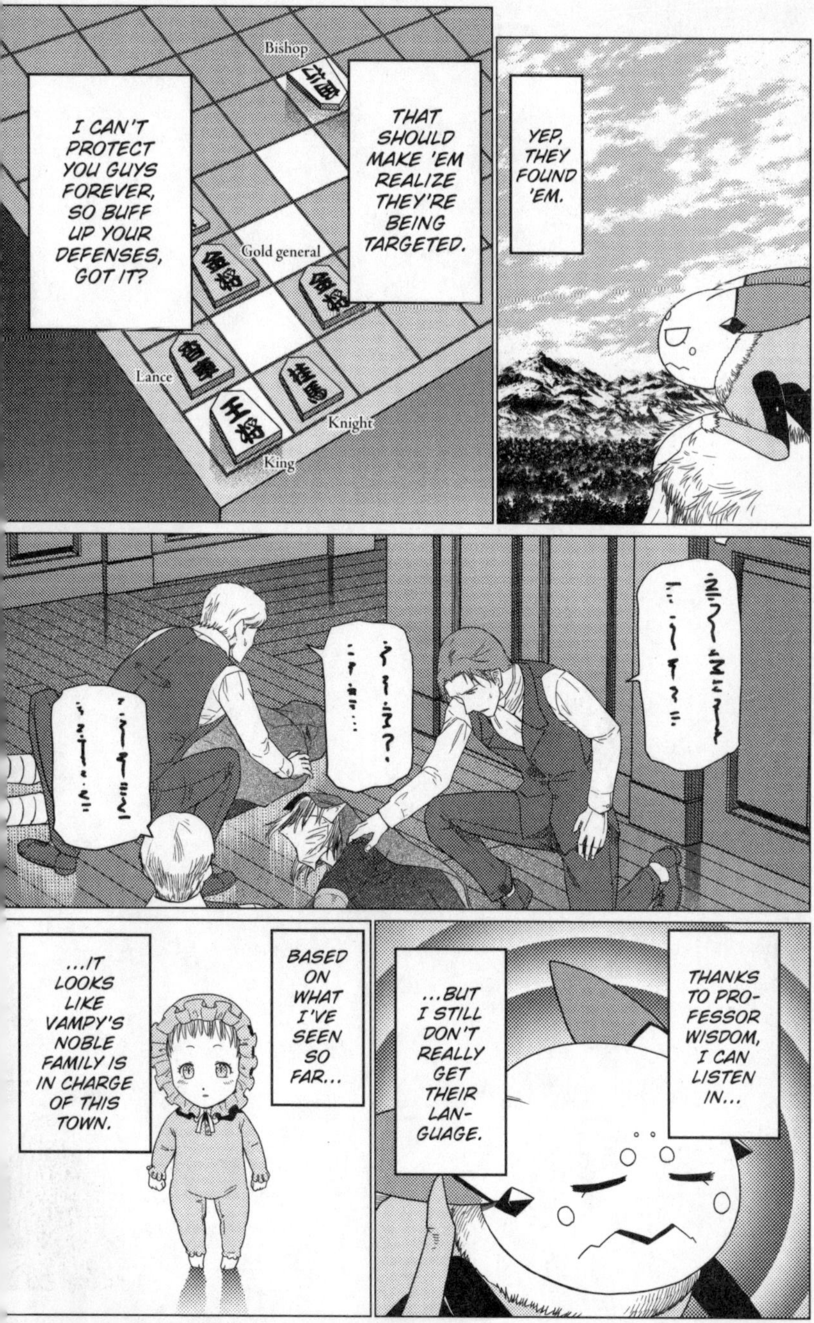
YEP, THEY FOUND 'EM.
THAT SHOULD MAKE 'EM REALIZE THEY'RE BEING TARGETED.
I CAN'T PROTECT YOU GUYS FOREVER, SO BUFF UP YOUR DEFENSES, GOT IT?
Bishop
Gold general
Lance
Knight
King
THANKS TO PROFESSOR WISDOM, I CAN LISTEN IN...
...BUT I STILL DON'T REALLY GET THEIR LANGUAGE.
BASED ON WHAT I'VE SEEN SO FAR...
...IT LOOKS LIKE VAMPY'S NOBLE FAMILY IS IN CHARGE OF THIS TOWN.

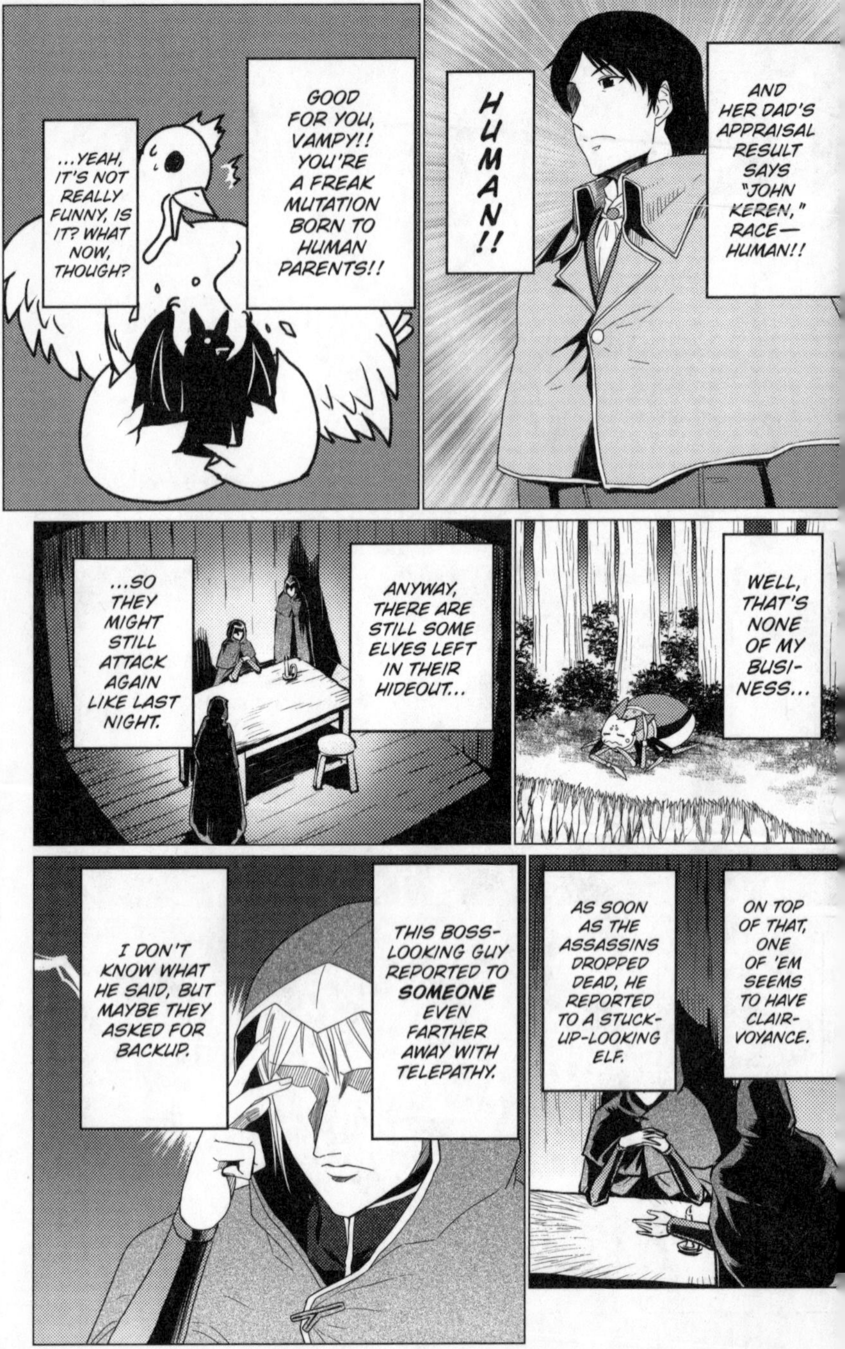
AND HER DAD'S APPRAISAL RESULT SAYS "JOHN KEREN," RACE— HUMAN!!
HUMAN!!
GOOD FOR YOU, VAMPY!! YOU'RE A FREAK MUTATION BORN TO HUMAN PARENTS!!
...YEAH, IT'S NOT REALLY FUNNY, IS IT? WHAT NOW, THOUGH?
WELL, THAT'S NONE OF MY BUSI- NESS...
ANYWAY, THERE ARE STILL SOME ELVES LEFT IN THEIR HIDEOUT...
...SO THEY MIGHT STILL ATTACK AGAIN LIKE LAST NIGHT.
ON TOP OF THAT, ONE OF 'EM SEEMS TO HAVE CLAIR- VOYANCE.
AS SOON AS THE ASSASSINS DROPPED DEAD, HE REPORTED TO A STUCK- UP-LOOKING ELF.
THIS BOSS- LOOKING GUY REPORTED TO SOMEONE EVEN FARTHER AWAY WITH TELEPATHY.
I DON'T KNOW WHAT HE SAID, BUT MAYBE THEY ASKED FOR BACKUP.

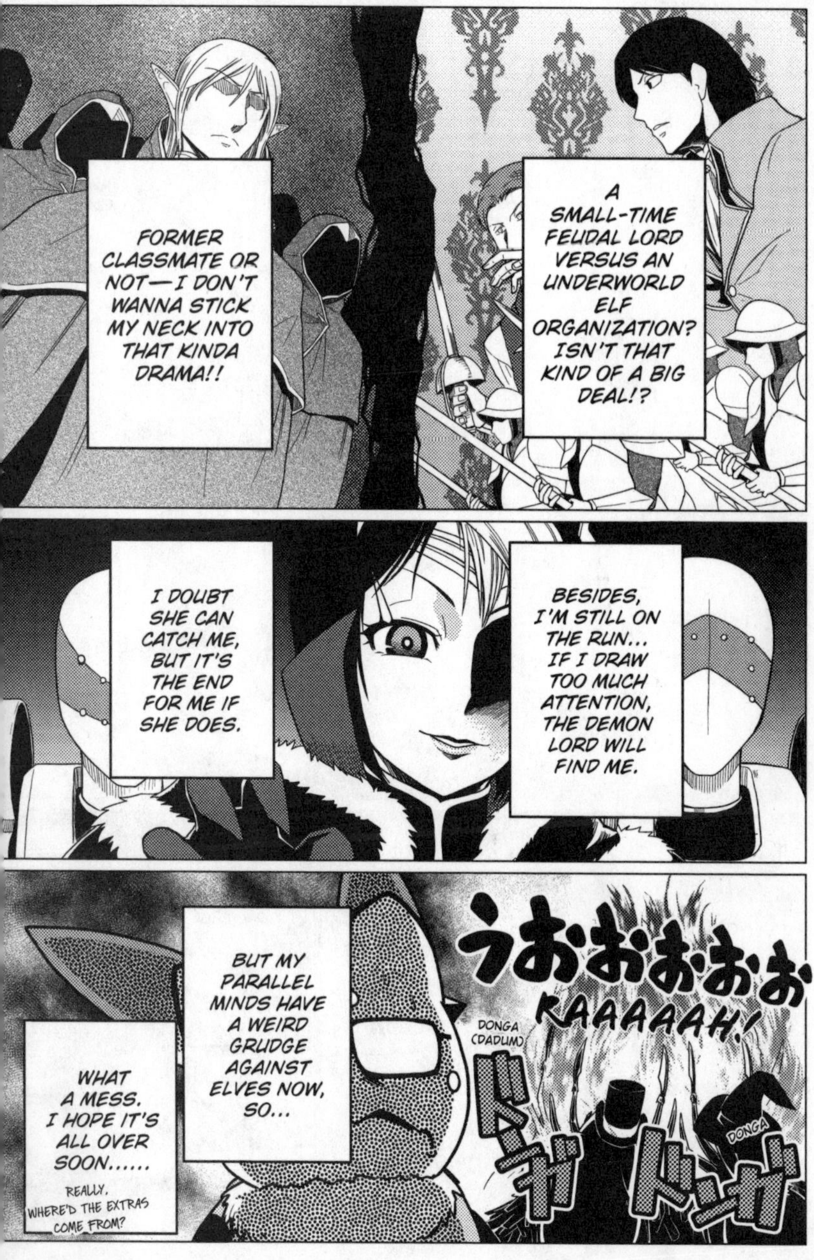
A SMALL-TIME FEUDAL LORD VERSUS AN UNDERWORLD ELF ORGANIZATION? ISN'T THAT KIND OF A BIG DEAL!?
FORMER CLASSMATE OR NOT—I DON'T WANNA STICK MY NECK INTO THAT KINDA DRAMA!!
BESIDES, I'M STILL ON THE RUN... IF I DRAW TOO MUCH ATTENTION, THE DEMON LORD WILL FIND ME.
I DOUBT SHE CAN CATCH ME, BUT IT'S THE END FOR ME IF SHE DOES.
うおおおおお
KAAAAAH!
ドガ ドガ
DONGA (DADUM)
DONGA
BUT MY PARALLEL MINDS HAVE A WEIRD GRUDGE AGAINST ELVES NOW, SO...
WHAT A MESS. I HOPE IT'S ALL OVER SOON......
REALLY, WHERE'D THE EXTRAS COME FROM?

END

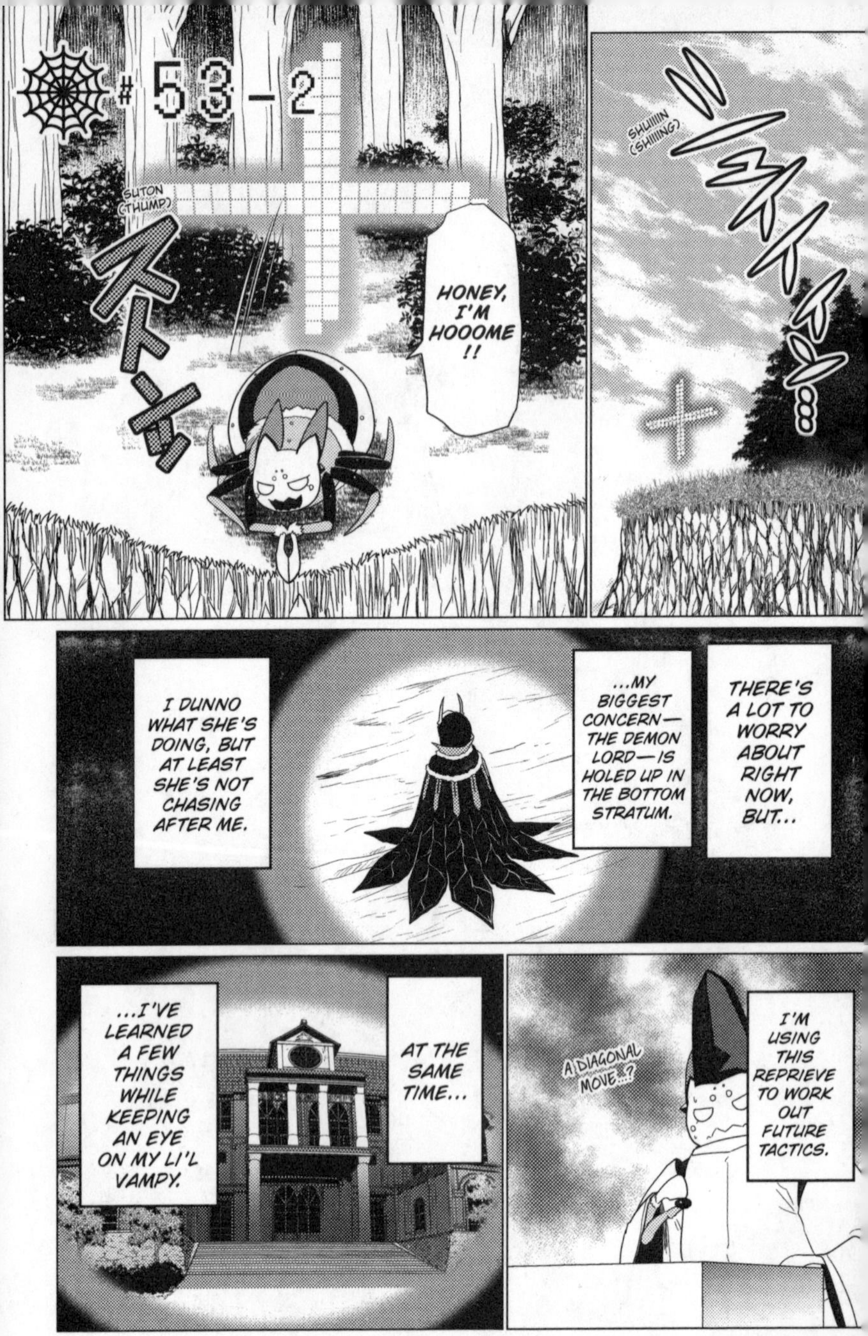
SHUIIIIN (SHIIIING)
#53-2
HONEY, I'M HOOOME!!
SUTON (THUMP)
THERE'S A LOT TO WORRY ABOUT RIGHT NOW, BUT...
...MY BIGGEST CONCERN—THE DEMON LORD—IS HOLED UP IN THE BOTTOM STRATUM.
I DUNNO WHAT SHE'S DOING, BUT AT LEAST SHE'S NOT CHASING AFTER ME.
I'M USING THIS REPRIEVE TO WORK OUT FUTURE TACTICS.
A DIAGONAL MOVE※...?
AT THE SAME TIME...
...I'VE LEARNED A FEW THINGS WHILE KEEPING AN EYE ON MY LI'L VAMPY.

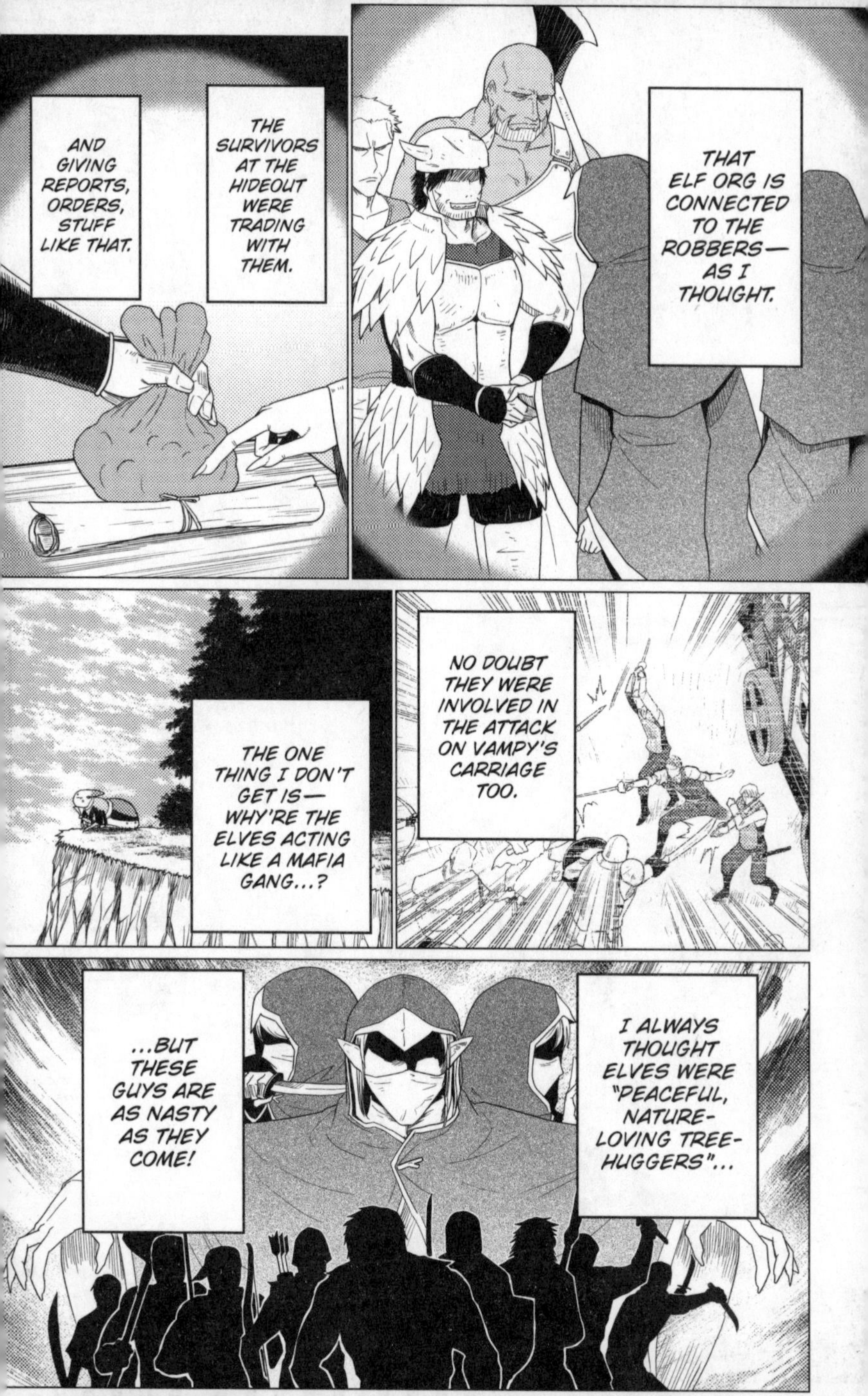
THAT ELF ORG IS CONNECTED TO THE ROBBERS—AS I THOUGHT.
THE SURVIVORS AT THE HIDEOUT WERE TRADING WITH THEM.
AND GIVING REPORTS, ORDERS, STUFF LIKE THAT.
NO DOUBT THEY WERE INVOLVED IN THE ATTACK ON VAMPY'S CARRIAGE TOO.
THE ONE THING I DON'T GET IS—WHY'RE THE ELVES ACTING LIKE A MAFIA GANG...?
I ALWAYS THOUGHT ELVES WERE "PEACEFUL, NATURE-LOVING TREE-HUGGERS"...
...BUT THESE GUYS ARE AS NASTY AS THEY COME!

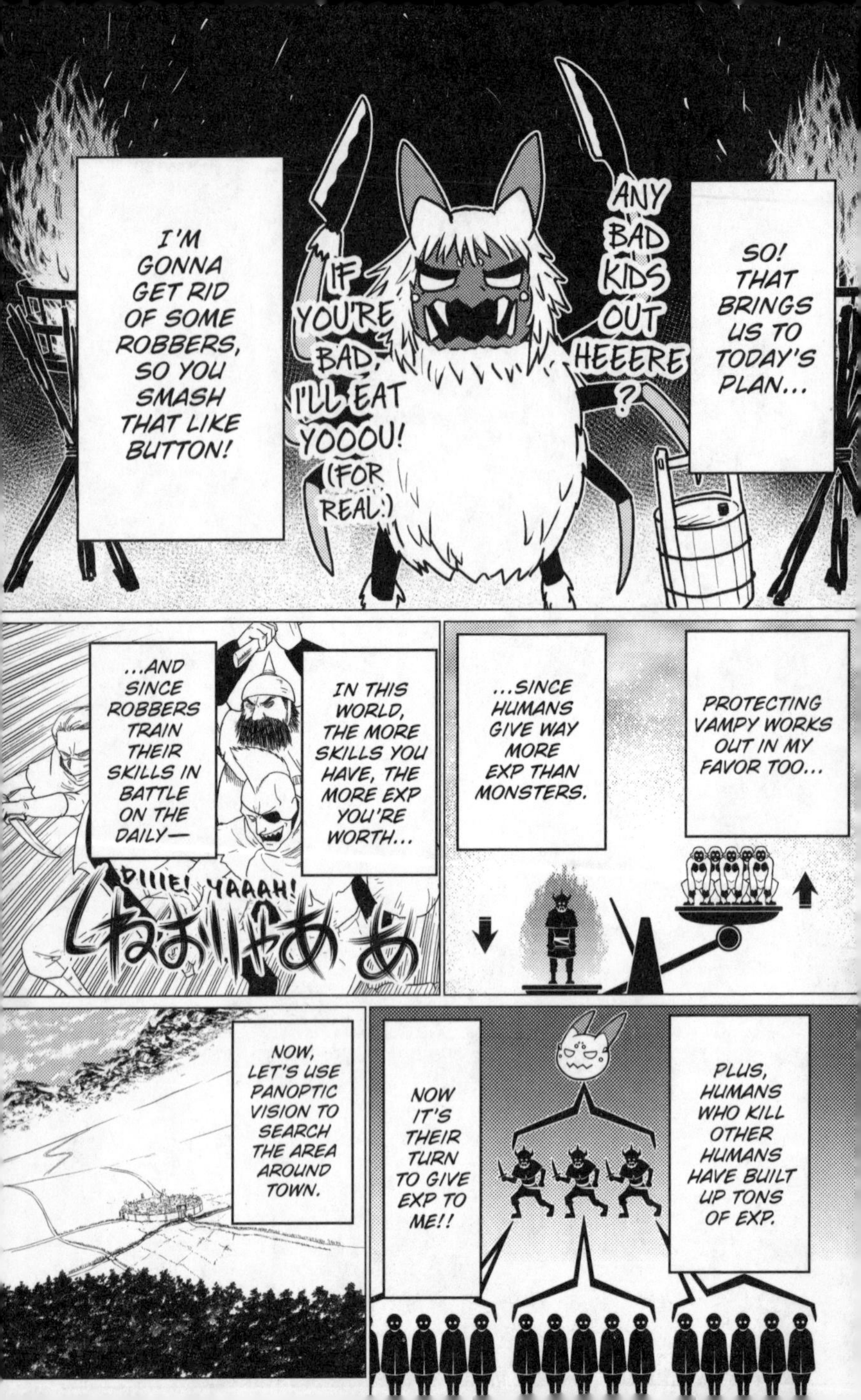
SO! THAT BRINGS US TO TODAY'S PLAN...
ANY BAD KIDS OUT HEEERE?
IF YOU'RE BAD, I'LL EAT YOOOU! (FOR REAL.)
I'M GONNA GET RID OF SOME ROBBERS, SO YOU SMASH THAT LIKE BUTTON!
PROTECTING VAMPY WORKS OUT IN MY FAVOR TOO...
...SINCE HUMANS GIVE WAY MORE EXP THAN MONSTERS.
IN THIS WORLD, THE MORE SKILLS YOU HAVE, THE MORE EXP YOU'RE WORTH...
...AND SINCE ROBBERS TRAIN THEIR SKILLS IN BATTLE ON THE DAILY—
YAAAH!
DIIIE!
PLUS, HUMANS WHO KILL OTHER HUMANS HAVE BUILT UP TONS OF EXP.
NOW IT'S THEIR TURN TO GIVE EXP TO ME!!
NOW, LET'S USE PANOPTIC VISION TO SEARCH THE AREA AROUND TOWN.

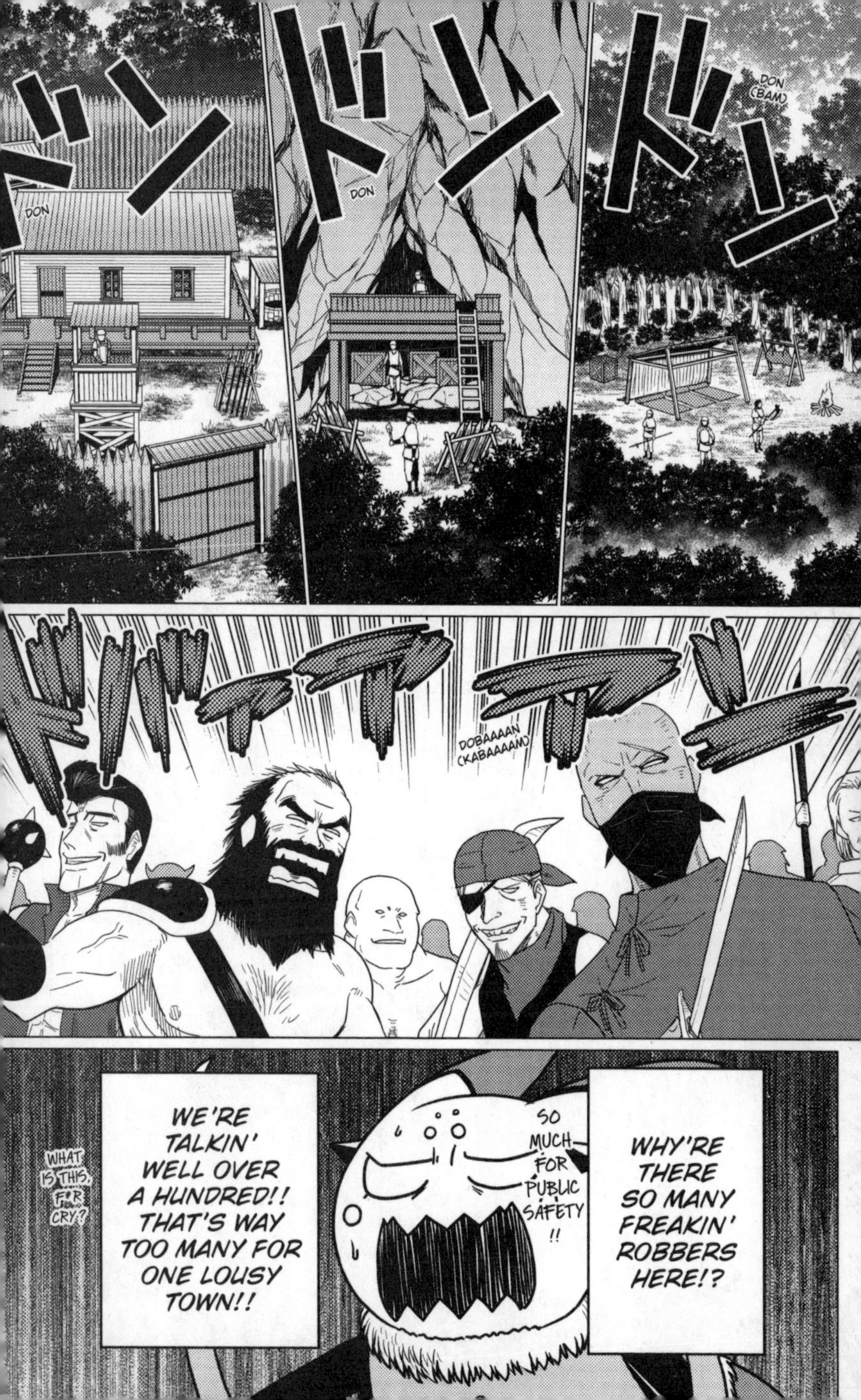
DON (BAM)
DON
DON
DOBAAAAN (KABAAAAM)
WHY'RE THERE SO MANY FREAKIN' ROBBERS HERE!?
SO MUCH FOR PUBLIC SAFETY!!
WE'RE TALKIN' WELL OVER A HUNDRED!! THAT'S WAY TOO MANY FOR ONE LOUSY TOWN!!
WHAT IS THIS, F*R CRY?

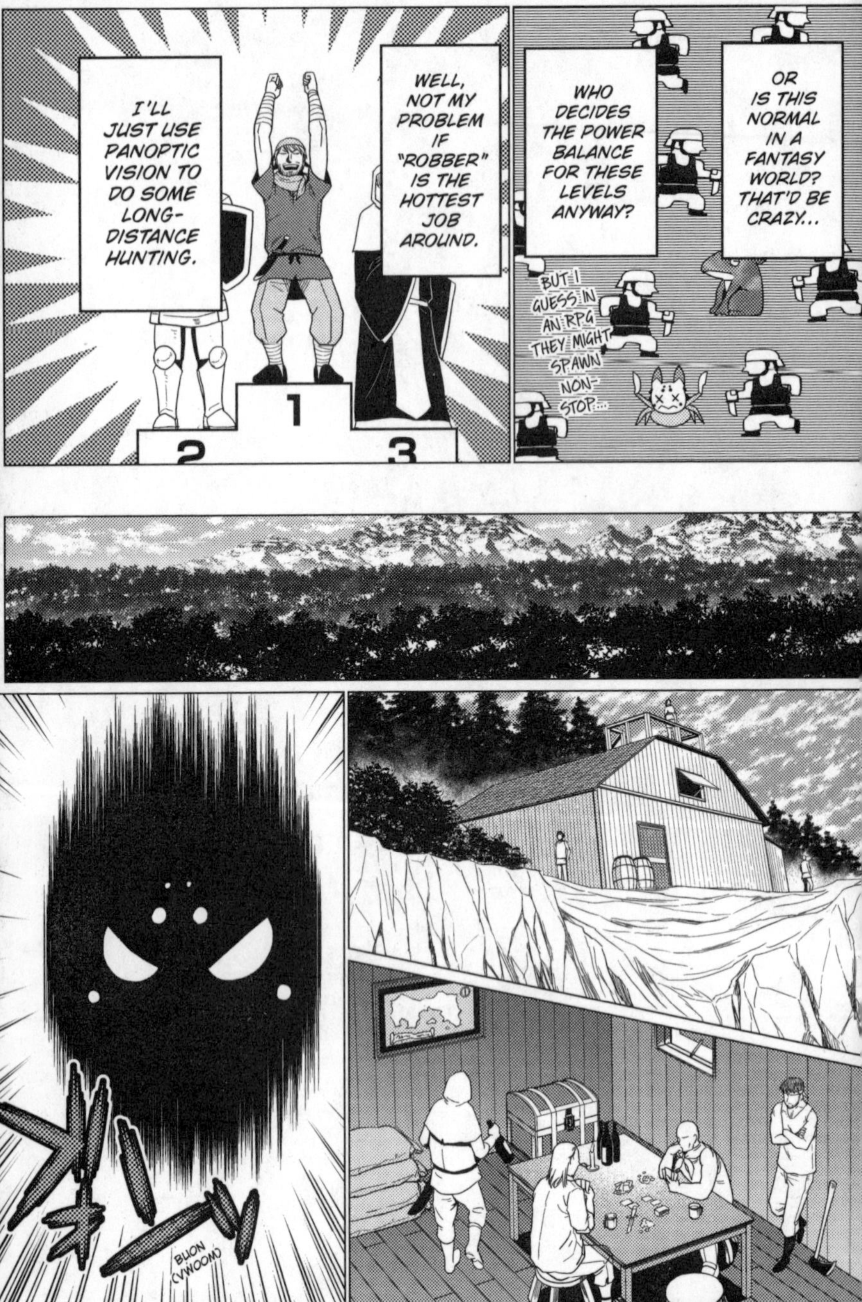
OR IS THIS NORMAL IN A FANTASY WORLD? THAT'D BE CRAZY...
WHO DECIDES THE POWER BALANCE FOR THESE LEVELS ANYWAY?
BUT I GUESS IN AN RPG THEY MIGHT SPAWN NON-STOP...
WELL, NOT MY PROBLEM IF "ROBBER" IS THE HOTTEST JOB AROUND.
I'LL JUST USE PANOPTIC VISION TO DO SOME LONG-DISTANCE HUNTING.
1
2
3
BUON (VWOOM)

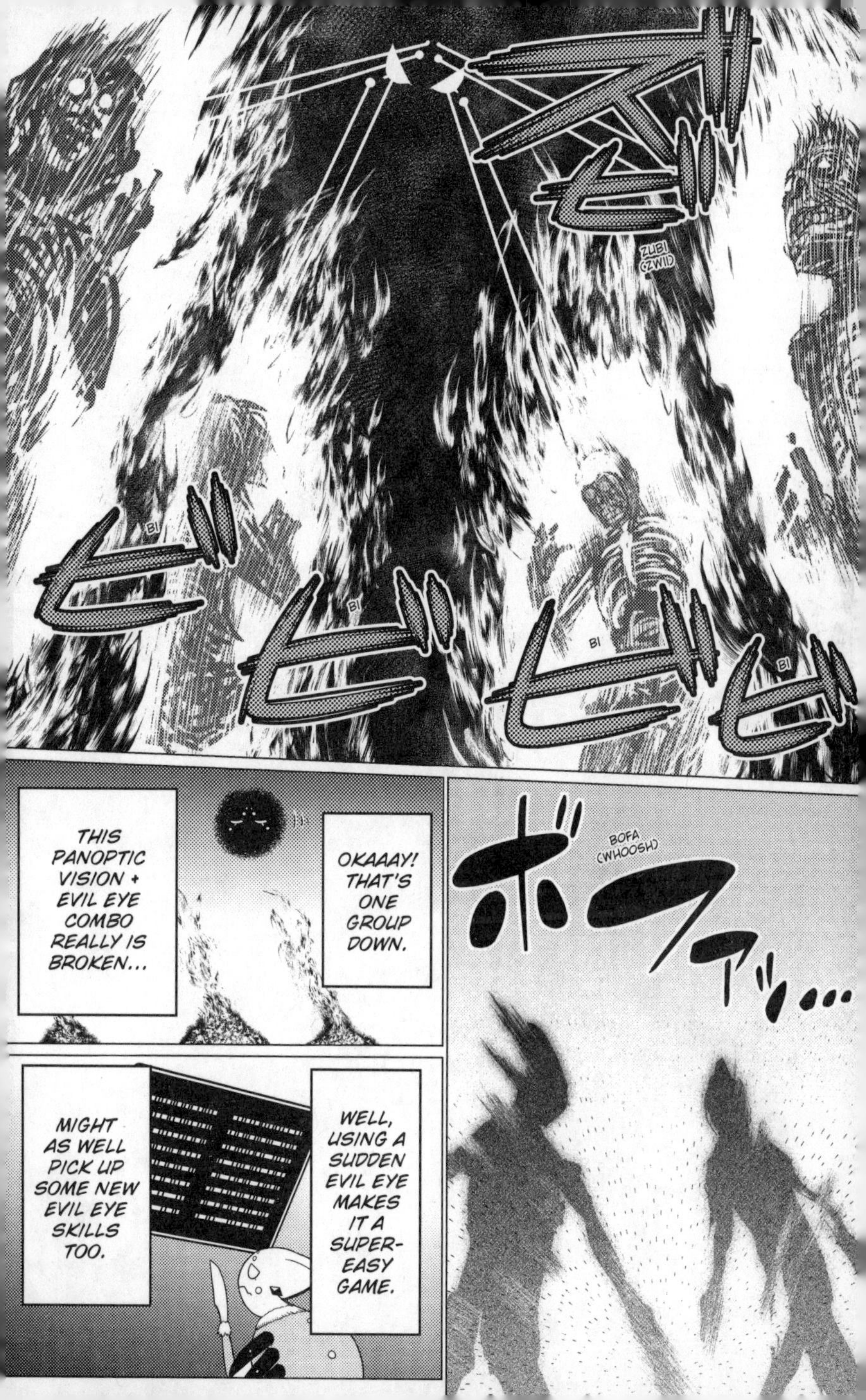
ZUBI (ZWII)
BI
BI
BI
BI
BOFA (WHOOSH)
OKAAAY! THAT'S ONE GROUP DOWN.
THIS PANOPTIC VISION + EVIL EYE COMBO REALLY IS BROKEN...
WELL, USING A SUDDEN EVIL EYE MAKES IT A SUPER-EASY GAME.
MIGHT AS WELL PICK UP SOME NEW EVIL EYE SKILLS TOO.

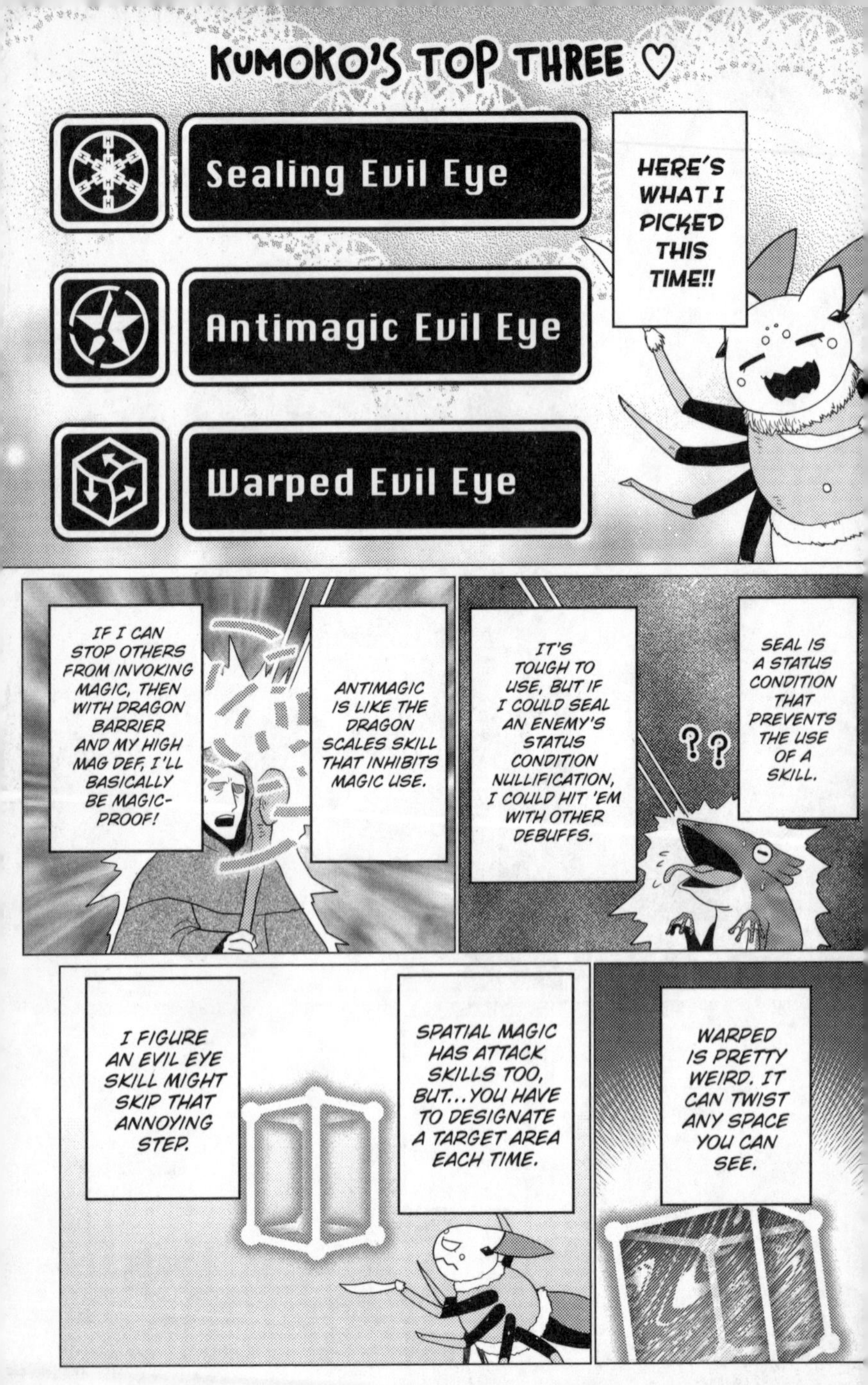
KUMOKO'S TOP THREE ♡
HERE'S WHAT I PICKED THIS TIME!!
Sealing Evil Eye
Antimagic Evil Eye
Warped Evil Eye
SEAL IS A STATUS CONDITION THAT PREVENTS THE USE OF A SKILL.
??
IT'S TOUGH TO USE, BUT IF I COULD SEAL AN ENEMY'S STATUS CONDITION NULLIFICATION, I COULD HIT 'EM WITH OTHER DEBUFFS.
ANTIMAGIC IS LIKE THE DRAGON SCALES SKILL THAT INHIBITS MAGIC USE.
IF I CAN STOP OTHERS FROM INVOKING MAGIC, THEN WITH DRAGON BARRIER AND MY HIGH MAG DEF, I'LL BASICALLY BE MAGIC-PROOF!
WARPED IS PRETTY WEIRD. IT CAN TWIST ANY SPACE YOU CAN SEE.
SPATIAL MAGIC HAS ATTACK SKILLS TOO, BUT...YOU HAVE TO DESIGNATE A TARGET AREA EACH TIME.
I FIGURE AN EVIL EYE SKILL MIGHT SKIP THAT ANNOYING STEP.

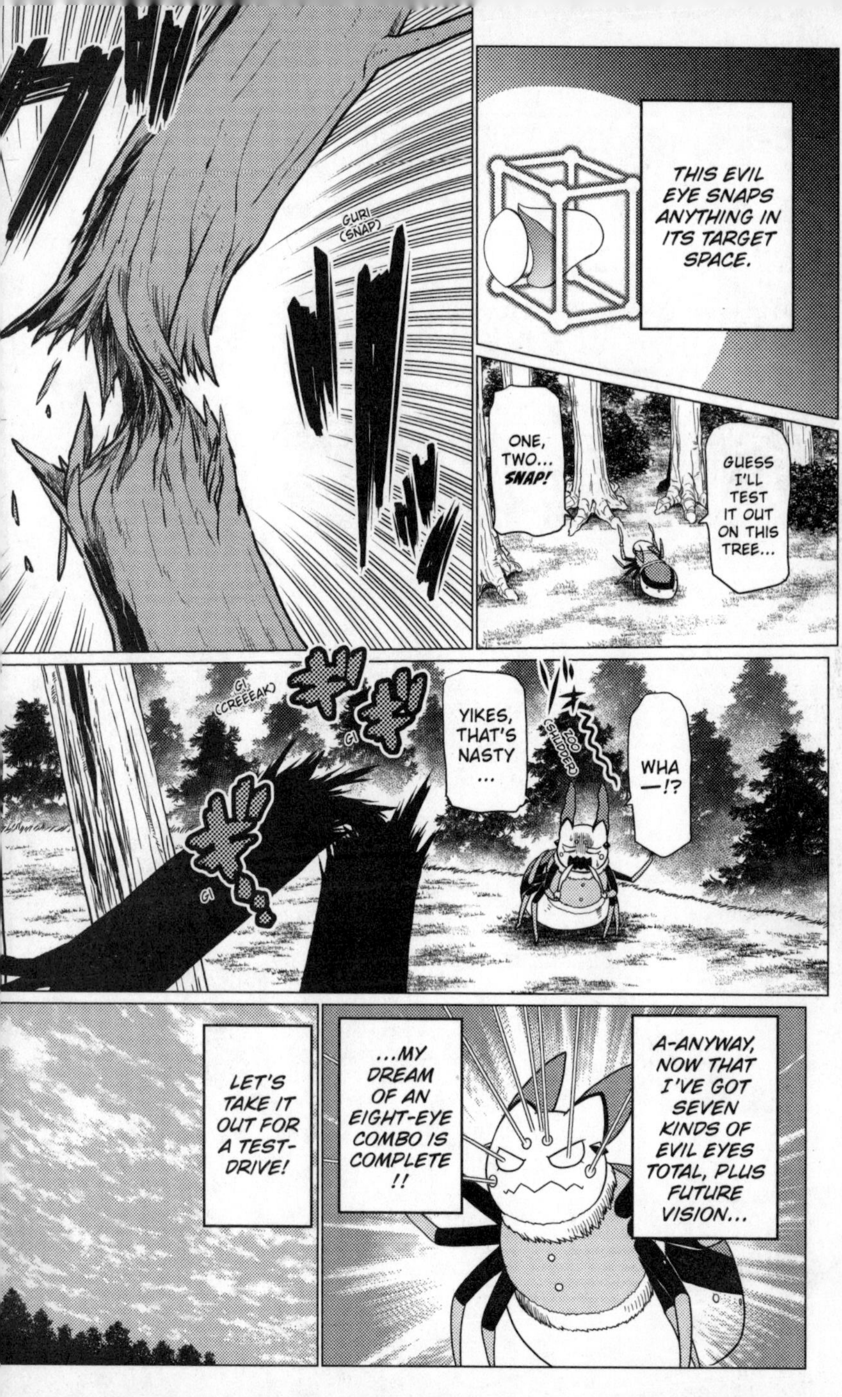
THIS EVIL EYE SNAPS ANYTHING IN ITS TARGET SPACE.
GUESS I'LL TEST IT OUT ON THIS TREE...
ONE, TWO... SNAP!
GURI (SNAP)
WHA—!?
ZOO (SHUDDER)
YIKES, THAT'S NASTY...
GI (CREEEAK)
GI
GI
A-ANYWAY, NOW THAT I'VE GOT SEVEN KINDS OF EVIL EYES TOTAL, PLUS FUTURE VISION...
...MY DREAM OF AN EIGHT-EYE COMBO IS COMPLETE!!
LET'S TAKE IT OUT FOR A TEST-DRIVE!

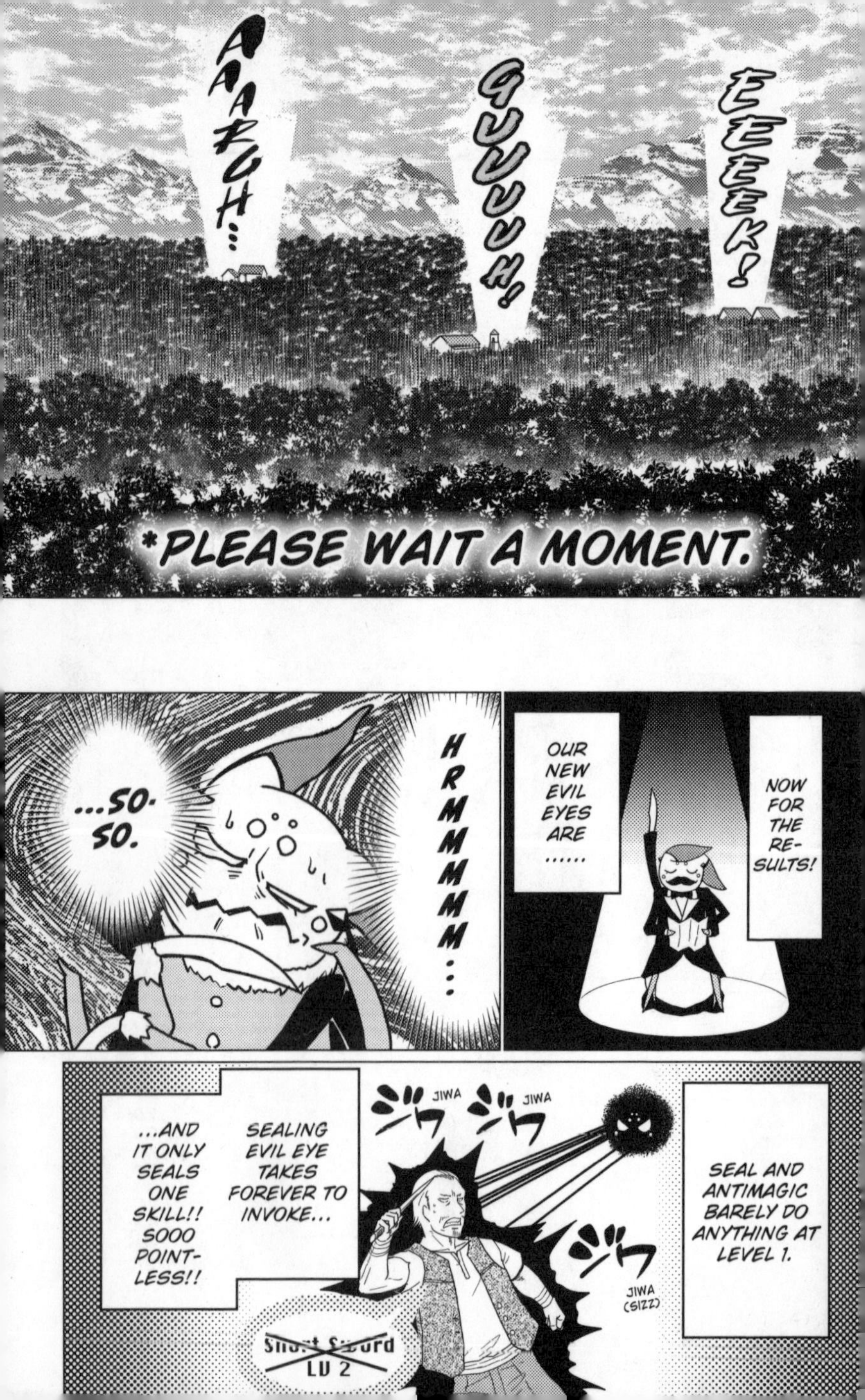
EEEEEK!
GUUUUH!
AAARUH...
*PLEASE WAIT A MOMENT.
NOW FOR THE RESULTS!
OUR NEW EVIL EYES ARE......
HRMMMMMM...
...SO-SO.
SEAL AND ANTIMAGIC BARELY DO ANYTHING AT LEVEL 1.
JIWA
JIWA
JIWA (SIZZ)
SEALING EVIL EYE TAKES FOREVER TO INVOKE...
...AND IT ONLY SEALS ONE SKILL!! SOOO POINTLESS!!
Short Sword
LV 2

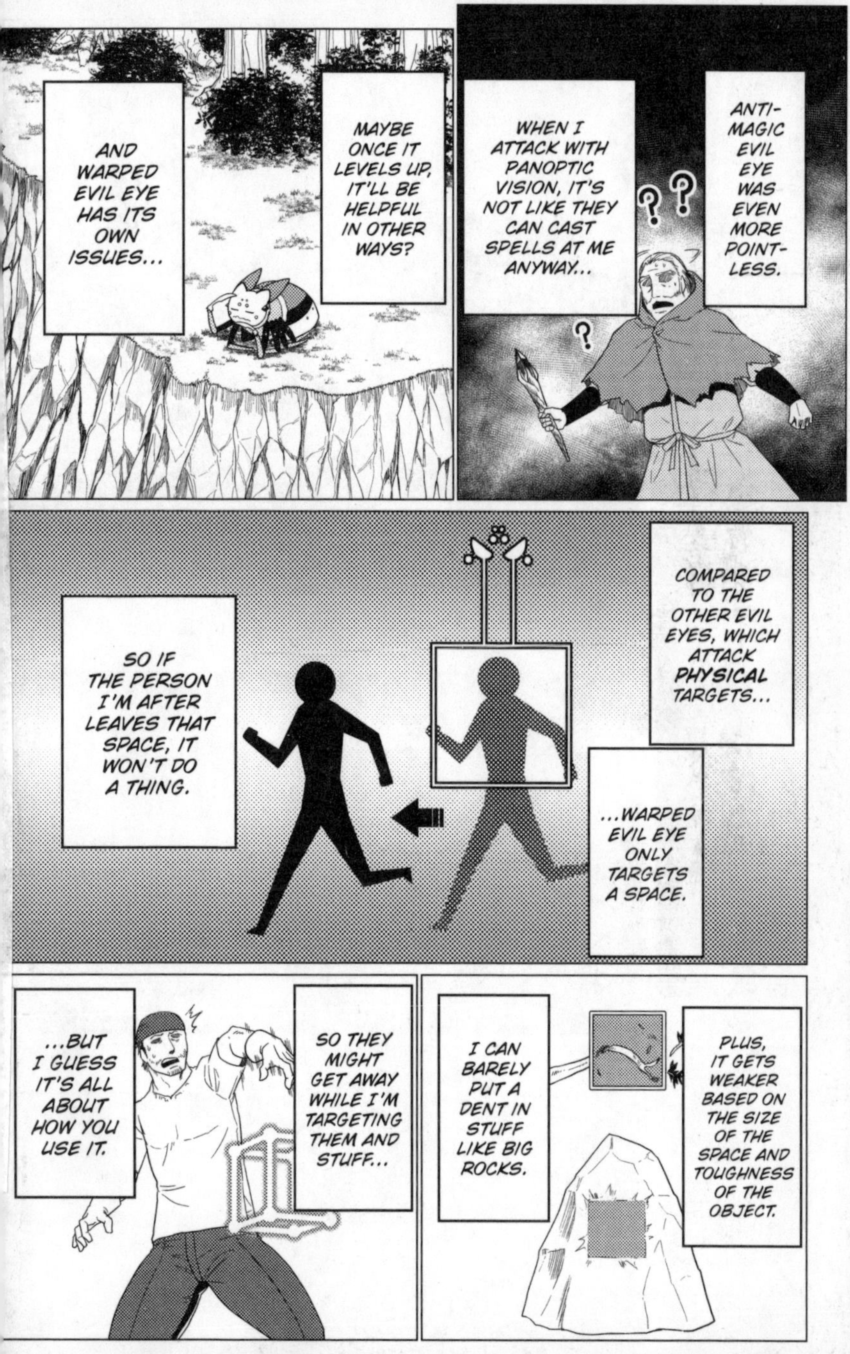
ANTI-MAGIC EVIL EYE WAS EVEN MORE POINTLESS.
WHEN I ATTACK WITH PANOPTIC VISION, IT'S NOT LIKE THEY CAN CAST SPELLS AT ME ANYWAY...
MAYBE ONCE IT LEVELS UP, IT'LL BE HELPFUL IN OTHER WAYS?
AND WARPED EVIL EYE HAS ITS OWN ISSUES...
COMPARED TO THE OTHER EVIL EYES, WHICH ATTACK **PHYSICAL** TARGETS...
...WARPED EVIL EYE ONLY TARGETS A SPACE.
SO IF THE PERSON I'M AFTER LEAVES THAT SPACE, IT WON'T DO A THING.
PLUS, IT GETS WEAKER BASED ON THE SIZE OF THE SPACE AND TOUGHNESS OF THE OBJECT.
I CAN BARELY PUT A DENT IN STUFF LIKE BIG ROCKS.
SO THEY MIGHT GET AWAY WHILE I'M TARGETING THEM AND STUFF...
...BUT I GUESS IT'S ALL ABOUT HOW YOU USE IT.

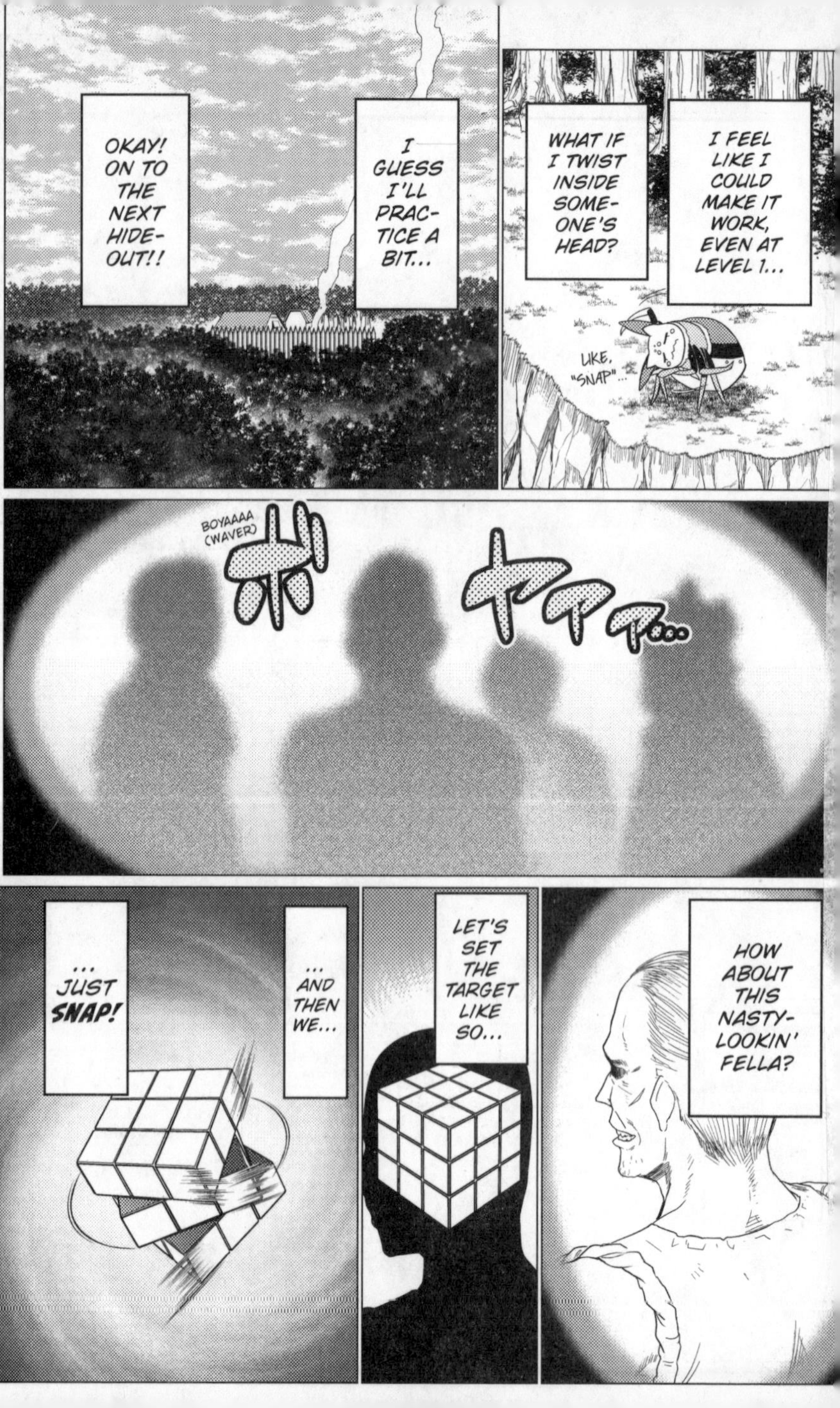
I FEEL LIKE I COULD MAKE IT WORK, EVEN AT LEVEL 1...
WHAT IF I TWIST INSIDE SOME-ONE'S HEAD?
LIKE, "SNAP"...
I GUESS I'LL PRAC-TICE A BIT...
OKAY! ON TO THE NEXT HIDE-OUT!!
BOYAAAA (WAVER)
ボヤァァ…
HOW ABOUT THIS NASTY-LOOKIN' FELLA?
LET'S SET THE TARGET LIKE SO...
...AND THEN WE...
...JUST **SNAP!**

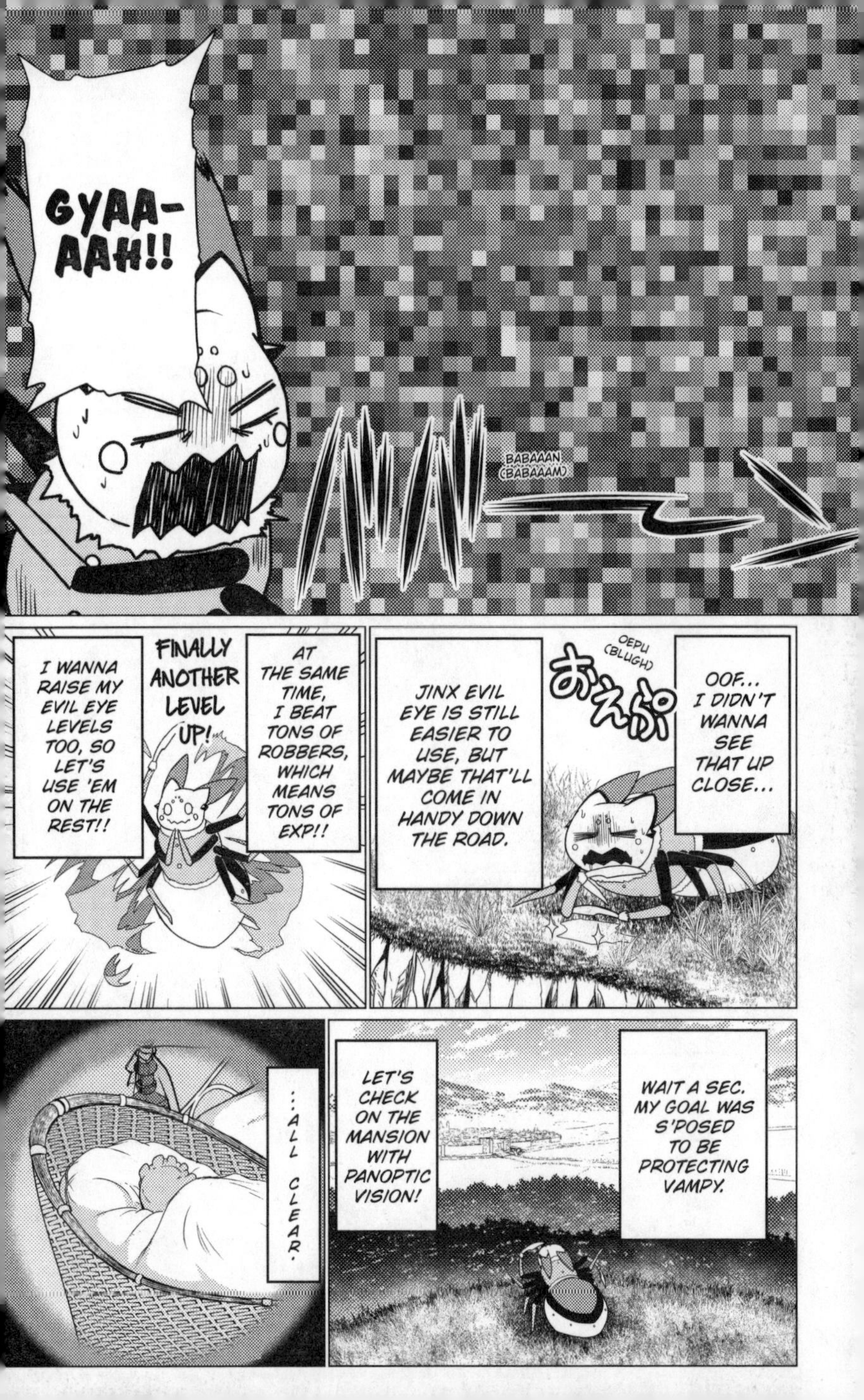
GYAA-AAH!!
BABAAAN (BABAAAM)
OOF... I DIDN'T WANNA SEE THAT UP CLOSE...
おえぷ
OEPU (BLUGH)
JINX EVIL EYE IS STILL EASIER TO USE, BUT MAYBE THAT'LL COME IN HANDY DOWN THE ROAD.
AT THE SAME TIME, I BEAT TONS OF ROBBERS, WHICH MEANS TONS OF EXP!!
FINALLY ANOTHER LEVEL UP!
I WANNA RAISE MY EVIL EYE LEVELS TOO, SO LET'S USE 'EM ON THE REST!!
WAIT A SEC. MY GOAL WAS S'POSED TO BE PROTECTING VAMPY.
LET'S CHECK ON THE MANSION WITH PANOPTIC VISION!
...ALL CLEAR.

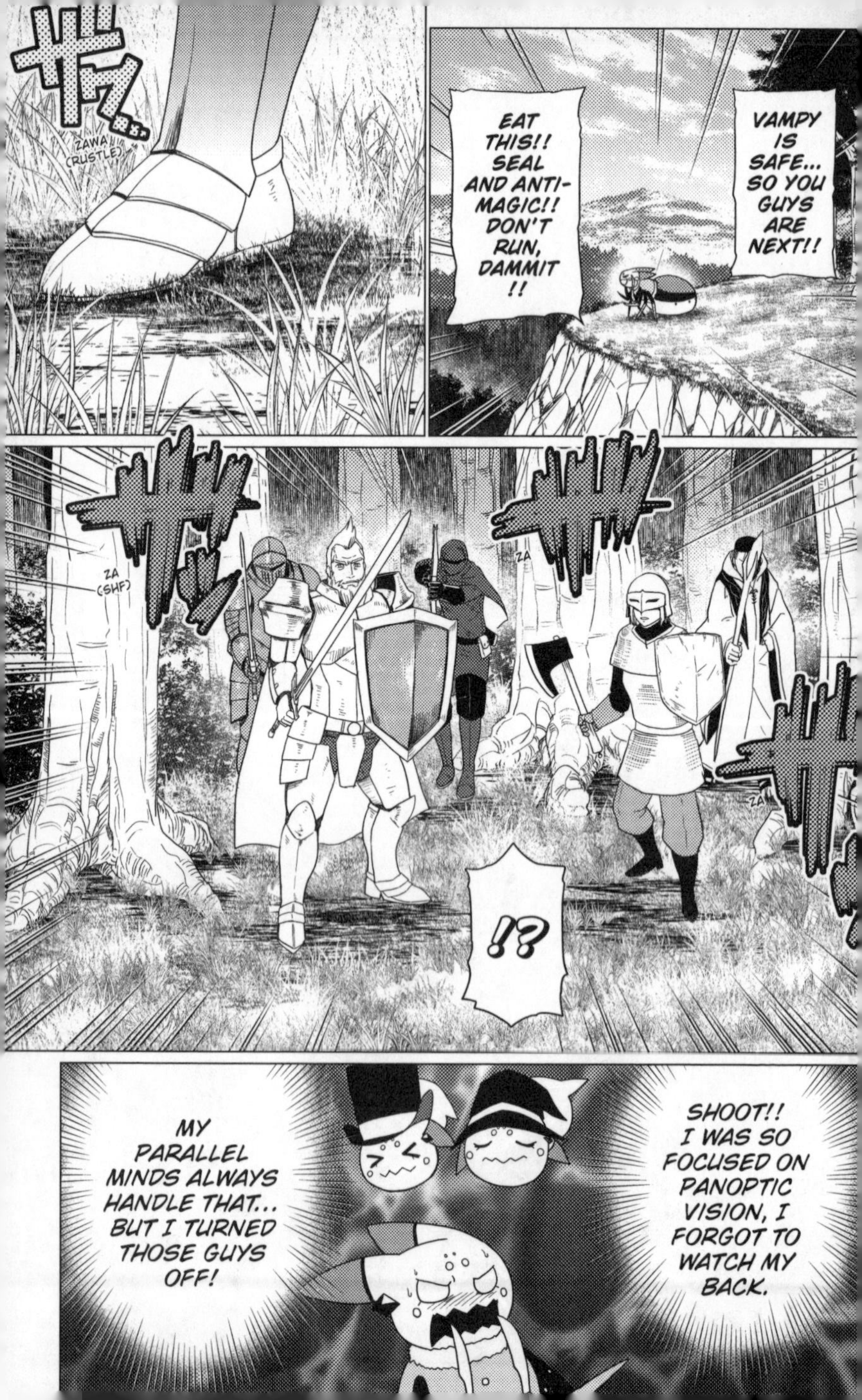
VAMPY IS SAFE... SO YOU GUYS ARE NEXT!!
EAT THIS!! SEAL AND ANTI-MAGIC!! DON'T RUN, DAMMIT!!
ZAWA (RUSTLE)
ZA
ZA
ZA (SHF)
!?
SHOOT!! I WAS SO FOCUSED ON PANOPTIC VISION, I FORGOT TO WATCH MY BACK.
MY PARALLEL MINDS ALWAYS HANDLE THAT... BUT I TURNED THOSE GUYS OFF!

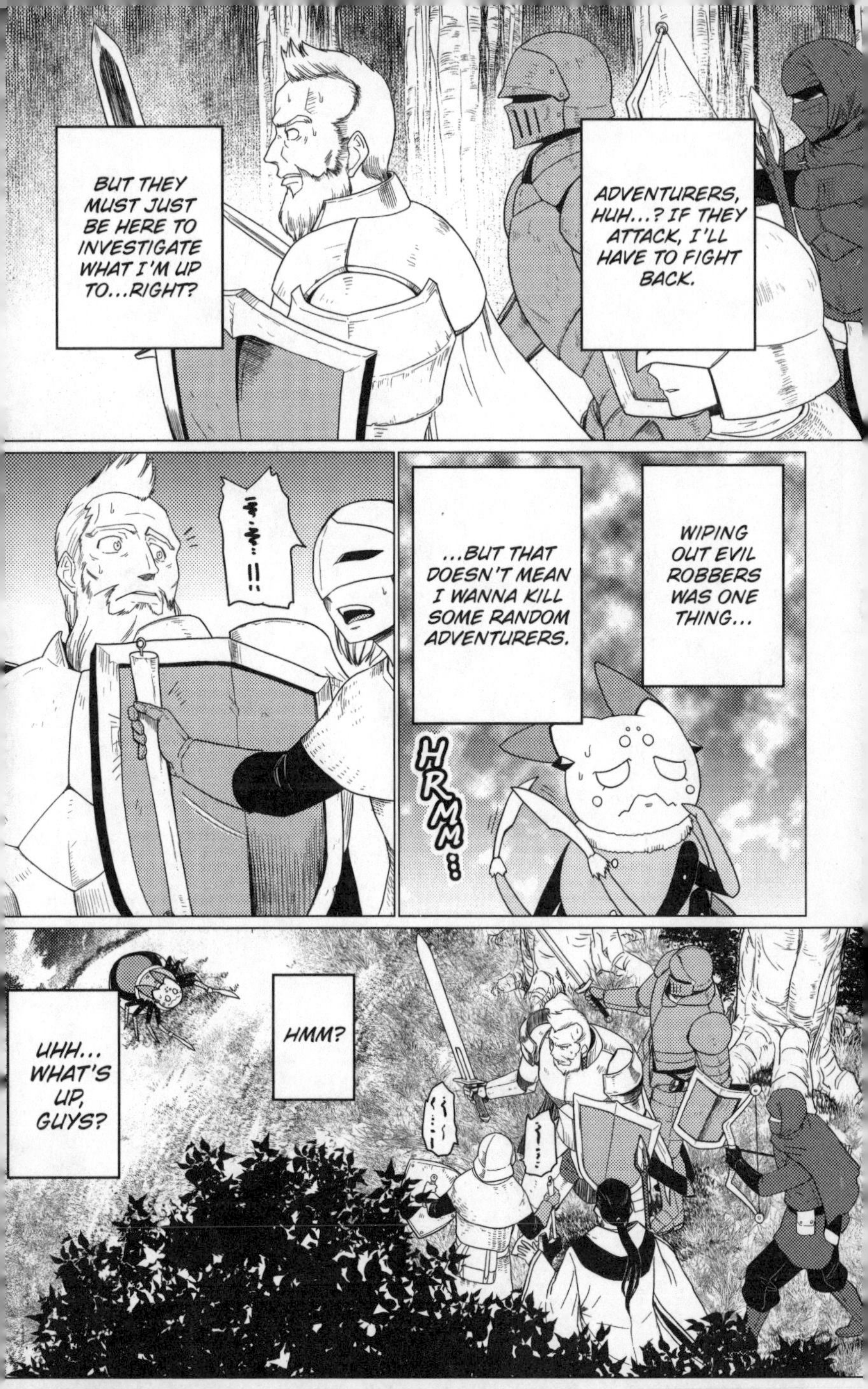
ADVENTURERS, HUH...? IF THEY ATTACK, I'LL HAVE TO FIGHT BACK.
BUT THEY MUST JUST BE HERE TO INVESTIGATE WHAT I'M UP TO...RIGHT?
WIPING OUT EVIL ROBBERS WAS ONE THING...
...BUT THAT DOESN'T MEAN I WANNA KILL SOME RANDOM ADVENTURERS.
HRMM..
HMM?
UHH... WHAT'S UP, GUYS?

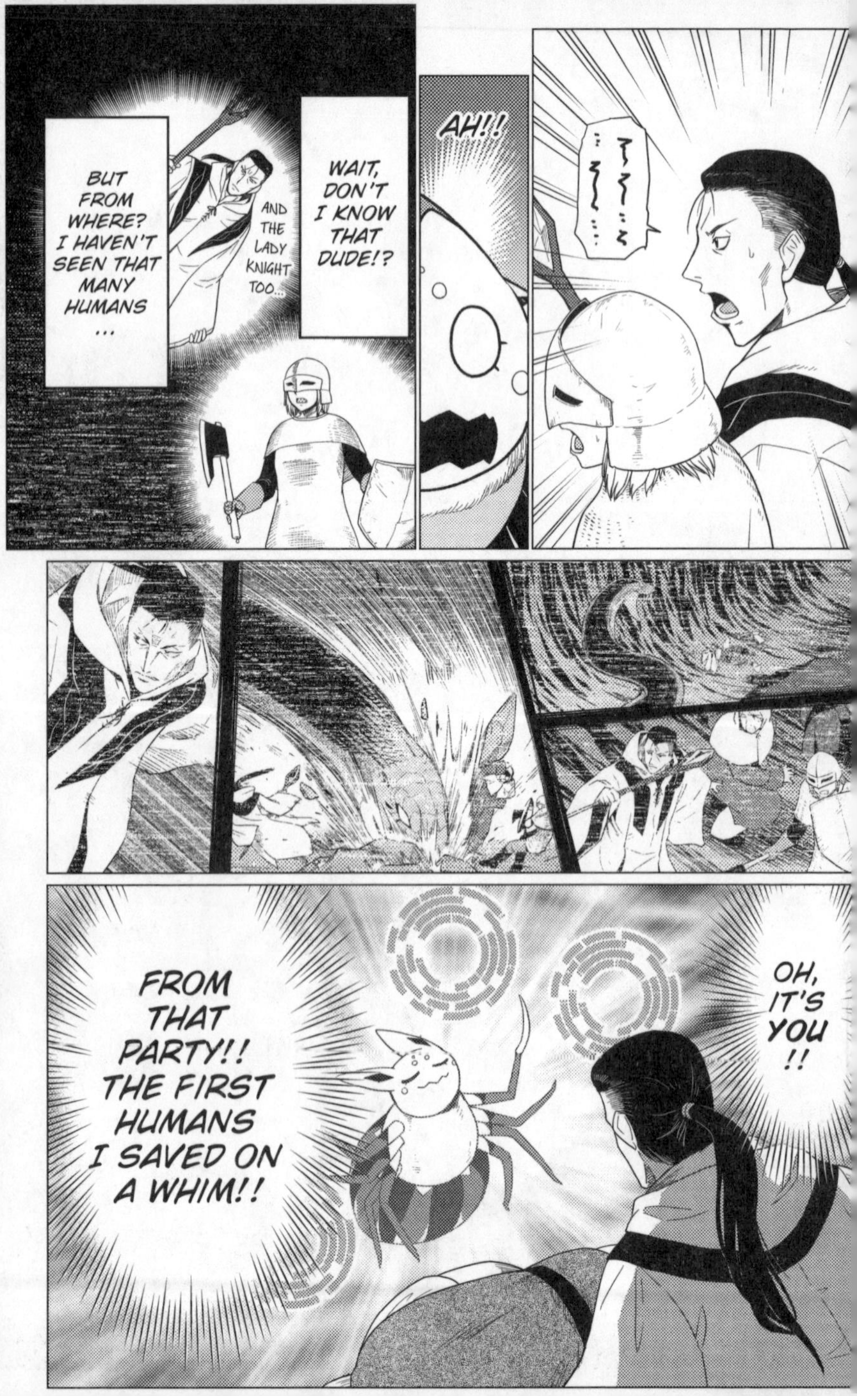
AH!!
WAIT, DON'T I KNOW THAT DUDE!?
AND THE LADY KNIGHT TOO...
BUT FROM WHERE? I HAVEN'T SEEN THAT MANY HUMANS ...
OH, IT'S YOU!!
FROM THAT PARTY!! THE FIRST HUMANS I SAVED ON A WHIM!!

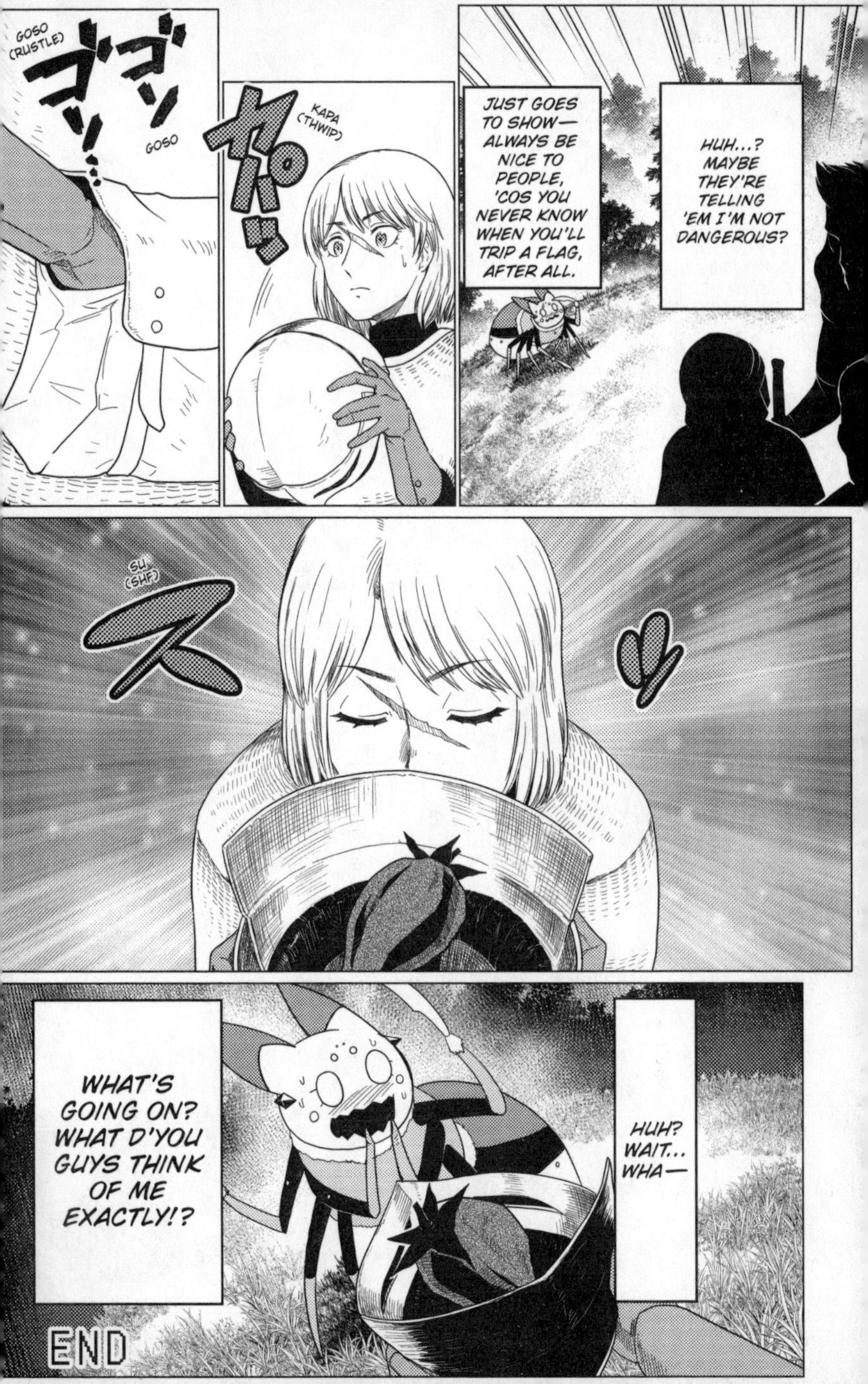
HUH...? MAYBE THEY'RE TELLING 'EM I'M NOT DANGEROUS?
JUST GOES TO SHOW— ALWAYS BE NICE TO PEOPLE, 'COS YOU NEVER KNOW WHEN YOU'LL TRIP A FLAG, AFTER ALL.
KAPA (THWIP)
GOSO (RUSTLE)
GOSO
SU (SHF)
HUH? WAIT... WHA—
WHAT'S GOING ON? WHAT D'YOU GUYS THINK OF ME EXACTLY!?
END

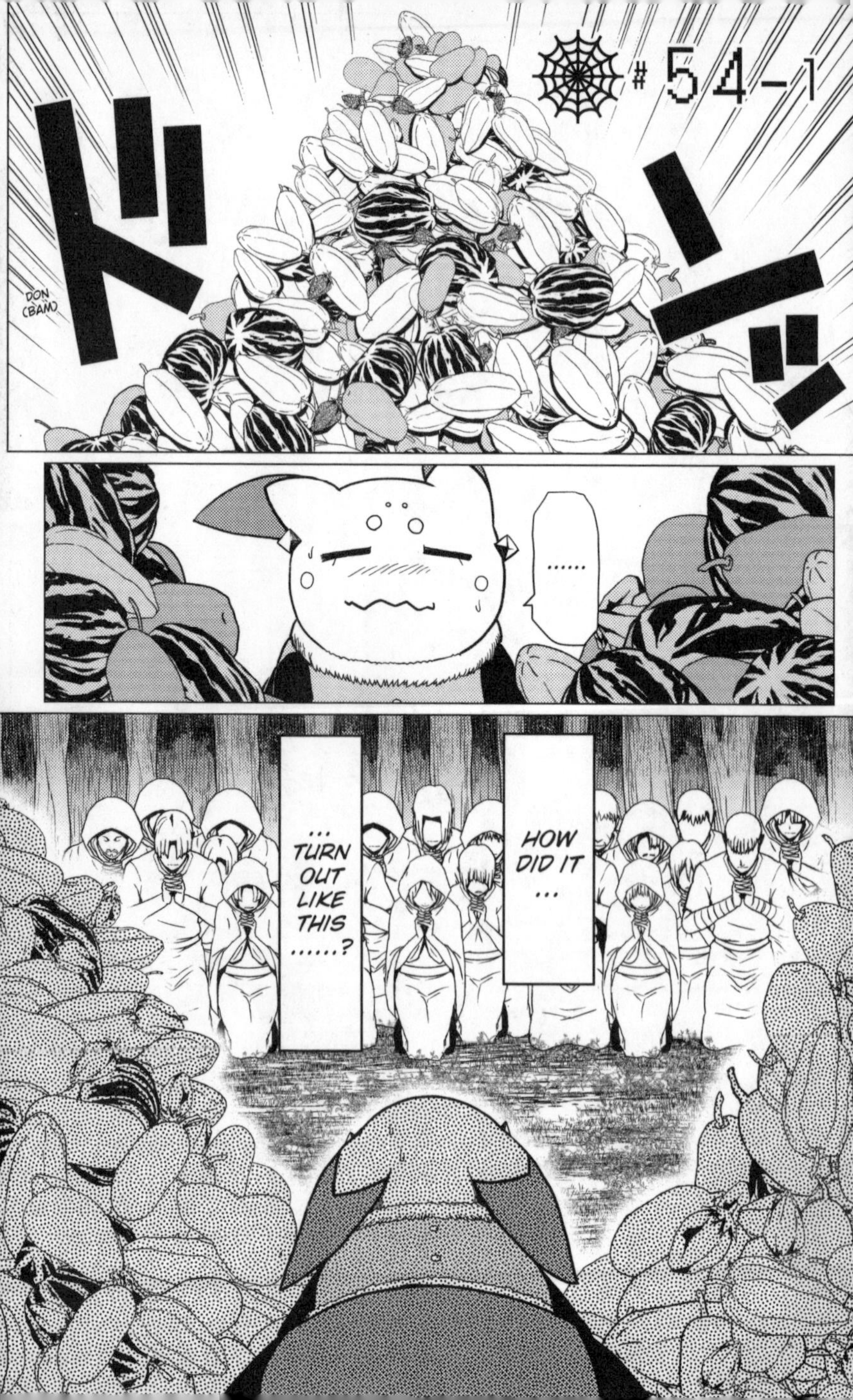
#54-1
ドーン
DON (BAM)
......
HOW DID IT ...
... TURN OUT LIKE THIS ......?

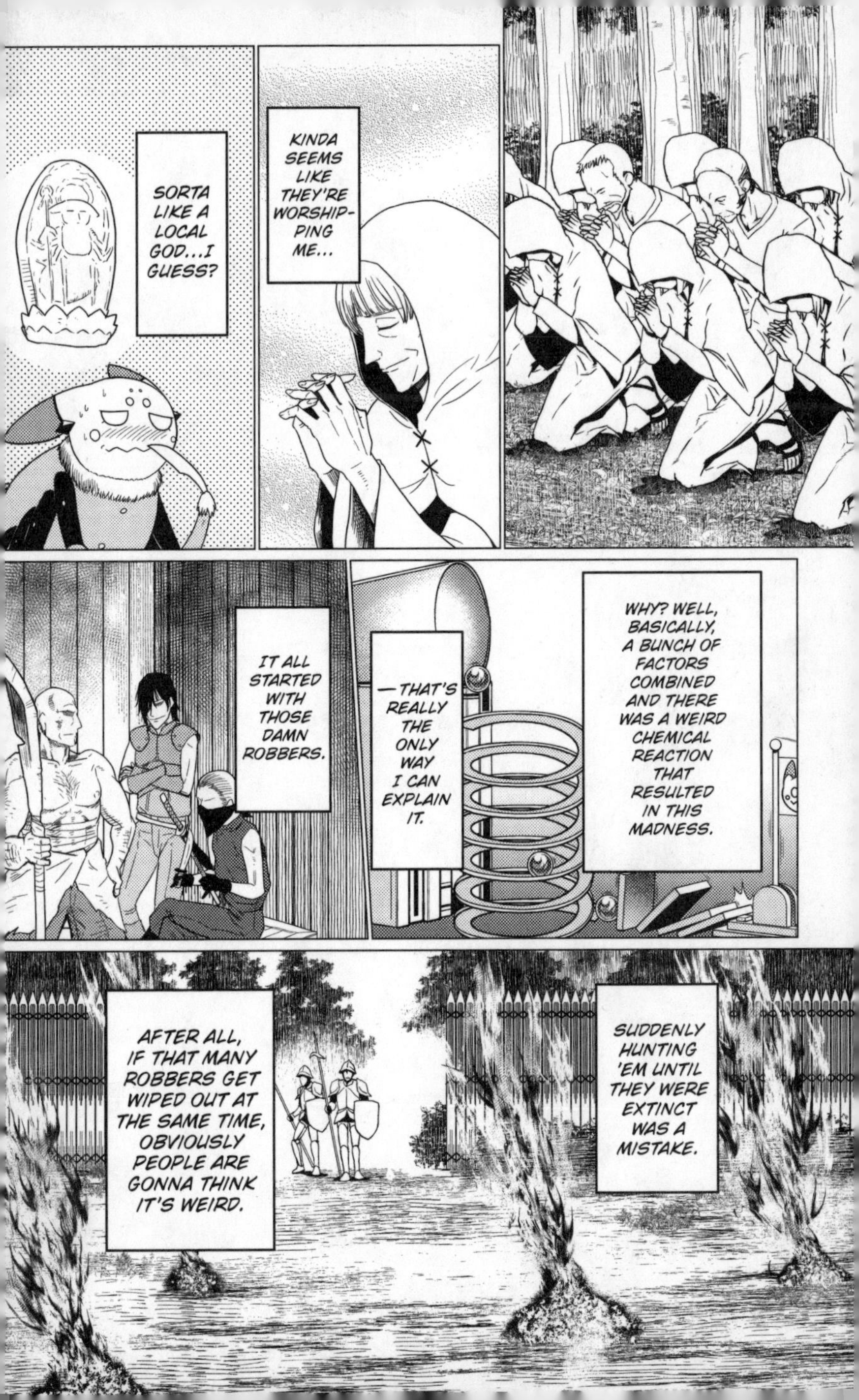
KINDA SEEMS LIKE THEY'RE WORSHIP-PING ME...
SORTA LIKE A LOCAL GOD...I GUESS?
WHY? WELL, BASICALLY, A BUNCH OF FACTORS COMBINED AND THERE WAS A WEIRD CHEMICAL REACTION THAT RESULTED IN THIS MADNESS.
—THAT'S REALLY THE ONLY WAY I CAN EXPLAIN IT.
IT ALL STARTED WITH THOSE DAMN ROBBERS.
SUDDENLY HUNTING 'EM UNTIL THEY WERE EXTINCT WAS A MISTAKE.
AFTER ALL, IF THAT MANY ROBBERS GET WIPED OUT AT THE SAME TIME, OBVIOUSLY PEOPLE ARE GONNA THINK IT'S WEIRD.

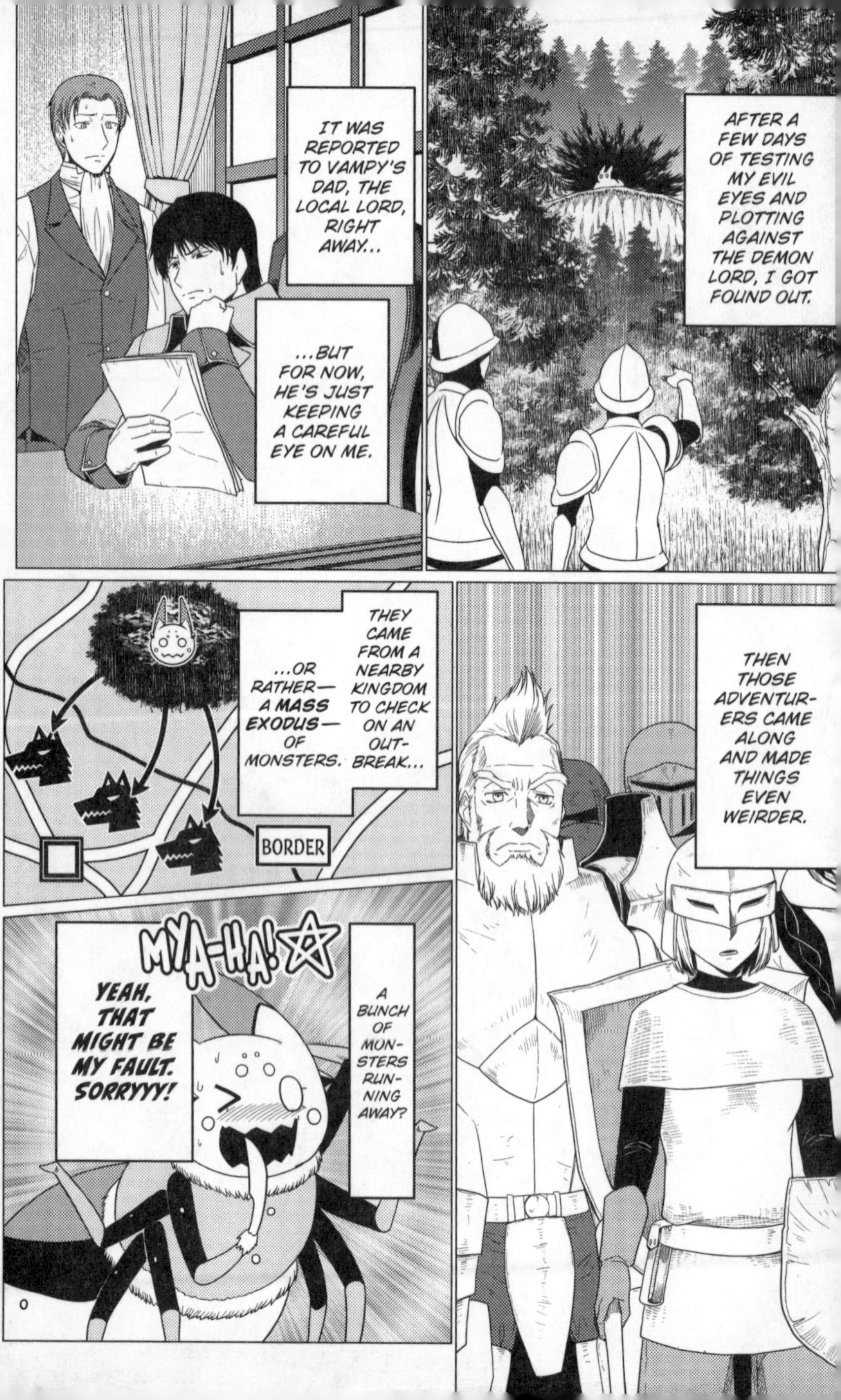
AFTER A FEW DAYS OF TESTING MY EVIL EYES AND PLOTTING AGAINST THE DEMON LORD, I GOT FOUND OUT.
IT WAS REPORTED TO VAMPY'S DAD, THE LOCAL LORD, RIGHT AWAY...
...BUT FOR NOW, HE'S JUST KEEPING A CAREFUL EYE ON ME.
THEN THOSE ADVENTURERS CAME ALONG AND MADE THINGS EVEN WEIRDER.
THEY CAME FROM A NEARBY KINGDOM TO CHECK ON AN OUTBREAK...
...OR RATHER—A **MASS EXODUS**—OF MONSTERS.
BORDER
A BUNCH OF MONSTERS RUNNING AWAY?
MYA-HA!☆
YEAH, THAT MIGHT BE MY FAULT. SORRYYY!

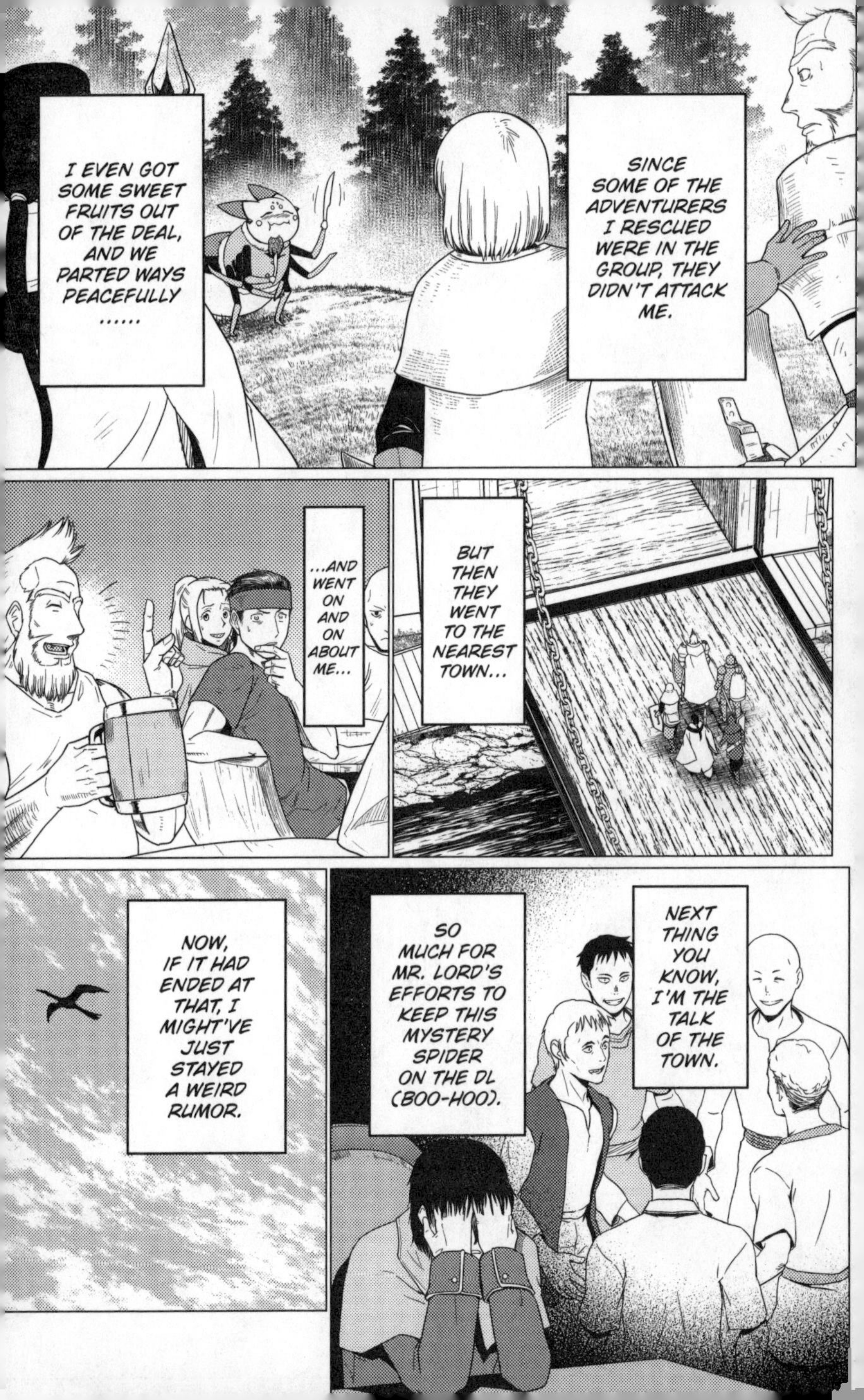
SINCE SOME OF THE ADVENTURERS I RESCUED WERE IN THE GROUP, THEY DIDN'T ATTACK ME.
I EVEN GOT SOME SWEET FRUITS OUT OF THE DEAL, AND WE PARTED WAYS PEACEFULLY ......
BUT THEN THEY WENT TO THE NEAREST TOWN...
...AND WENT ON AND ON ABOUT ME...
NEXT THING YOU KNOW, I'M THE TALK OF THE TOWN.
SO MUCH FOR MR. LORD'S EFFORTS TO KEEP THIS MYSTERY SPIDER ON THE DL (BOO-HOO).
NOW, IF IT HAD ENDED AT THAT, I MIGHT'VE JUST STAYED A WEIRD RUMOR.

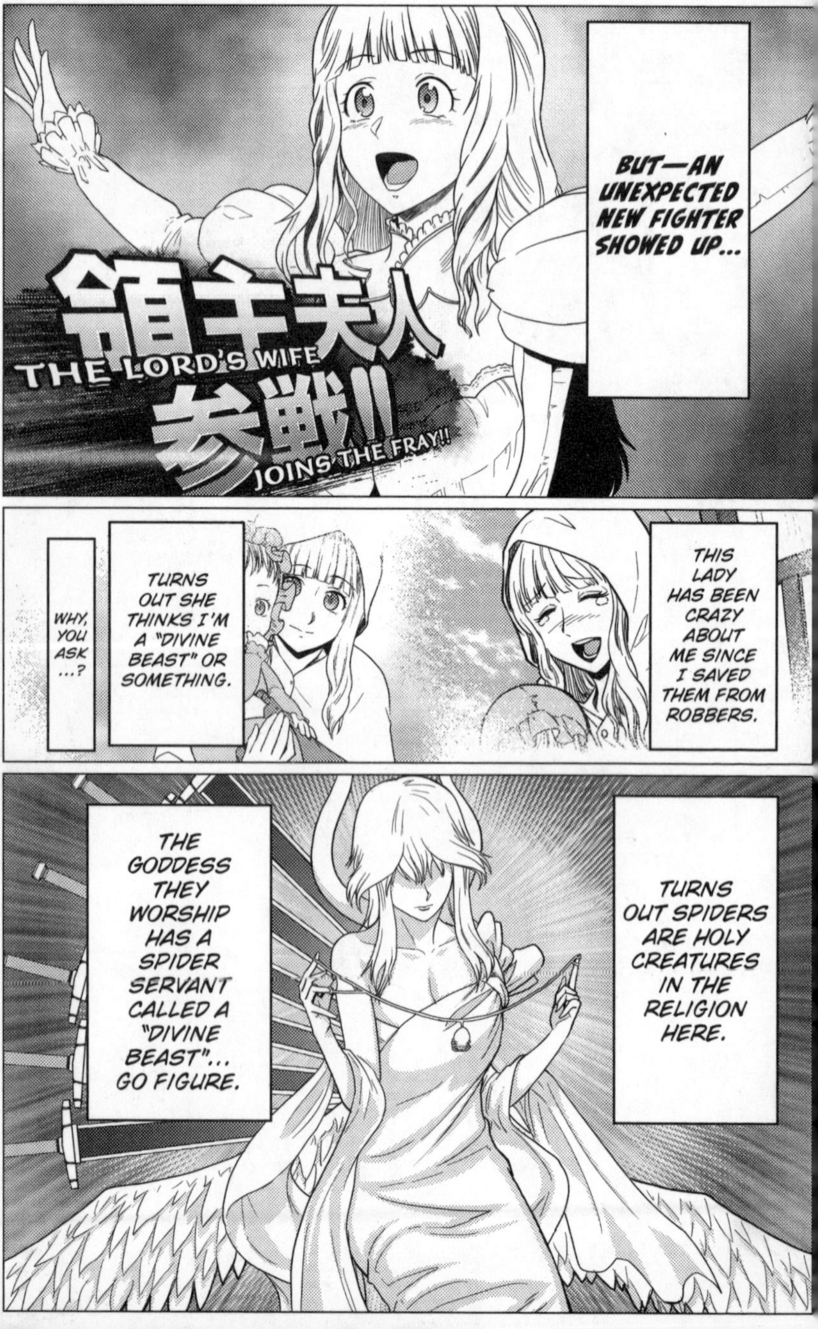
BUT—AN UNEXPECTED NEW FIGHTER SHOWED UP...
領主夫人
THE LORD'S WIFE
参戦!!
JOINS THE FRAY!!
THIS LADY HAS BEEN CRAZY ABOUT ME SINCE I SAVED THEM FROM ROBBERS.
TURNS OUT SHE THINKS I'M A "DIVINE BEAST" OR SOMETHING.
WHY, YOU ASK...?
TURNS OUT SPIDERS ARE HOLY CREATURES IN THE RELIGION HERE.
THE GODDESS THEY WORSHIP HAS A SPIDER SERVANT CALLED A "DIVINE BEAST"... GO FIGURE.

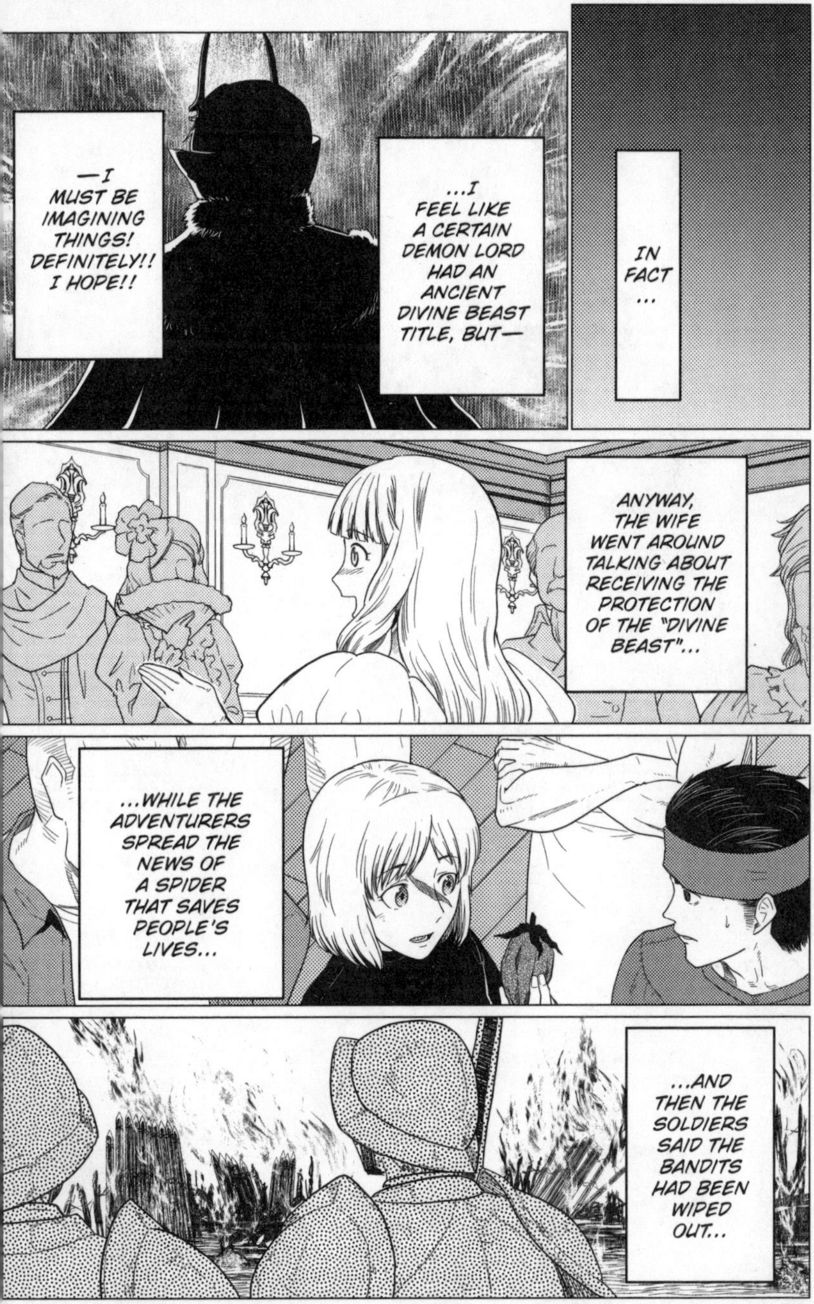
IN FACT...
...I FEEL LIKE A CERTAIN DEMON LORD HAD AN ANCIENT DIVINE BEAST TITLE, BUT—
—I MUST BE IMAGINING THINGS! DEFINITELY!! I HOPE!!
ANYWAY, THE WIFE WENT AROUND TALKING ABOUT RECEIVING THE PROTECTION OF THE "DIVINE BEAST"...
...WHILE THE ADVENTURERS SPREAD THE NEWS OF A SPIDER THAT SAVES PEOPLE'S LIVES...
...AND THEN THE SOLDIERS SAID THE BANDITS HAD BEEN WIPED OUT...

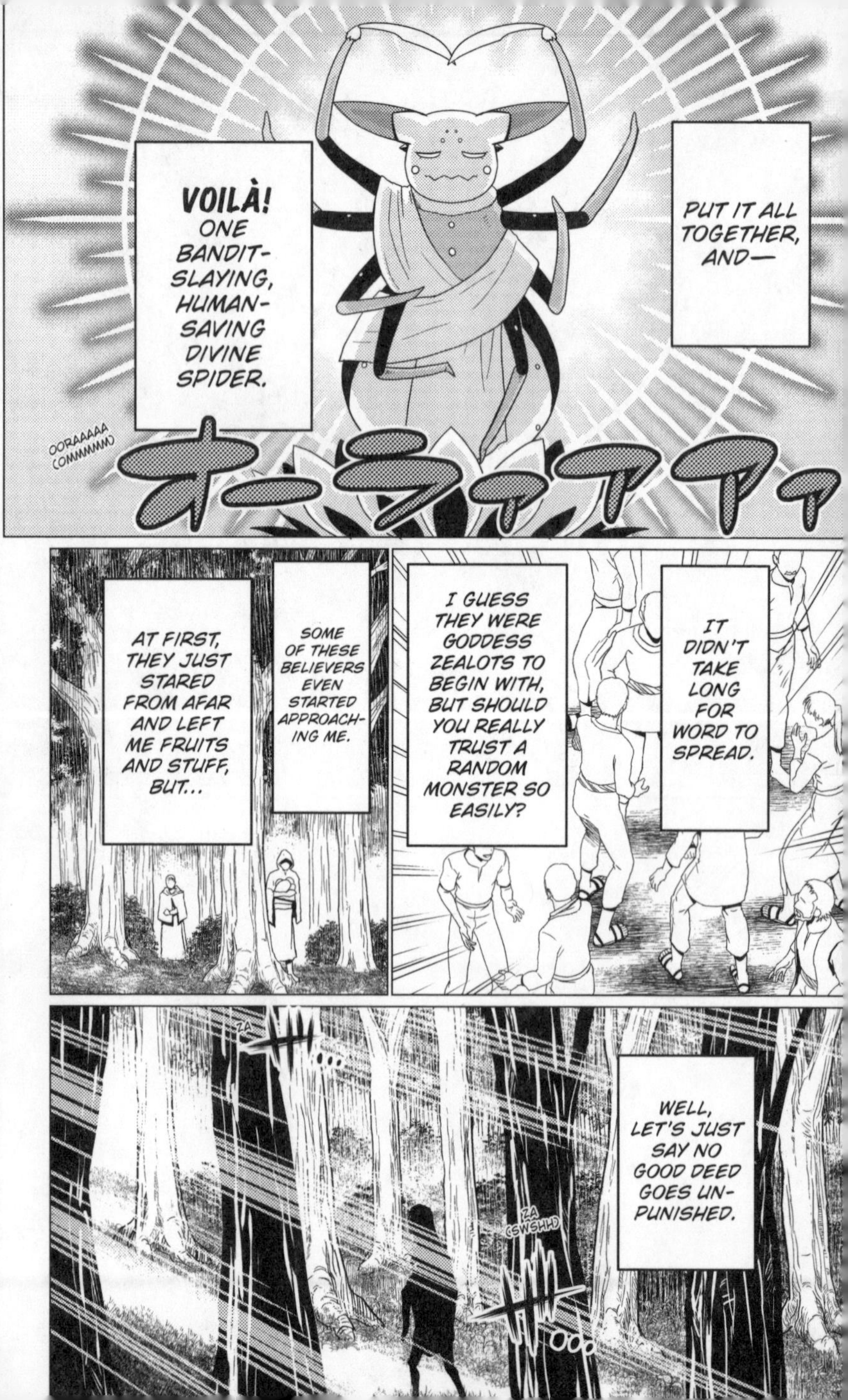
PUT IT ALL TOGETHER, AND—
VOILÀ! ONE BANDIT-SLAYING, HUMAN-SAVING DIVINE SPIDER.
OORAAAAA (OMMMMM)
オーラァァァ
IT DIDN'T TAKE LONG FOR WORD TO SPREAD.
I GUESS THEY WERE GODDESS ZEALOTS TO BEGIN WITH, BUT SHOULD YOU REALLY TRUST A RANDOM MONSTER SO EASILY?
SOME OF THESE BELIEVERS EVEN STARTED APPROACHING ME.
AT FIRST, THEY JUST STARED FROM AFAR AND LEFT ME FRUITS AND STUFF, BUT...
WELL, LET'S JUST SAY NO GOOD DEED GOES UNPUNISHED.
ZA
ZA (SWSHH)

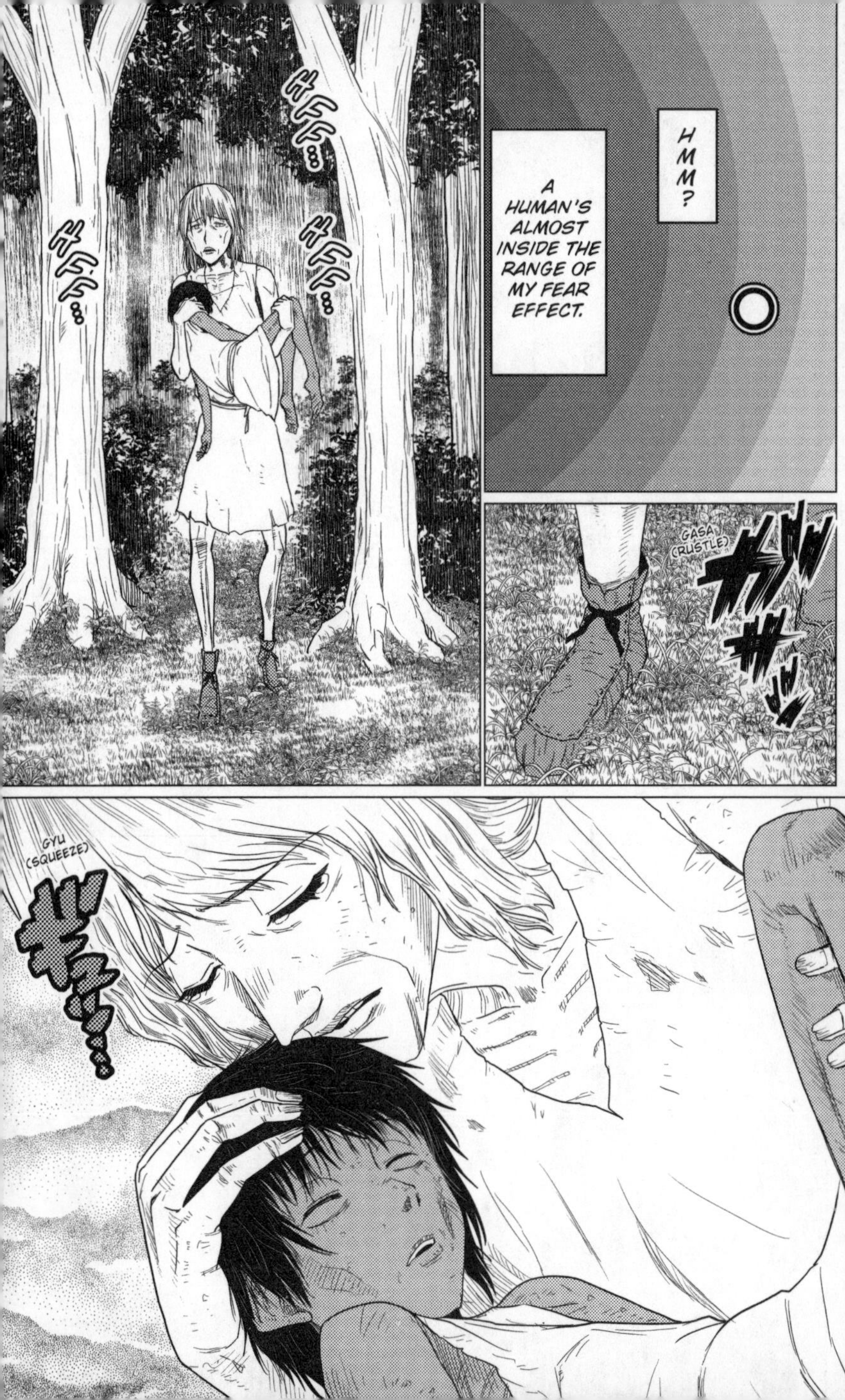
HMM?
A HUMAN'S ALMOST INSIDE THE RANGE OF MY FEAR EFFECT.
GASA (RUSTLE)
HFF...
HFF...
HFF...
GYU (SQUEEZE)

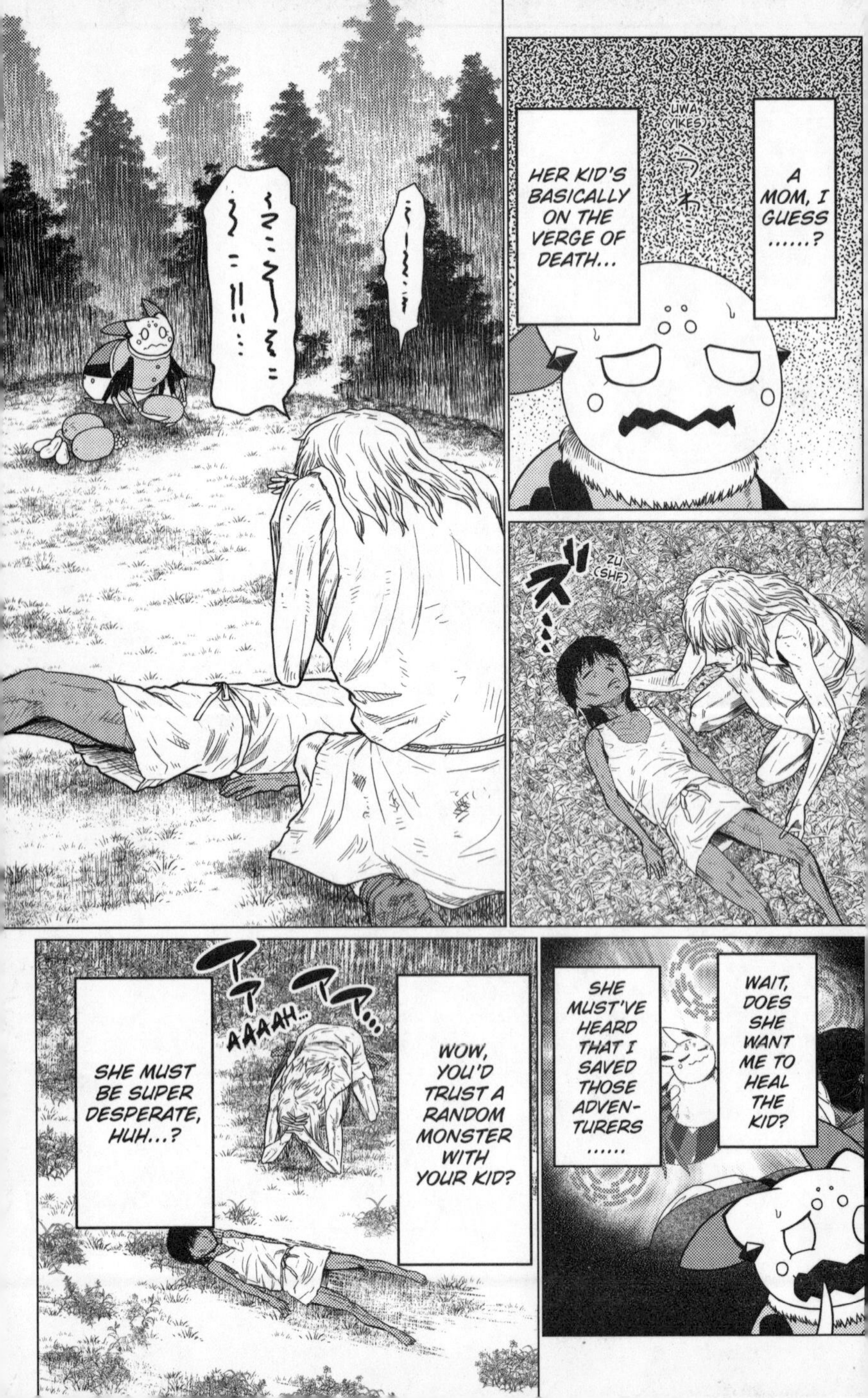
A MOM, I GUESS......?
UWA (YIKES)
HER KID'S BASICALLY ON THE VERGE OF DEATH...
ZU (SHF)
WAIT, DOES SHE WANT ME TO HEAL THE KID?
SHE MUST'VE HEARD THAT I SAVED THOSE ADVENTURERS......
AAAAH...
WOW, YOU'D TRUST A RANDOM MONSTER WITH YOUR KID?
SHE MUST BE SUPER DESPERATE, HUH...?

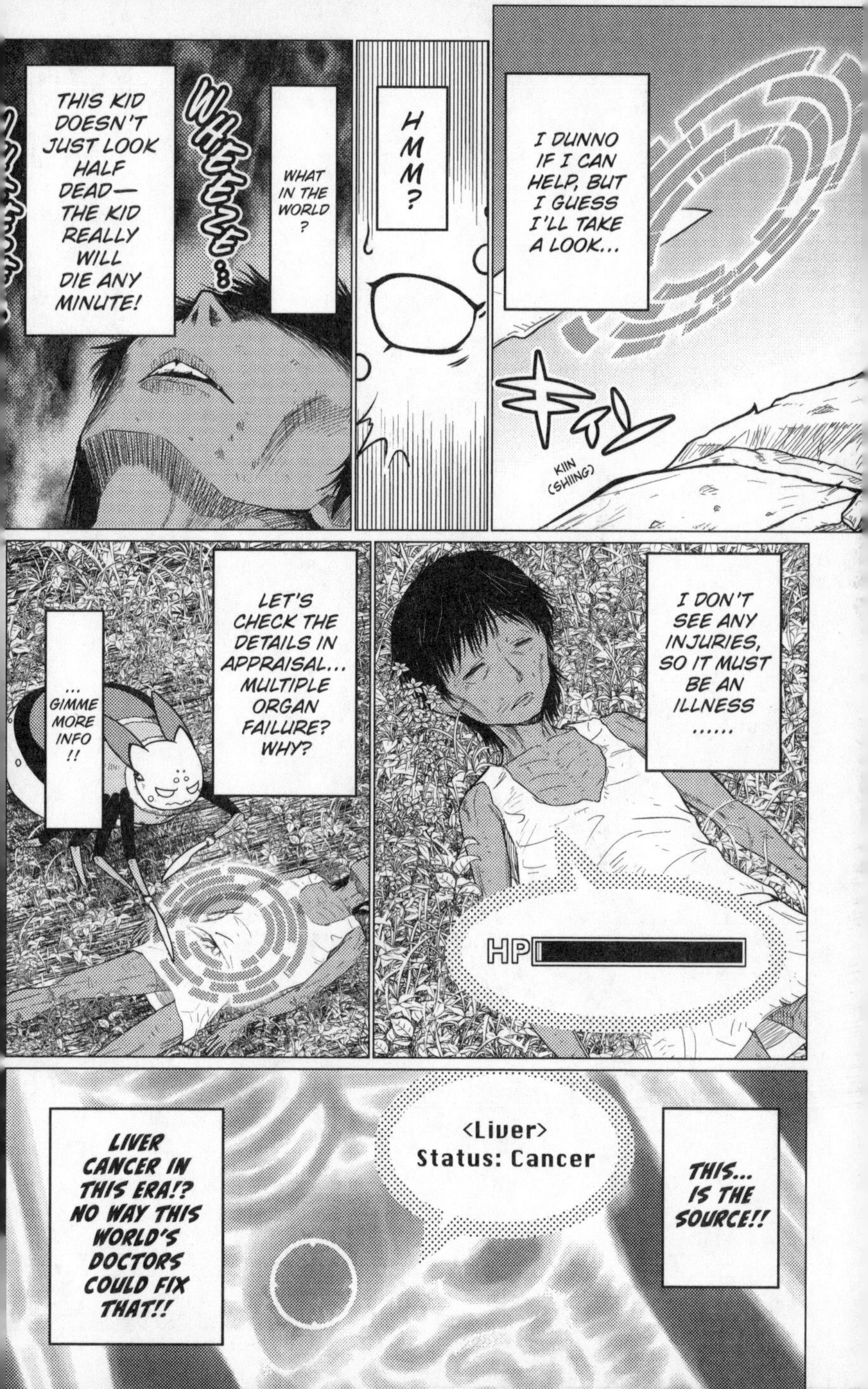
I DUNNO IF I CAN HELP, BUT I GUESS I'LL TAKE A LOOK...
KIIN (SHIING)
HMM?
WHAT IN THE WORLD?
THIS KID DOESN'T JUST LOOK HALF DEAD—THE KID REALLY WILL DIE ANY MINUTE!
I DON'T SEE ANY INJURIES, SO IT MUST BE AN ILLNESS ......
HP
LET'S CHECK THE DETAILS IN APPRAISAL... MULTIPLE ORGAN FAILURE? WHY?
...GIMME MORE INFO!!
THIS... IS THE SOURCE!!
<Liver> Status: Cancer
LIVER CANCER IN THIS ERA!? NO WAY THIS WORLD'S DOCTORS COULD FIX THAT!!

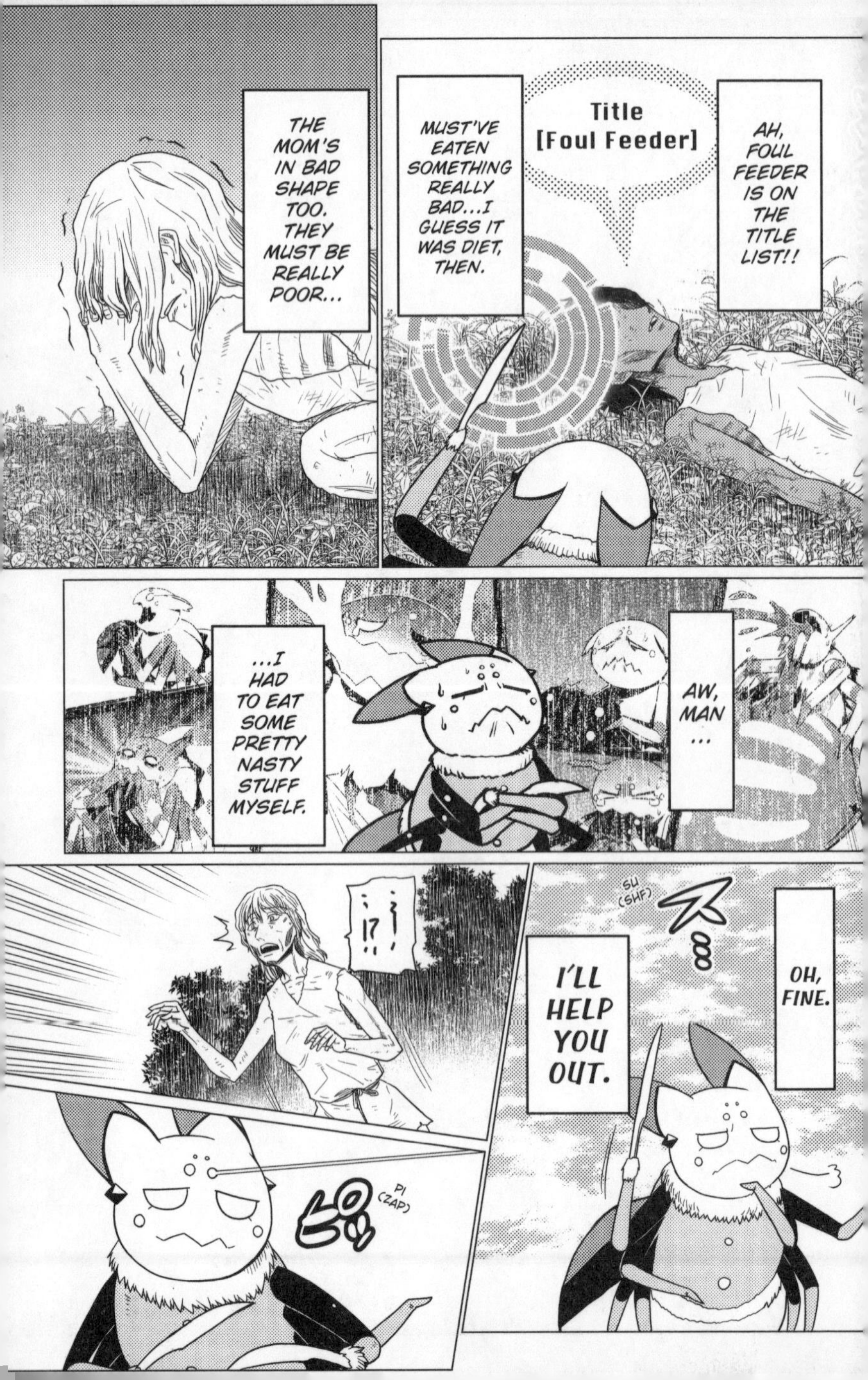

AH, FOUL FEEDER IS ON THE TITLE LIST!!
Title [Foul Feeder]
MUST'VE EATEN SOMETHING REALLY BAD...I GUESS IT WAS DIET, THEN.
THE MOM'S IN BAD SHAPE TOO. THEY MUST BE REALLY POOR...
AW, MAN ...
...I HAD TO EAT SOME PRETTY NASTY STUFF MYSELF.
OH, FINE.
SU (SHF)
I'LL HELP YOU OUT.
!?
PI (ZAP)

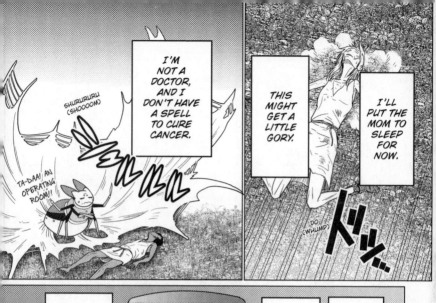

I'LL PUT THE MOM TO SLEEP FOR NOW.
THIS MIGHT GET A LITTLE GORY.
DO (WHUMP)
I'M NOT A DOCTOR, AND I DON'T HAVE A SPELL TO CURE CANCER.
SHURURURU (SHOOOOM)
TA-DAA! AN OPERATING ROOM!!
SO I'LL JUST USE THE POWER OF RAW MAGIC.
I'LL CUT OUT THE BAD PARTS OF THE LIVER...
...AND USE HEALING MAGIC TO REGROW IT.
WELL, THEN—
LET THE OPERATION BEGIN!!

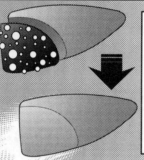

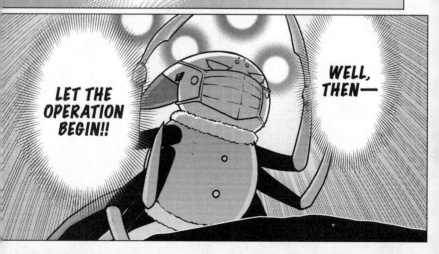

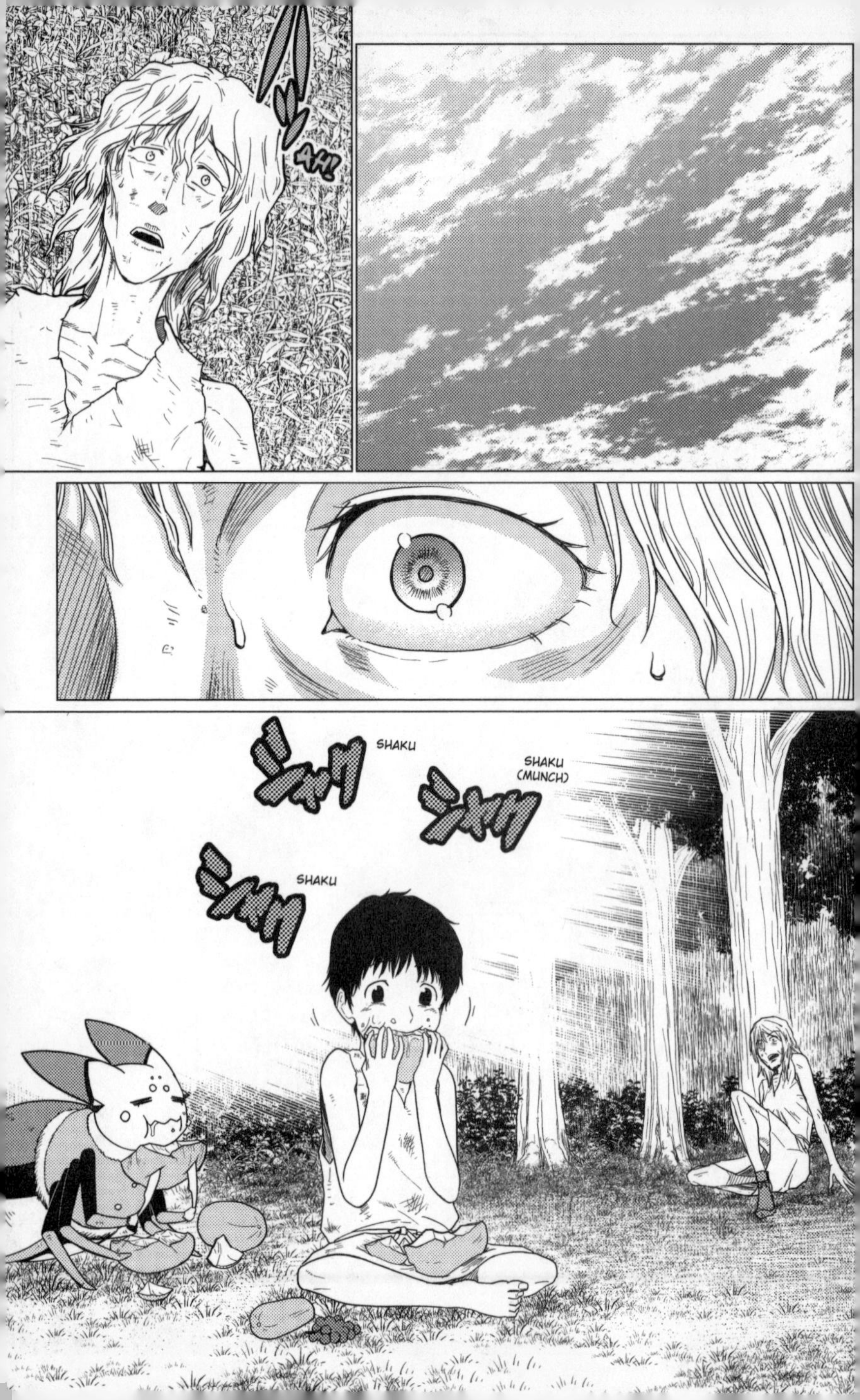
AH!
SHAKU (MUNCH)
SHAKU
SHAKU

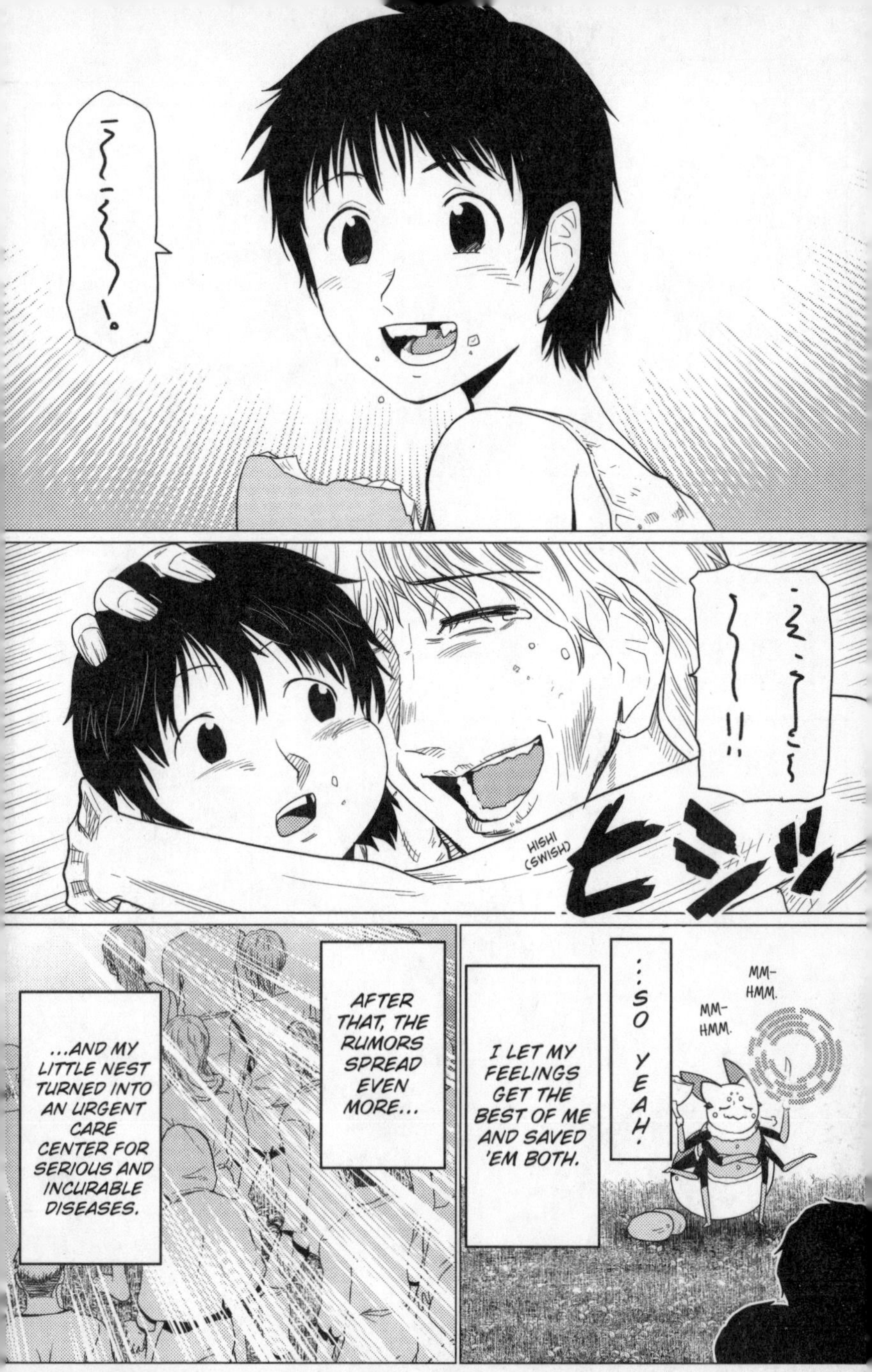
HISHI (SWISH)
MM-HMM.
MM-HMM.
...SO YEAH!
I LET MY FEELINGS GET THE BEST OF ME AND SAVED 'EM BOTH.
AFTER THAT, THE RUMORS SPREAD EVEN MORE...
...AND MY LITTLE NEST TURNED INTO AN URGENT CARE CENTER FOR SERIOUS AND INCURABLE DISEASES.

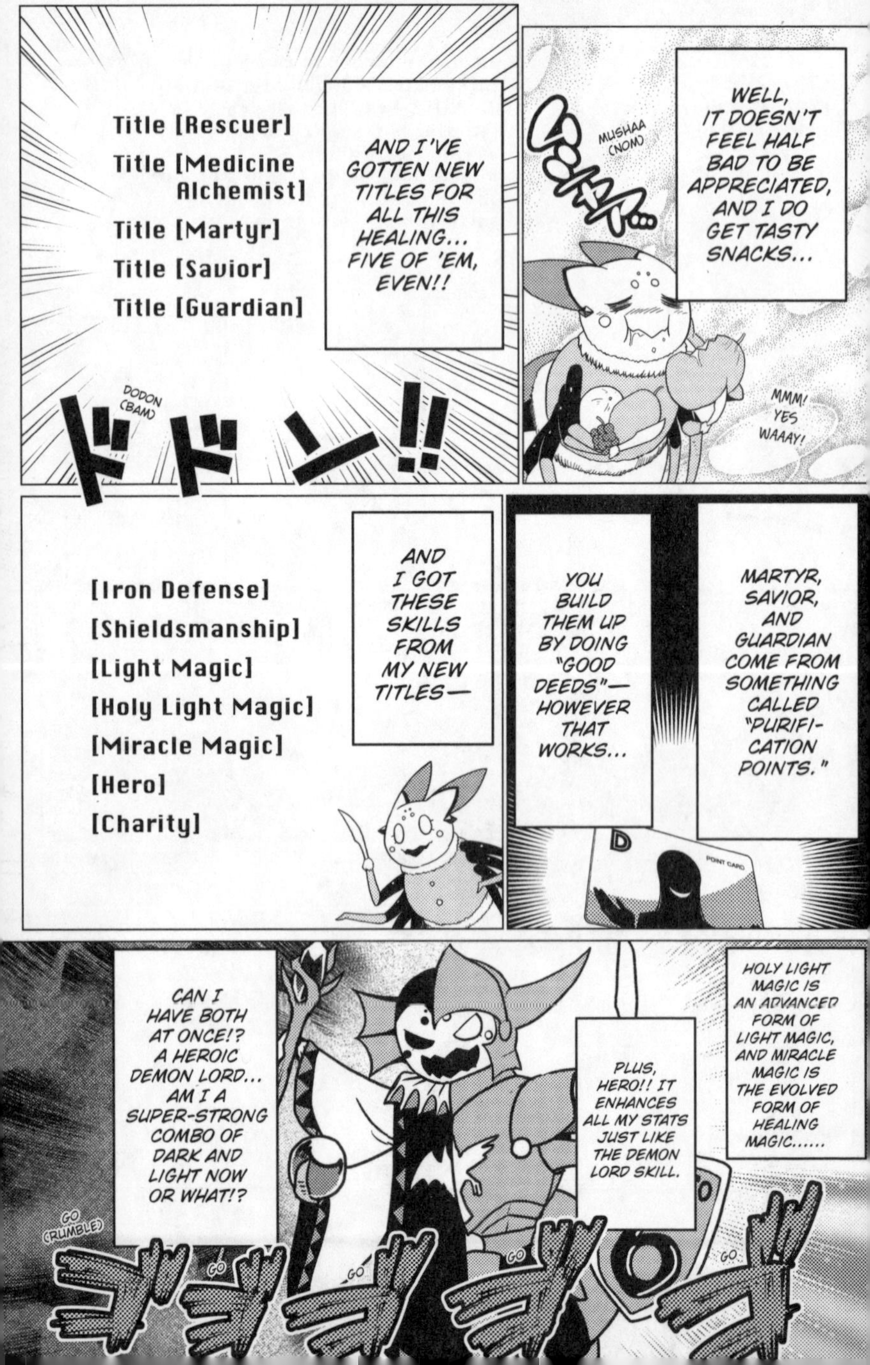

WELL, IT DOESN'T FEEL HALF BAD TO BE APPRECIATED, AND I DO GET TASTY SNACKS...
MUSHAA (NOM)
MMM! YES WAAAY!
AND I'VE GOTTEN NEW TITLES FOR ALL THIS HEALING... FIVE OF 'EM, EVEN!!
Title [Rescuer]
Title [Medicine Alchemist]
Title [Martyr]
Title [Savior]
Title [Guardian]
DODON (BAM)
ドドン!!
MARTYR, SAVIOR, AND GUARDIAN COME FROM SOMETHING CALLED "PURIFICATION POINTS."
YOU BUILD THEM UP BY DOING "GOOD DEEDS"—HOWEVER THAT WORKS...
D
POINT CARD
AND I GOT THESE SKILLS FROM MY NEW TITLES—
[Iron Defense]
[Shieldsmanship]
[Light Magic]
[Holy Light Magic]
[Miracle Magic]
[Hero]
[Charity]
HOLY LIGHT MAGIC IS AN ADVANCED FORM OF LIGHT MAGIC, AND MIRACLE MAGIC IS THE EVOLVED FORM OF HEALING MAGIC......
PLUS, HERO!! IT ENHANCES ALL MY STATS JUST LIKE THE DEMON LORD SKILL.
CAN I HAVE BOTH AT ONCE!? A HEROIC DEMON LORD... AM I A SUPER-STRONG COMBO OF DARK AND LIGHT NOW OR WHAT!?
GO (RUMBLE)
GO
GO
GO
GO

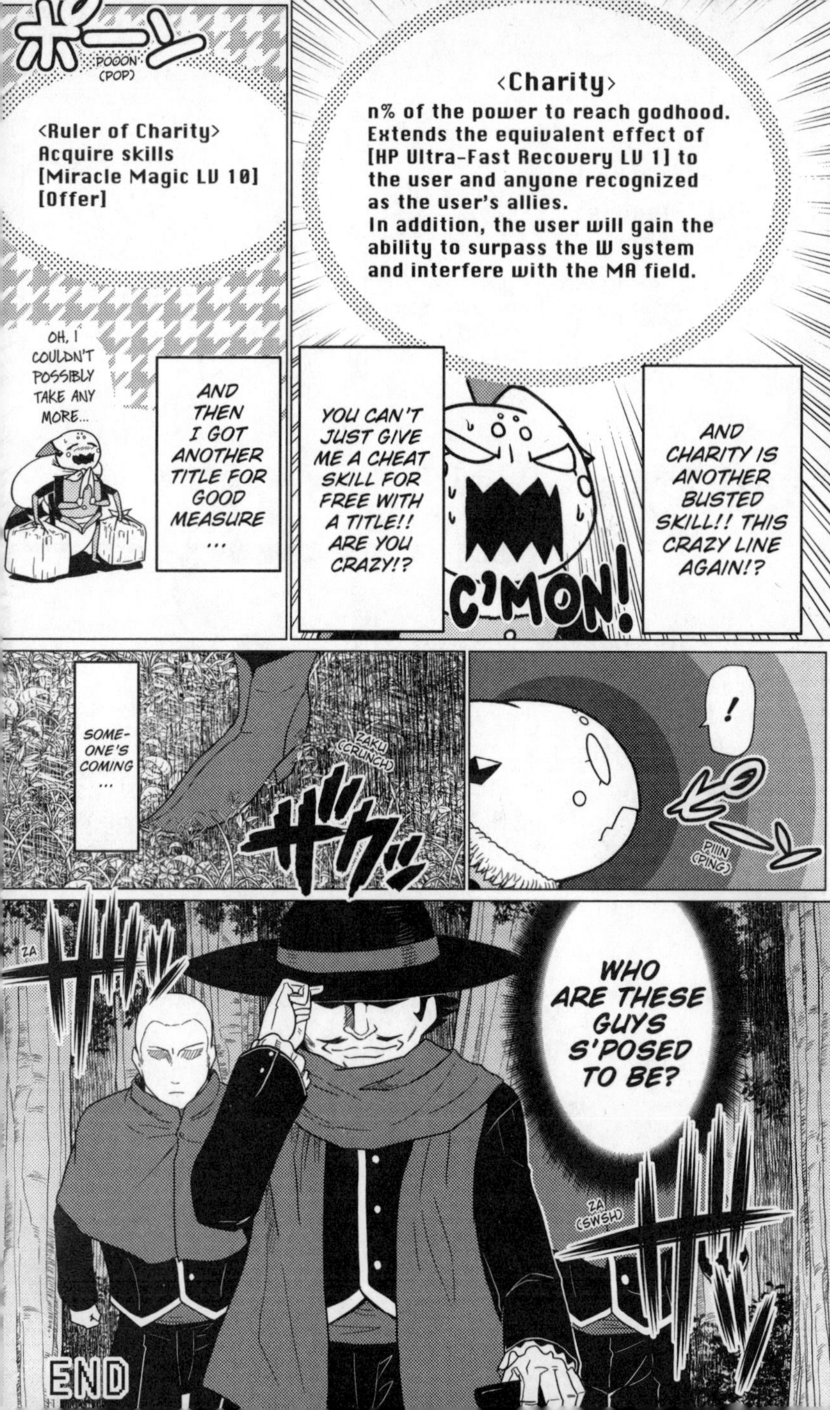

<Charity>
n% of the power to reach godhood. Extends the equivalent effect of [HP Ultra-Fast Recovery LV 1] to the user and anyone recognized as the user's allies. In addition, the user will gain the ability to surpass the W system and interfere with the MA field.
AND CHARITY IS ANOTHER BUSTED SKILL!! THIS CRAZY LINE AGAIN!?
C'MON!
YOU CAN'T JUST GIVE ME A CHEAT SKILL FOR FREE WITH A TITLE!! ARE YOU CRAZY!?
ポーン
POOON (POP)
<Ruler of Charity> Acquire skills [Miracle Magic LV 10] [Offer]
AND THEN I GOT ANOTHER TITLE FOR GOOD MEASURE ...
OH, I COULDN'T POSSIBLY TAKE ANY MORE...
!
PIIIN (PING)
SOME-ONE'S COMING ...
ZAKU (CRUNCH)
ザクッ
WHO ARE THESE GUYS S'POSED TO BE?
ZA (SWSH)
ザッ
ZA
ザッ
END

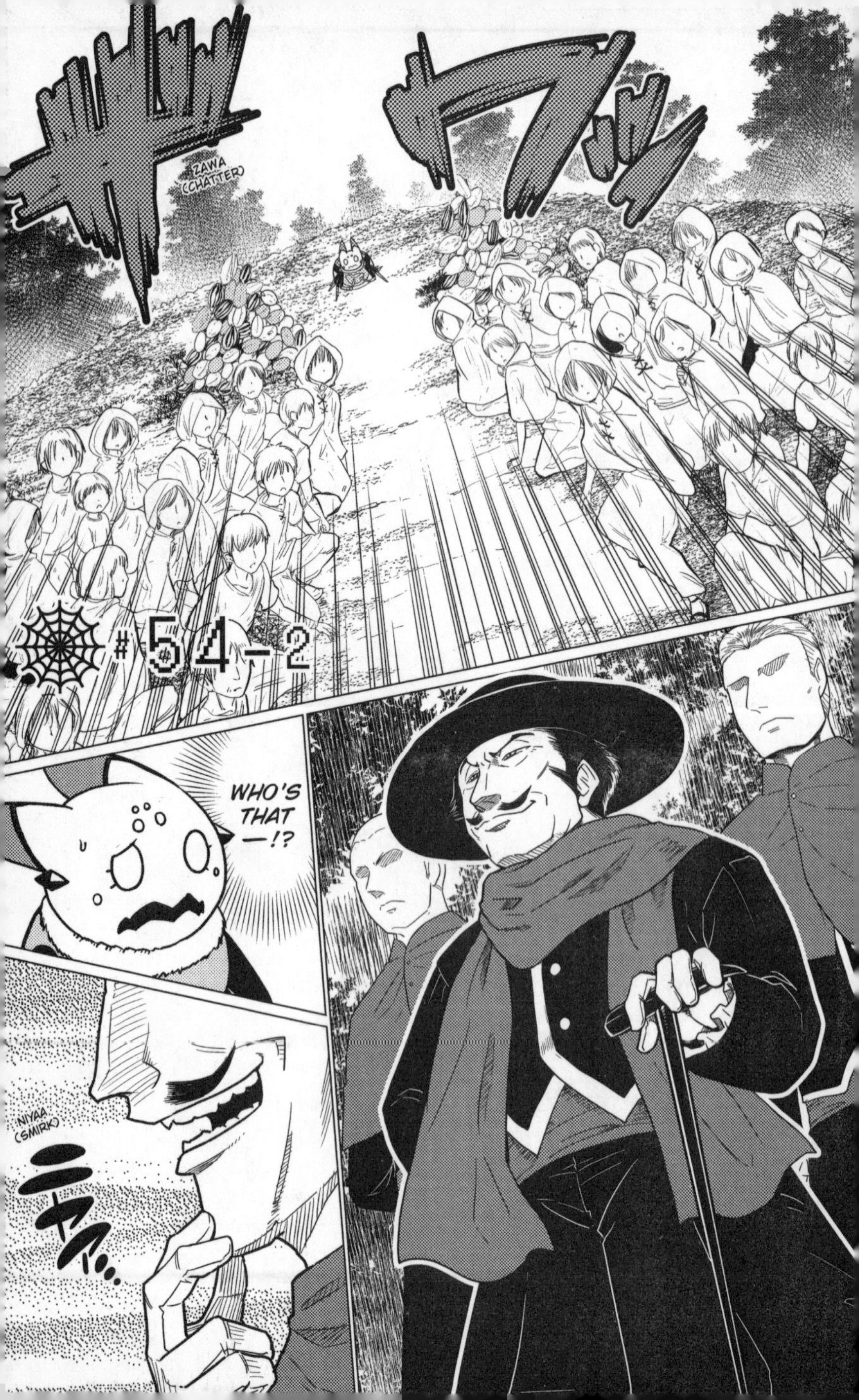
ZAWA (CHATTER)
#54-2
WHO'S THAT—!?
NIYAA (SMIRK)

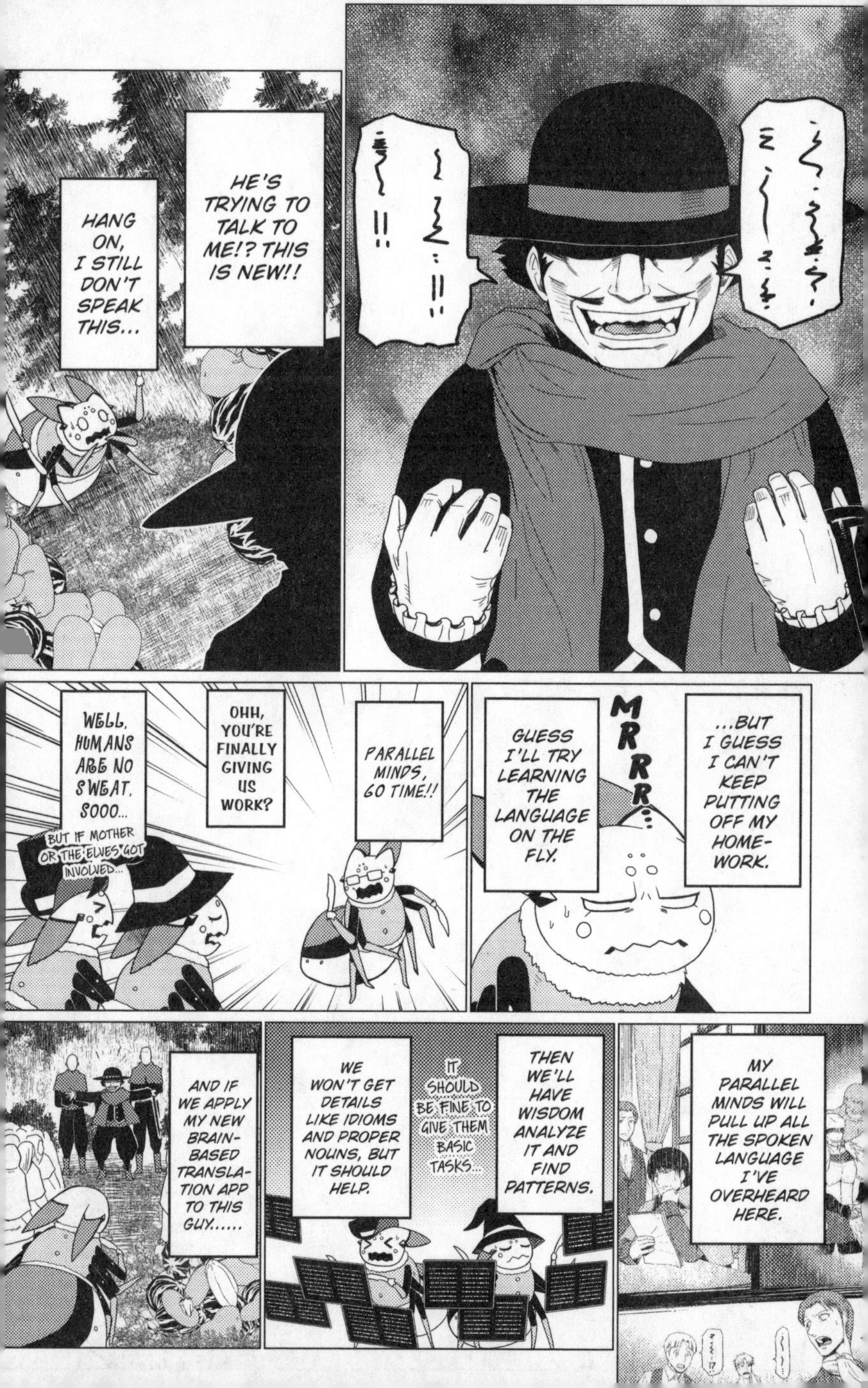
HE'S TRYING TO TALK TO ME!? THIS IS NEW!!
HANG ON, I STILL DON'T SPEAK THIS...
...BUT I GUESS I CAN'T KEEP PUTTING OFF MY HOMEWORK.
MRRR...
GUESS I'LL TRY LEARNING THE LANGUAGE ON THE FLY.
PARALLEL MINDS, GO TIME!!
OHH, YOU'RE FINALLY GIVING US WORK?
WELL, HUMANS ARE NO SWEAT. SOOO...
BUT IF MOTHER OR THE ELVES GOT INVOLVED...
MY PARALLEL MINDS WILL PULL UP ALL THE SPOKEN LANGUAGE I'VE OVERHEARD HERE.
THEN WE'LL HAVE WISDOM ANALYZE IT AND FIND PATTERNS.
IT SHOULD BE FINE TO GIVE THEM BASIC TASKS...
WE WON'T GET DETAILS LIKE IDIOMS AND PROPER NOUNS, BUT IT SHOULD HELP.
AND IF WE APPLY MY NEW BRAIN-BASED TRANSLATION APP TO THIS GUY......

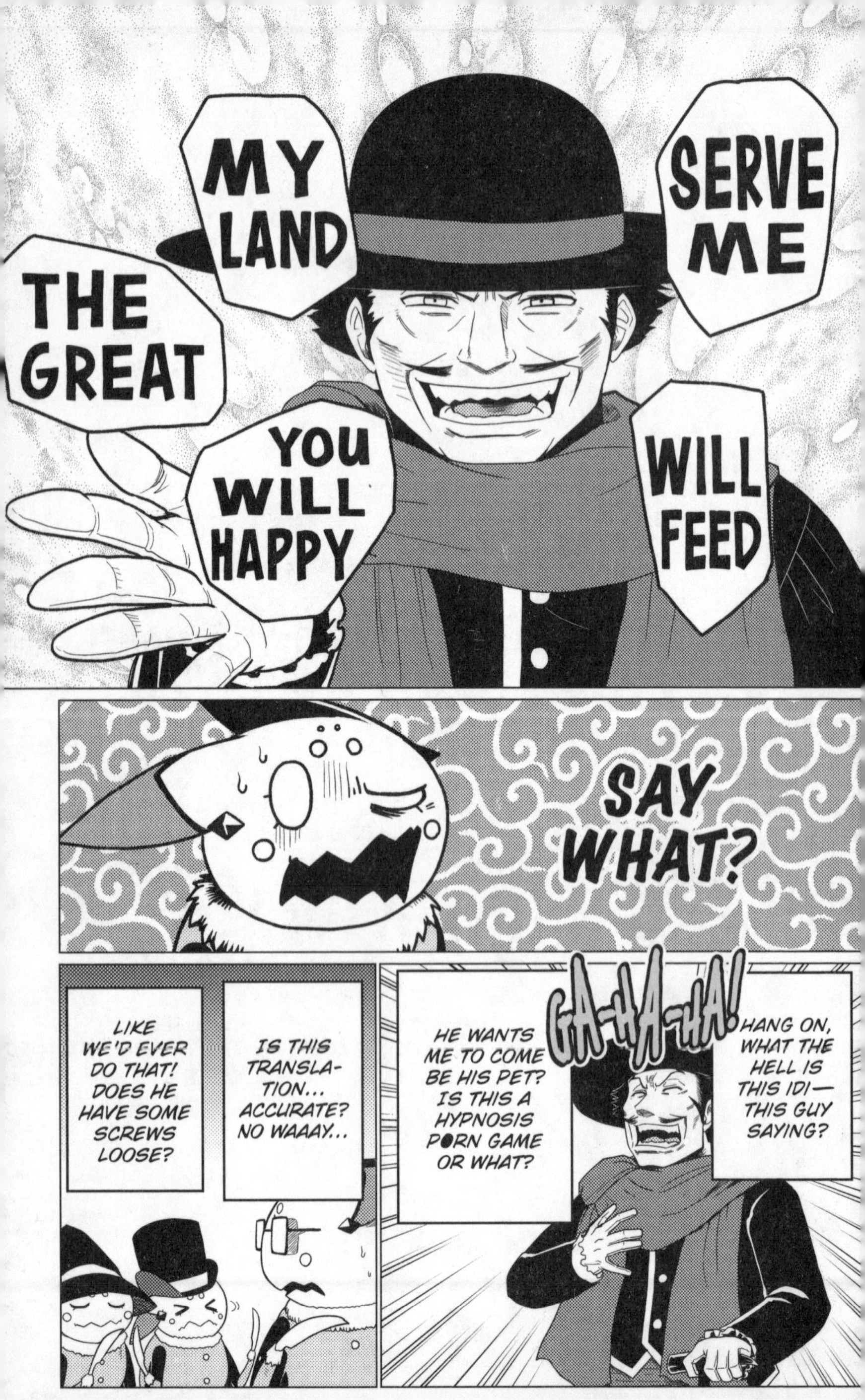
SERVE ME
MY LAND
THE GREAT
WILL FEED
YOU WILL HAPPY
SAY WHAT?
GA-HA-HA!
HANG ON, WHAT THE HELL IS THIS IDI— THIS GUY SAYING?
HE WANTS ME TO COME BE HIS PET? IS THIS A HYPNOSIS P●RN GAME OR WHAT?
IS THIS TRANSLA-TION... ACCURATE? NO WAAAY...
LIKE WE'D EVER DO THAT! DOES HE HAVE SOME SCREWS LOOSE?

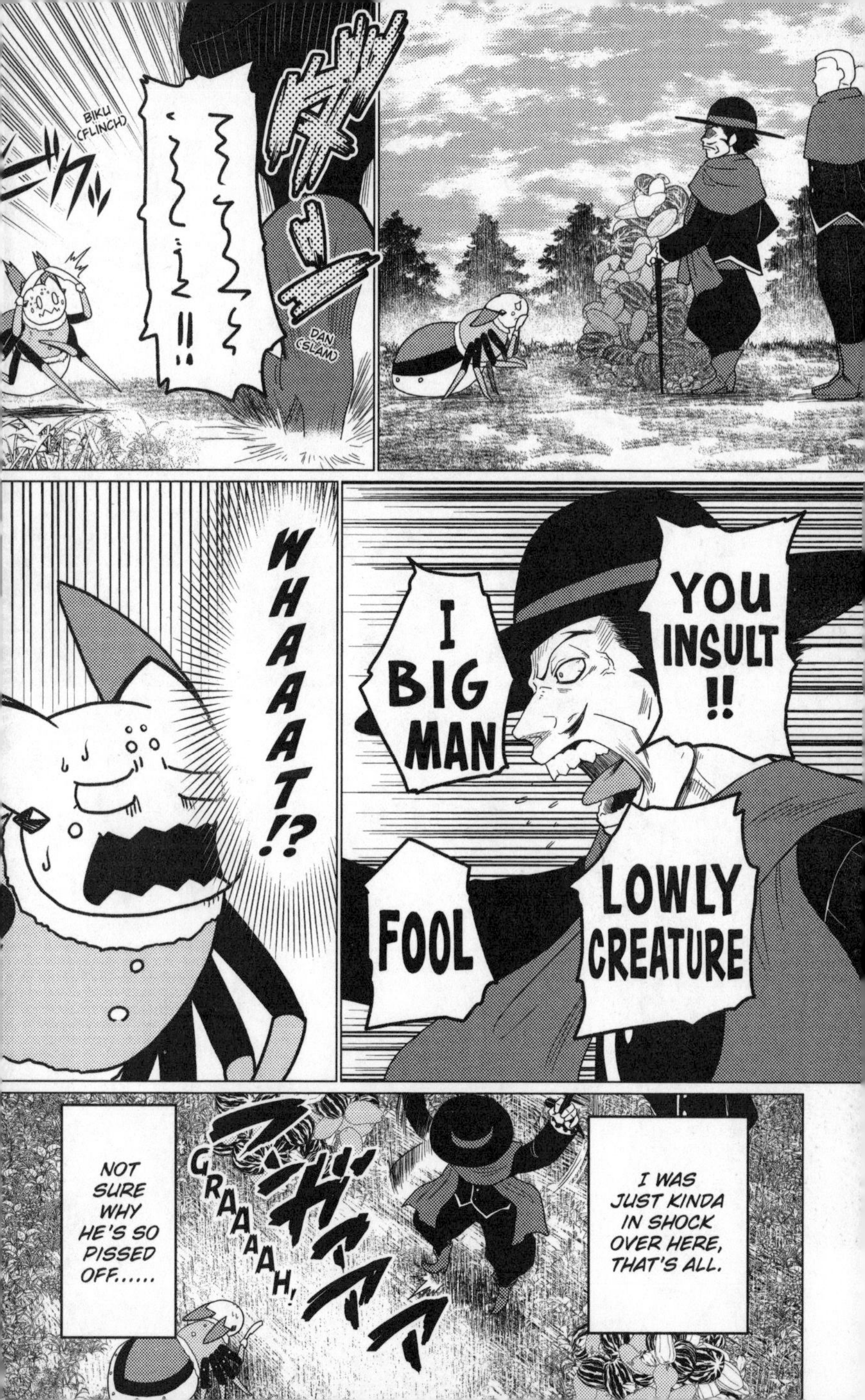
DAN (SLAM)
BIKU (FLINCH)
YOU INSULT!!
I BIG MAN
LOWLY CREATURE
FOOL
WHAAAAAT!?
I WAS JUST KINDA IN SHOCK OVER HERE, THAT'S ALL.
GRAAAAAH!
NOT SURE WHY HE'S SO PISSED OFF......

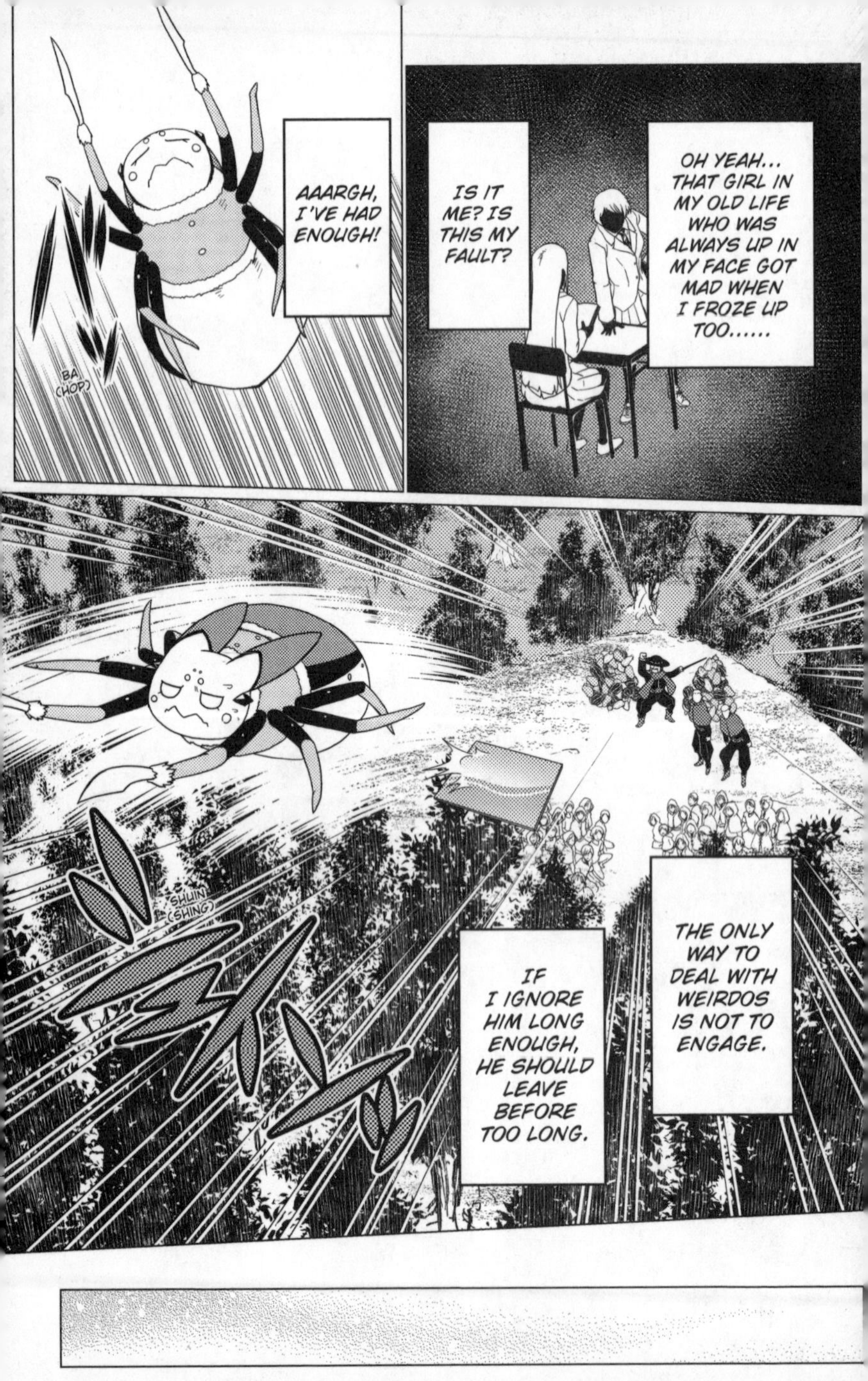
OH YEAH... THAT GIRL IN MY OLD LIFE WHO WAS ALWAYS UP IN MY FACE GOT MAD WHEN I FROZE UP TOO......
IS IT ME? IS THIS MY FAULT?
AAARGH, I'VE HAD ENOUGH!
BA (HOP)
THE ONLY WAY TO DEAL WITH WEIRDOS IS NOT TO ENGAGE.
IF I IGNORE HIM LONG ENOUGH, HE SHOULD LEAVE BEFORE TOO LONG.
SHUIN (SHING)

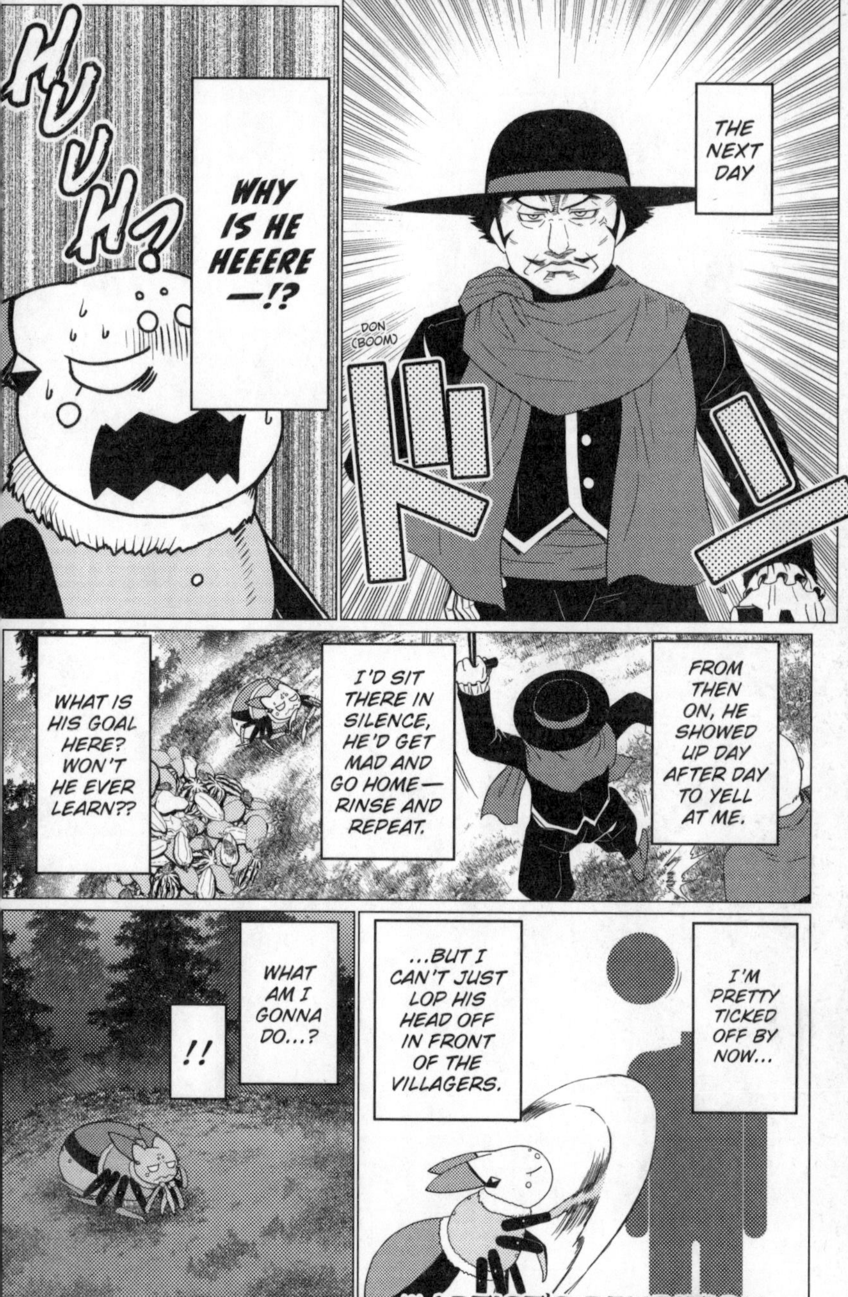
THE NEXT DAY
DON (BOOM)
HUUH?
WHY IS HE HEEERE—!?
FROM THEN ON, HE SHOWED UP DAY AFTER DAY TO YELL AT ME.
I'D SIT THERE IN SILENCE, HE'D GET MAD AND GO HOME—RINSE AND REPEAT.
WHAT IS HIS GOAL HERE? WON'T HE EVER LEARN??
I'M PRETTY TICKED OFF BY NOW...
...BUT I CAN'T JUST LOP HIS HEAD OFF IN FRONT OF THE VILLAGERS.
※ARTIST'S RENDITION
WHAT AM I GONNA DO...?
!!

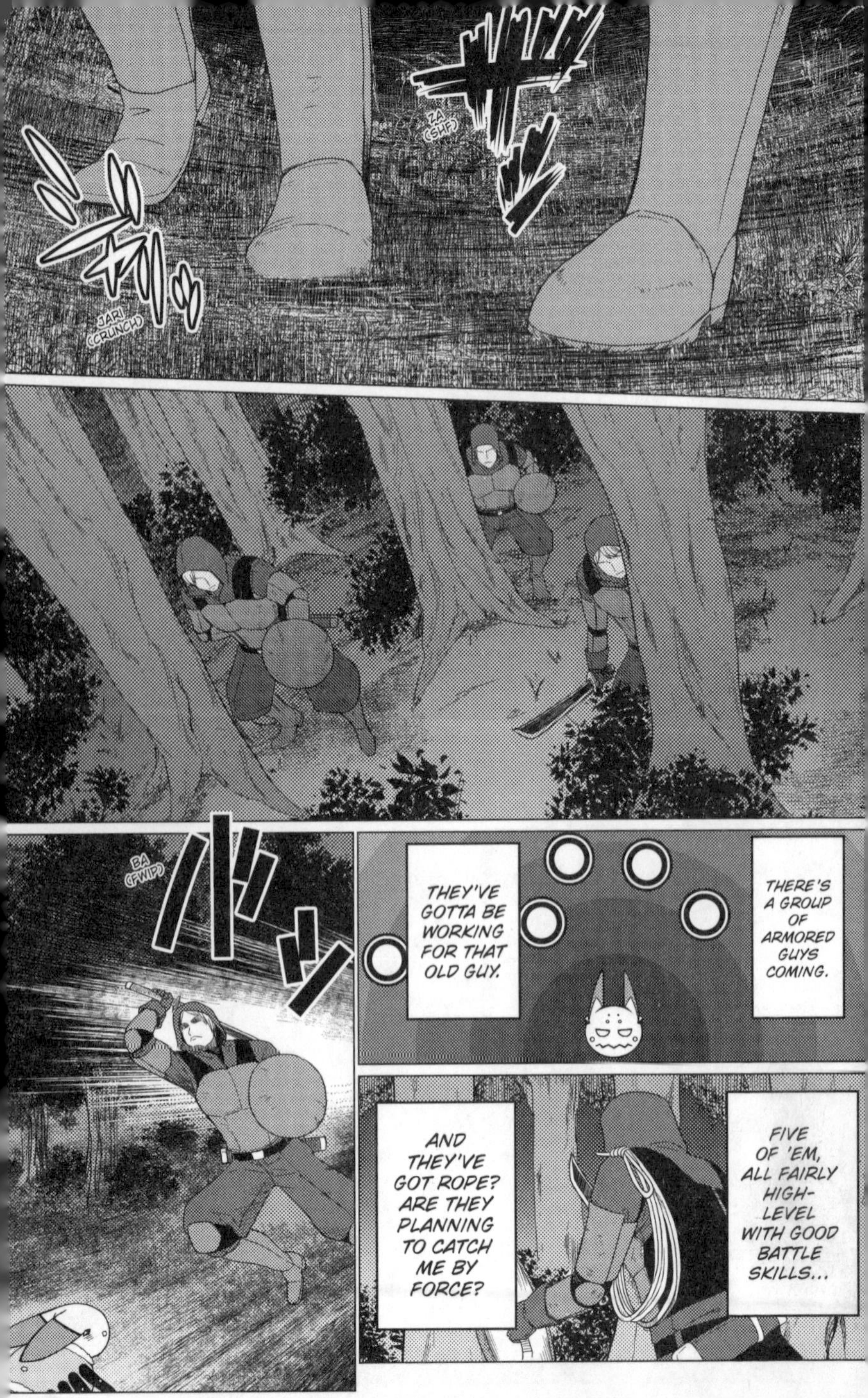
ZA (SHF)
JARI (CRUNCH)
THERE'S A GROUP OF ARMORED GUYS COMING.
THEY'VE GOTTA BE WORKING FOR THAT OLD GUY.
FIVE OF 'EM, ALL FAIRLY HIGH-LEVEL WITH GOOD BATTLE SKILLS...
AND THEY'VE GOT ROPE? ARE THEY PLANNING TO CATCH ME BY FORCE?
BA (FWIP)

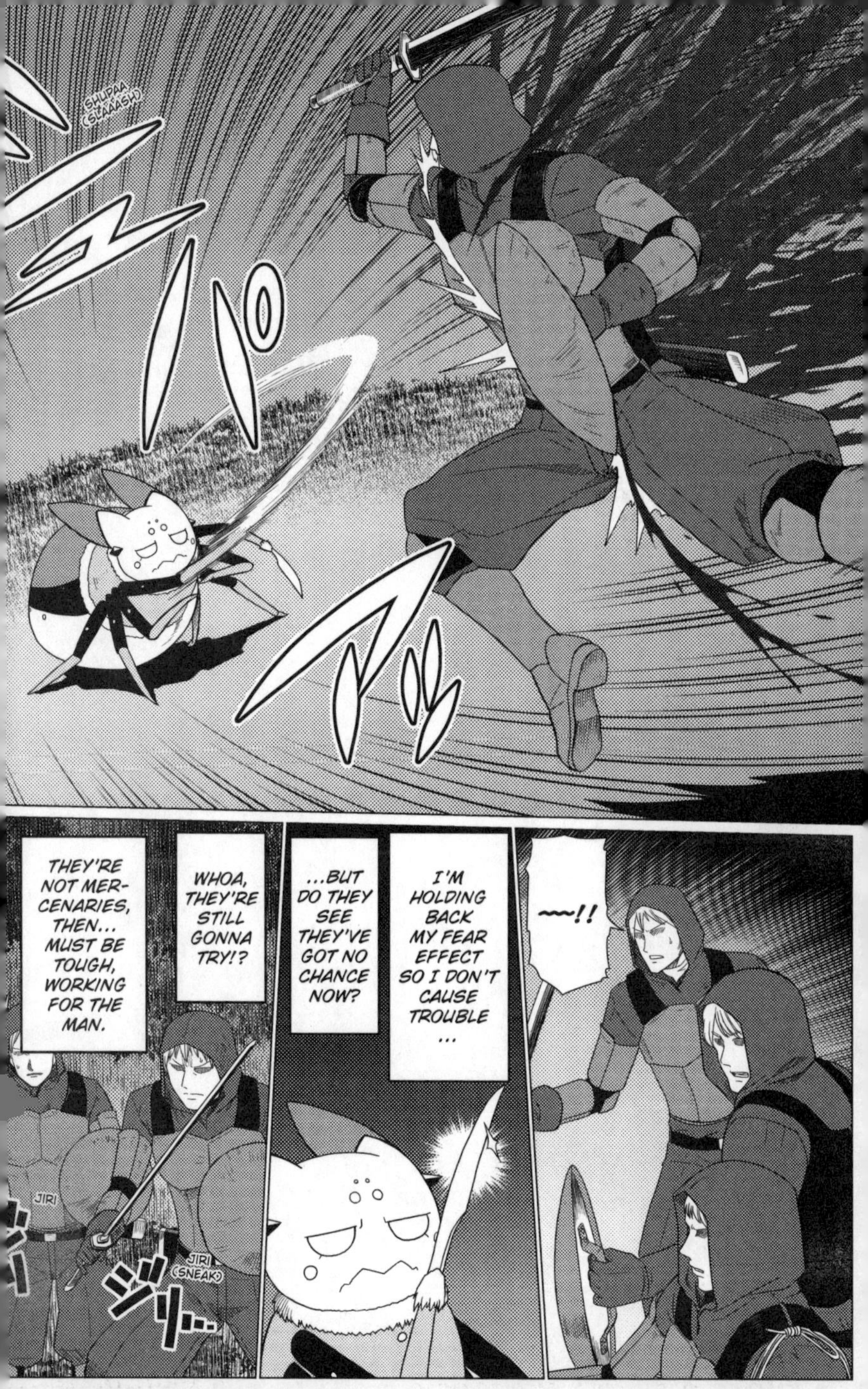
SHUPAA (SLAAASH)
~~!!
I'M HOLDING BACK MY FEAR EFFECT SO I DON'T CAUSE TROUBLE...
...BUT DO THEY SEE THEY'VE GOT NO CHANCE NOW?
WHOA, THEY'RE STILL GONNA TRY!?
THEY'RE NOT MER-CENARIES, THEN... MUST BE TOUGH, WORKING FOR THE MAN.
JIRI
JIRI (SNEAK)

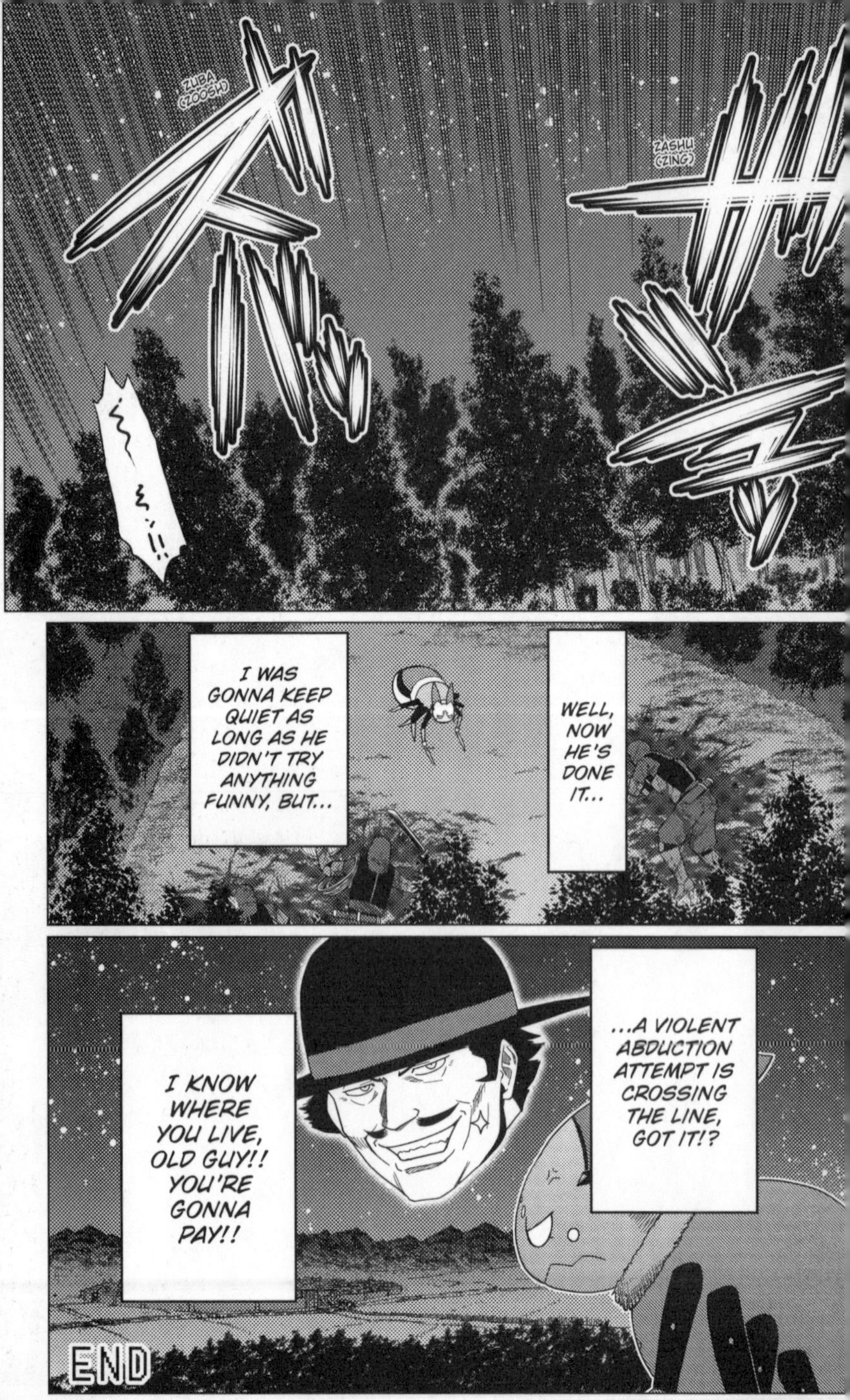
ZASHU (ZING)
ZUBA (ZOOSH)
WELL, NOW HE'S DONE IT...
I WAS GONNA KEEP QUIET AS LONG AS HE DIDN'T TRY ANYTHING FUNNY, BUT...
...A VIOLENT ABDUCTION ATTEMPT IS CROSSING THE LINE, GOT IT!?
I KNOW WHERE YOU LIVE, OLD GUY!! YOU'RE GONNA PAY!!
END

So I'm a Spider, So What?

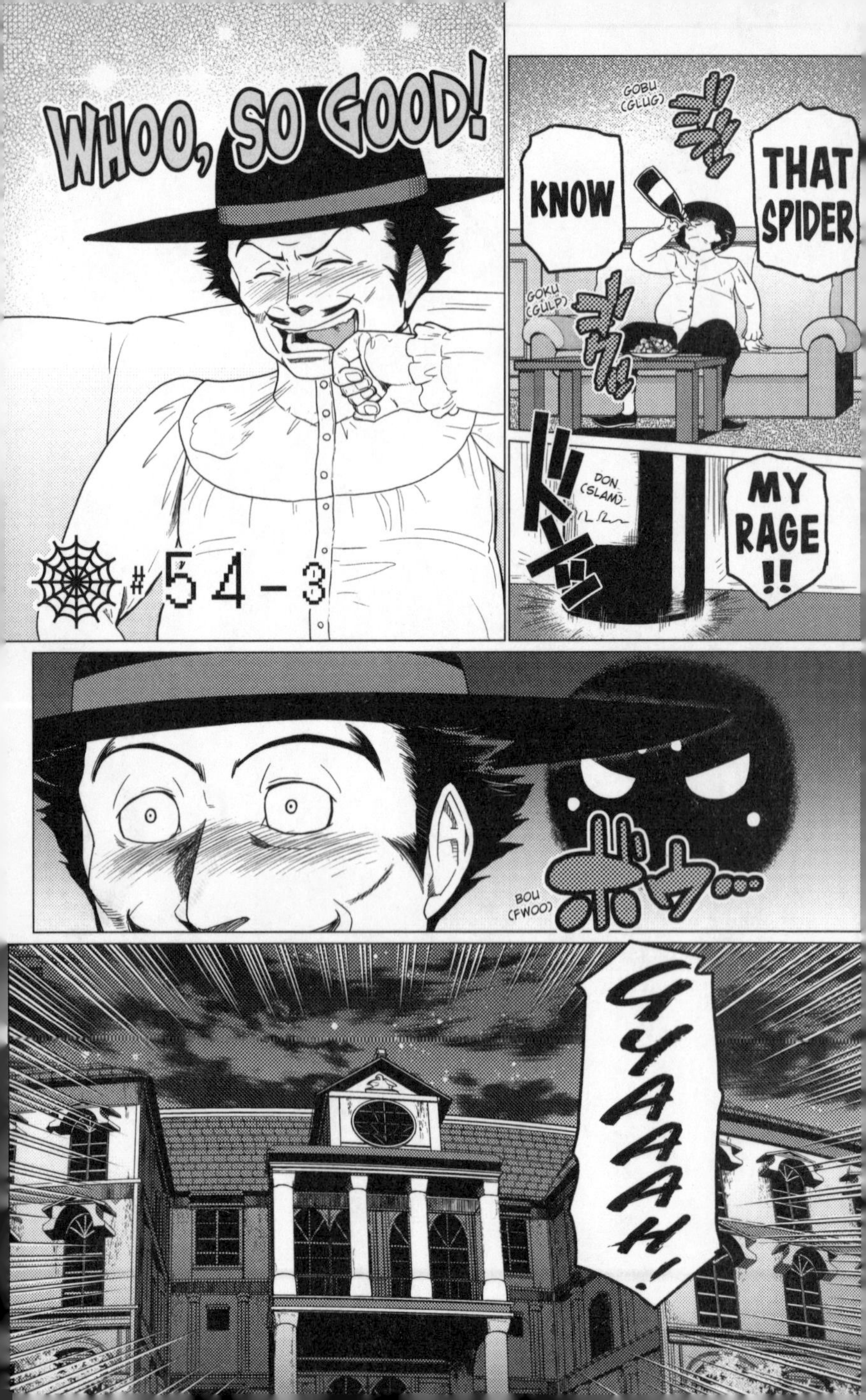
GOBU (GLUG)
THAT SPIDER
KNOW
GOKU (GULP)
MY RAGE!!
DON (SLAM)
WHOO, SO GOOD!
#54-3
BOU (FWOO)
GYAAAAAH!

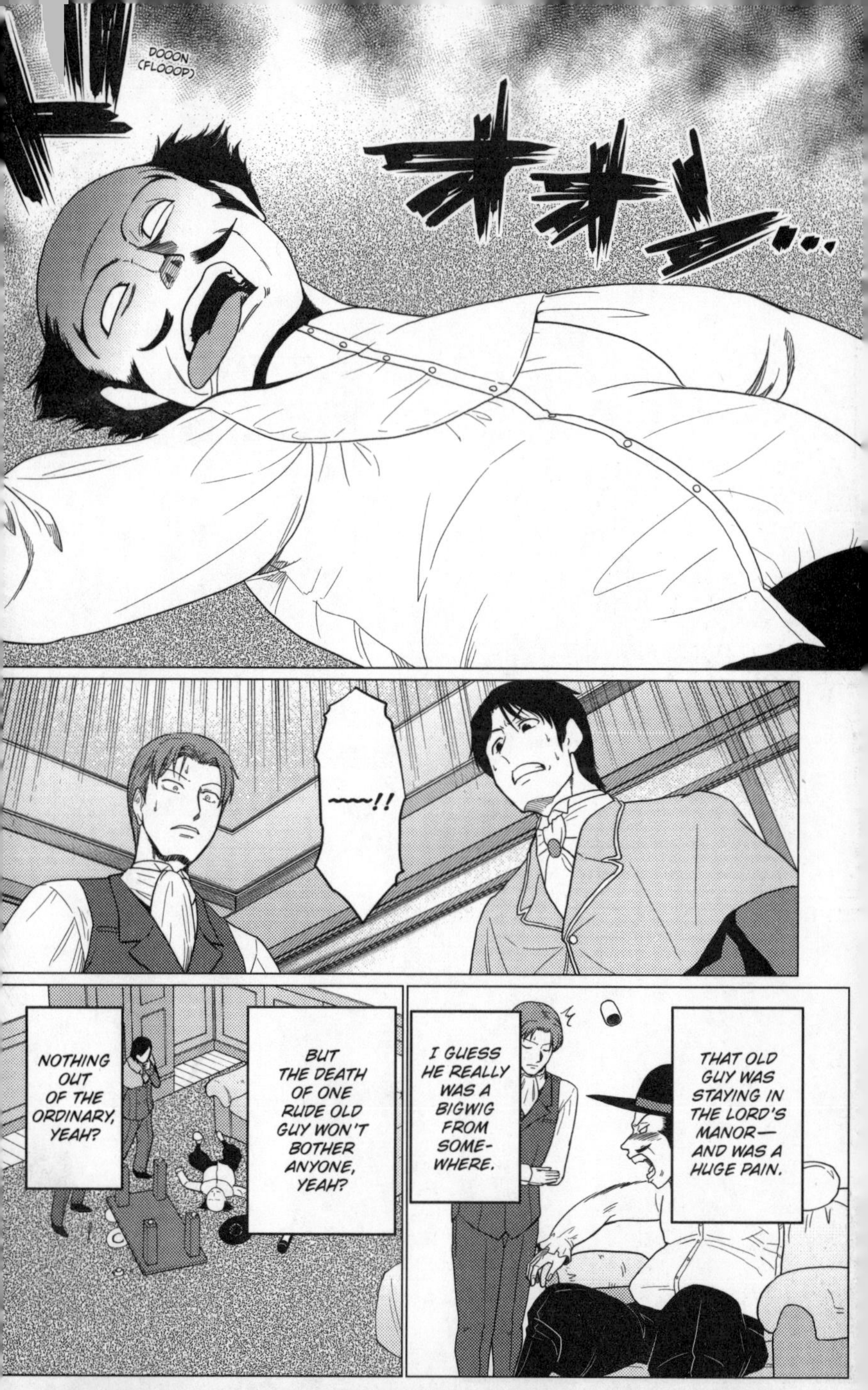
DOOON
(FLOOOP)
~~~~!!
THAT OLD GUY WAS STAYING IN THE LORD'S MANOR—AND WAS A HUGE PAIN.
I GUESS HE REALLY WAS A BIGWIG FROM SOME-WHERE.
BUT THE DEATH OF ONE RUDE OLD GUY WON'T BOTHER ANYONE, YEAH?
NOTHING OUT OF THE ORDINARY, YEAH?
~~~~

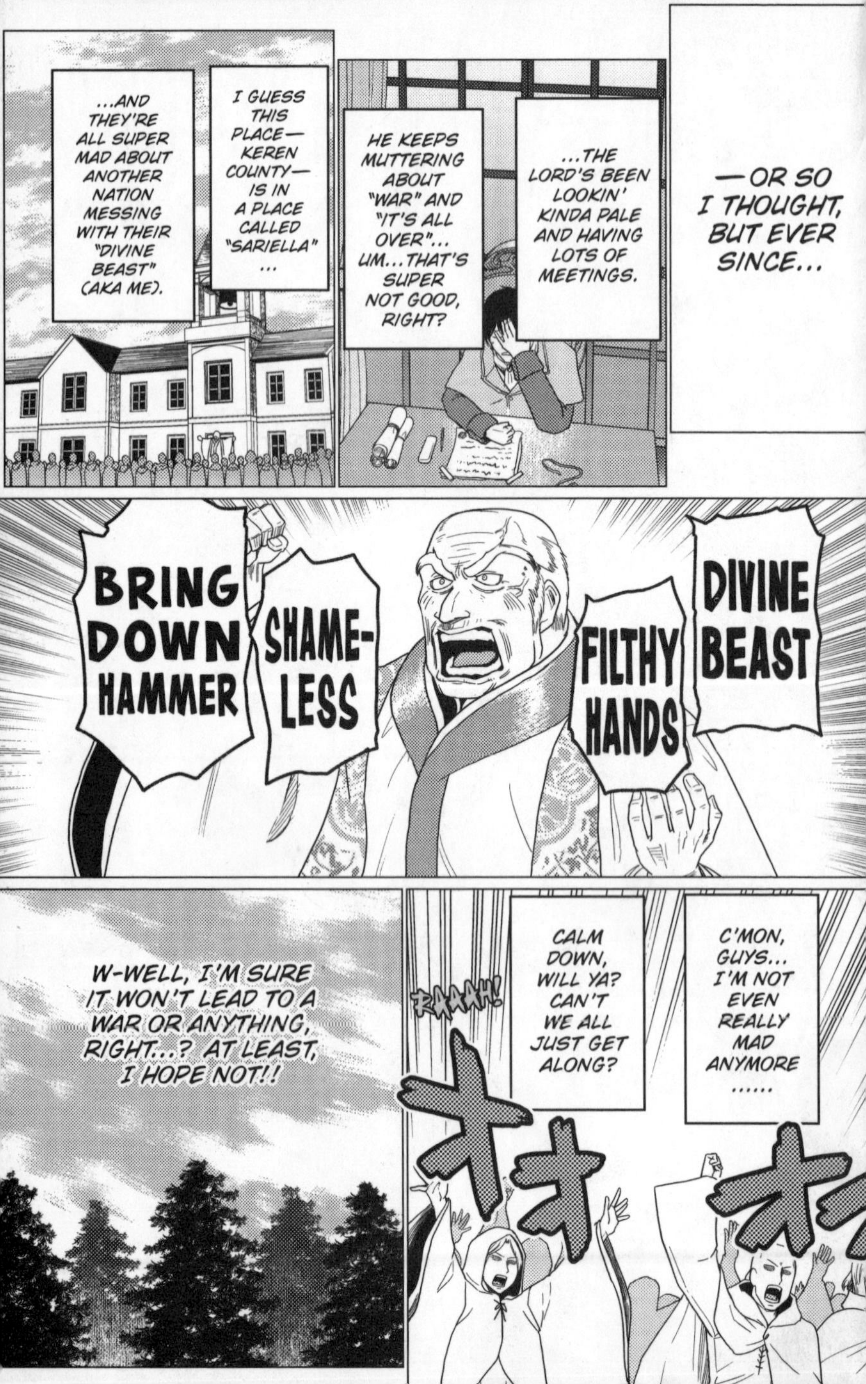
—OR SO I THOUGHT, BUT EVER SINCE...
...THE LORD'S BEEN LOOKIN' KINDA PALE AND HAVING LOTS OF MEETINGS.
HE KEEPS MUTTERING ABOUT "WAR" AND "IT'S ALL OVER"... UM...THAT'S SUPER NOT GOOD, RIGHT?
I GUESS THIS PLACE—KEREN COUNTY—IS IN A PLACE CALLED "SARIELLA"...
...AND THEY'RE ALL SUPER MAD ABOUT ANOTHER NATION MESSING WITH THEIR "DIVINE BEAST" (AKA ME).
DIVINE BEAST
FILTHY HANDS
SHAME-LESS
BRING DOWN HAMMER
C'MON, GUYS... I'M NOT EVEN REALLY MAD ANYMORE ......
CALM DOWN, WILL YA? CAN'T WE ALL JUST GET ALONG?
RAAAH!
W-WELL, I'M SURE IT WON'T LEAD TO A WAR OR ANYTHING, RIGHT...? AT LEAST, I HOPE NOT!!

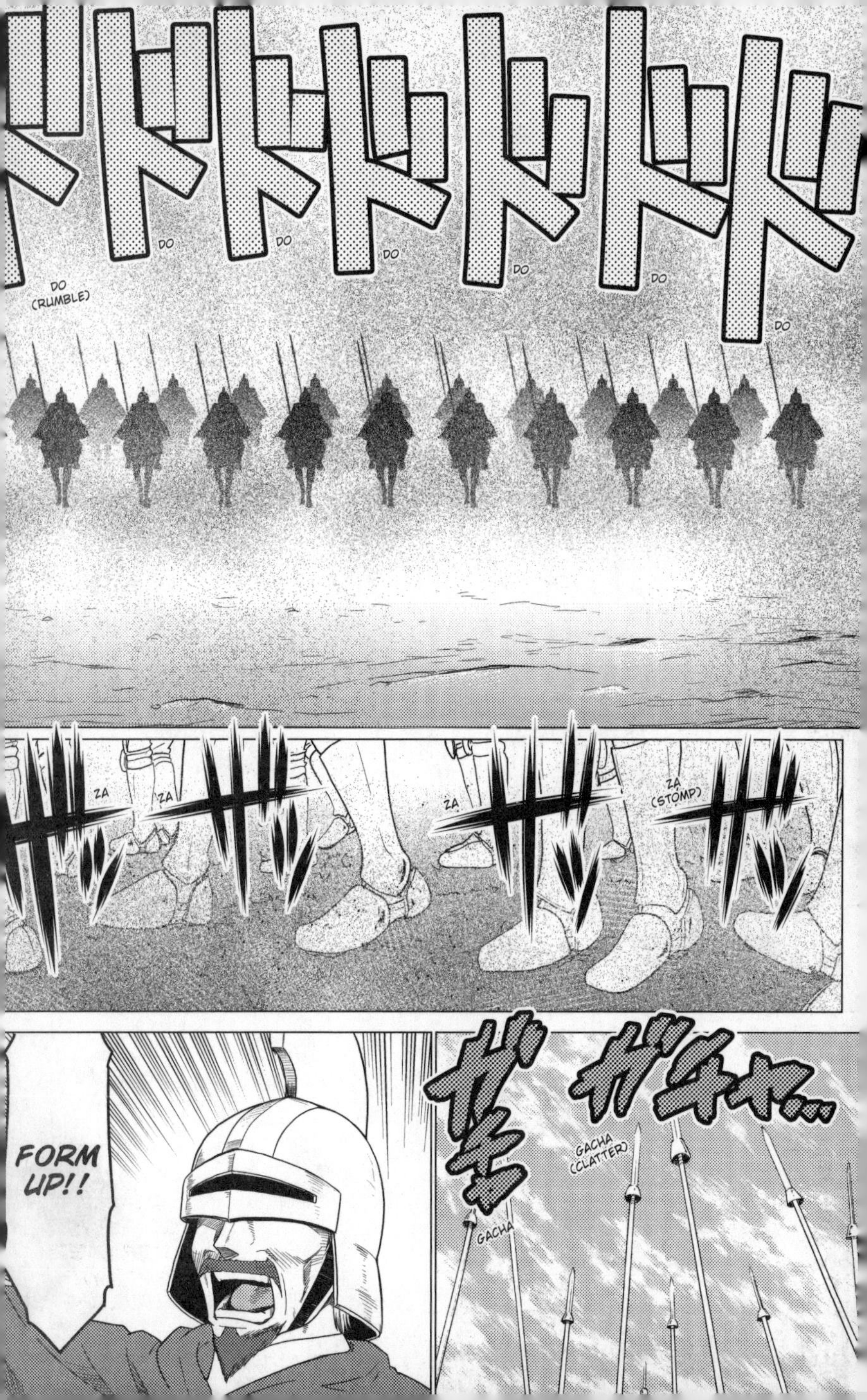
DO
DO
DO
DO
DO
DO
DO (RUMBLE)
ZA (STOMP)
ZA
ZA
ZA
GACHA (CLATTER)
GACHA
FORM UP!!

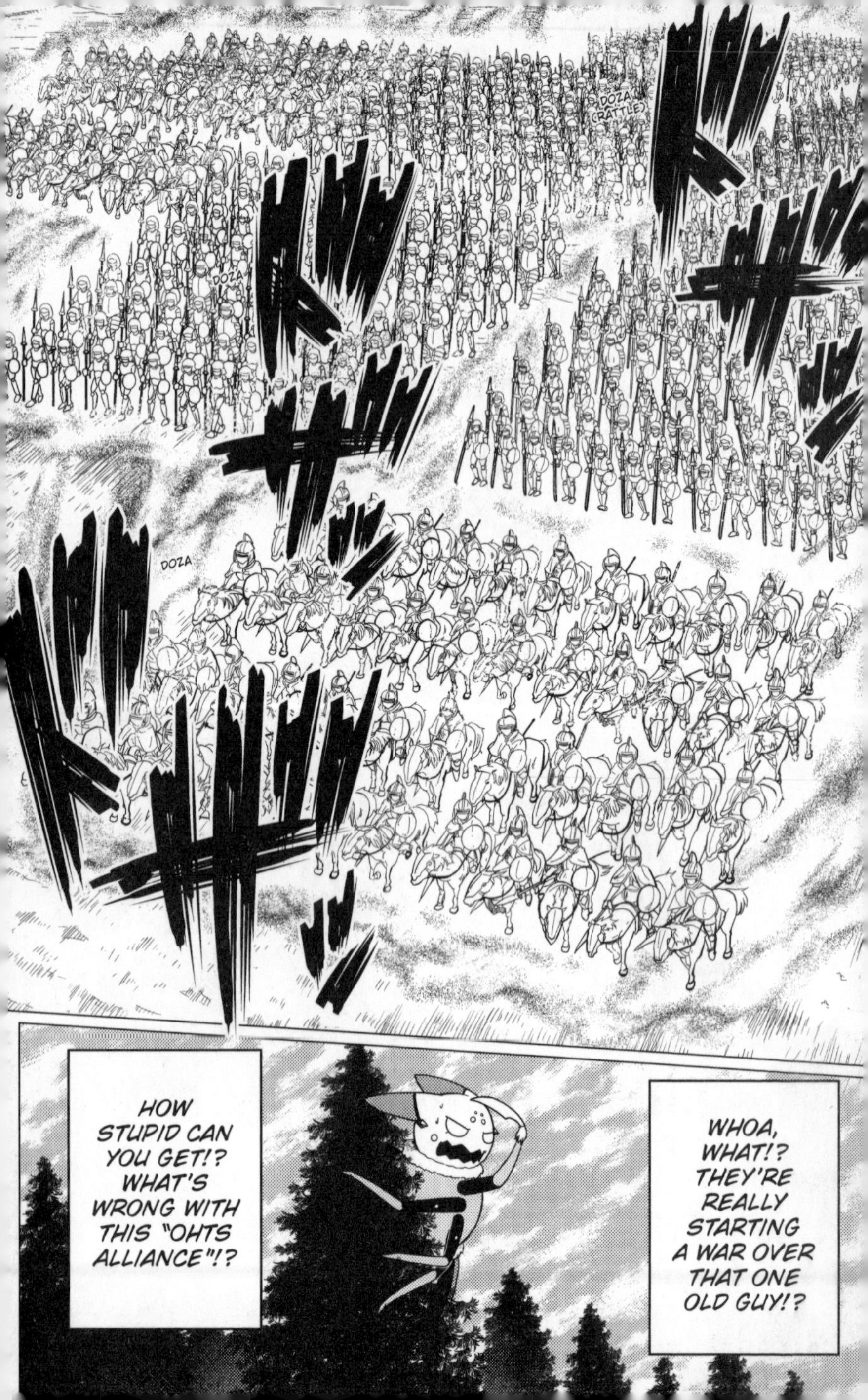
DOZA
(RATTLE)
DOZA
DOZA
WHOA, WHAT!? THEY'RE REALLY STARTING A WAR OVER THAT ONE OLD GUY!?
HOW STUPID CAN YOU GET!? WHAT'S WRONG WITH THIS "OHTS ALLIANCE"!?

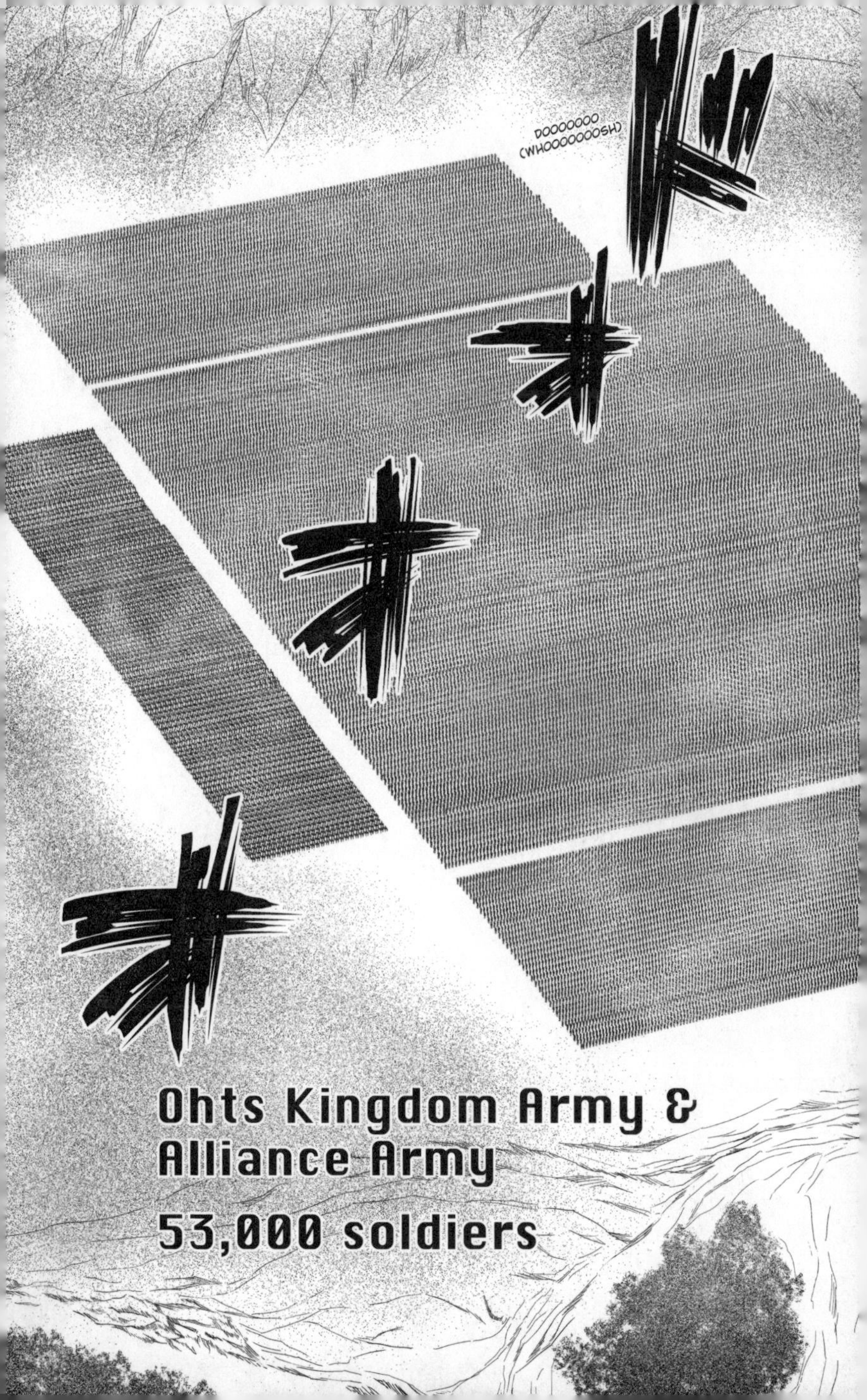
DOOOOOOO
(WHOOOOOOOSH)
Ohts Kingdom Army &
Alliance Army
53,000 soldiers

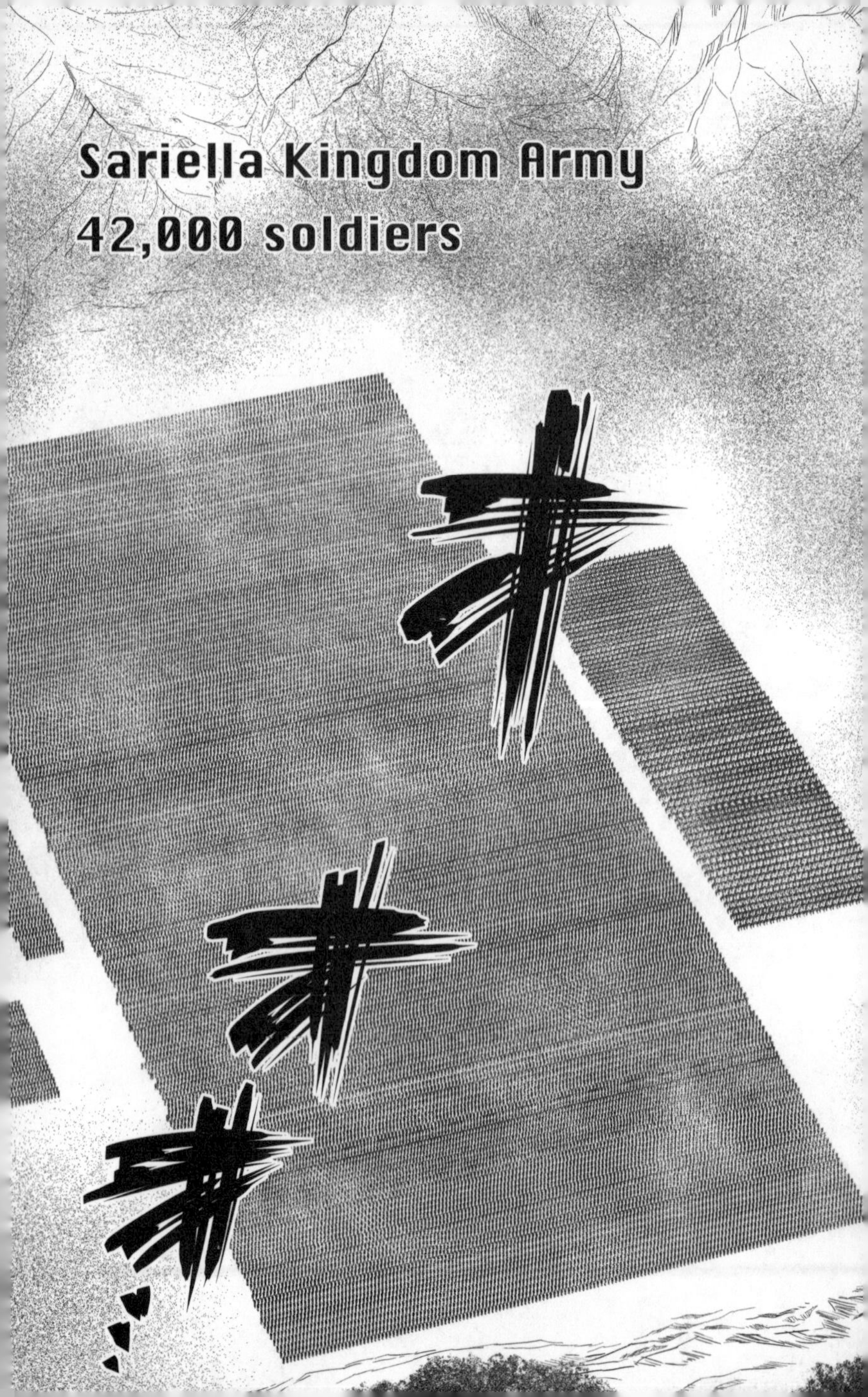
Sariella Kingdom Army
42,000 soldiers

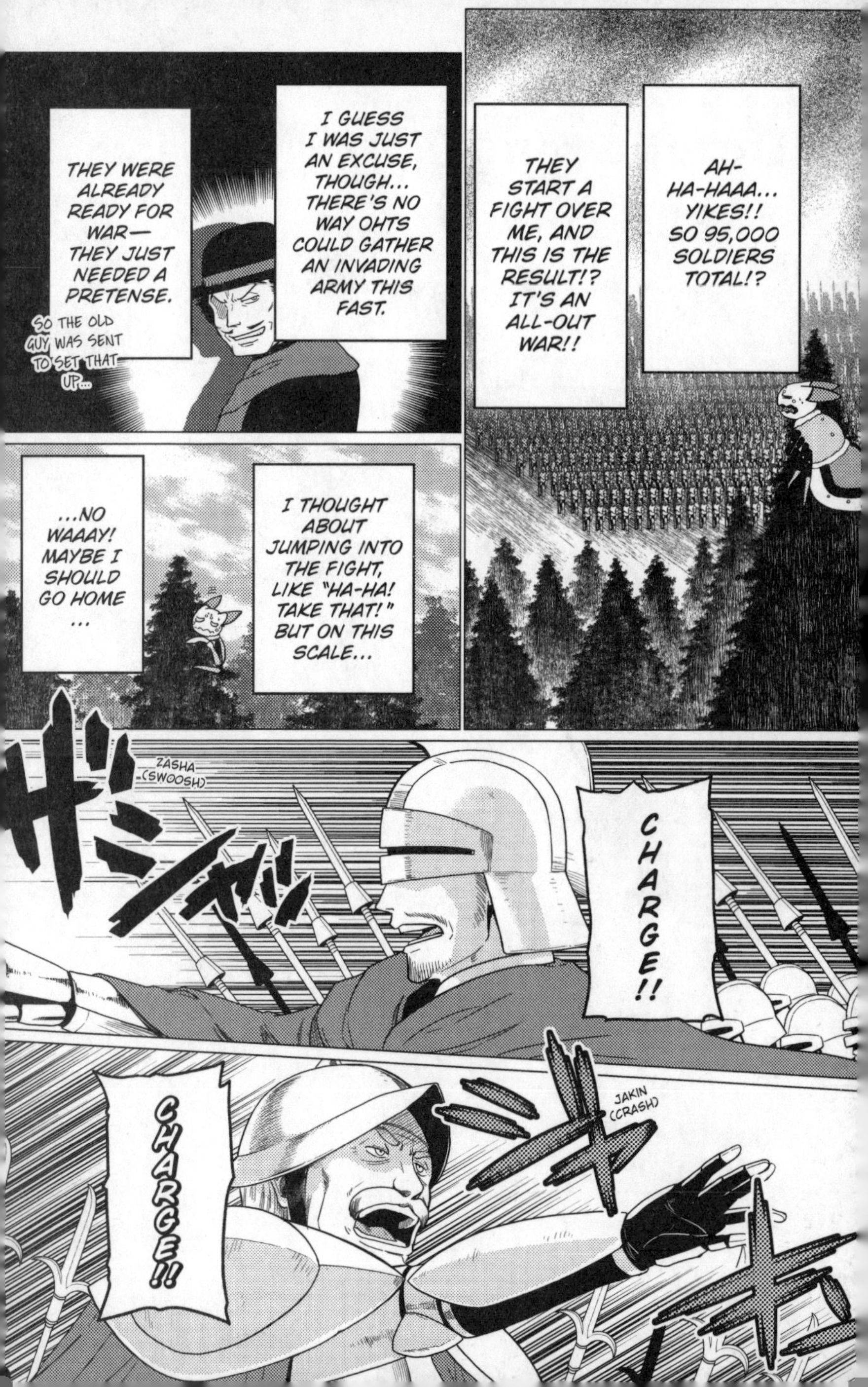

AH-HA-HAAA... YIKES!! SO 95,000 SOLDIERS TOTAL!?
THEY START A FIGHT OVER ME, AND THIS IS THE RESULT!? IT'S AN ALL-OUT WAR!!
I GUESS I WAS JUST AN EXCUSE, THOUGH... THERE'S NO WAY OHTS COULD GATHER AN INVADING ARMY THIS FAST.
THEY WERE ALREADY READY FOR WAR—THEY JUST NEEDED A PRETENSE.
SO THE OLD GUY WAS SENT TO SET THAT UP...
I THOUGHT ABOUT JUMPING INTO THE FIGHT, LIKE "HA-HA! TAKE THAT!" BUT ON THIS SCALE...
...NO WAAAY! MAYBE I SHOULD GO HOME...
CHARGE!!
ZASHA (SWOOSH)
JAKIN (CRASH)
CHARGE!!

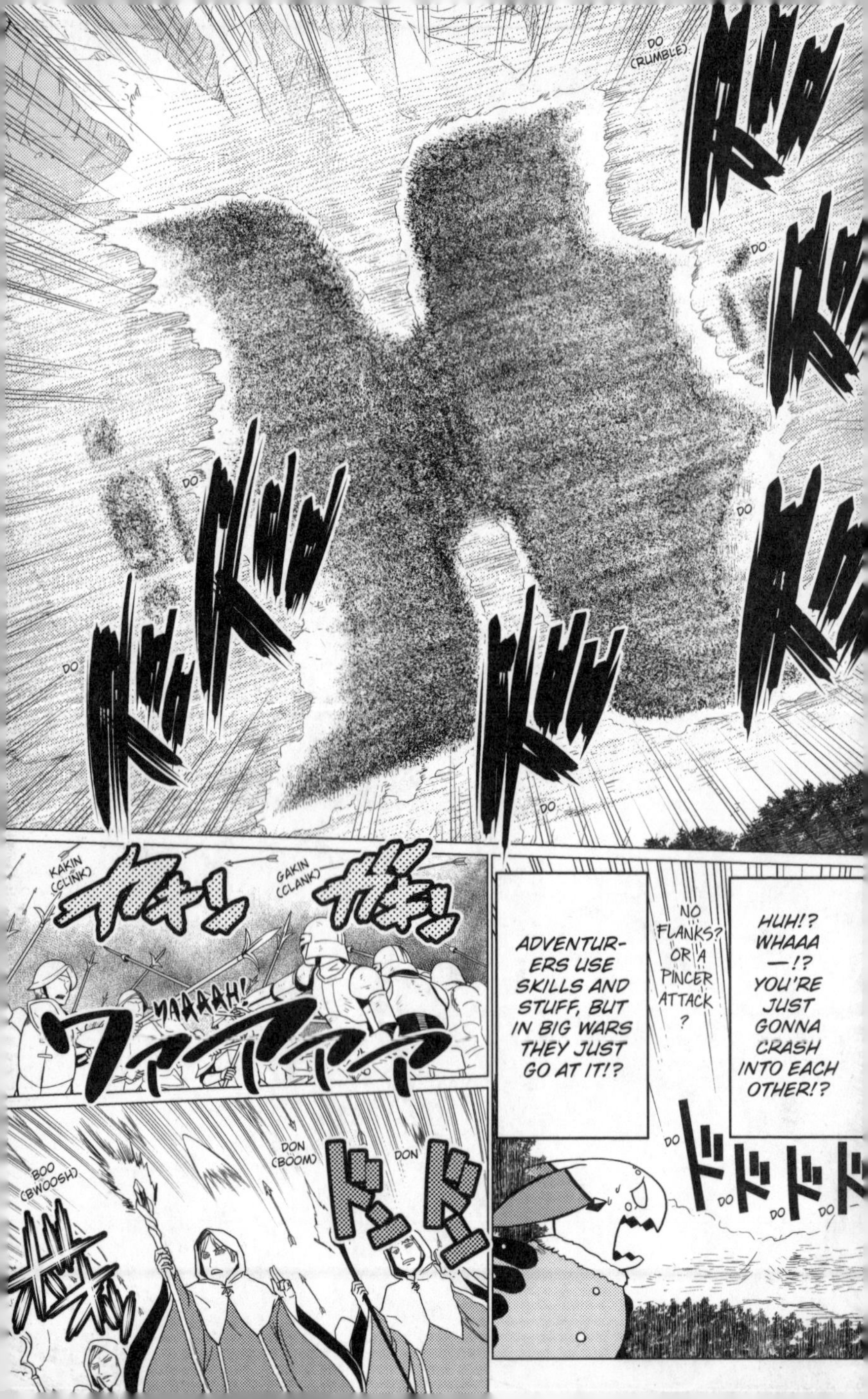
DO (RUMBLE)
DO
DO
DO
DO
DO
HUH!? WHAAA—!? YOU'RE JUST GONNA CRASH INTO EACH OTHER!?
NO FLANKS? OR A PINCER ATTACK?
ADVENTURERS USE SKILLS AND STUFF, BUT IN BIG WARS THEY JUST GO AT IT!?
DO
DO
DO
DO
GAKIN (CLANK)
KAKIN (CLINK)
WAAAAH!
DON
DON (BOOM)
BOO (BWOOSH)

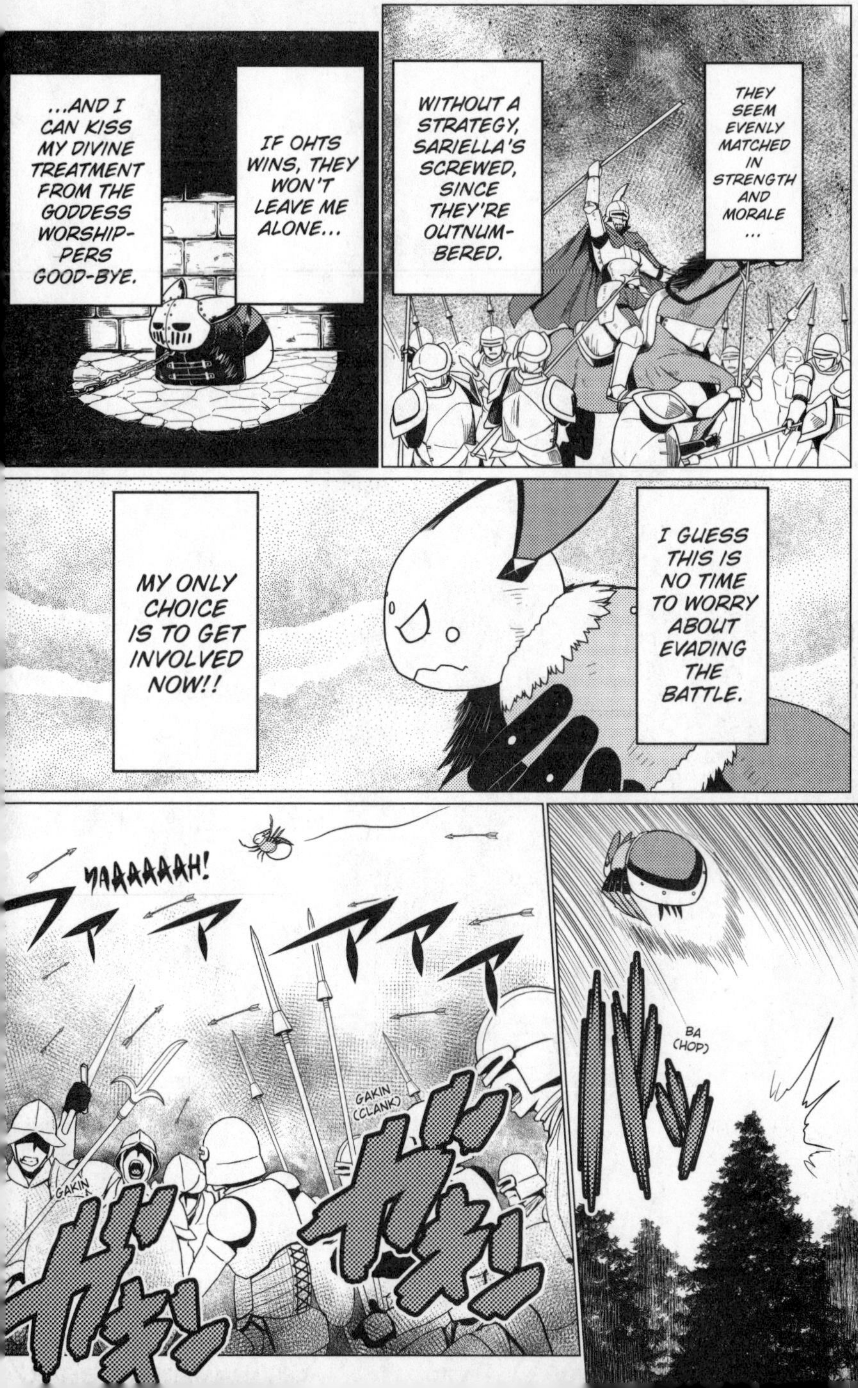
THEY SEEM EVENLY MATCHED IN STRENGTH AND MORALE...
WITHOUT A STRATEGY, SARIELLA'S SCREWED, SINCE THEY'RE OUTNUMBERED.
IF OHTS WINS, THEY WON'T LEAVE ME ALONE...
...AND I CAN KISS MY DIVINE TREATMENT FROM THE GODDESS WORSHIPPERS GOOD-BYE.
I GUESS THIS IS NO TIME TO WORRY ABOUT EVADING THE BATTLE.
MY ONLY CHOICE IS TO GET INVOLVED NOW!!
BA (HOP)
YAAAAAAH!
GAKIN (CLANK)
GAKIN

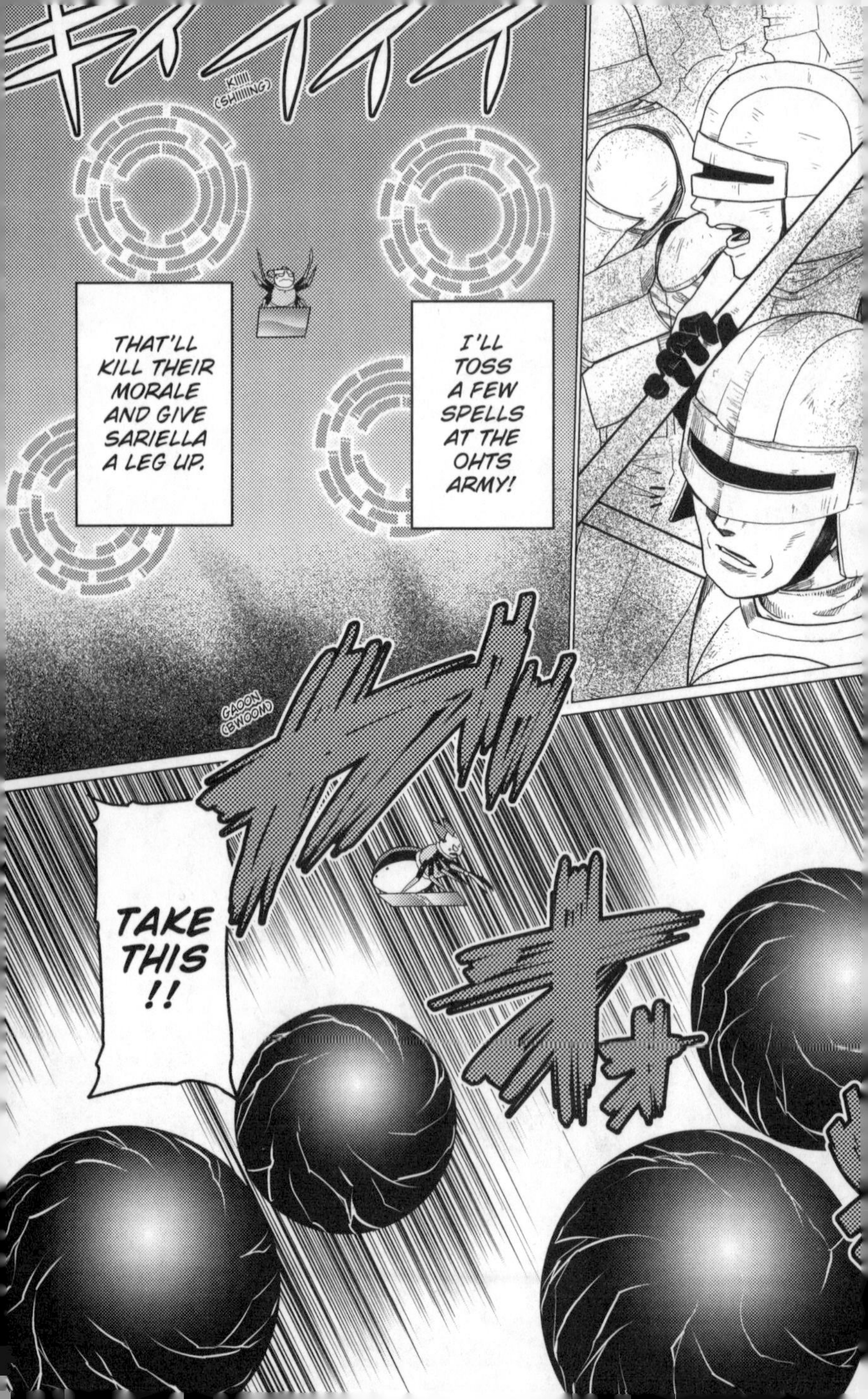
KIIII
(SHIIIING)
I'LL TOSS A FEW SPELLS AT THE OHTS ARMY!
THAT'LL KILL THEIR MORALE AND GIVE SARIELLA A LEG UP.
GAOON
(BWOOM)
TAKE THIS!!

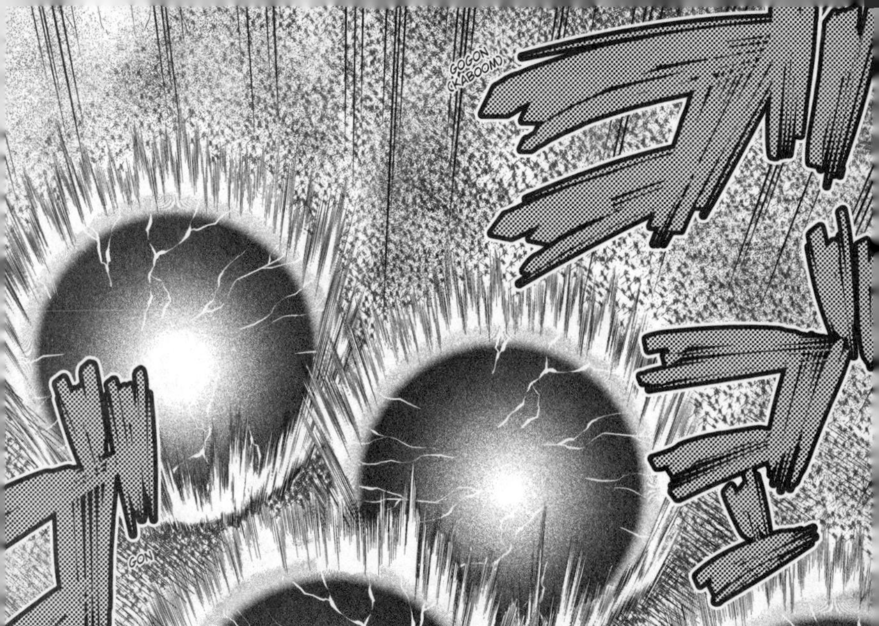
GOGON (KABOOM)
GON
GON
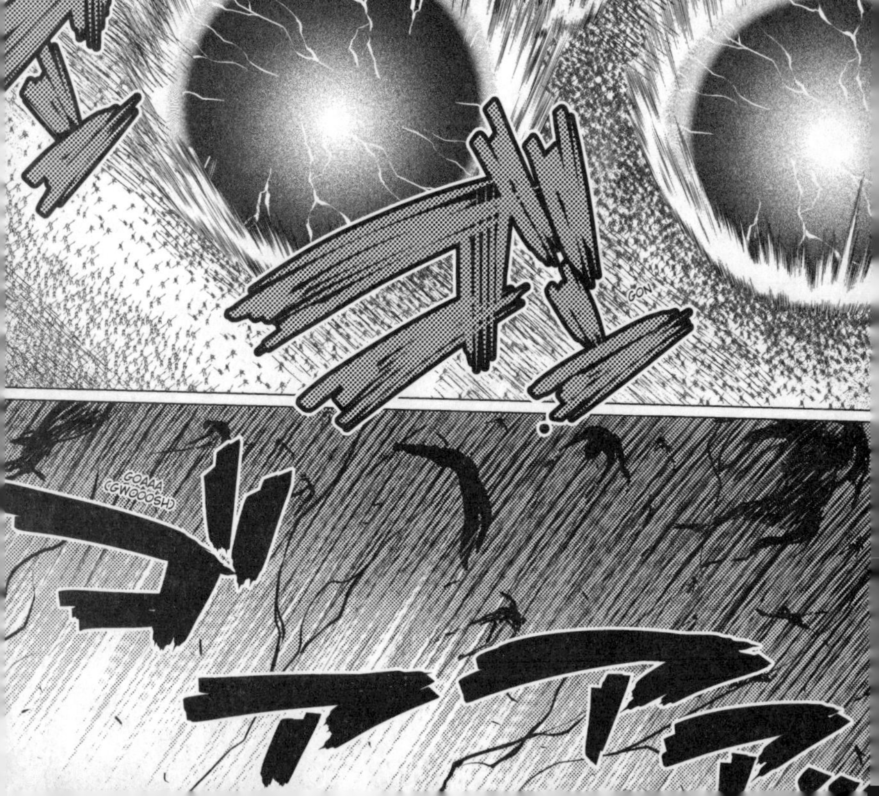
GOAAA (GWOOOSH)

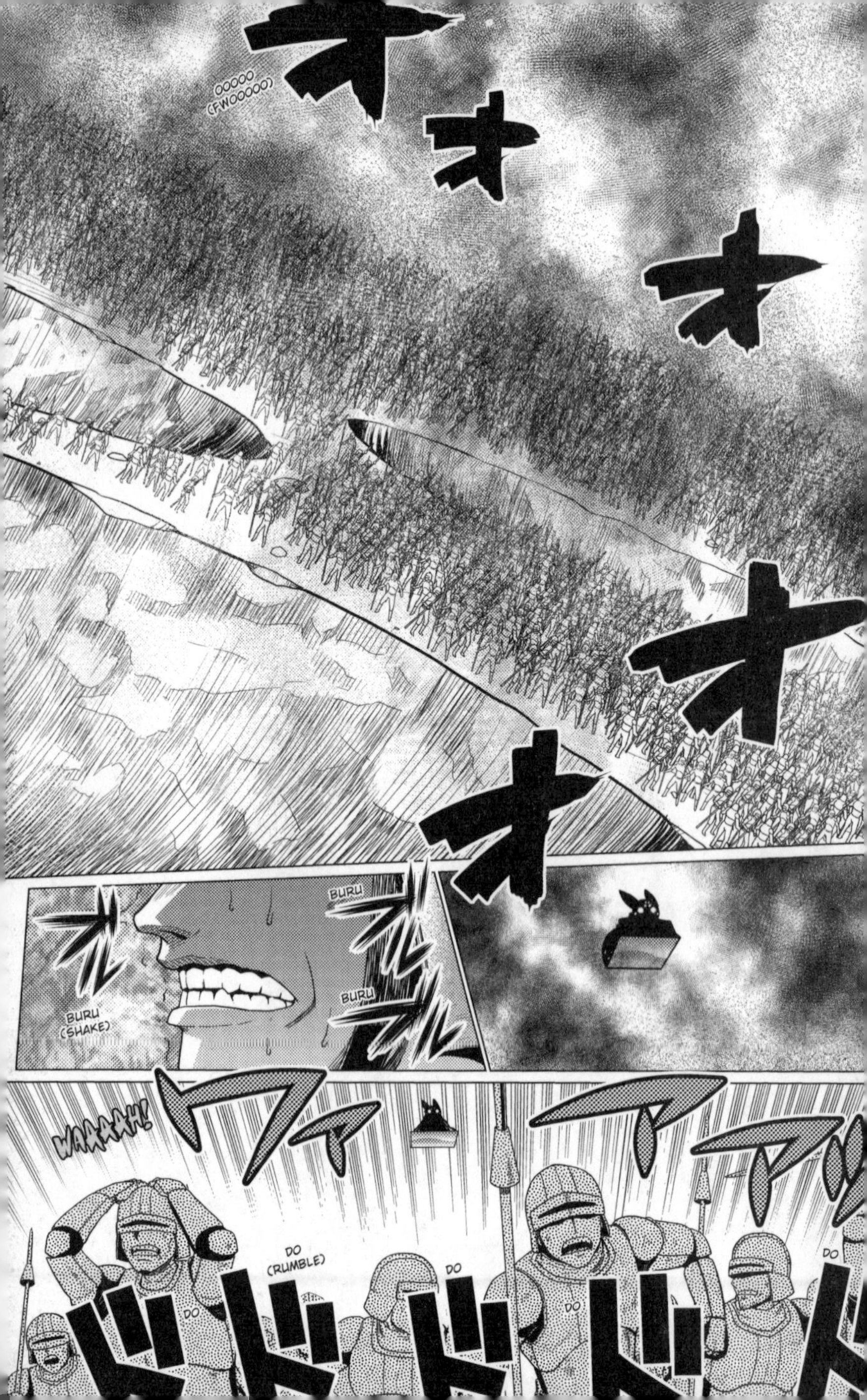

OOOOO (FWOOOOO)
BURU
BURU
BURU (SHAKE)
WAAAAH!
DO
DO
DO
DO (RUMBLE)
DO

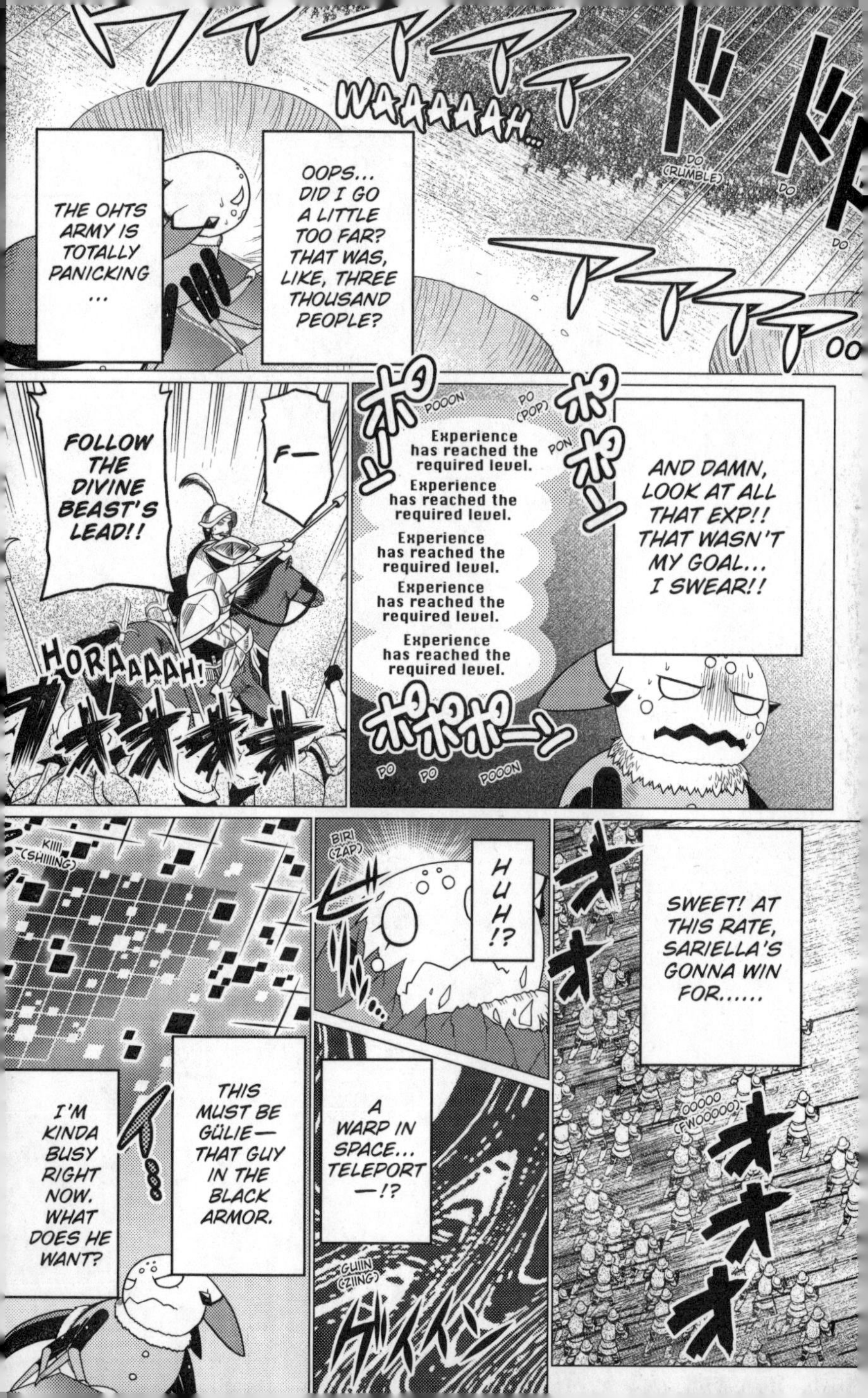
DO (RUMBLE)
DO
DO
WAAAAAAH...
OOPS... DID I GO A LITTLE TOO FAR? THAT WAS, LIKE, THREE THOUSAND PEOPLE?
THE OHTS ARMY IS TOTALLY PANICKING ...
OO
AND DAMN, LOOK AT ALL THAT EXP!! THAT WASN'T MY GOAL... I SWEAR!!
PO (POP)
PON
POOON
Experience has reached the required level.
Experience has reached the required level.
Experience has reached the required level.
Experience has reached the required level.
Experience has reached the required level.
PO PO POOON
F—
FOLLOW THE DIVINE BEAST'S LEAD!!
HORAAAAH!
SWEET! AT THIS RATE, SARIELLA'S GONNA WIN FOR......
OOOOO (FWOOOOO)
HUH!?
BIRI (ZAP)
A WARP IN SPACE... TELEPORT—!?
GUIIN (ZIING)
KIIII (SHIIING)
THIS MUST BE GÜLIE—THAT GUY IN THE BLACK ARMOR.
I'M KINDA BUSY RIGHT NOW. WHAT DOES HE WANT?

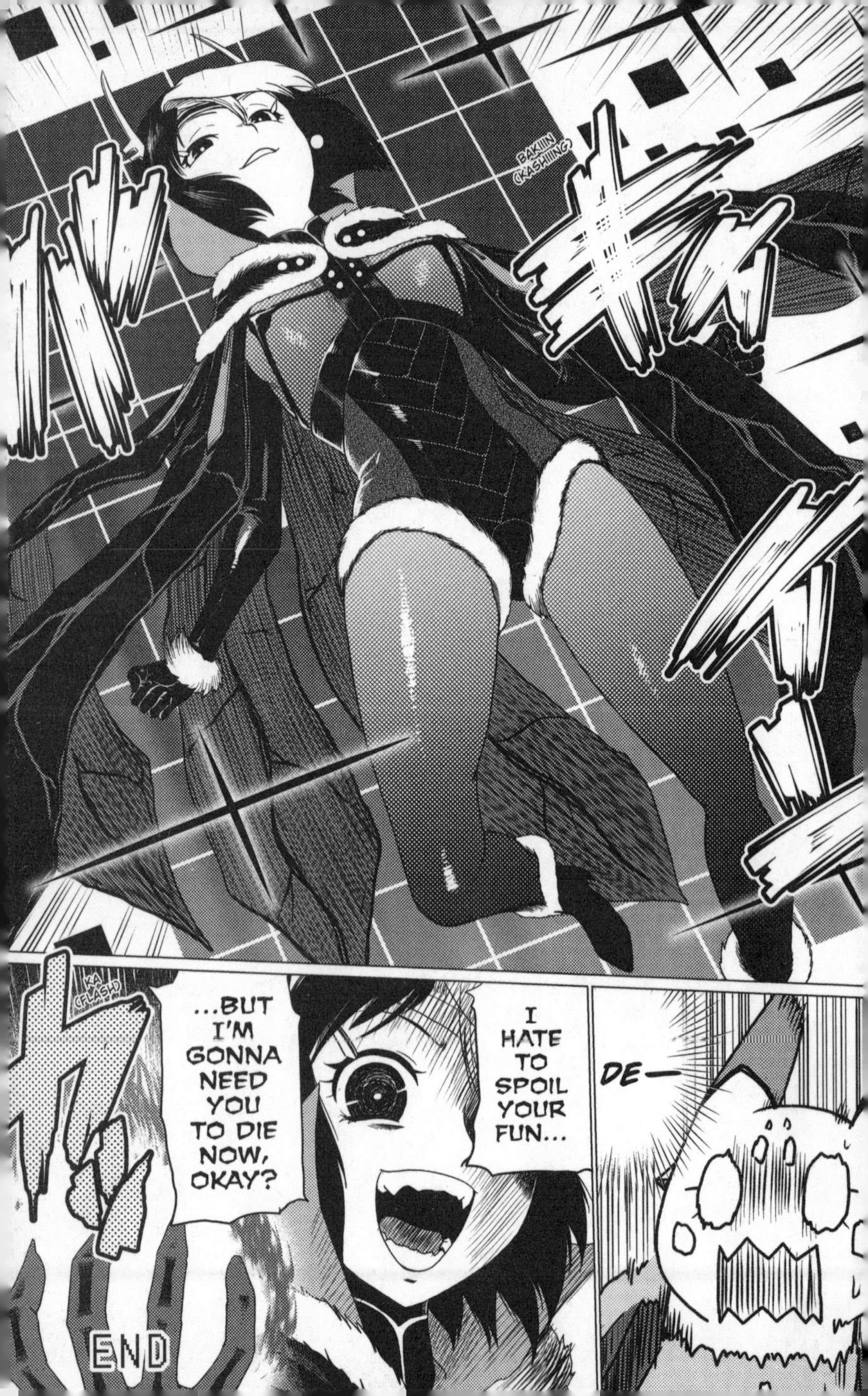
BAKIIN (KASHIING)
DE—
I HATE TO SPOIL YOUR FUN...
...BUT I'M GONNA NEED YOU TO DIE NOW, OKAY?
KA (FLASH)
END

So I'm a Spider, So What?

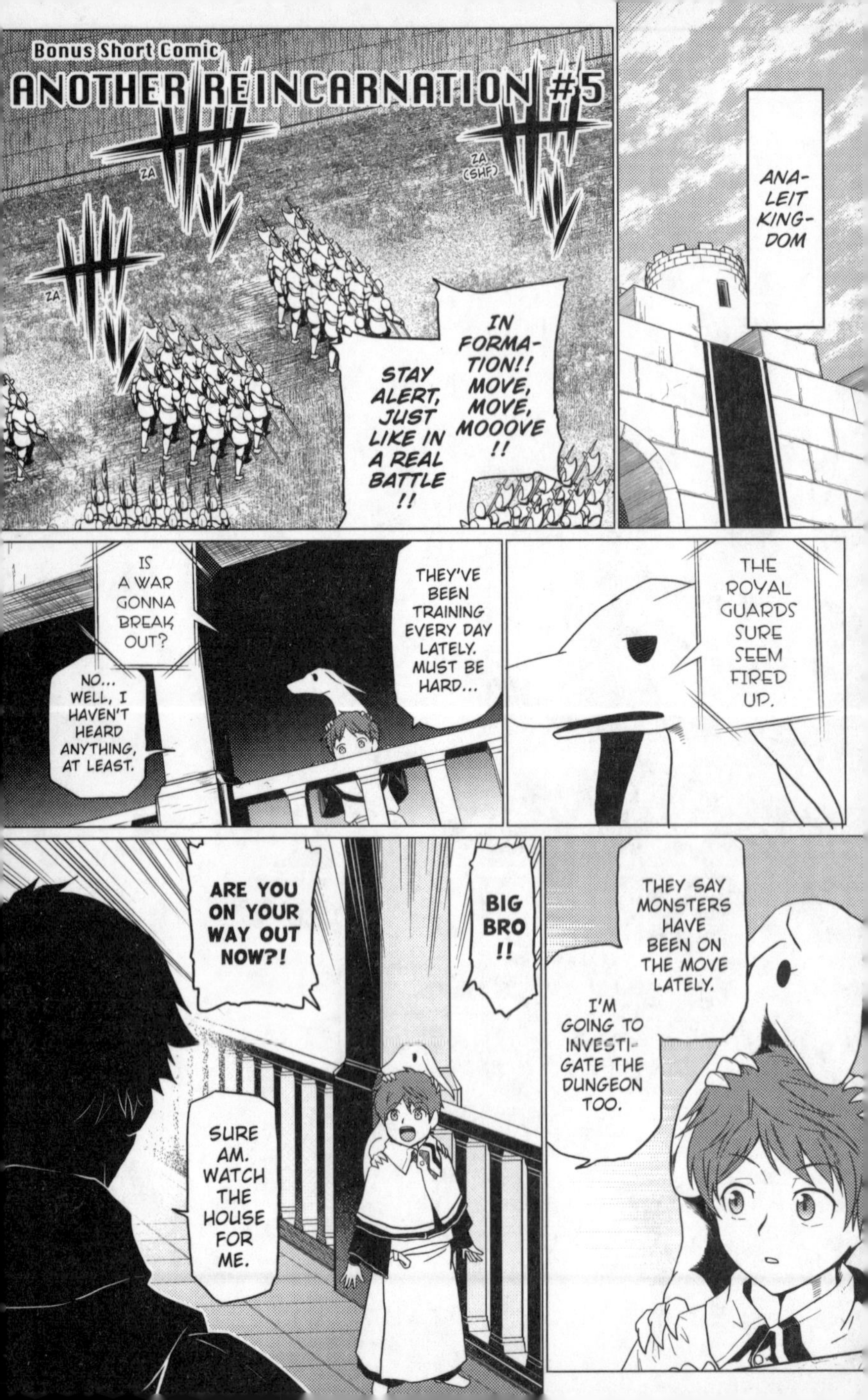
ANA-LEIT KINGDOM
Bonus Short Comic
ANOTHER REINCARNATION #5
ZA (SHF)
ZA
ZA
IN FORMATION!! MOVE, MOVE, MOOOVE!!
STAY ALERT, JUST LIKE IN A REAL BATTLE!!
THE ROYAL GUARDS SURE SEEM FIRED UP.
THEY'VE BEEN TRAINING EVERY DAY LATELY. MUST BE HARD...
IS A WAR GONNA BREAK OUT?
NO... WELL, I HAVEN'T HEARD ANYTHING, AT LEAST.
THEY SAY MONSTERS HAVE BEEN ON THE MOVE LATELY.
I'M GOING TO INVESTI-GATE THE DUNGEON TOO.
BIG BRO!!
ARE YOU ON YOUR WAY OUT NOW?!
SURE AM. WATCH THE HOUSE FOR ME.

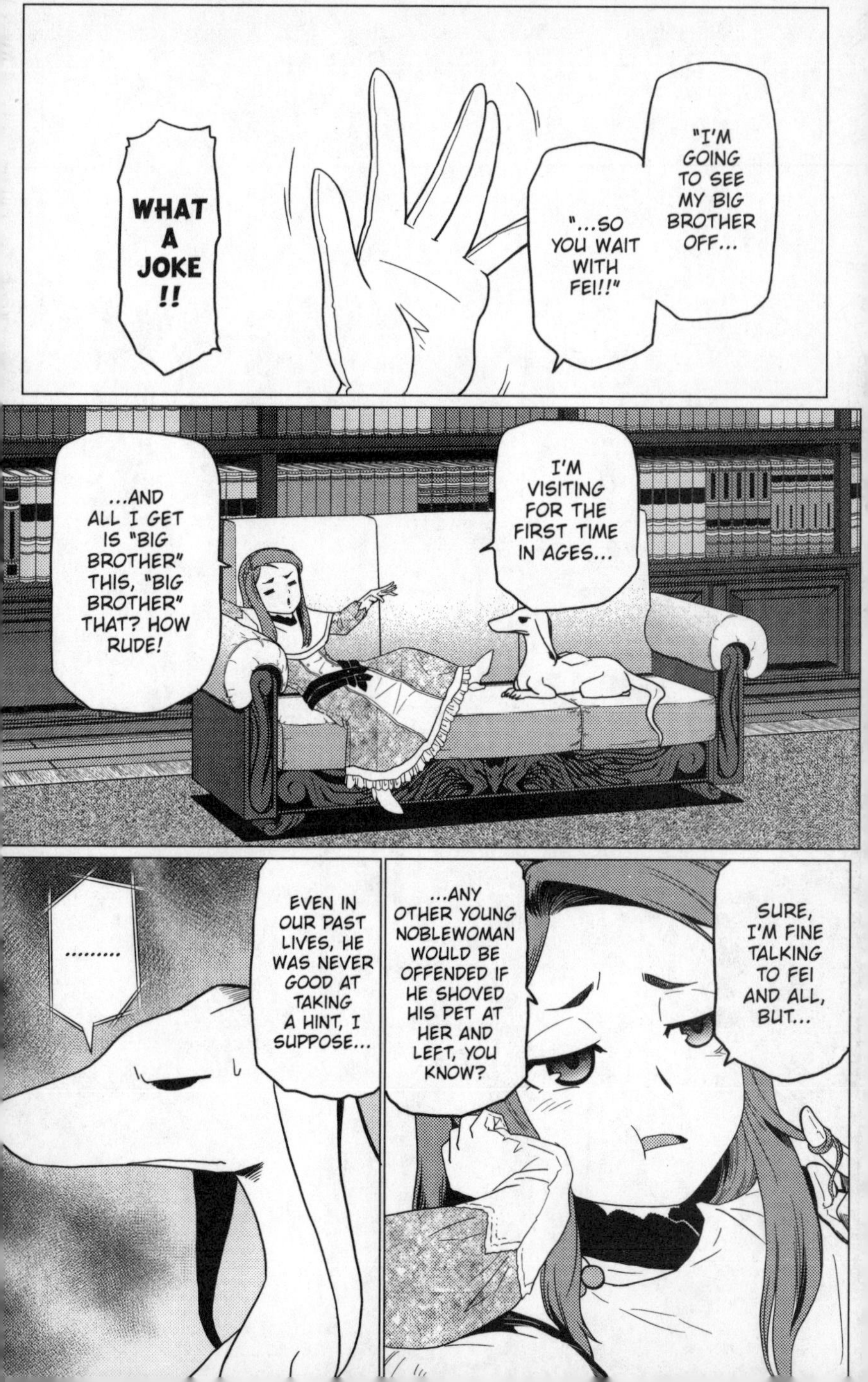
"I'M GOING TO SEE MY BIG BROTHER OFF...
"...SO YOU WAIT WITH FEI!!"
WHAT A JOKE!!
I'M VISITING FOR THE FIRST TIME IN AGES...
...AND ALL I GET IS "BIG BROTHER" THIS, "BIG BROTHER" THAT? HOW RUDE!
SURE, I'M FINE TALKING TO FEI AND ALL, BUT...
...ANY OTHER YOUNG NOBLEWOMAN WOULD BE OFFENDED IF HE SHOVED HIS PET AT HER AND LEFT, YOU KNOW?
EVEN IN OUR PAST LIVES, HE WAS NEVER GOOD AT TAKING A HINT, I SUPPOSE...
....

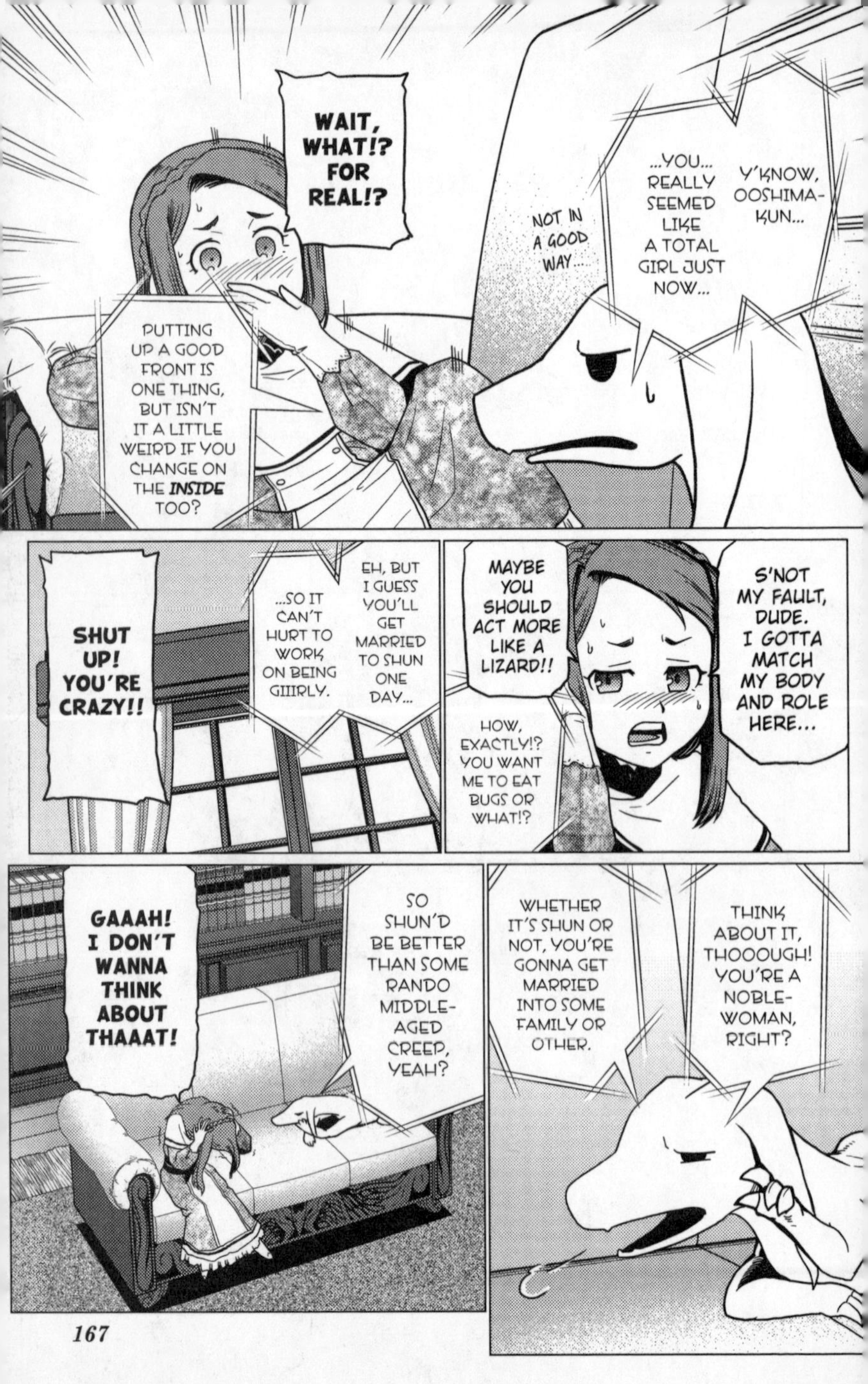
Y'KNOW, OOSHIMA-KUN...
...YOU... REALLY SEEMED LIKE A TOTAL GIRL JUST NOW...
NOT IN A GOOD WAY...
WAIT, WHAT!? FOR REAL!?
PUTTING UP A GOOD FRONT IS ONE THING, BUT ISN'T IT A LITTLE WEIRD IF YOU CHANGE ON THE *INSIDE* TOO?
S'NOT MY FAULT, DUDE. I GOTTA MATCH MY BODY AND ROLE HERE...
MAYBE YOU SHOULD ACT MORE LIKE A LIZARD!!
HOW, EXACTLY!? YOU WANT ME TO EAT BUGS OR WHAT!?
EH, BUT I GUESS YOU'LL GET MARRIED TO SHUN ONE DAY...
...SO IT CAN'T HURT TO WORK ON BEING GIIIRLY.
SHUT UP! YOU'RE CRAZY!!
THINK ABOUT IT, THOOOUGH! YOU'RE A NOBLE-WOMAN, RIGHT?
WHETHER IT'S SHUN OR NOT, YOU'RE GONNA GET MARRIED INTO SOME FAMILY OR OTHER.
SO SHUN'D BE BETTER THAN SOME RANDO MIDDLE-AGED CREEP, YEAH?
GAAAH! I DON'T WANNA THINK ABOUT THAAAT!

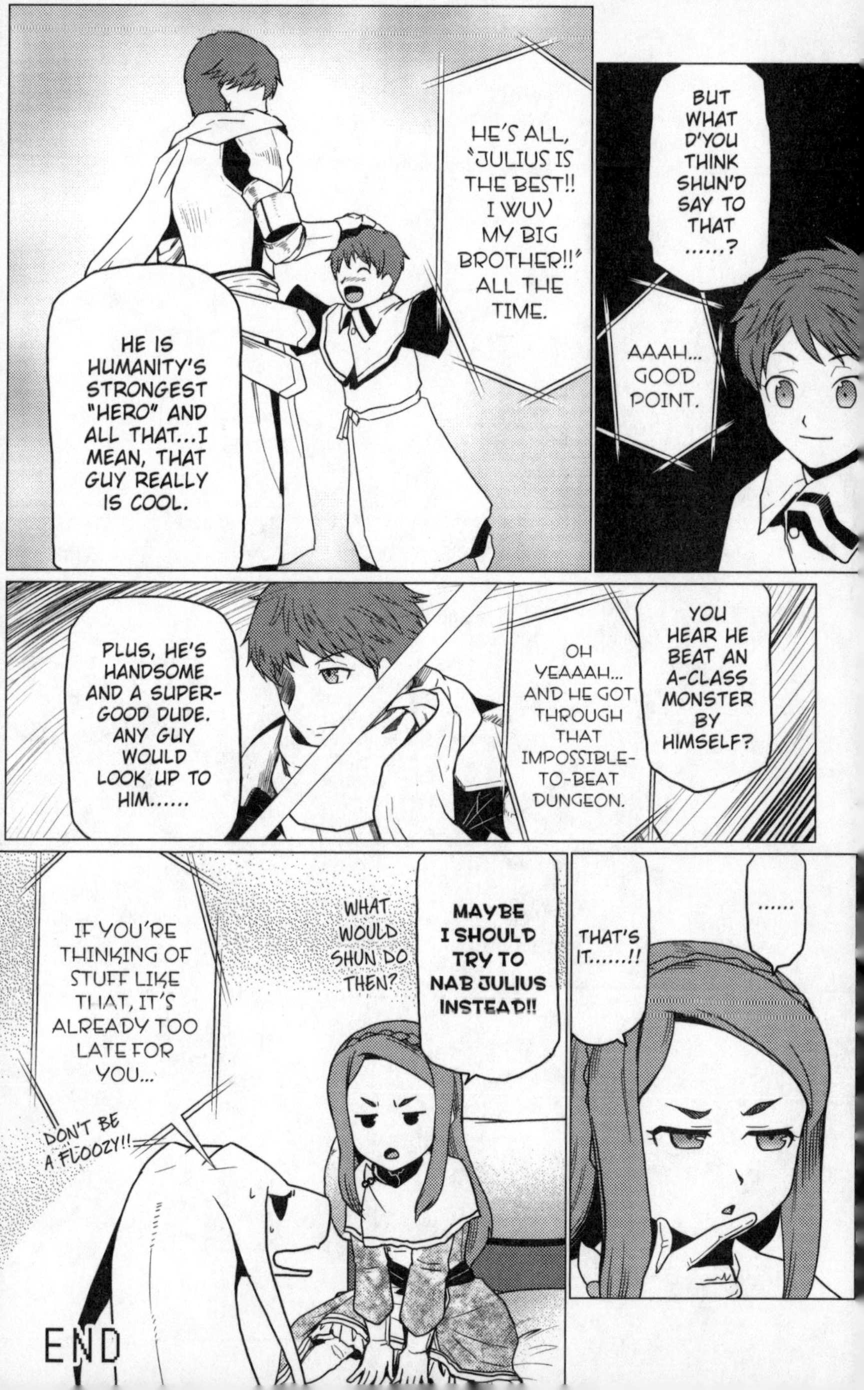
BUT WHAT D'YOU THINK SHUN'D SAY TO THAT ......?
AAAH... GOOD POINT.
HE'S ALL, "JULIUS IS THE BEST!! I WUV MY BIG BROTHER!!" ALL THE TIME.
HE IS HUMANITY'S STRONGEST "HERO" AND ALL THAT...I MEAN, THAT GUY REALLY IS COOL.
YOU HEAR HE BEAT AN A-CLASS MONSTER BY HIMSELF?
OH YEAAAH... AND HE GOT THROUGH THAT IMPOSSIBLE-TO-BEAT DUNGEON.
PLUS, HE'S HANDSOME AND A SUPER-GOOD DUDE. ANY GUY WOULD LOOK UP TO HIM......
......
THAT'S IT......!!
MAYBE I SHOULD TRY TO NAB JULIUS INSTEAD!!
WHAT WOULD SHUN DO THEN?
IF YOU'RE THINKING OF STUFF LIKE THAT, IT'S ALREADY TOO LATE FOR YOU...
DON'T BE A FLOOZY!!
END

So I'm a Spider, So What?

AFTERWORD
ORIGINAL CREATOR: OKINA BABA

HELLO. I'M THE ORIGINAL AUTHOR, OKINA BABA.

THE FIGHT WITH MOTHER FINALLY COMES TO A HEAD!

WHICH MEANS OUR SPIDER HEROINE'S LONG STANDOFF WITH MOTHER ENDS AT LAST IN THIS VOLUME.

THINKING BACK, IN THE FIRST CHAPTER OF THE FIRST VOLUME, MOTHER TOOK UP A WHOLE PAGE WITH A BIG FIRST APPEARANCE.

THE STORY BEGINS WITH KUMOKO'S NARROW ESCAPE FROM GETTING EATEN BY MOTHER!

THEY SAY LIONS DROP THEIR YOUNG INTO A RAVINE, BUT MOTHER'S ARE DROPPED INTO HER STOMACH...

NO WONDER KUMOKO HAD TO GET AWAY FROM MOTHER ASAP.

AND EVEN THOUGH SHE APPEARED AT THE VERY BEGINNING, MOTHER'S AS STRONG AS ANY FINAL BOSS.

A FITTING VILLAIN FOR THE BIG MILESTONE OF VOLUME 10 OF THE MANGA!

AFTER SETTLING THE SCORE WITH MOTHER, WE SEE MORE INTERACTION WITH HUMANS, BRINGING THE STORY TO A TURNING POINT.

WHAT'S GOING TO HAPPEN NEXT!?

AND AFTER THOSE BIG SWARMS OF MONSTERS, WHAT WILL HAPPEN TO KAKASHI-SENSEI, WHO HAS TO DRAW HUGE ARMIES OF HUMANS NEXT!?

YOU'LL HAVE TO FIND OUT WITH YOUR OWN EYES...

HANG IN THERE, KAKASHI-SENSEI!

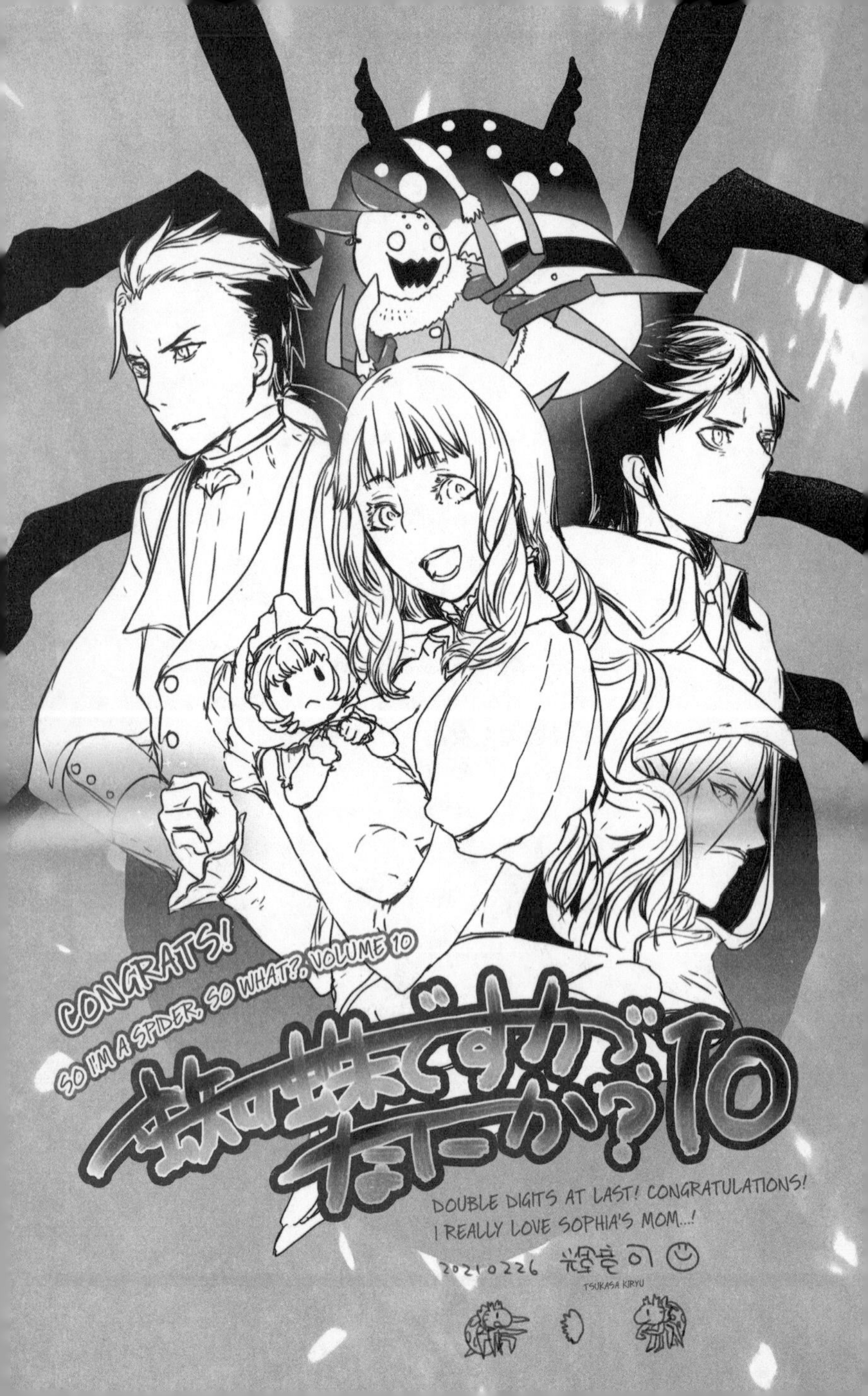
CONGRATS!
SO I'M A SPIDER, SO WHAT?, VOLUME 10
蜘蛛ですが、なにか？10
DOUBLE DIGITS AT LAST! CONGRATULATIONS!
I REALLY LOVE SOPHIA'S MOM...!
20210226
TSUKASA KIRYU

STAFF LIST

The author

ASAHIRO KAKASHI

Assistants

TERUO HATANAKA

REI HASEKURA

HIROTSUGU FUJIWARA

Design

R design studio

(Shinji Yamaguchi, Yuwa Tojo, Chie Ooshima)

You're reading
the wrong way!
Turn the page to read
a bonus short story by
So I'm a Spider, So What?
original creator
Okina Baba!

They have glass windows too.

Glass windows are a relatively new technology on Earth, aren't they?

Somewhere around the eighteenth century, if I remember right?

And at the time, I'm pretty sure they were super expensive, so only rich nobles used them or something.

......But even the average houses in this town have glass windows, y'know?

And the robbers' booze bottles are made out of glass, too!

Basically, what I'm saying is, fantasy worlds are wild.

Since there are skills and stats here, it makes sense they'd have different developments than Earth. Stuff like architecture, metalworking, and glasswork don't seem like they'd be super related to that, though.

So this parallel world is more advanced than I expected.

At the very least, it's gotta be further along than the Middle Ages.

Guess that Middle-Ages-in-Europe aesthetic is just for show.

[The End]

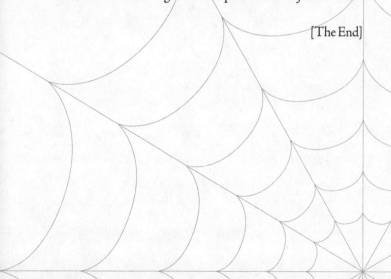

Well, since there are monsters and such in this world, I guess it must've been pretty important to develop sturdy houses and walls. So it makes sense that their architecture would be fairly advanced.

Necessity is the mother of invention, after all.

By the same token, it makes sense that they'd develop weapons and armor and so on and so forth, too.

Every soldier in town is decked out in metal armor and the like.

Which means their metalworking technology is pretty far along—enough that even soldiers in a small town have decent armor, y'know?

I mean, armor has a pretty long history on Earth too, so it's not surprising to see soldiers in armor here.

......Or so you'd think, right?

But consider it a little more deeply. This world has stats, remember?

Thanks to stats, these soldiers can become way more powerful than any soldier on Earth.

So is their armor the same as the kind in the Middle Ages on Earth?

No way! It's gotta have way higher defense!

Otherwise there'd be no point in wearing it!

Is the base metal just naturally harder, or is it made that way with some kind of magical process?

I don't know...but either way, it's gotta involve pretty advanced technology.

Actually, let's go back to the subject of buildings for a minute.

So I'm a Spider, So What?

Europe in the Middle Ages?

Okina Baba

After I defeated Mother, I started living near town to keep an eye on Vampy.

I've been messing with the local bandits while watching over the town.

It's basically the kind of Middle Ages European-style town most Japanese people might picture.

But the more I look at it, the more I get to thinking...

Is it just me, or are they surprisingly advanced?

The first things that catch my eye are the walls.

The walls.

The big, tall, sturdy walls that surround the whole town.

You can tell at a glance that they must've been really hard to build, right?

Which must mean they have the technology to make things like that.

That alone proves that this world's architecture is pretty impressive...but the houses and stuff inside the walls are pretty darn well-made, too.

......In fact, even the robbers' hideouts and whatnot look way too well put-together to have been built on the fly.